Street by S

OXFORDSHIRE
PLUS HIGHWORTH, MORETON-IN-MARSH, READING
Enlarged Areas Banbury, Oxford

M000005058

Ist edition May 2001

© Automobile Association Developments Limited 2001

Published by AA Publishing (a trading name of Automobile Association Developments Limited, whose registered office is Norfolk House, Priestley Road, Basingstoke, Hampshire, RG24 9NY. Registered number 1878835).

Mapping produced by the Cartographic Department of The Automobile Association.

A CIP Catalogue record for this book is available from the British Library.

Printed by in Italy by Printer Trento srl

Key to map pages ii-iii

Key to map symbols iv-1

Enlarged scale pages 2-5

Street by Street 6-335

Index – towns & villages 336-338

Index – streets 340-371

Index – featured places 371-377

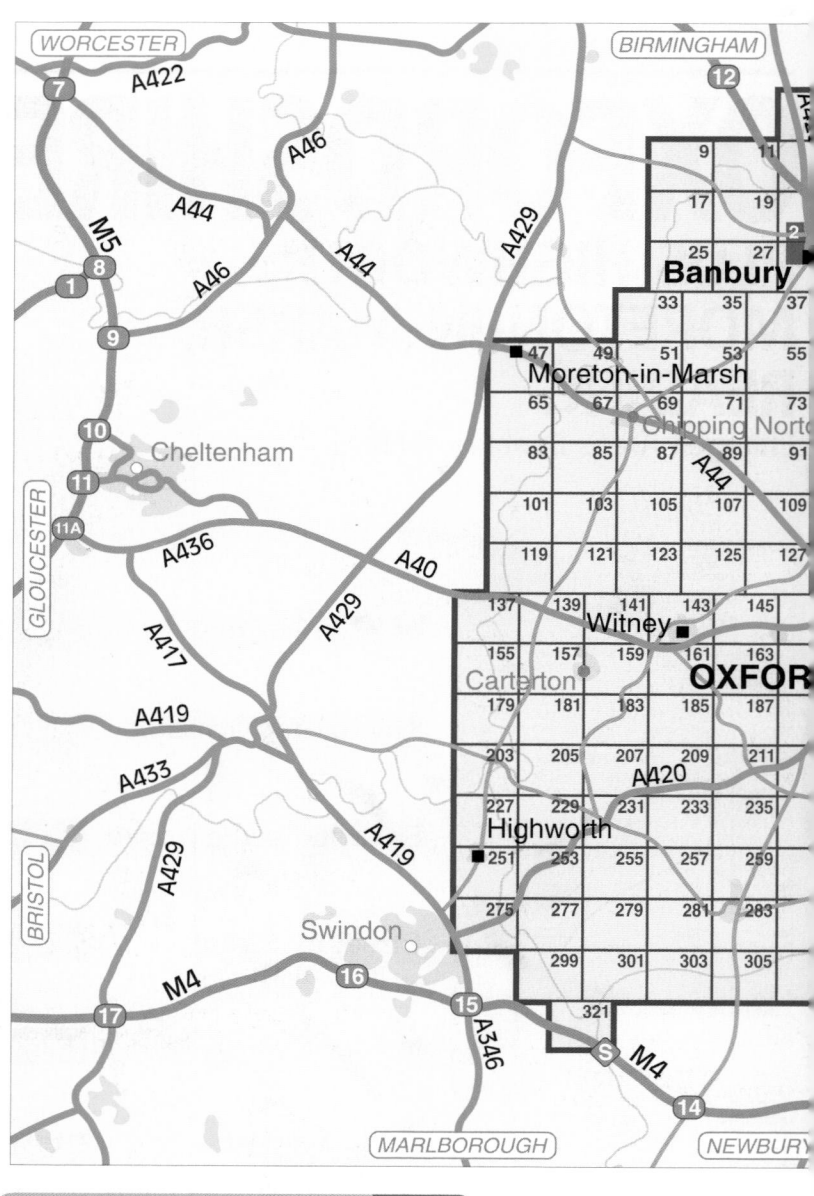

Enlarged scale pages | 1:17,500 | 3.6 inches to 1 mile

0   1/2   miles   1

0   1/2   1   kilometres   1 1/2

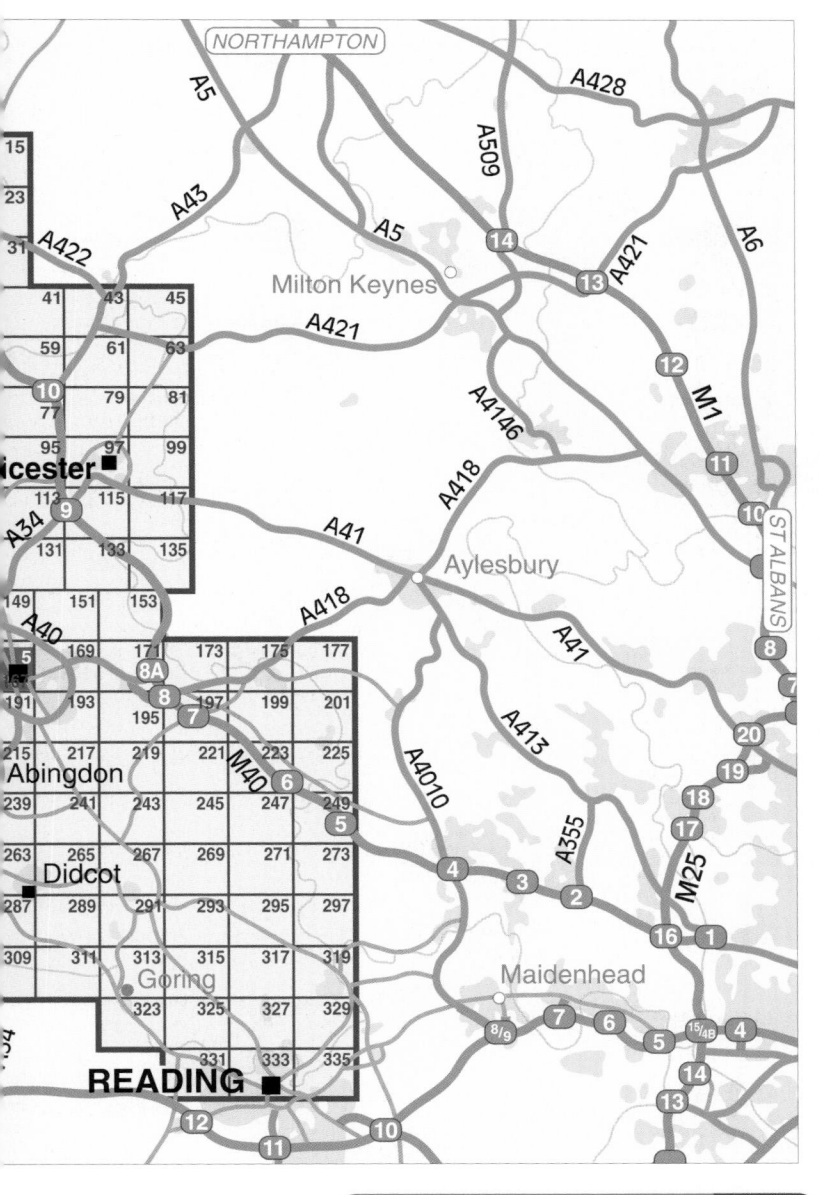

2.5 inches to 1 mile **Scale of main map pages** 1:25,000

iv

Junction 9	Motorway & junction	**P+**	Park & Ride
Services	Motorway service area		Bus/coach station
	Primary road single/dual carriageway		Railway & main railway station
Services	Primary road service area		Railway & minor railway station
	A road single/dual carriageway	⊖	Underground station
	B road single/dual carriageway	⊖	Light railway & station
	Other road single/dual carriageway	++++++++	Preserved private railway
	Restricted road	*LC*	Level crossing
	Private road	●—●—●—	Tramway
← ←	One way street	---------	Ferry route
	Pedestrian street	....	Airport runway
=========	Track/ footpath	— · — · — ·	Boundaries- borough/ district
	Road under construction	◥◥◥◥◥◥	Mounds
⊱ = = = ⊰	Road tunnel	**93**	Page continuation 1:25,000
P	Parking	**7**	Page continuation to enlarged scale 1:17,500

River/canal lake, pier		Toilet with disabled facilities
Aqueduct lock, weir		Petrol station
465 Winter Hill Peak (with height in metres)		Public house
Beach		Post Office
Coniferous woodland		Public library
Broadleaved woodland		Tourist Information Centre
Mixed woodland		Castle
Park		Historic house/ building
Cemetery		Wakehurst Place NT National Trust property
Built-up area		Museum/ art gallery
Featured building		Church/chapel
City wall		Country park
A&E Accident & Emergency hospital		Theatre/ performing arts
Toilet		Cinema

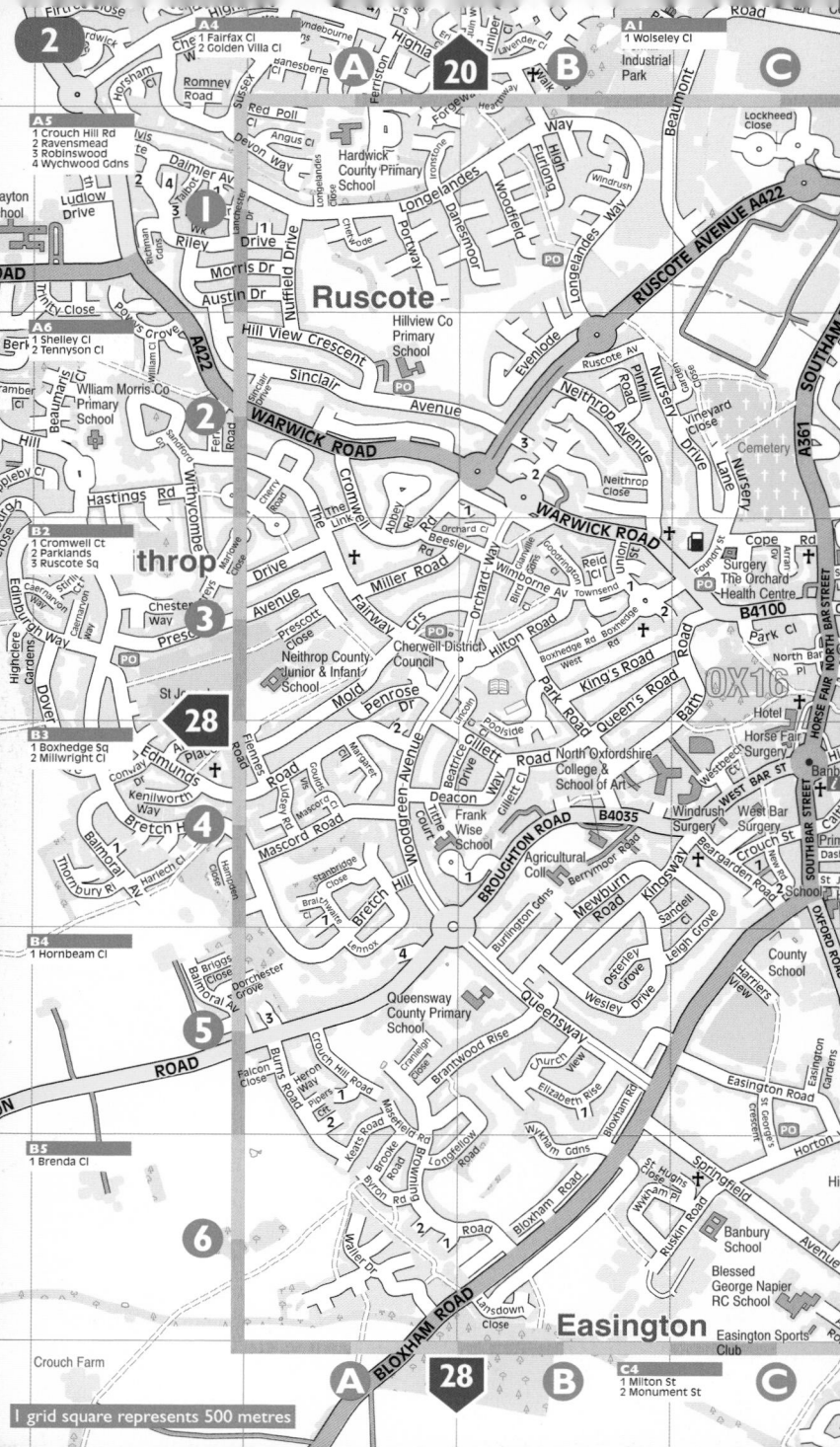

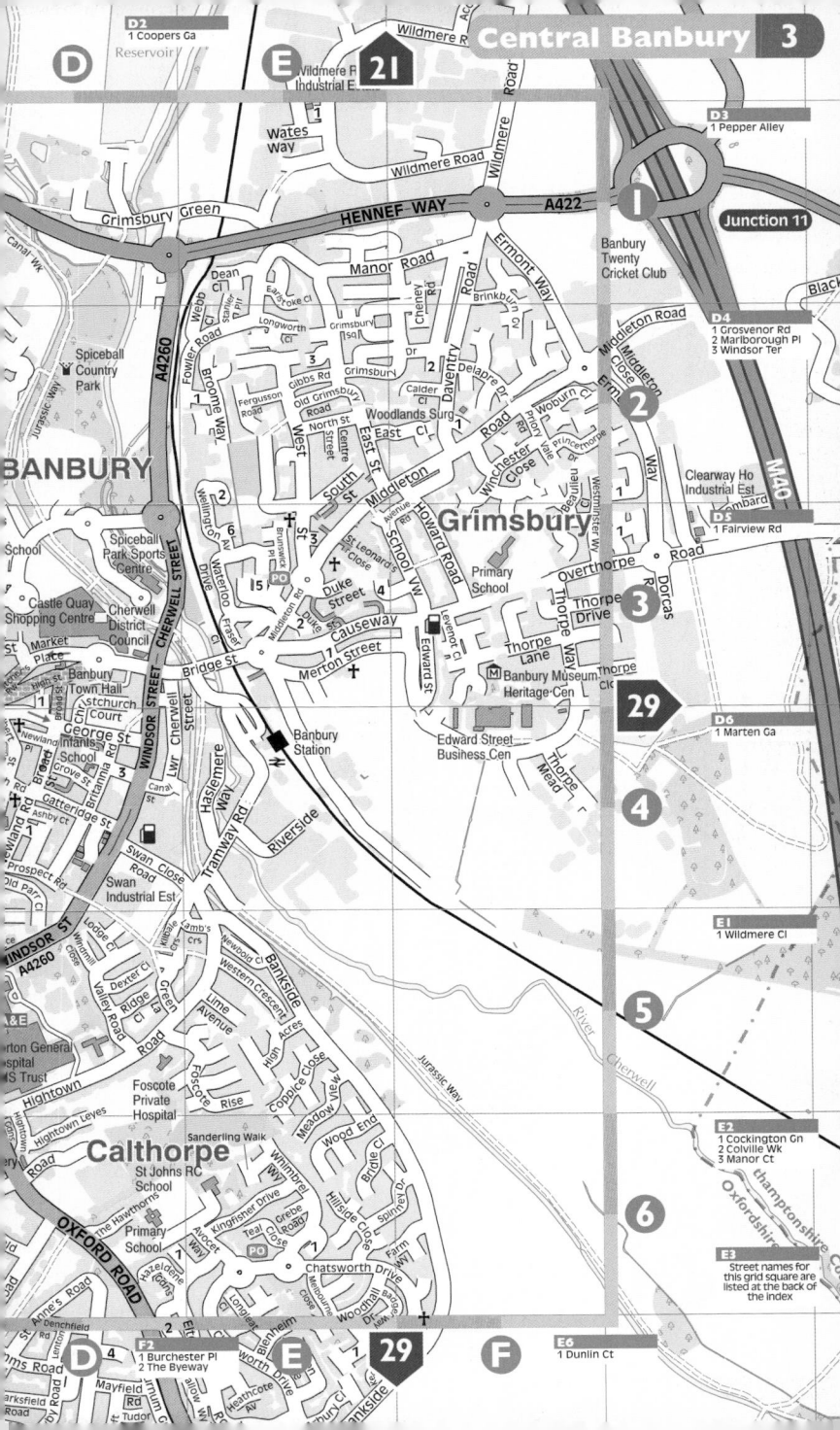

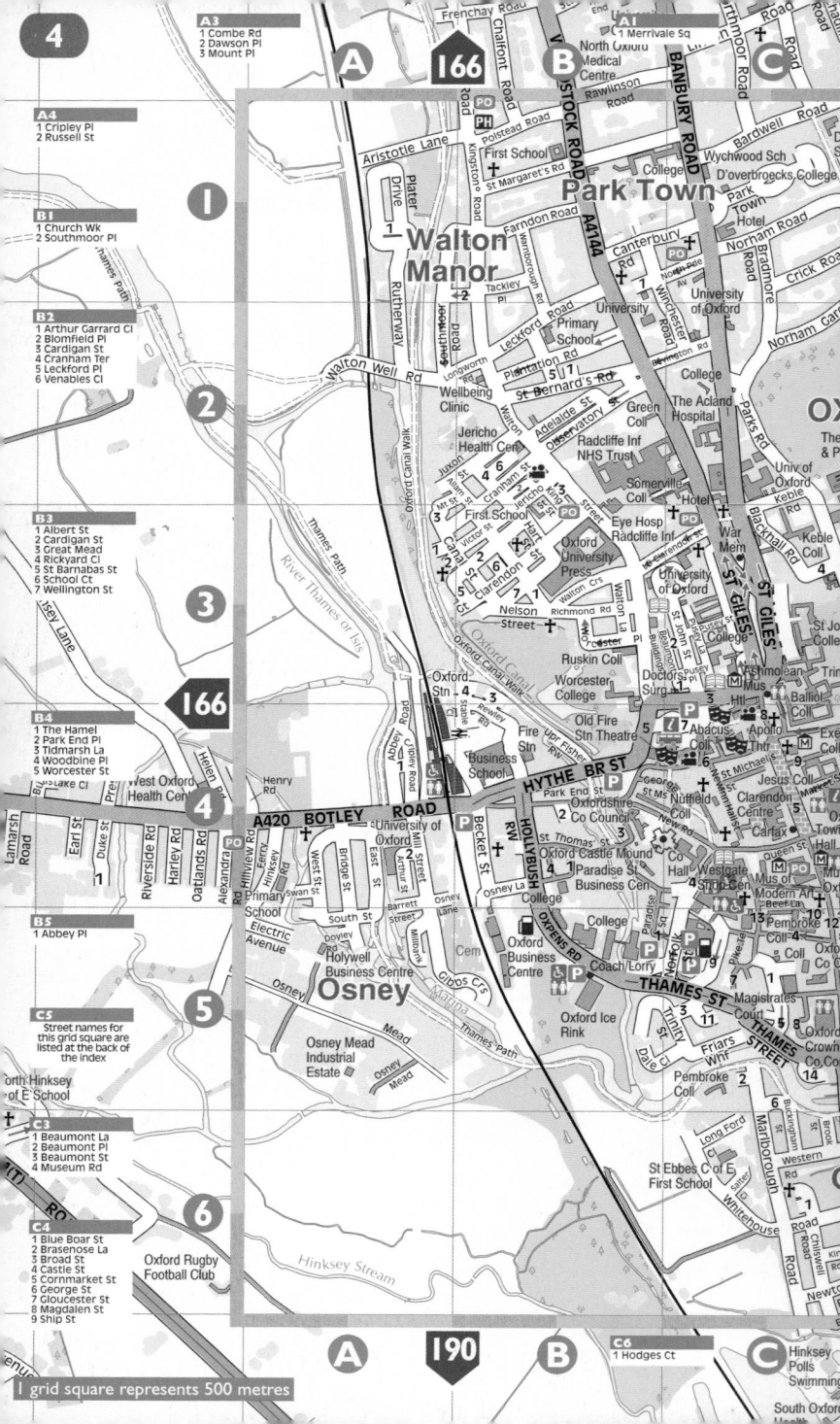

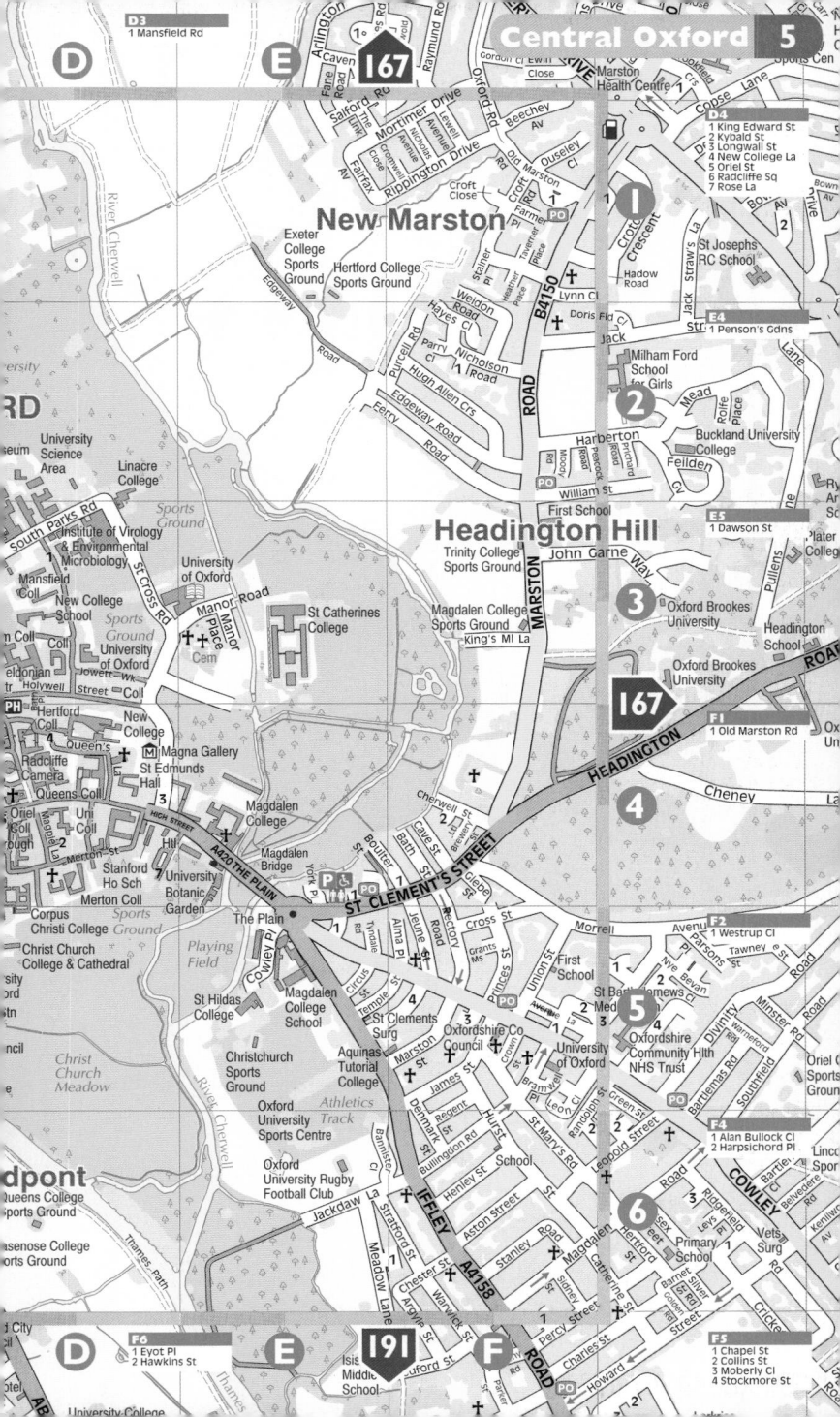

Frog Lane

Upper
Boddington

Primary School

Church Road

I

Spella
House

**Lower
Boddington**

Three
Shires

Road

2

H Paddock

Owl End
Lane

Banbury

Cedars
Farm

Claydon Hay
Farm

3

Northamptonshire County

Oxfordshire County

Oxfordshire County

4

Springfield
Farm

5

ord Canal

Macmillan Way

6

Boddington Road

on

Bygones
Museum

Bignolds
Close

Oxford Canal Walk

Macmillan Way

Apptree

7

attercote

8

Claydon Road

Canal Walk

River Cherwell

Oathill
Farm

F G H J K

B4086

I

Knowle
End

2

Radway

3

Old Road

New Road

Centenary Way

Westcote
Farm

The Grange

Ratl

Centenary Way

Grange
Grange

Townhill

High Street

Chapel
Lane

PH

4

PH

Edgehill

10

5

Warwickshire County
Oxfordshire County

Westcote
Manor

Edgehill
Farm

6

Hornton Hill
Farm

Centenary Way

Uplands
Farm

RISING HILL

A422

7

Sun
Rising

Centenary Way

Sugarswell Lane

Upton
House (NT)

PH

A422

8

F G H 17 J K

Temple
Pool

10

A B C D E

1

B4086

Arlescote

Knowle
End

2

Nadbury
House

Edgehill
Country Park

3

Crescent Way

Ratley

New
Lane

Chapel
Cottage

B4086

CAM

Macmillan

Townhill

High Street

Chapel Lane

Edge **4** ✝ PH

9

5

Sor Brook

Warwickshire County

Oxfordshire County

6

Hornton Hill
Farm

Poplars
Farm

7

Horley Fields
Farm

A422

Hornton
Hall

Millers Lane

8

Savee
Farm

Church Lane

East Gate

PO

✝ ✝ Church
Street

Hornton

A B **18** West End C D E

Bell Street

I grid square represents 500 metres

F G H J K

1

Farnborough Park

College Farm

2

Warwickshire County
Oxfordshire County

3

Macmillan Way

Village Road

Mollington Lane

March Road

M40

armington

Macmillan Way

Chapel St

Court La

Soot La

Church Hill

4

March Road

Fir Tree Farm

BANBURY ROAD

B4100

Manor Farm

12

5

Brook

Valley Farm

6

7

Mollington Lane

Shutt La

New Road

Middle Lane

Shotteswell

8

Warwickshire County
Oxfordshire County

B4100

F G H 19 J K

H5
1 Orchard Vw
2 Vicarage Gdns

attercote

F   G   H   7   J   K

I

Claydon Road

Oathill
Farm

Oxford Canal Walk

River Cherwell

ropredy
wn

Oxford Canal

2

3

Prescote Manor
Farm

Oxhey Hill

4

Claydon Road

Everts Corner

Crampot La

Oxford Canal Walk

Prescote
Manor

14

Cropredy

5

Cup and
Saucer

Battle Site
(1644)

The Surgery

6

Wardington
Grange

Cropredy
C of E
School

eat
urton

well La

Station Road

School La

The Green

Crow La

Bourton
House

Oxford Canal Walk

Williamscot

7

Foxden Way

Mill Lane

Peewit
Farm

8

F   G   H   21   J   K   A5 WILLIAMSCOT HILL

F G H J K

Macmillan Way

Welsh Road

River Cherwell

Trafford House

1

River Cherwell

2

Trafford Bridge

Trafford Bridge Farm

Wadground Barn

3

4

Danes Moor

Edgcote Lodge Farm

5

6

Northamptonshire County
Oxfordshire County

7

Lower Thorp

Hill Farm

8

Banbury Lane

F G H 23 J K

Fenny Hill

The Hill

Thorpe Mand

Townsend Lane PH

Oxfordshir

F G H **9** J K

I

Temple Pool

Macmillan Way

2

Hornton Grounds

Sugarswell Farm

The Bungalow

3

STRATFORD ROAD

4

18

The Surgery

Stocking Lane

Kennill Road

PH

School

Shenington

PO

The Level

Marmings PO

Macmillan Way

Alkerton

Well La

5

Rattlecombe Road

6

Rough Hill Farm

7

Alkerton Grounds

8

Macmillan Way

Epwell Grounds Farm

F G H **25** J Grounds Farm K

well

K7
1 Metcalfe Cl

F   G   H   I   J   K

Warwickshire County
Oxfordshire County

Horley

Manor
Orch
Lane
Cl
Quinten Cl

I

2

3

WARWICK

4

20

5
Drayton
Lodge

6

Cemetery

SILVER STREET   A422

Hotel

The First

ROAD
ORD
Main
Street
Mills Lane
Horley Path rd.
Church Street
Park
Tadmarts
Wroxton
C of E
Primary
School

Fairleigh Dickinson
University

Wroxton

Mill Lane

Drayton

Drayton
Schoo

7

STRATFORD   ROAD

Bretch
Brami

8

Penrhyn
Close

Castle
Bank

F   G   H   27   J   K

Newington Grounds
Farm

F7
1 Braggintons La
2 Lexton Gdns
3 Manor Cl
4 Salmons La

F8
1 Ashlade
2 Tulbrook Stones

F G H **15** J K

Fern Hill

The Hill

Thorpe Mande

Townsend Lane

PH

Oxfordshire County
Northamptonshire County

Thorpe Lodge Farm

Banbury Lane

Chacombe Lodge Farm

B4525

BANBURY LANE

B4525

Thenford Grounds Farm

Rectory Farm

Marston St Lawrence

Thenford Road

Lower Middleton Cheney

Main Road

Thenford

F G H **31** J K

A422

F
G
H
17
J
K

I

Epwell Grounds
Farm

Shutford Grounds
Farm

well

Epwell Road

2 tford

Cemetery

the Dovehouse

3

Chilaway
Farm

Farmington
Farm

Sibford Road

4

Blenheim
Farm

26

5

Brakelands
Farm

B4035

6

Green Lane

Tyne Hill
Farm

Lane

B4035

Swalcliffe Park
School

7

0X15

Hawkes
The Surgery

Burdrop

Elm
Farm

Bakers
Lane

Swalcliffe

8

hool
Main

PO

Street

Folly
Court

Small house

k Lane

**Sibford
Ferris**

Grange Lane

Park Lane

Sibford School

F
G
H
34
J
K

valcliffe
ange

Sibford Grounds
Farm

F ANBURY

Grimsbury

F **G** **H** **21** **J** **K**

I

F3
1 Fairview Rd

2
F4
1 Marten Ga

3
F5
1 Ashridge Cl
2 Birchwood
3 Briar Cl
4 Willoughby Rd

4

30

5
F6
1 Maple Cl

6
G1
1 Junction Rd
2 Mckeevor Pl
3 Moorfield Ct
4 Old School Pl
5 Victoria Pl
6 Wellesley Cl

7
G4
1 Dunlin Ct

8

Banbury Station

Banbury Museum
Heritage Cen

Edward Street
Business Cen

Calthorpe

St Johns RC
Primary School

Bishop Loveday
C of E Primary
School

Cherwell
District
Council

Banbury
Rugby Union
Football Club

Cotefield House

Bodicote
Mill House

Manor Farm

Paddock Farm

F **G** **H** **38** **J** **K**

Bloxham
1 Waltham Gdns

G6
1 Broad End
2 Park End Ct

G5
1 Harewood Rd
2 Homestead Rd
3 Poplar Cl

Greenhill House

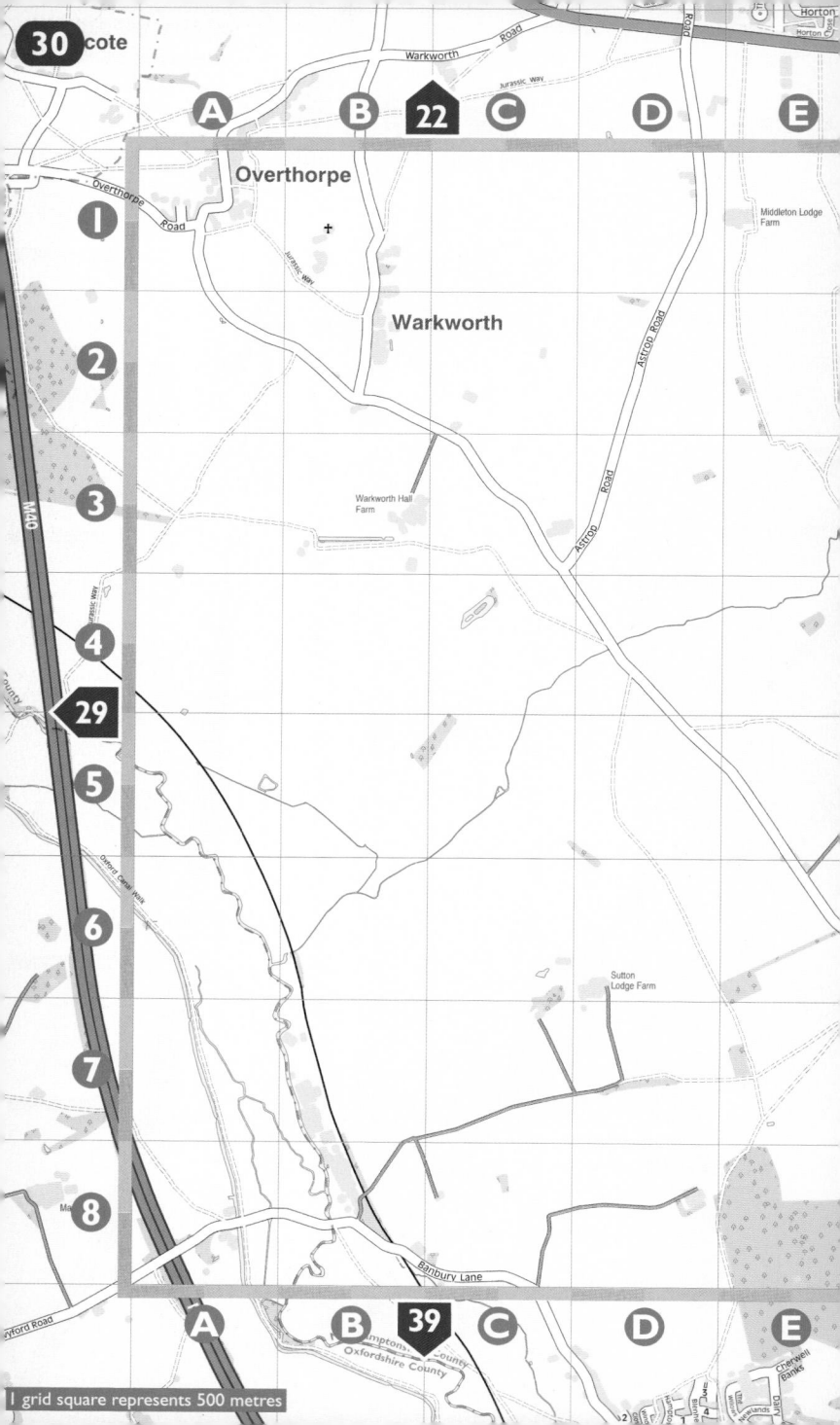

cote

A   B   **22**   C   D   E

Warkworth   Road

Jurassic Way

Horton

Road

I Overthorpe   Road

Overthorpe

Middleton Lodge
Farm

Jurassic Way

✝

Warkworth

2

3

Warkworth Hall
Farm

Astrop   Road

Astrop   Road

4

29

5

Oxford Canal Walk

6

7

Sutton
Lodge Farm

8

Ma

Banbury Lane

A   B   **39**   C   D   E

Oxfordshire County
amptons   County

Cherwell
Banks

Middleton
Cheney

F G H **23** J K

I

2

3

4

5

6

7

8

A422

A422

Great
Purston

Little
Purston

Buston
Farm

Farthinghoe
Lodge

Astrophill
Farm

Rosamond's
Bower

Upper Astrop

Robin
Wood

Newbottle

F G H **40** J K

Astrop House

Nature
Reserve

St Rumbald's
Well

Newbottle
Spinney

New Road

Clarks Lane

PO
Old

Force
Farm

Road

ton-under-Brailes

A   B   C   D   E

I

Chinslade Farm

Sutton Mill

Whichford Mill

2

Farnicombe

Lanes End Farm

3

Stourton Hill

North Leasow

4

Macmillan Way

5

Barratts Hill

De Mohun Crescent

Ascott Road

Whichford

Ascott Road

Ascott

Ascott Hill

Macmillan Way

6

Doctor's Barn

7

Yerdley Coppice

Gottenham

Whichford Hill Farm

8

A   B   **50**   C   D   E

grid square represents 500 metres

Sibford School

Main Street
Small House
Folly Court
PO
Back Lane
Woodway Rd
Hook Norton Road

A

Sibford School

Sibford
Ferris

B

25

Grange Lane

C

A8
1 The Green
2 Middle Hl
3 Queen St
4 Sibford Rd

D

E

I

Swalcliffe
Grange

Sibford Grounds
Farm

2

Bacon
Farm

3

Isle
Farm

Lower Nill
Farm

4

Lodge
Farm

33

Nill
Farm

5

Withycombe
Farm

6

7

Hook Norton
C of E Primary
School

Orchard Road
Hollybrunn Road
Station Road
Austin's Wy

East End

Ironstone
Hollow

Bourne Lane
Sibford Road
Rectory Lane

Manor Farm

The
Old
School
End

Hook Norton
Surgery

Bourne

Bell's Lane
Chapel
Street
East End
Nicolls Lane
Down
End
Titt Lane
Cemetery

8

Scotland End
Brookside

Netting Street

Well
Bank

Park Road

PH
PH

Bell Hill
High
Street
Park End

Park Farm

Clay Bank

Hook Norton

Bell's Croft Road
Croft's Lane

Park Road
Beargarth Rd

A

Southrop

Park Farm

B

52

grounds

C

D

E

I grid square represents 500 metres

Lower Tadmarton

36

B4035

E3
1 Bradford Ct
2 Goose Wk
3 Hawke La
4 Unicorn St

E2
1 Workhouse La

B6
1 Newcombe Cl

Ell's Farm

A **B** **27** **C** **D** **E**

Ell's Lane

1

E4
1 Cumberford
2 Orchard Gv

Tadmarton Lodge

Tadmarton House Farm

Firs Hill

2

Bloxham

Tadmarton Road

3

Bloxham C of E School

Courtington

Quarry Close

The Avenue

4

A361

35

Bloxham Road

5

Happy Farm

The Green

Milcombe

Portland

New Road

SOUTH NEWINGTON ROAD

6

Brickfield Farm

7

A361

River Swere

South Newington

8

Wigginton Road

High Street

Moor Lane

A361

A **B** **54** **C** **D** **E**

Barford Road

Rignell Farm

Rignell Hall

Buttermilk

I grid square represents 500 metres

F3
1 Humber St
2 Merrivale's La

G2
1 Greens Garth

F G H **28** J K

Sor Brook

Furlong

Boticote
Mill House

I

Bloxham Grove Road

BANBURY ROAD

Bloxham
Grove

School

A361

Calcotters
Close

Strawberry
Ter

Bloxham
School

Chapel Street

Steeple
Close

The
Surgery

PH

Wayhouse
Farm

Oldbarn
Farm

2

3

4

Barford
Road

Milton Road

Chapel
Lane

Milton

Milton **38**

5

6

7

Bloxham Road

**Barford
St John**

8

Mead
Road

F **Barford
G St Michael** H **55** J K

PH

Lower St

Church
Street

Fir
Rock

Horn Hill

Deddington Mill

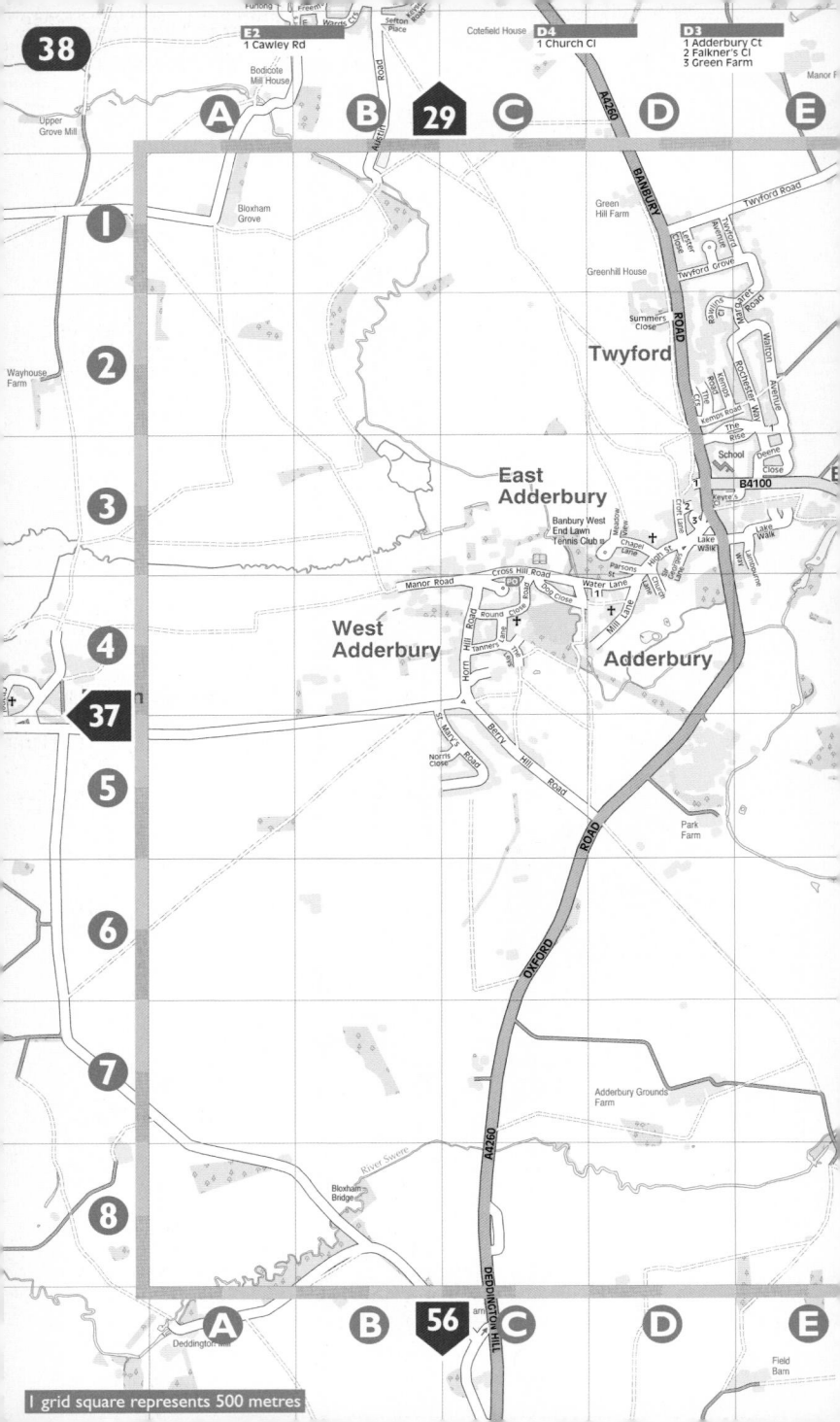

I1
1 Balmoral Wy
2 Barton Cl
3 Kensington Cl
4 Marlborough Cl

J2
1 Church Av
2 The Square

F G H 30 J K

Banbury Lane

Northamptonshire County
Oxfordshire County

River Cherwell

M40

I

K2
1 Dobbins Cl

Astrop

2

Kings Sutton Station

Kings
Sutton

3

Cemetery

ROAD

B4100

Trinity Way

Oxford Canal Walk

Bo-Peep Farm

Mill House
Farm

4

40

Walton
Grounds

5

Aynho Road

Nell
Bridge

Banbury
Golf Club

6

River Swere

7

B4100

Nellbridge Farm

Oxford Canal Walk

M40

8

River Cherwell

ROAD

F G H 57 J K

Tithe Lane

AYNHO ROAD

B4031

Hazel
Hedge

F G H J K

H7
1 Chapel End

J7
1 Church End

Wardrobe Farm

Hinton-in-
the-Hedges

Forceleap
Farm

Airfield

1

2

Charlton
House Farm

arlton

3

4

42

Rowler

5

6

Warren
Farm

Cem

7

Wheeler's

Croughton
C of E School

HIGH STREET

Brackley Road

BLENHEIM   B4031

Mill La

Church

PARK END

Portway

B4031

8

Croughton

Portway
Crs

Portway Drive

Sixth Street

Fifth Av

Fifth St E

Fifth St

Fourth
Avenue

PO

F G H **59** J K

Third St

Second St

First
Street

New
Buildings

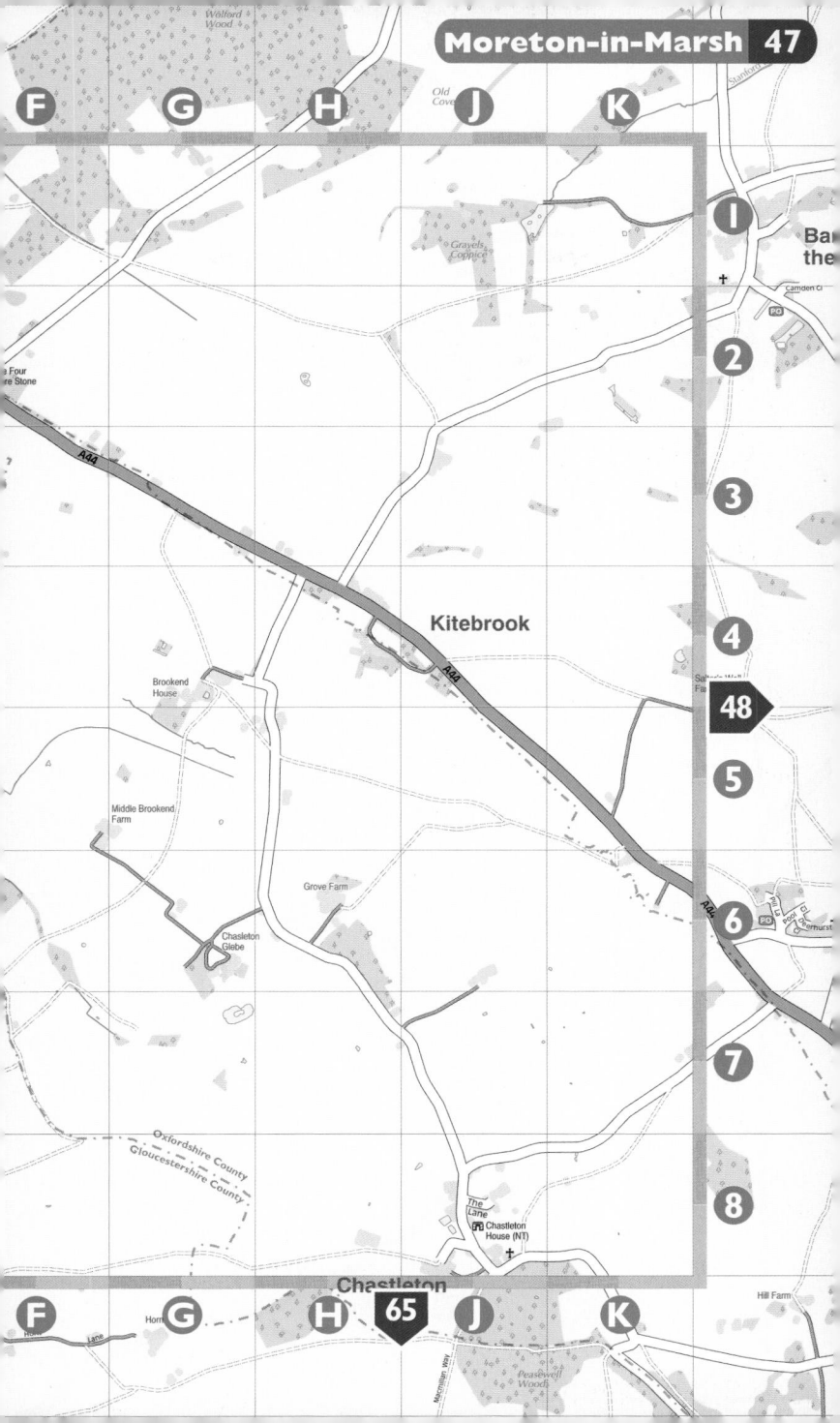

A B C **Barton Road** D E

I

Barton-on-the-Heath

Camden Cl

2

3

4

47

5

Salter's Well Farm

Hawton Farm

Slade Farm

Cemetery

Oakham Road Oakham

6 Willow End

Little Compton

New Town

7

8

Warwickshire County
Oxfordshire County

A B 66 C D E

Hill Farm

A436

SHIPSTON ROAD

Crockwell St

F

G

Long Compton

H

J

K

Kenhill Lane

Malthouse La

PO

Vicarage Lane

Broad Street

East street

Weston Ct

Wood Cl

Butlers Cl

Long Compton
Junior & Infant
School

Butlers La

A3400

Barn Cl

Clarks Lane

Butlers Road

I

Oxfordshire County
Warwickshire County

2

Butlers Road
Farm

3

Butlers Road

Butlers Hill
Farm

Macmillan Way

The Hollows

South Hill
Farm

A3400

4

50

Warwickshire County
Oxfordshire County

Kings Men

Whispering
Knights

5

6

**Little
Rollright**

7

Choicehill
Farm

8

Hirons
Hill Farm

Spri
Fa

F

G

H

67

J

K

50

E4
1 Church End

D4
1 Chapel End
2 Cotswold Cnr
3 The Green

A   B   **32**   C   D   E

I

Coombe Farm

Hutton Grange Farm

2

Bullers Road Farm

3

Hill Barn Farm

Oxfordshire County
Warwickshire County

Butlers Road

Church End

Hook   Norton   Road

Great Rollright C of E Primary School

Manor House

Butlers Hill Farm

4   A3400

49

High Street

Old Forge Road

PO

Great Rollrig

South End   Robins Close

5

6

Half Farm

A3400

7

Choicehill Farm

Hull Farm

8

Sandfields Farm

B4026

A   B   **68**   C   D   E

Choicehill Road

Rollright Hill

Over Norton House

I grid square represents 500 metres

Court Farm

Berryfield Farm

Scotland End

Ewery Lane

School End

Hook Norton

Croft's Lane

Fanville Farm

Rollright Heath Farm

Duckpool Farm

well Farm

Coltscombe

Coldharbour Farm

Priory Mill

Walk Farm

A361

Over Norton Common

Show Farm

A361

BANBURY ROAD

Green Lane

F G H 33 J K I South

2

3

4

52

5

6

7

8

F G H 69 J K

South

Chipping Norton Road

Swerford Road

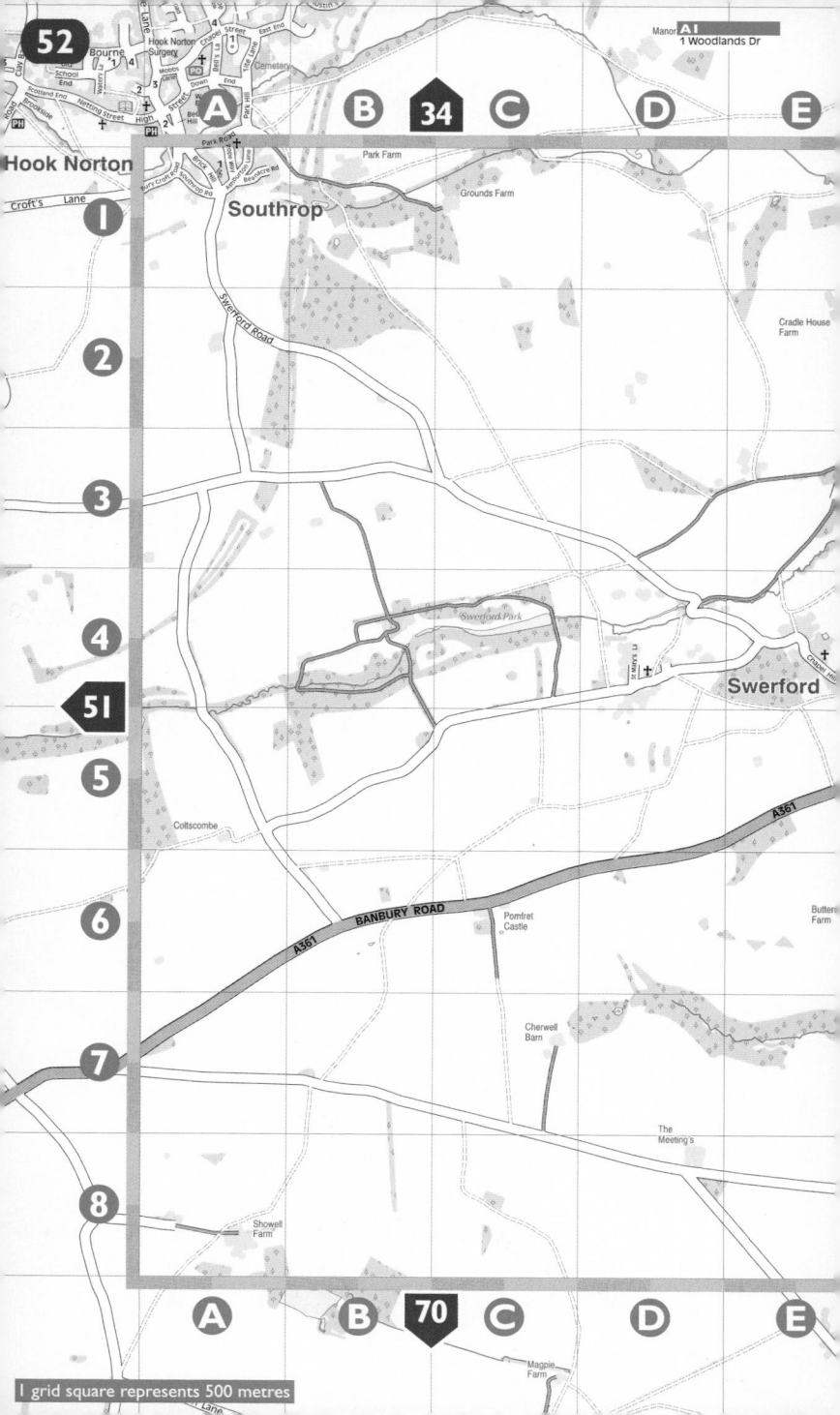

A B **34** C D E

Hook Norton

Croft's Lane

1

Park Farm

Southrop

Grounds Farm

Cradle House Farm

Swerford Road

2

3

Swerford Park

St Mary's La

Swerford

Chase Hill

4

51

5

Coltscombe

A361

A361 BANBURY ROAD

Pomfret Castle

Butter Farm

6

Cherwell Barn

The Meeting's

7

8

Showell Farm

A B **70** C D E

Magpie Farm

F1
1 Bishops Cl

St John

Barford
St Michael

Mead
Road

PH
PO
Lower St
The Rock
Horn Hill
Church Street
Broad Close
High Street
Robins
Townsend
Nethertworton Road

B4031 STEEPNESS HILL

St John's Way
Snakehill
Lane
The Lane

Hempton

B4031

Cemetery

Ilbury Farm

56

Tomwell
Farm

Newhouse
Farm

Over
Worton

Lower Farm

Rest
Hill Farm

Worton
House

Duns
Tew

Manor
House

Hill Farm Lane

F G H 37 J K

I
2
3
4
5
6
7
8

F G H 73 J K

I grid square represents 500 metres

A421

Northamptonshire County
Oxfordshire County

The Hulls

F   **G**   **H**   **43**   **J**   **K**

1

Middle Farm

The Pits

2

Coldharbour Farm

Featherbed Lane

3

Shelswell Plantation

4

Cottisford

62

Shelswell Park

Shelswell

5

Fox Covert

6

Coneygre Farm

7

Willaston Farm

Hethe

Main Street

Hardwick Road

8

Tangley Farm

Bainton Road

PRESCOTT Lane

Fringford

F   **G**   **H**   **79**   **J**   **K**   Fringford

Fringford C of E School

64
Barrow

Heath Barn

A

B

46

C

+

D

E

D7
1 Embrook

Green Lane

Church Lane

Horn

Evenlode

1

North Rye House

Cownham Farm

Lane

2

3

Foxes Row

Millbrook Ley

Quinmoor Farm

Chapel Street

Broadwell

Evenlode Farm

River Evenlode

4

5

Broadwell Hill

Sydenham Farm

Black Pit

6

Bro

7

Back Lane

Lo
Od

A436

Upper Oddington

8

B4450

Martin's Hill

Cotswold Crest

A

B

82

C

D

E

B4450

I grid square represents 500 metres

Ⓐ   Ⓑ   **48**   Ⓒ   Ⓓ   Ⓔ

Hill Farm

Greygoose Lane

A436

A44

I

Chastleton
Barrow

2

A436

Park
Farm

3

A436

Glebe
Farm

4

Cornwell

Cornwell
Manor

A436

◀ **65**

5

Daylesford
Hill Farm

Daylesford
House

6

The
Dell

Gloucestershire County
Oxfordshire County

Kingham Hill
Farm

Slade
Farm

Kingham Hill
School

7

Kingham Hill
School

8

Ⓐ   Ⓑ   **84**   Ⓒ   Ⓓ   Ⓔ

I grid square represents 500 metres

F G H 49 J K

I
2
3
4
68
5
6
7
8

Hirons
Hill Farm

Springhill
Farm

The
Green

Chapel Lane

Roses Lane

Cooks Lane

Orchard
Close

Lower End

Salford

A44

Primsdown
Industrial
Estate

Cemetery

WORCESTER ROAD

WORCESTER ROAD

A44

Kennel
Lane

Coe Lane

Toy Lane

Common
Lane

Lewis Road

Tudor Road

Webb
Cresc

The
Levs

Alexandra
Square

Lords Piece Road

Thisley
Road

CHURCHILL ROAD

COTMAN ROAD

Meads
Farm

B4450

Churchill
Grounds Farm

Boulter's Barn

Besbury Lane

B4450

Sarsgrove
Farm

F G H 85 J K

F G H **53** J **Great Tew** K

Brook Rd.
PO
The Lane
Great Tew
Old Road
BUTCHER'S ROAD
New Road
I

Great Tew Park

1

2

West Lane
Eltstone Road
Little Tew
The Lodge
B4022

Hookerswell Farm

Beaconsfield Farm

3

4

72

Mill Covert

Tracey Farm

5

6

7

Cuckold's Holt Farm

B4030

8

B4031

F G H **89** J K **Gagingwell**

Drystone Hill House

O G7
1 Crossway
Worton

F **G** **H** 55 **J** **K**

Lower Farm

Worton
House

Heath Farm

I
**Duns
Tew**

Manor
House

Hill Farm Lane

Main Street

Glebe Court

Middle Barton Road

2

3

Down Hill
Farm

Horsehay
Farm

4

74

5

Cockley Brook

6

Orchard Way
Hillside Road

Worton Road

**Middle
Barton**

Colliers

Crescent

Kiddy Close

Rectory Cl

Farmers Rd

Frances Road

NORTH STREET

Jacobs Yard

Fox Lane

South Street

Mill Lane

Middle Barton
Primary
School

B4030

Barlongate

7
Whistlow

8

B4030

Church Lane

Pack Lane

F **G** **H** 91 **J**
**Steeple
Barton**

K
**Barton
Abbey**

Church Lane

A B **58** C D E

I

2

3

4

◀ 75

5

6

7

8

A B **94** C D E

B8
1 Carswell Cir

No B7
1 Brice Rd
2 Carswell Crs
3 Portal Dr
4 Whitley Dr

Portway
Farm

Street

Forge Place

Forge Place East

Ardley Road

Bainhouse Lane

Village
Farm

Troy Farm

Mudginwell
Farm

Upper Heyford
Airfield

Trenchard
Circle

Chilgrove Drive

Road

Egan St

Homestead
Crescent

Kirtlington Road

Port Way

Soden Road

Larsen Road

Camp Road

Gordon Road

Roper Rd

Chestnut Rd

Dacey Drive

Eadle Road

Portal

Gibson Dr

Tait Dr

Bader Dr

Harris Road

Nettleton
Drive

Drive St

The
Heath

I grid square represents 500 metres

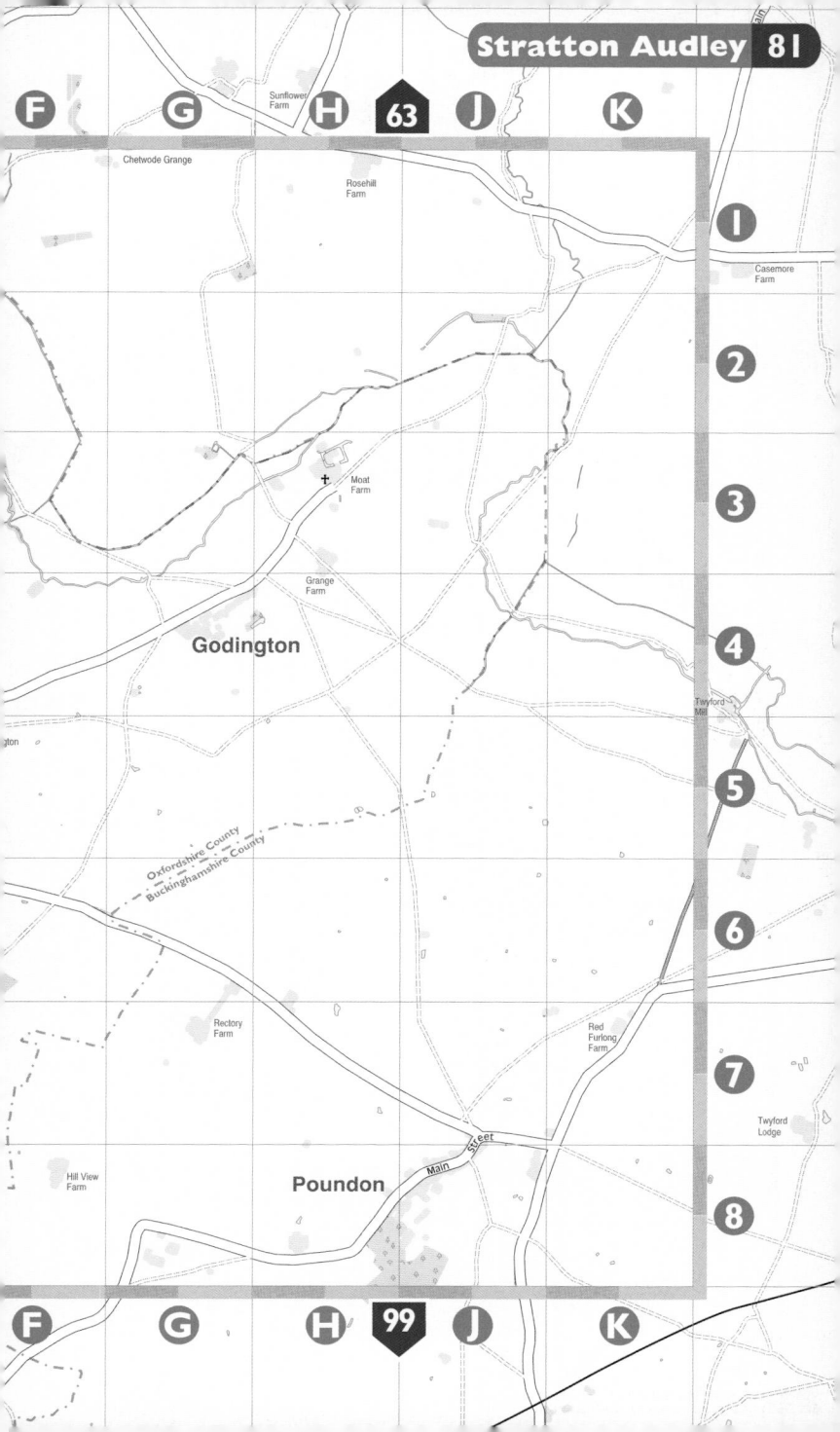

F G H 63 J K

I

Chetwode Grange

Sunflower Farm

Rosehill Farm

Casemore Farm

2

3

Moat Farm

Grange Farm

4

Godington

Twyford Mill

5

Oxfordshire County

Buckinghamshire County

6

Rectory Farm

Red Furlong Farm

7

Twyford Lodge

Hill View Farm

Main Street

Poundon

8

F G H **65** J K

I

2

3

4

84

5

6

7

8

F G H **101** J K

River Evenlode

Bledington Heath

Bledington Grounds

Mickland's Hill

B4450

STOW ROAD

CHAPEL ST

Chapel Street

MAIN STREET

PH

Church Street

Church Lane

Old Forge Cottage

Bledington County Primary School

OLD BURFORD ROAD

Oxfordmore Way

Bledington

B4450

STATION

Oxfordmore Way

Gloucestershire County

Oxfordshire County

Ilcote Brook

Foscot

Foxholes Farm

Nature Reserve

Fifield Heath

The Moors

West End

Green Close

PO

Cornood Cl

Meadow W

New Road

Field Road

Station Road

Station Road

Hotel

ROAD

Kingham Station

Bou

84

A B **66** C D E

I

Sarsd Halt

2

Kingham County Primary School
Churchill Road

The Mall
Main's Close
West Street
The Green
Chapel Lane
Church St
West End
Coach's Lane
The Grapes
Fowler's Road

Kingham

3

Coxmoor
Meadow Way
New
Field Road
Station Road

Hotel

4

B4450

83

5

Kingham Station

Rynehill Farm

ROAD

STATION

B4450

Churchill Heath Farm

6

B4450

7

Sarsden Lodge

8

Foxholes Farm

Nature Reserve

A B **102** C D E

Lyneham Golf Club

River Evenlode

LC

I grid square represents 500 metres

F G H **71** J K

Gagingwell

1

2

Cleveley

3

Radfordbridge

Drystone Hill
House

4

90

5

A44

Deadman's
Riding Wood

A44

Asterleigh
Farm

6

Dog
Kennel

Kiddington Drive

7

Grimsdyke
Farm

8

Ditchley
Park

F G H **107** J K

Out
Wood

90

A   B   **72**   C   D   E

Gagingwell

1

Oathill
Farm

2

Radford

White
House Farm

3

Radfordbridge

4

89

Heath
Farm

Kiddington

5

Asterleigh
Farm

6

Home
Farm

Over
Kiddington

7

Glympton
Park

Gly

Kiddington Drive

Grimsdyke
Farm

B4027

New Road

PO

8

Hill
Wood

Copping
Knoll

A   B   **108**   C   D   E

Hill
Farm

Gars
Wood

1 grid square represents 500 metres

G1
1 knapton's Cft

F G H 75 J K

I

2

3

4

94

5

6

7

8

Heyford
Station
STATION ROAD

Lower
Heyford

Church La
The Lane
Freehold
Mill Lane
Station
View
Cherwell Bank
Street
Bromeswell
Close

B4030

Port Way

LOWER HEYF
Caulcott

South Street

Greenway

The
Cleeves

Fir Tree
Farm

Oxford Canal

Northbrook

Port Way

Manor
Farm

Oxford Canal Walk

The Ridge

F G H III J K

Nethercott

Nethercott

Tackley
Station

PORT WAY

A4095

Gibz
Tait
Reid

F G H **77** J K

I

2

3

4

96

5

6

7

8

Upper Farm

Dewars Farm

Bucknell Lodge

B430

ARDLEY ROAD

HEYFORD ROAD

Park Lane

School Lane

Hotel

OXFORD ROAD

BICESTER ROAD   B4030

Middleton Stoney

B4030

M40

Chesterton Fields Farm

Bignell Park Farm

Bignell Park Farm

A4095

B430

Simms Farm

Bignell Park Farm

Chesterton Country Golf Club

Spring Well Farm

A4095

Alchester

Hotel

Bignell House

The Woodlands

Green

F G H **113** J K

B450

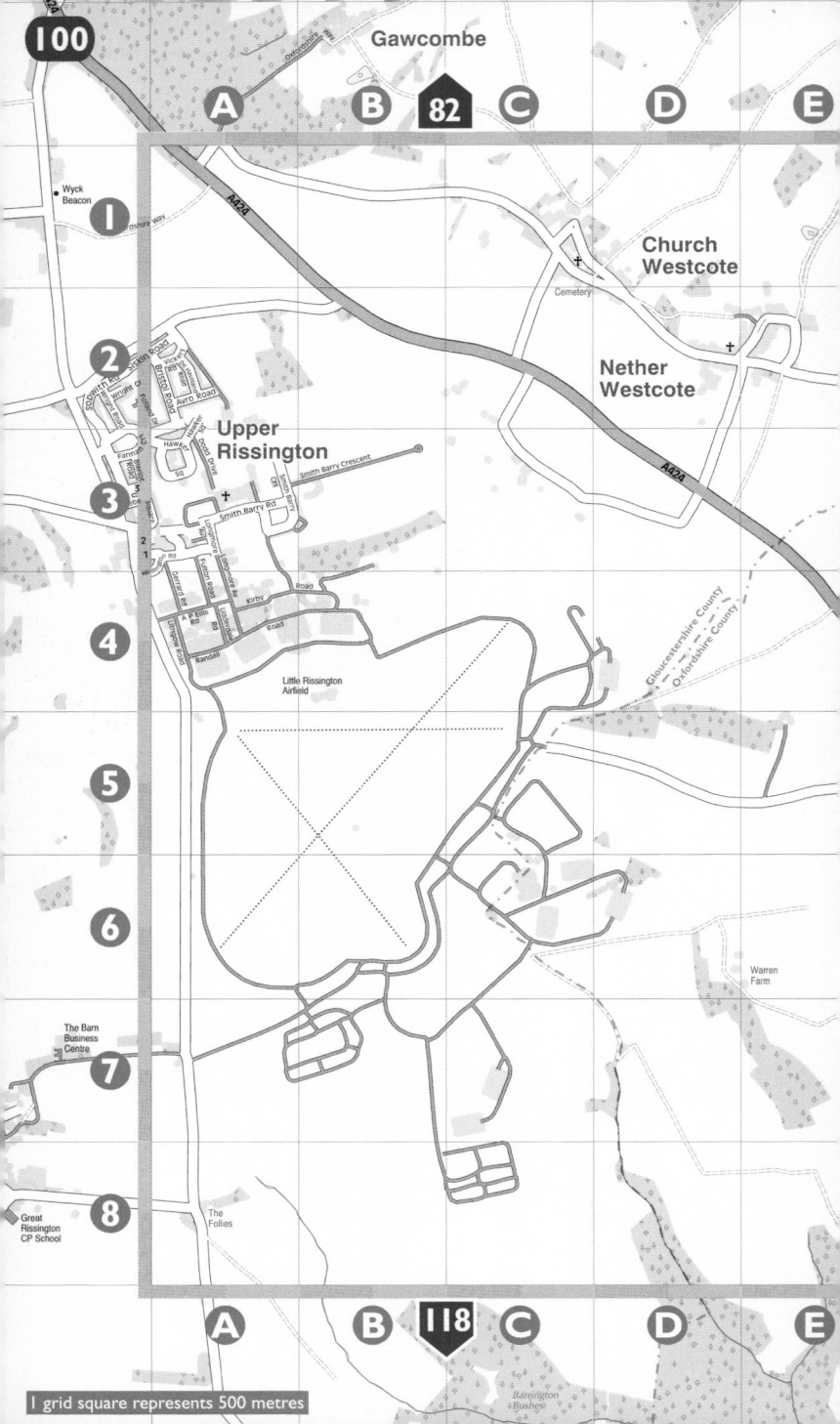

F G H 83 J K

Foxholes Farm

I

Fifield Heath

Bould

Nature Reserve

2

Church St

Idbury

3

Herbert's Heath

Sacred Flame

4

102

Grange Fm

Fifield

5

High St

Merrymouth Road

Church Street

6

Milton u Wychwe

Hill Farm

7

A424

Tangley Woods

High Lodge Farm

8

Tangley Hall

A424

Springhill Farm

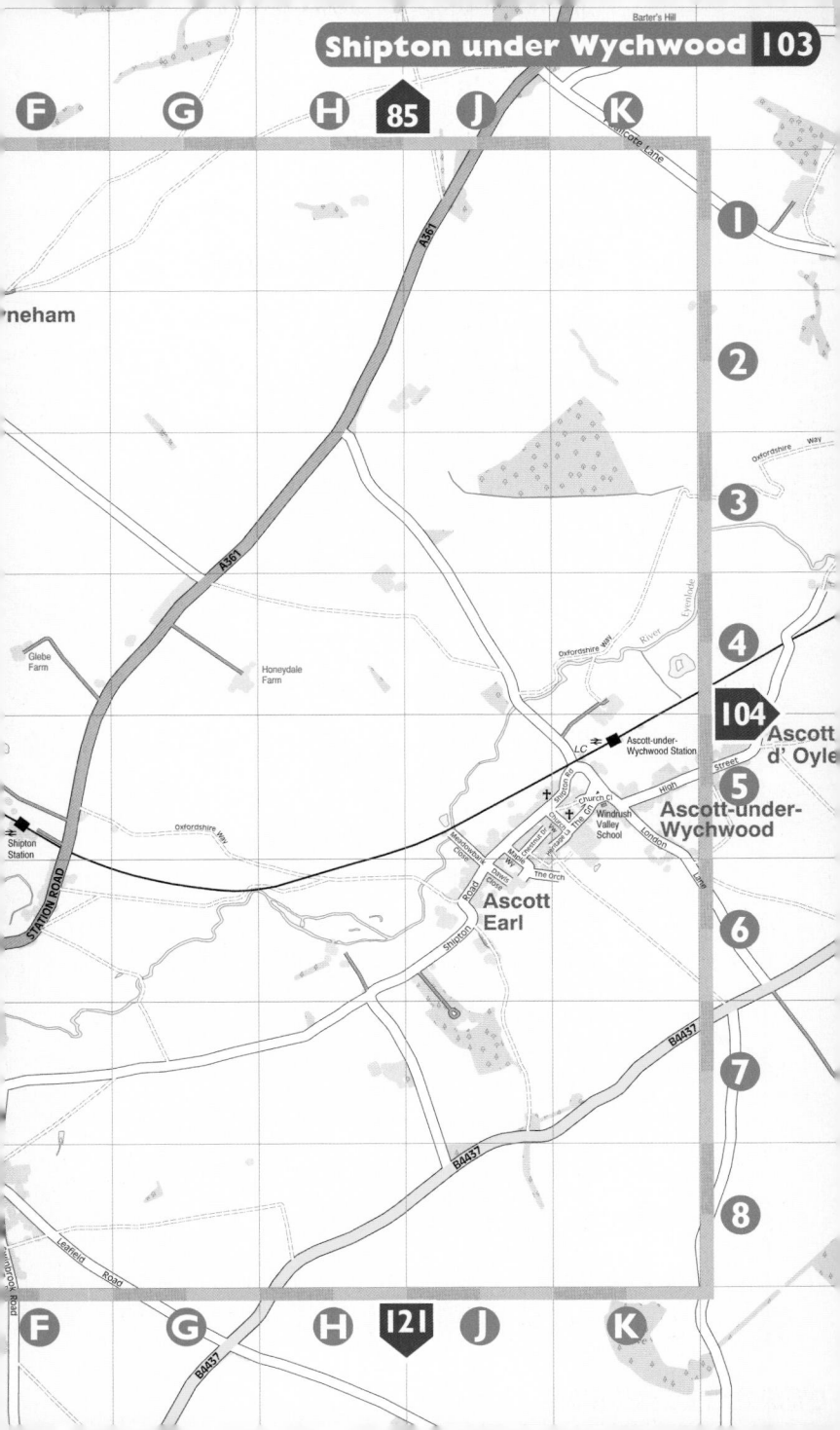

F G H `85` J K

`I`

`2`

`3`

`4`

`104` Ascott d' Oyle

`5`

`6`

`7`

`8`

Barter's Hill

Wilcote Lane

A361

neham

Glebe Farm

Honeydale Farm

Oxfordshire Way

River Evenlode

Oxfordshire Way

Ascott-under-Wychwood Station

LC

High Street

Church Cl

Windrush Valley School

The Orch

London Lane

Ascott-under-Wychwood

STATION ROAD

Shipton Station

Oxfordshire Way

Mawle

WI

Manchester Close

Shipton Rd

De Breos Dr

Priory Cl

Shipton Rd

Ascott Earl

B4437

B4437

Leafield Road

Swinbrook Road

F G H `121` J K

B4437

H8
1 Barrett's Cl
2 Cockshoot Cl
3 Friends' Cl
4 Hunt's Cl
5 Maltsters
6 Prospect Cl
7 St James Ct

F **G** **H** **89** **J** **K**

I

Out Wood

2

Wood Farm

3

Kingswood Farm

Lodge Farm

Model Farm

Ash Copse

B4437 B447 **4**

Sheer's Copse

B4437

108

King's Wood

5

Stonesfield Road

Callow Farm

6

Hill Barn Farm

Oxfordshire Way

7

Oaklands Farm

Wootton End

Farley

Longore

Stonesfield

Greenfield Crescent

8

The Ridings

Brook St

Peaks Lane

Pond Hill

Longore

Bushy

Stonesfield Primary Sch

High Street

Woodstock Road

Church St

Combe Road

Church Fields

Cemetery

Oxfordshire Way

F **G** **H** **125** **J** **K**

Oakland's Farm

Noroaks Wood

G3
1 Walnut Cl

H8
1 Marlborough Crs
2 Vermont Dr

F G H 91 J K

I

2

3

4

110

5 B4027

6

Banbury Road

7

8

Wootton

B4027 GLYMPTON ROAD

Tew Lane

Burditch Bank

Castle Road

Manor Farm Court

Primary School

Milford Place

Open View

Lamb's La

River Glyne

West End

OX20

Holly Bank

Lower Dornford Farm

Hordley Farm

Stratford Lane

Stratford Bridge

A44

Oxfordshire Way

Furze Platt

Field Barn

Old Woodstock

Hill Rise

MANOR ROAD

A44

Green Lane

River Glyne

Cemetery

Great Park

Column of Victory

Hensington

Banbury Road

Buards Cl

Marlborough School

C of E

Woodstock Swimming Pool

Hensington Close

F G H 127 J K

Oxfordshire County Museum

Park St

WAY

PO

Union St

Hotel

Park St

Cockpit Close

Bear Close

Hensington Road

New Road

Kenwood Terr

Shipton Road

Queen Pool

Doctors Surgery

Lane

WOODSTOCK

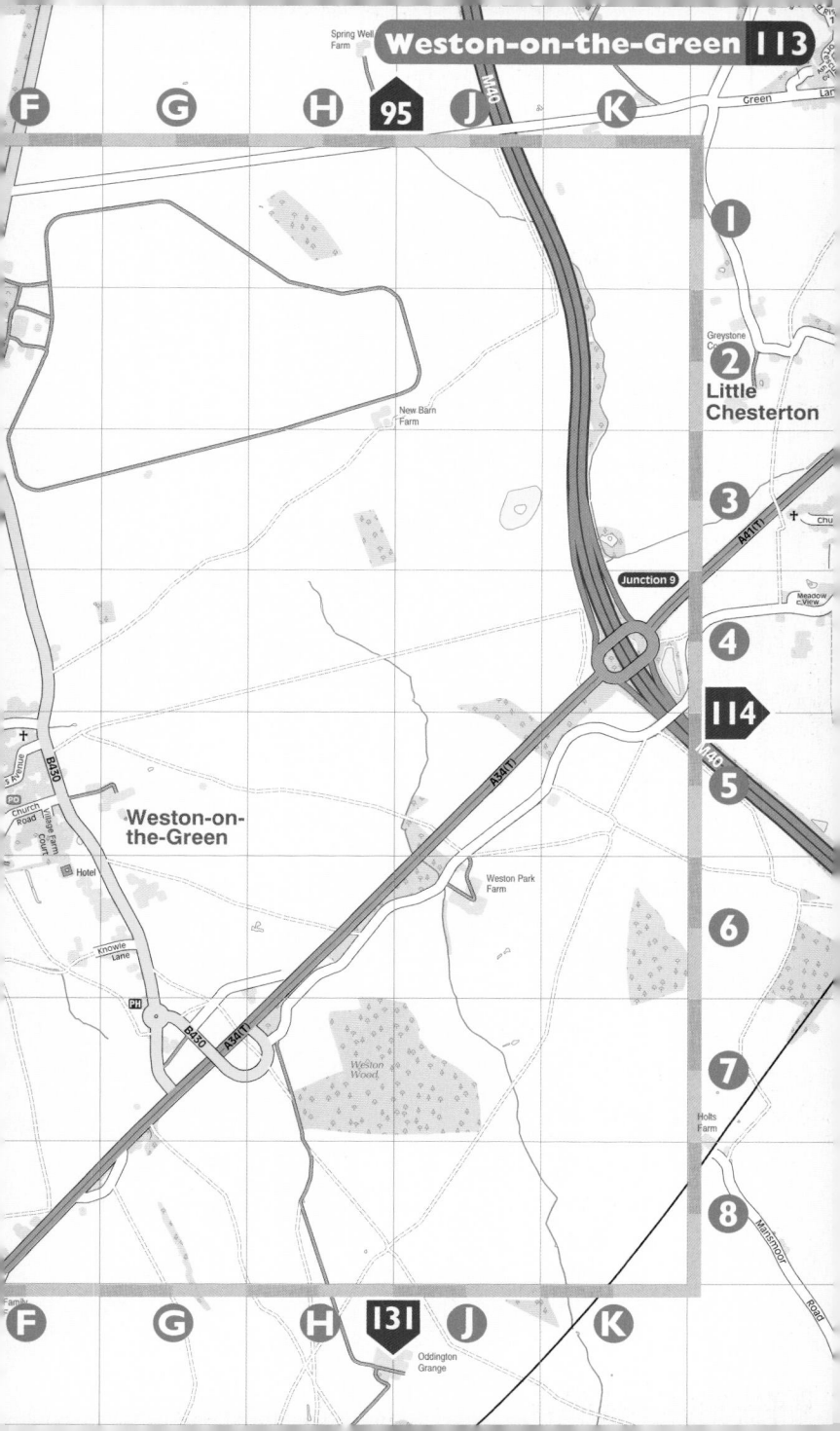

F
G
H
95
J
K

Spring Well Farm

Green Lane

I

Greystone Co...

2
Little Chesterton

New Barn Farm

3
A34(1)
✝ Chu

Meadow View

Junction 9

4

114

M40

5

✝
BA30
3 Avenue
Church Road
Village Farm Court
PO
Hotel
Weston-on-the-Green

Weston Park Farm

6

Knowle Lane

PH
B430
A34(1)

Weston Wood

7

Holts Farm

8
Mansmoor Road

Family

F
G
H
131
J
K

Oddington Grange

F G H **99** J K

I

Essex Farm

Heet Farm

2

Grange Farm

Three Points

Heath Bridge

A41(T)

White House Farm

3

Buckinghamshire County
Oxfordshire County

Piddington Cow Leys

4

5

New Barn Farm

6

Piddington Road

7

Arncott Road

Uxbridge Road

Lower End

8

Glebe Farm

Eastbrook Close

Piddington

Thame Road

Vicarage Lane

Buck

F G H 103 J K

I

Leafield Road

B4457

B4457

Priest Grove

Fairspear Farm

2

Farfield Corner

3

Swinbrook Road

Leafield Road

Forest Farm

Langley Farm

Langley

4

122

South Lawn

Potter's Hill

5

6

Hens Grove

Fordwells

7

8

Stokkley Copse

Asthall Leigh

F G H 140 J K

The Olde Farm

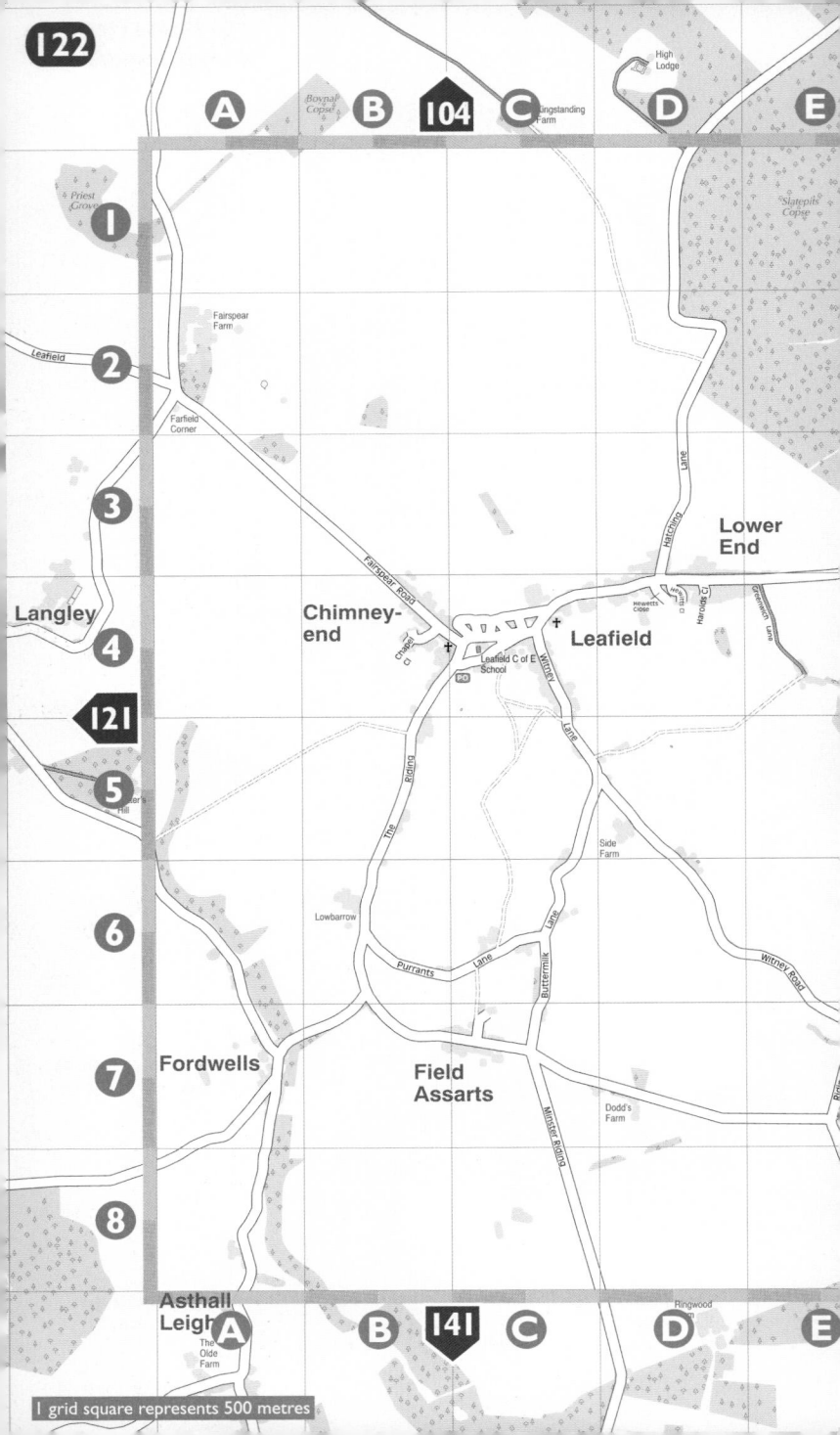

I22

A B **104** C D E

I Priest Grove

Boynal Copse

High Lodge

Ungstanding Farm

Slatepits Copse

2 Leafield

Fairspear Farm

3 Farfield Corner

Hatching Lane

Lower End

Langley

4 Chimney-end

Chapel

Leafield C of E School

Leafield

newetts Copse

Harolde Cl

Greenwich Lane

I2I

5 r's Hill

The Riding

Side Farm

6 Lowbarrow

Witney Lane

7 Fordwells

Purrants Lane

Buttermilk Lane

Witney Road

Field Assarts

Dodd's Farm

8

Minster Riding

Ringwood

Asthall Leigh

The Olde Farm

A B **141** C D E

I grid square represents 500 metres

F **G** **H** **105** **J** **K**

I

WITNEY ROAD

Finstc
Prima

2

High Street

Ramsden
Heath

Mount
Skipp **3**

B4022

Skippett Lane

High Street

Woodcote **4**

Brize's
Lodge

Cemetery

124

5

Saint John's Lane

6

Chasewood
Farm

Blackbird Lane

Whiteoak
Green

Singe
Wood

Gigley
Farm

Wood Lane

PH

7

Turley Lane

Wood Lane

Showells
Farm

Leafield Road

B4022

Manor House

Delly Cl

De 8 End

DELLY HILL

Hailey

F **G** **H** **142** **J** **K**

Riding Lane

Broken
Hatch
Farm

Church Lane

124

A **B** **106** **C** **D** **E**

B2
1 Walker's Height

Fawler

LC

I

CHARLBURY ROAD

School Road

Church Rd

Ward's Lane

Finstock C of E
Primary School

Topples
Wood

WITNEY ROAD

Hill Crs

Main Ht

2

Finstock

PH

High Street

Wilcote Riding

Wilcote Riding

Skippett Lane

3 **Mount
Skippett**

Wilcote
House

Wilcote
Manor

Wilcote
House

4

High Street

PH

Woodcote Lane

The
Hays

Wilcote
Grange

Cemetery

123

Ramsden

5

Holly
Grove

Bridewell
Farm

6

Assarts Lane

Blackbird Lane

Shakenoak
Farm

7

Gigley
Farm

Whitings Lane

North Leigh Lane

Wood Lane

Manor House

Delly Cl

8

Delly End

Pitts Lane

New Yatt Lane

**New
Yatt**

New Yatt
Business
Centre

Hailey

Primary
School

A **B** **143** **C** **D** **E**

Hartford

Job's Copse

**Poffley
End**

1 grid square represents 500 metres

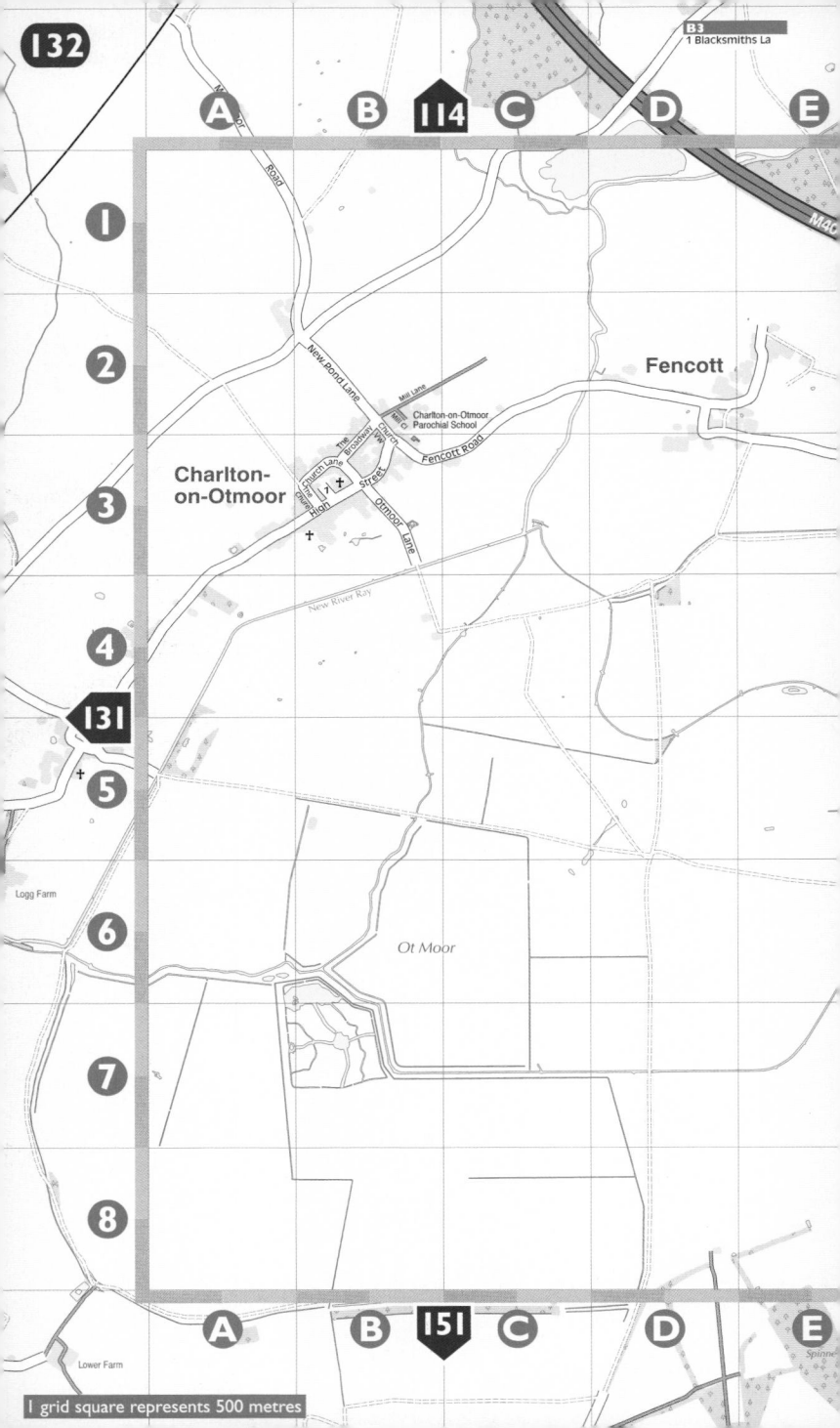

B3
1 Blacksmiths La

A　　B　**114**　C　　D　　E

M40

1

2　　　　　　　　　　　　　　　**Fencott**

New Bond Lane

Mill Lane

Charlton-on-Otmoor
Parochial School

Charlton-　　　Church Lane　Fencott Road
on-Otmoor　　The Brookham　Church Street

3

Otmoor Lane

New River Ray

4

5

Logg Farm

6　　　　　　　　　　　*Ot Moor*

7

8

A　　　　B　**151**　C　　　D　　E

Lower Farm　　　　　　　　　　　　　　　Spinne

F **G** **H** 115 **J** **K**

I

2

3

River Ray

M40

New Park
Farm

Marlake
House

PH
Murcott

Four Winds
Farm
4

Buckinghamshire County

Oxfordshire County
M40

Panshill
Fms
134

Whitecross
Green

5

Whitecross
Green Wood

6

7

Warren
Farm

Bonnell's Lane

Gardner's Barn

8

West Hill
Farm

Church Lane

F **G** **H** **117** **J** **K**

I

2

3

4

5

6

7

8

F **G** **H** **J** **K**

Piddington

Arncott Road

Ludgershall Road

Blackbrook

Glebe Farm

Thame

Vicarage Lane

Buckinghamshire County
Oxfordshire County

Chilling Place Stud

Corble Farm

Poletree Farm

Muswellhill Farm

198
Muswell Hill

Tramway Business Park

Oakcroft Farm

B4011

Middle Farm

Brillbury Hall Farm

Tramhill

Tramhill

Touchbridge

Brill

The Square

Windmill

PH

Brae Hill

Brae Hill Close

School Lane

Temple Land Close

High Street

Temple Street

Church Street

Brill C of E Combined School

The Spa Close

Green

Castle Farm Close

Doctors Surgery

Brill House

Oakley Road

Thame Road

B4011

Nashway Farm

Fenny Farm

FORESTERS

BICESTER RD

Hillside Farm

A B Windrush C D E

† Church Lane

A40(T)

Camp Barn

udgehill Wood

I

2

3

4

5

6

7

8

A40(T)

P

Hill Barn

B4425

Barrington Downs Farm

No Man's Land
tion

A B 154 C D E

1 grid square represents 500 metres

F G H **118** J K

1

A40(T)

Little
Barrington

Minnow Lane

Road

Middle

Home
Farm

2

A40(T)

Gloucestershire County

Oxfordshire County

B4425

Upper
Dow

3

Hurst Barn
Farm

4

138

5

6

Westwell

7

Downs
Farm

8

Hol

Westwell
Copse

F G H **155** J K

Holwell Downs
Farm

F1
1 Dolphin La

F **F** **G** rook **H** **120** **J** **K**

I

2 inbrook
Swin Lane

3

Widford

4

Flat Barn
Farm

140

5

Sturt Farm
and Stud

6

A40(T)

Burford Road

Stonelands

7

Lingermans

8

Whitehill
Farm
White Hill
A40(T)

Whitehills
Farm

Shilton Downs
Farm

Churn Lane
Upr End
Beech Grove
361
Orchard
Meadow
Lane

Fuzzy
Lease s

Handley
Plain

Farm

Windrush
River

Well
Head

F **F** G **G** **H** **157** **J** K **K**

B4020
Ladd

Kilkenny
Farm

Carterton Town
Football Club
Kilkenny Lane

GS
1 O'connors Rd
2 St Kenelm's Cl

F G H 122 J K

Riding Lane

I

Ringwood
Farm

2

3

Col
Farm

Minster Riding

4

† Minster Lovell
Hall

142

Little
Minster

Lower
Crescent

School Lane

School Hill

PH

PH

Minster
Lovell

B4047

Upper Crescent

Edwards

Charterville Close

St Kenelms
C of E
School

Wenrisc

Drive

Ripley's

Lovell

Cotswold Cl

5

BURFORD ROAD

Bromag
Industrial
Estate

Minster Industrial
Estate

Supergas
Industrial
Estate

Northwood
Road

Windrush Ind Park

Southwood
Road

6

Charterville
Allotments

Witney Town
Football Club

Road

7

BRIZE NORTON ROAD

Bushey
Ground

Downs

B4477

A40(T)

Peashell
Farm

A40(T)

8

F G H 159 Witn J K

Curbridge

Main Road

Lane

PO

†

F5
1 Bakers Piece

F6
1 Jacobs Cl
2 The Old
Coachyard

Yatt Lane

New
Yatt

New Yatt
Busin
Cent

New Yatt Lane

Perrot

F **G** **H** **124** **J** **K**

1

F7
1 Marlborough La

2

G5
1 Maidley Cl

3

H7
1 Stanton Harcourt
Rd

4

144 **JX29**

5

6

7

8

Poffley
End

Job's
Copse

Swanhall
Farm

New Yatt Road

Merryfield
Farm

Kings
School

Middlefield
Farm

A4095

Osney Hill
Farm

HAILEY ROAD

West
Oxfordshire
District Council

WOODSTOCK ROAD

The Crs

Woodgreen

WOODGREEN HILL

Woodgreen
Comprehensive
School

WEST END

BRIDGE ST

NEWLAND

WITNEY

Newland

Woolgate
Shopping
Centre

Witney Leisure
Centre

St Mary's C of E
Infant School

OXFORD HILL

B4022

A40(T)

B4022

Shores
Green

Two Rivers
Industrial Estate

Cogges

Cogges Manor
Farm Museum

The Blake
C of E Primary
School

Cogges Hill
Surgery

A40(T)

Lindsey
Farm

F **G** **H** **161** **J** **K**

Avenue
Three

A40(T)

High
Cogges

A B **131** C D E

Noke

Oxfordshire Way

1

Prattle
Wood

Lower

2

Home
Farm

Lower Woods
Farm

3 Woodeaton

B4027

4

Woodeaton
Wood

149

Forest Farm

5

Long
Wood

Wick
Copse

6 Elsfield

OX3

Home
Farm

7

8

A40(T)

Elsfield

A B **168** C D E

1 grid square represents 500 metres

Ⓐ Ⓑ **133** Ⓒ Ⓓ Ⓔ

Gardner's Barn

Randall's Lane

1 Thea Spinn

West Hill Farm

Church Lane

2 ✝ Church Lane

Mill Lane

The Green

PO

Horton-cum-Studley

Hotel

Studley Wood Golf Club

Brill Road

3 Oxfordshire Way

Oxfordshire Way

Studley Wood

4 Middle Park Farm

Blackwater Wood

Stanton Little Wood

The Moat

151

5 Oxfordshire Way

Danesbrook Farm

Oxfordshire Way

Danes Brook

6 Woodperry

Holly Wood

Me Gu

7 Street

Mill Lane

8 ✝ Middle Lane

Cocke Lane

PO

PH

PH

Stanton St John

Courtfield Road

Stanton Great Wood

A

Lane

B

Ⓐ Ⓑ **170** Ⓒ Ⓓ Ⓔ

Oxfordshire Way

I grid square represents 500 metres

F G H 134 J K

Honeyburge

Burstall
Wood

I

Slatters
Farm

2

Danes Brook

Pasture
Farm

New
Farm

M40

Jericho
Farm

3

Oakley
Wood

4

Oxfordshire
way

Alex Road

Corner
Farm

Shabbington
Wood

5

York's
Wood

M40

6

Hell
Coppice

7

Field
Farm

Wood
Farm

Joshua
Farm

8

Waterperry Common

M40

Waterperry
Wood

Thomley Hall
Farm

Oxford's
Corner

F G H 171 J K

Farm

Oxfordshire Way

No Man's Land
Plantation

Eastleach
Downs Farm

Macaroni Downs
Farm

River Leach

Lappingwell
Wood

East Leach
Folly

Beer Furlong
Buildings

Macaroni
Farm

Blu...
Ha...

PO

Eastleach
Turville

Macaroni
Wood

1 grid square represents 500 metres

F G H **137** J K

Ho

+

I

2

3

4

156

5

6

7

8

F G H **179** J K

Westwell Copse

Holwell Downs Farm

...rdshire County
...re County

Filkins Down Farm

Broughtondowns Plantation

Furze Ground

College Farm

Sheephouse Farm

...ocombe Hill

Oxleaze Farm

Filkins Farm

tleach
tin

Shire

J5
1 Arundel Cl

K2
1 Stoneleigh Dr

Lingermans

Well Head

Kilkenny Farm

Kilkenny

K3
1 Rowan Cl
2 Shilideane Dr

B4020

Carterton Town Football Club

Church

Shilton

SHILTON ROAD

OX18

Glenmore Road

Braemar Close

K4
1 Finchdale Cl
2 Lime Tree Cl
3 Poultney Pl
4 Robinson Cl

Shilbrook Av

Wychendon

Manor Rd

Sunnymook

Lovatt Rd

Hearne

Bracken

Bonham

Beve

K5
1 Hollybush Rd
2 Magdalen Pl

Scholars Acre

Connolly Dr

BURFORD RD

Hill

Hill View

Carterton Community College

Cottenwood

Downs

Upavon

Buxford Way

UPAVON WAY

Heron

Kestrel

Merlin

Kenley

Emsworth

Rd

Garden

Carterton County Primary School

158

Rock Road

Northolt

Rock Close

Sycamore

Arkell Avenue

Brize

Alvescot Down

B4020

Carr Av

String

Richens

Hobbs

Rose

5

Wycombe Way

Alvescot Health Centre

Carterton Town Hall

K6
1 Hawthorn Gv
2 Hayward Dr
3 Whittington Pl

Primary School

Edith Moorhouse Primary School

Lawton

Langdale

Edgeworth

Kingham

Butlers

Field Farm

Minty Cl

Alvescot

Mayfield Cl

Oakfield Rd

Clarkston Road

Ashfield Road

Pamaps Road

6

Carterton Industrial Estate

Kenn's Farm

ALVESCOT ROAD

Colbert Road

The Moors

Milestone

Belle Terrace

7

Clare Terrace

The Crs

Lazarford

8

St Peter's School

181

20

Mill Lane

Kencot

Alvescot

F7
1 Willowbrook

G7
1 The Close
2 Flexneys
Paddock

F G H **145** J K

I

B4449

2

Oakfield
Industrial
Estate

Lane

3

Lower Farm

B4449

Foxley
Farm

Limb Brook

4

164

B4449

5

Friar's Farm

Sutton
Green

6

Sutton

Sutton Lane

Burr Close

Duck End Lane

7

Edmund
Close

Bury Mead

Stanton
Harcourt

Blackditch

B4449

The Green

Blackditch

Steady's Lane

8

Tawney's
Farm

F G H **187** J K

Thames Path

Pimm

The County
Gallery

Manor
Close

Burnstone

Swan St

Abbey Pl

Abbey St

High St

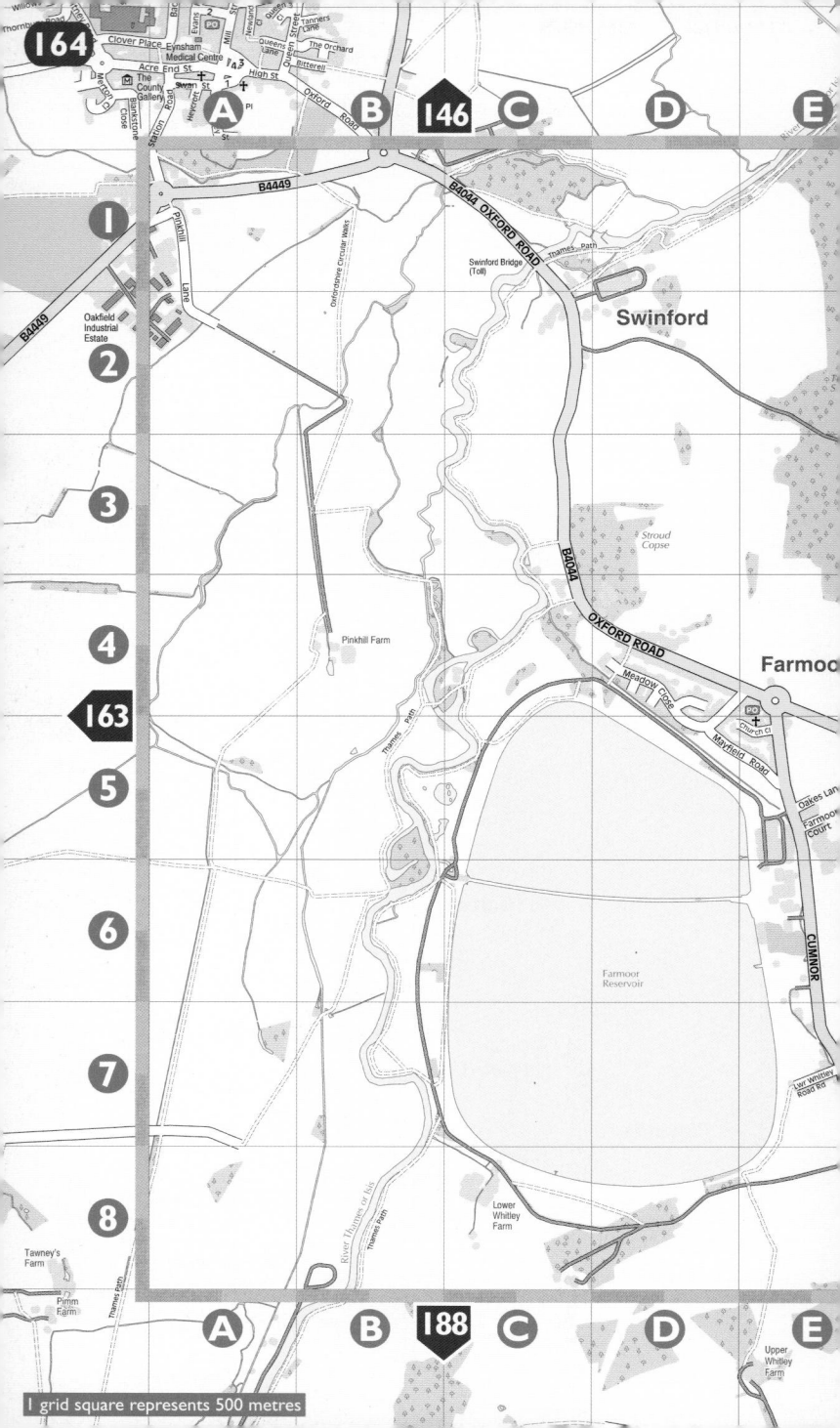

164
146
163
188

Clover Place
Eynsham Medical Centre
The County Gallery
Acre End St
Swan St
High St
The Orchard
Bitterell
Queens Lane
Tanners Lane
Mill
Newland St
Thornbury
Willow

A B C D E

B4449

Oxford Road

1

B4449

Oxfordshire Circular Walks

Oakfield Industrial Estate

2

3

Pinkhill Lane

B4044 OXFORD ROAD

Thames Path

Swinford Bridge (Toll)

Swinford

Stroud Copse

B4044

4

OXFORD ROAD

Farmoor

Meadow Close

Marfield Road

Church Cl.

Pinkhill Farm

Thames Path

Oakes Lane

Farmoor Court

5

CUMNOR

6

Farmoor Reservoir

7

Lwr Whitley Road Rd

8

Tawney's Farm

River Thames or Isis

Thames Path

Lower Whitley Farm

Pimm Farm

Upper Whitley Farm

A B C D E

1 grid square represents 500 metres

J7
1 Browns Cl
2 Stubble Cl

K6
1 Deanfield Rd

F G H **147** J K

A34(T)

Wytham

PH

Wytham Park

1

2

WEST...

A34(T)

Radbrook Common

Marley Wood

3

ON...

4

166

Woodend Farm

Oaken Holt

5

Tilb...

EYNSHAM ROAD

B4044

A420(T)

Botley

Botley Medical Centre

6

Seacourt Road

WEST

Red House Farm

West Way Health Centre

Tudor Court

Nobles Lane

EYNSHAM ROAD

B4044

Rose Gdns

Evenlode

7

mpstead

Denman's Farm

Orchard Road

A420(T)

Pinnocks Wy

Pinnocks Way

Third Acre Rise

Dean Co...

Cumnor Rise Rd

Stanville Rd

8

Arnold...

Way

Matthew Arnold County Secondary School

Scholar Pl

Cumnor Hill

F G H **189** J K

rove Down

Chawley Lan...

Turnpike Road

Hurst Lane

Chawley

F G H J K

Ford
PH
Ford Farm
Chapel Road
Water
Froud
Close
Lime
Burgess
Lane
Aylesbury RING
HP17

1

Chess Road

2

Aston
Mullins

Lower Waldridge
Farm

3

Aston
Sandford

4

Black Barn
Farm

5

Pasture
Farm

Whirlbush
Farm

A4129

6

A4129

Ray
Farm

Bumpers

7

Ilmer

Meadows Way

8

F G H 201 J K

Oxdeaze
Farm

F
G
H 155 J
K

I

Shire
Gate

The
Pills

2

field

3

Langford Downs
Farm

A361

4

180 ▶

Gloucestershire County
Oxfordshire County

5

Common Barn
Farm

A361

6

Hulse Ground
Farm

Great Lemhill
Farm

7

**Little
Faringdon**

Langford
House

8

Little Lemhill
Farm

F
G
H A361 203 J
K

Horseshoe
Lake

Filkins Farm

A   B   156   C   D   E

1

The Pills

2

3

4

A561

179

5

6

Little Faringdon

7

8

A   B   204   C   D   E

Cross Tree La

Woolen Mill

Filkins

Manor Farm

Manor Farm

Broughton Poggs

Broadwell Brook

Colston House Tennis Club

King's Lane

Broadwell Road

Filkins Road

Bro

PH

Langfo

Lechlade Road

St Christophers C of E School

Rectory Farm

Hooks Close

Hulse Grounds Farm

Langford Brook

1 grid square represents 500 metres

J2
1 Pemscott Cl

F G H **157** J K

1

Kencot

2

St Peter's
School

Alvescot

Bla
Bo

STATION
RD

3

B4020

4

182

Bazeland

5

BLACK BOURT

Broadwell
Mill

Calcroft Lane

6

Edgerly
Farm

Hotel

Pound La

7

Mill Lane

Queen's
Cls

High
House

8

Little
Clanfield

Glebe
Farm

MAIN

Friar's CC

F G H **205** J K

Grafton

A7
1 Furlong Rw

A

B **158** C D E

Lower Haddon
Farm

Elmwood
House

1

Mill Lane

**Black
Bourton** PH

2

Church La

STATION RD

School La

Mill Farm

3

4

◀ **181**

B4020

5

BLACK BOURTON ROAD

A4095

Black Bourton Brook

6

Hotel

Bourton
Close

BAMPTON ROAD

Pound
La

Bailey's Close

PO

Wick
Close

Clanfield

Mill Lane

7

Bakery La

Queen's
Crs

HIGH
HOUSE
CI

Clanfield Parish
School

Marsh
Lane

Marsh Lane

MAIN STREET

8

Friar's Court

Friar's
Court

A B **206** C D E

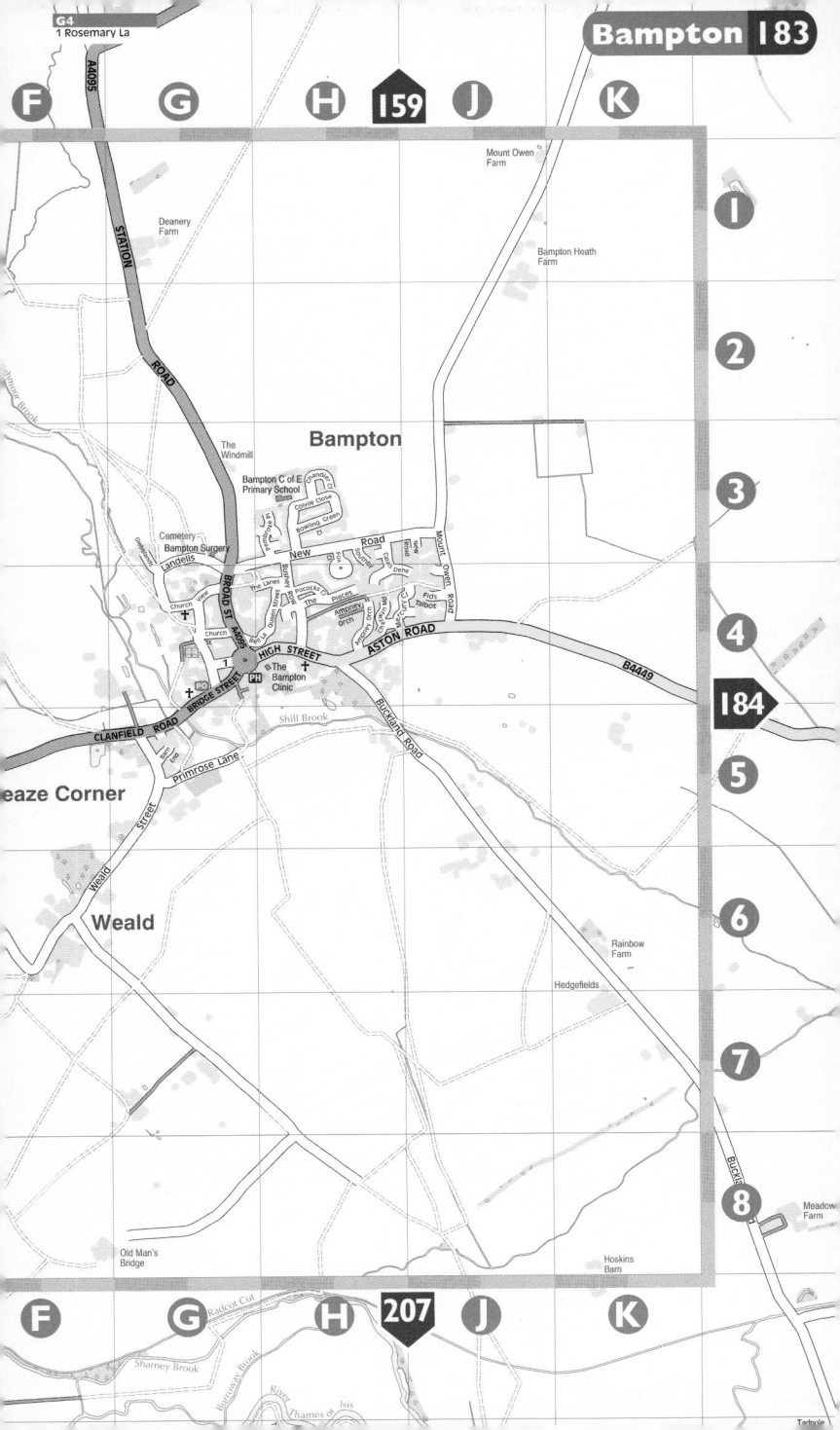

F G H 161 J K

Breach
Cottage

Calais Road

Westfield
Farm

Hawthorn
Farm

I

Works

Yelford

A415

2
Calais Road

WITNEY RO

3

ROAD

New Shifford
Farm

4

T S C
186

B4449

B4449

South
Farm

5

6

Shifford

7
Thames Path

8

River Thames or Isis

Shifford
Lock

F
Chimney

G

H 209 J K

Thames Path

Ⓐ   Ⓑ   164   Ⓒ   Ⓓ   Ⓔ

Tawney's Farm

Pimm Farm

1

Lower Whitley Farm

Upper Whitley Farm

Leys Road

Long Leys Farm

2

West End

Bablock Hythe

Thames Path

Bablock Hythe Road

3

Watkins Farm

Eaton Heath

4

Thames Path

Bablock Hythe Road

Eaton

Eaton Practice

187

River Thames or Isis

5

Thames Path

Eaton Road

6

7

Badswell Lane

Church Rd

PO

Appleton

Manor House

Park Lane

Fortnum Close

8

Bessels Leigh School

Tubney Manor Farm

Appleton Lower Common

Ⓐ   Millway Lane   Ⓑ   212   Ⓒ   Ⓓ   Ⓔ

Netherton Road

Oakmere

G3
1 Abingdon Rd
2 Kenilworth Rd
3 Robsart Pl

F **G** **H** **165** **J** **K**

Matthew Arnold
County Seconda
School

Cumnor
Hill

1

Songe Close

Hill's
Close Rd

Ashmare Way

Colgrove Down

Cotswold Rd

Hurst Lane

Turnpike Road

Chawley

2

Chawley
Lane

Norreys   Road

Cumnor C of E
Primary School

Denman's Lane

Bertie Road

Oxford   Road

A420(T)

Cumnor Hill

Cumnor Hill

LEDOWN HILL

HIGH STREET

PO

PH   Cumnor
The
Park
Road

PH

GLEBE RD

CLOSE

The Glebe

Leys
2
3
Pound
Lane
1

Robsart
Place

3

FARINGDON ROAD

Bradley
Farm

B4017

Whitebarn

4

190

Henwood
Farm

5

Sandy   Lane

Henwood

B4017

CUMNOR

Henwood Dr

Vine Hill Lane

6 Boars
Hill

Orchard
La

Bessels
Leigh

A420(T)

Besselsleigh Road

Hill
View La

ROAD

Wootton C of E
Primary School

7

8

Wootton

Besselsleigh Road

Leigh Cft.
Beech Cl.

PO
Berry
Croft

Matthews

Home
Close

Lamborough
Hill

F **G** **H** **213** **J** **K**

Great Park
Farm

Isnet   Lane

Besselsleigh Road

Raleigh Road

Coupland Rd

Arthur Evans

St Edwin's
Way

Dudley
Close

LOUGH HILL

Fox Lane

The Field

Dry Sandford County
Primary School

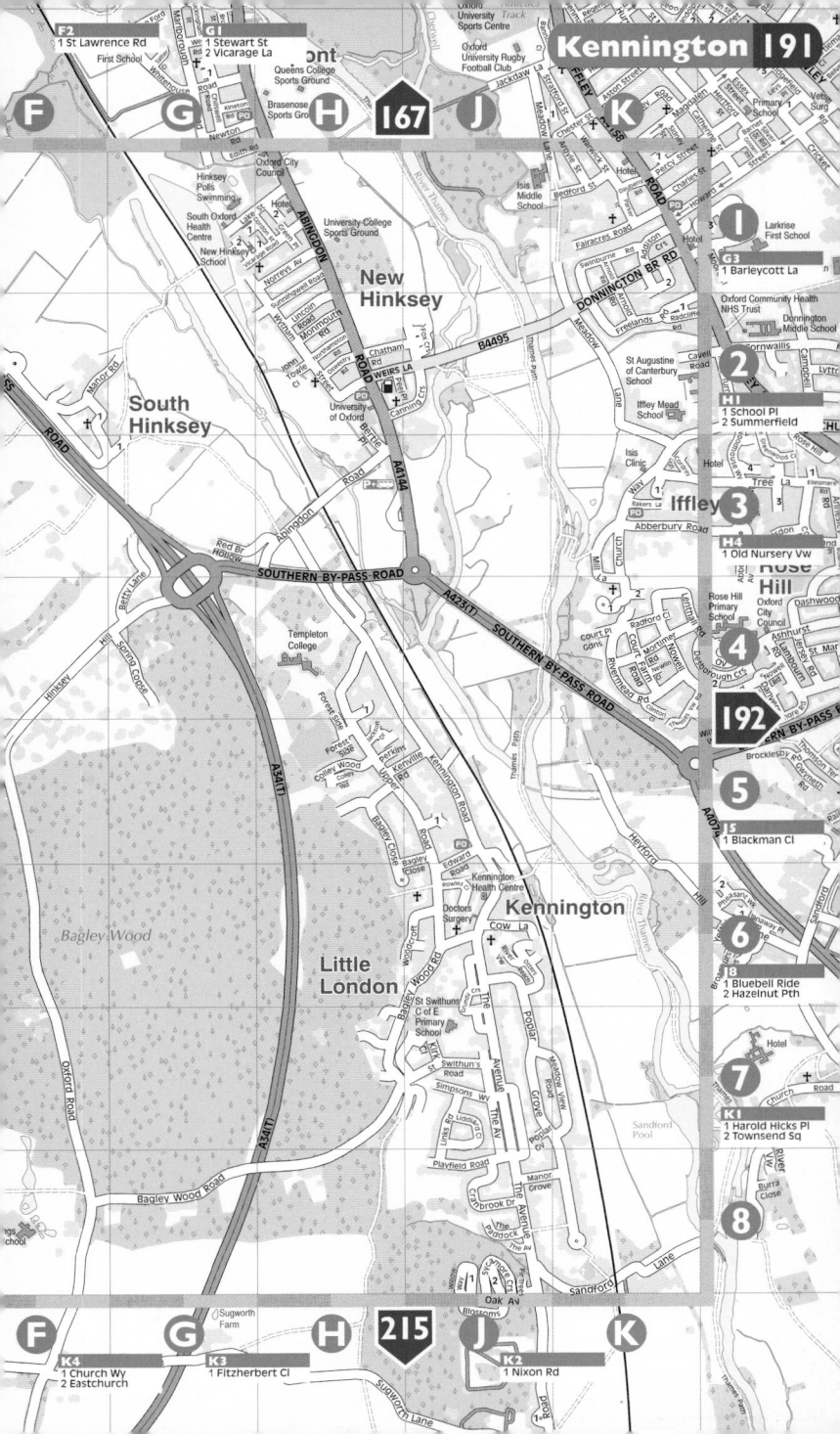

F2
1 St Lawrence Rd
First School

G1
1 Stewart St
2 Vicarage La

167

J

K

I
Larkrise
First School

G3
1 Barleycott La

2
H1
1 School Pl
2 Summerfield

3
Iffley

H4
1 Old Nursery Vw

Rose
Hill

4

192

5
J5
1 Blackman Cl

6
J6
1 Bluebell Ride
2 Hazelnut Pth

7
K1
1 Harold Hicks Pl
2 Townsend Sq

8

New
Hinksey

South
Hinksey

SOUTHERN BY-PASS ROAD

Templeton
College

Bagley Wood

Little
London

Kennington

F
G
H
215
J
K

K4
1 Church Wy
2 Eastchurch

K3
1 Fitzherbert Cl

K2
1 Nixon Rd

A B 170 C D E

Gidley Way

Horspa 1
Coombe House

Cuddesdon Road

Hill Farm 2

Wheatley Road 3

Coombe Wood

Slay Barn

City Farm 4
Boundary Business Park

193
Church Close
Cuddesdo

Birch Road
Blenheim 5
Upperfield Farm

PH

Garsington C of E Primary School
Garsington Sports Club
Denton Lane Denton Lane

High St

Denton Hill

Denton

Garsington 6

Southend

Pettiwell 7
Southend

The Platt

8
Southend

A B 218 C D E

1 grid square represents 500 metres

F
G
H
173
J
K

I

Oxfordshire Way

Rycote Lake

The Oxfordshire Golf Club

Rycote

✝ Chapel

Field Farm

RYCOTE LANE

2

A329

Old Paddock

Lobbersdown Farm

Oxfordshire Way

RYCOTE LANE

3

Golf Course

Cmp Industrial Estate

A329

Rycotelane Farm

Oxfordshire Way

on
mmon

Hill Farm

4

N ROAD A40

Lower Farm

198

M40

5

ools

A40

M40

Lobb Farm

Tetsworth Common

6

Tetsworth

M40

Manor Farm

7

Jointer's Farm

8

Latchford

Haseley Brook

F
G
H
221
J
K

A **B** 174 **C** **D** **E**

B8
1 Oak Farm Cl

B7
1 Cygnet Cl
2 Parkers Hl
3 Yew Tree Cl

1

RYCOTE LANE

Oxfordshire Way

Moreton

2

3

Golf Course

Oxfordshire Way

4

Hill

197

5

Moreton Field
Farm

Spencer's
Farm

6

Tetsworth
Common

Oxfordshire Way

Marsh End

M40

Tetsworth

B4012

7

Manor
Farm

Tetsworth County
Primary School

The
Leather
3
Chiltern
View

Elm Cl

2

HIGH

STREET

A329

8

Harlesford
House

Oxfordshire Way

Harlesford
Farm

M40

A **B** 222 **C** **D** **E**

200

Thame Road

Windmill Close

Court Cl Road

Church Cl

Towersey

A B **176** C D E

Manor Road

Chinnor Road

1

Manor Road

2

Grovehill Farm

Penn Farm

New Close Farm

Westbrook Farm

3

B4445

Waterlands Farm

Great Covert

4

199

5

Manor Farm

6

Emmington

Plough Corner

Sydenham

7

Sydenham Road

Lupins Lane

The Slades

B4445 THAME ROAD

Halliers Close

8

Mill Lane County Primary School

Malyns Close

LOWER

Wellington Practice

Mill Lane

Jan Clements

Beech Road

CHAPEL

Miller's Turn

Rigers Way

Van N

OAKLEY LANE

COWLEAZE

OAKLEY ROAD

A B **224** C D E

I grid square represents 500 metres

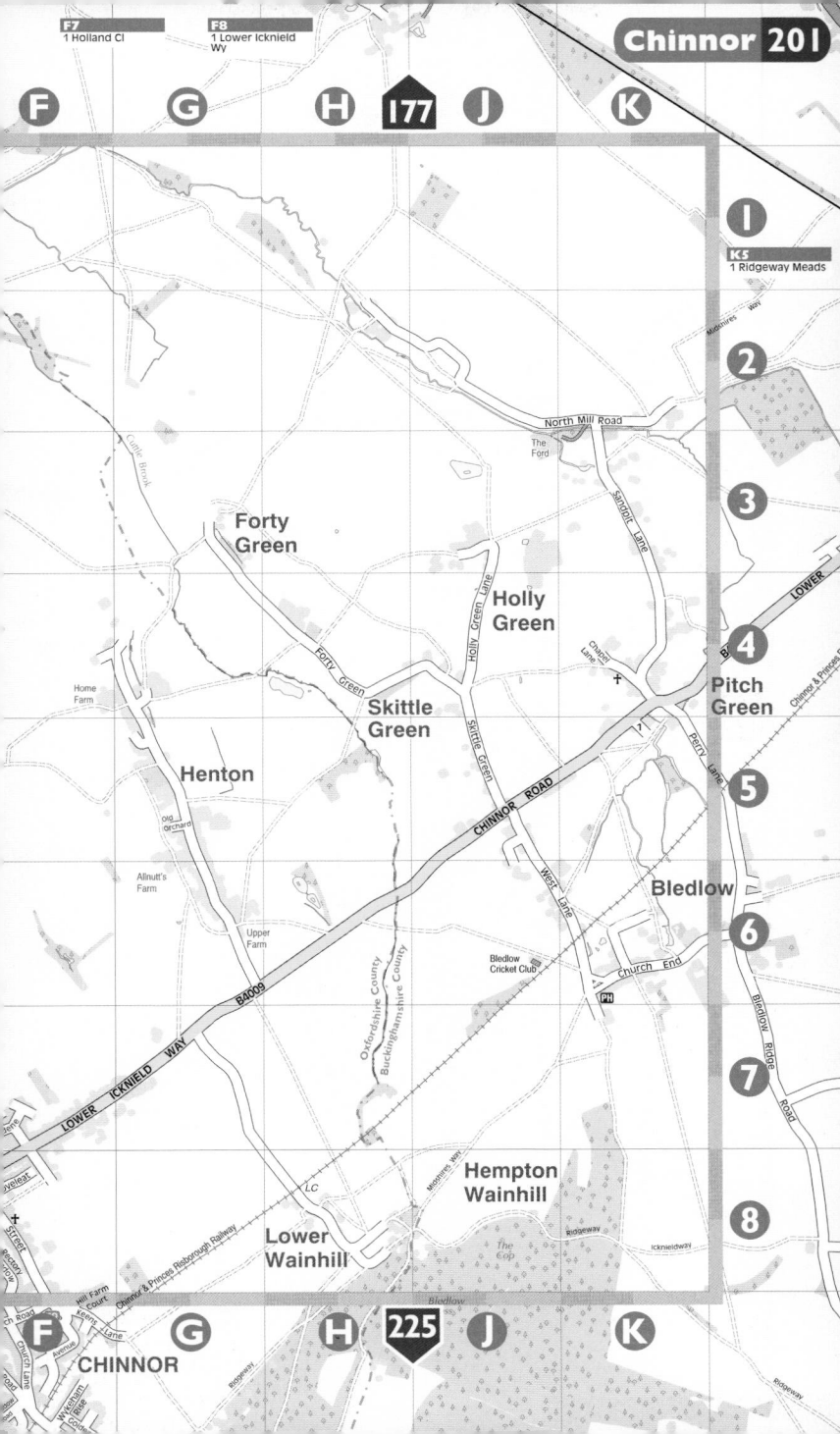

F7 1 Holland Cl

F8 1 Lower Icknield Wy

F G H **177** J K

I

K5 1 Ridgeway Meads

2

3

North Mill Road

The Ford

Cuttle Brook

Forty Green

Holly Green

Chute Lane

LOWER

4

Pitch Green

Chinnor & Princes R...

Skittle Green

Home Farm

Henton

Perry Lane

5

West Lane

Old Orchard

Allnut's Farm

Bledlow

Upper Farm

6

Bledlow Cricket Club

Church End

PH

CHINNOR ROAD

Oxfordshire County

Buckinghamshire County

B4009

7

Bledlow Ridge Road

LOWER ICKNIELD WAY

Chinnor & Princes Risborough Railway

Hempton Wainhill

Ridgeway

Icknieldway

8

LC

Lower Wainhill

The Cop

Bledlow

Hill Farm Court

F **CHINNOR** G H **225** J K

Avenue

Church Lane

Wyshall...

202

A   B   178   C   D   E

1

Snowstorm
Gorse

Thornhill Farm

Claydon
Fields

2

Claydon
House

Warren's Cross
Farm

A417

3

4

Cotswold
Water Park

5

River Coln

Inglesh

6

Dudgrove
Farm

Gloucestershire County
Swindon

7

am
arm

8

A   B   226   C   D   E

Bywooth Lane

River Thames or Isis

I grid square represents 500 metres

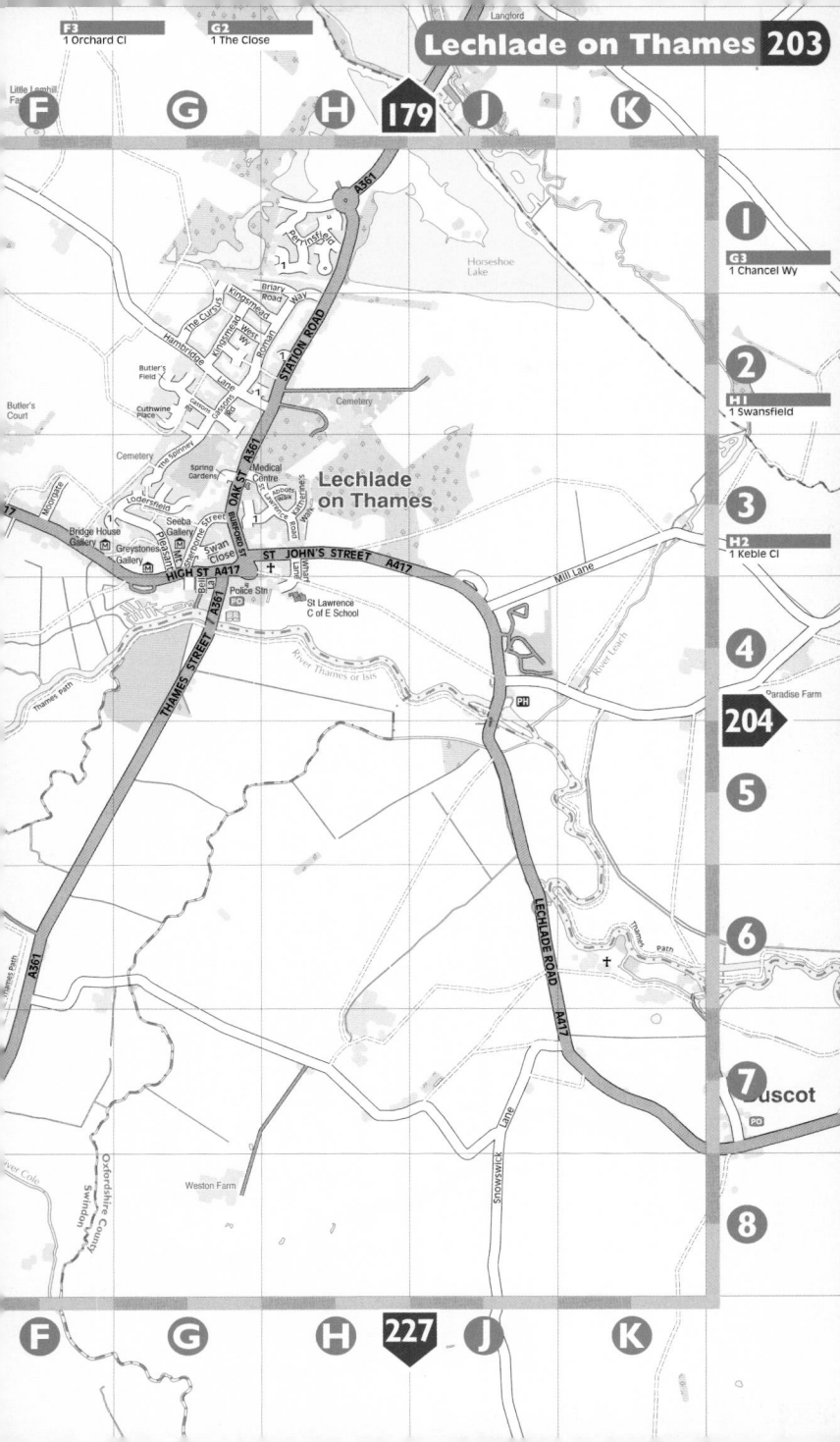

F3
1 Orchard Cl

G2
1 The Close

F **G** **H** 179 **J** **K**

I

G3
1 Chancel Wy

2

H1
1 Swansfield

3

H2
1 Keble Cl

4

204

5

6

7

8

F **G** **H** 227 **J** **K**

Langford

Horseshoe Lake

Cemetery

Lechlade on Thames

Little Lemhill

Butler's Court

Butler's Field

Cuthwine Place

Cemetery

Spring Gardens

Medical Centre

STATION ROAD

Briary Road

The Curvs

Kingspead

Hambridge Lane

Bridge House Gallery

Greystones Gallery

Seeba Gallery

Lodersfield

Moorgate

HIGH ST A417

ST JOHN'S STREET A417

Swan Close

Police Stn

PO

St Lawrence C of E School

River Thames or Isis

Thames Path

Thames Street / A361

A361

OAK ST A361

A361

Mill Lane

River Leach

PH

Paradise Farm

uscot

PO

LECHLADE ROAD A417

Thames Path

†

Snowswick Lane

Oxfordshire County Swindon

Weston Farm

River Cole

A361

Thames Path

204

A   B   180   C   D   E

Langford Brook

1

2

3

Hill Lane

4

Paradise Farm

203

Oxfordshire County
Gloucestershire County

Kelmscot

PH

5

River Leach

6

River Thames or Isis

7

Buscot

PO

Kilmester's
Farm

8

LECHLADE ROAD A417

A   B   228   C   D   E

Buscot
Park (NT)

1 grid square represents 500 metres

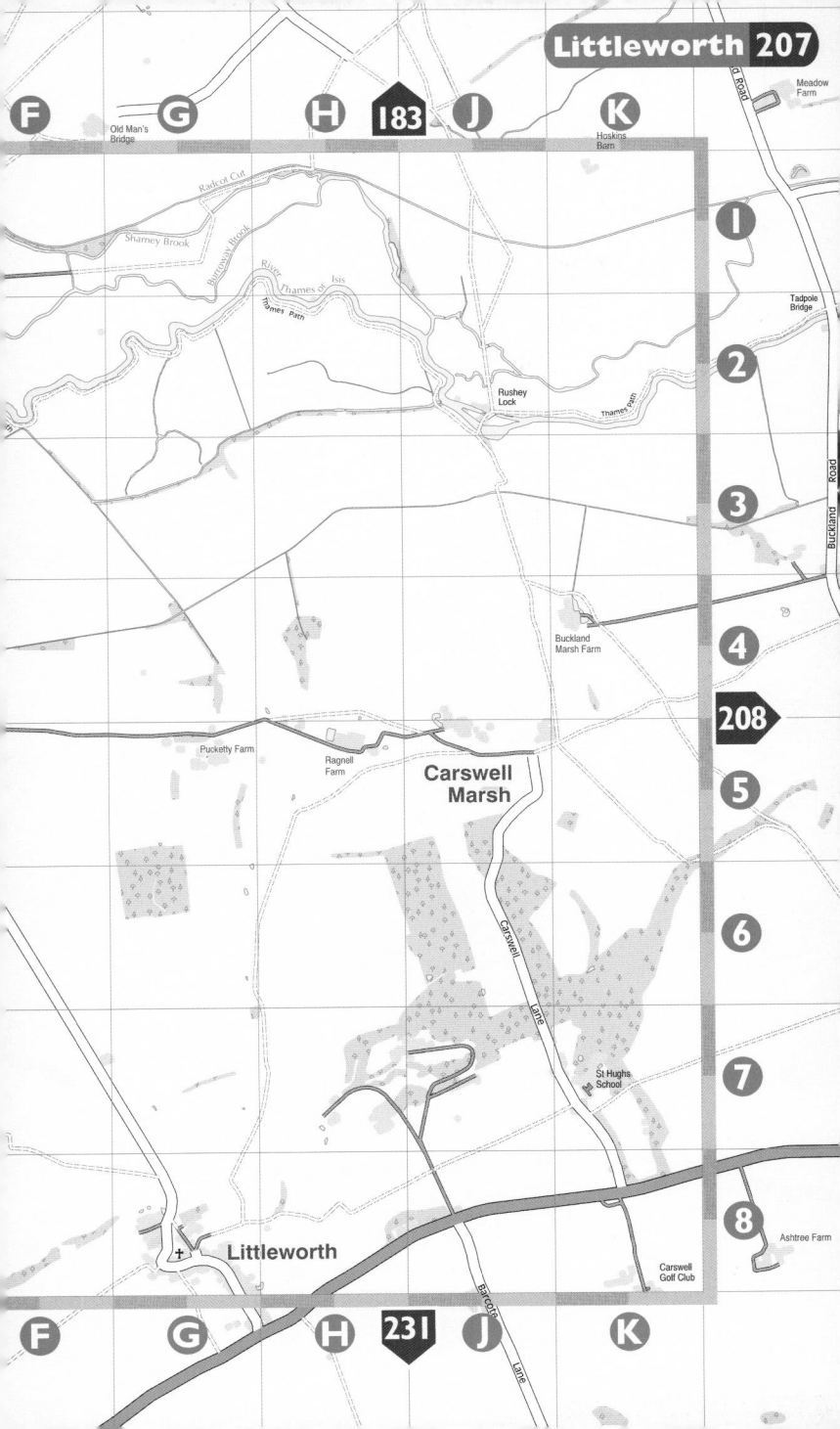

Hoskins Barn

Meadow Farm

A **B** **184** **C** **D** **E**

I

Tadpole Bridge

Thames Path

PH

2

Thames Path

Thames Path

3

Buckland Road

Buckland Marsh

Buckland Marsh Farm

4

Gore Farm

207

5

6

St Hughs School

7

St George's

Buckland

PH

Summerside Road

Oxford Road

Buckland School

A420(T)

8

Ashtree Farm

Carswell Golf Club

Mount Pleasant Farm

Buckland Road

A **B** **232** **C** **D** **E**

K5
1 Laggots Cl

F G H 185 J K

Chimney

Duxford

Duxford Farm

Thames Path

Thames Path

Duxford

Hinton
Waldrist

Church Road

Priors Lane

High Street

St Thomas's
St Clicut's

210 Hinton P

ry Farm

Welmore Farm

A420(T)

B4508

Pusey

F G H 233 J K

Lovell's
Court Farm

Pusey
Lodge Farm

I
2
3
4
5
6
7
8

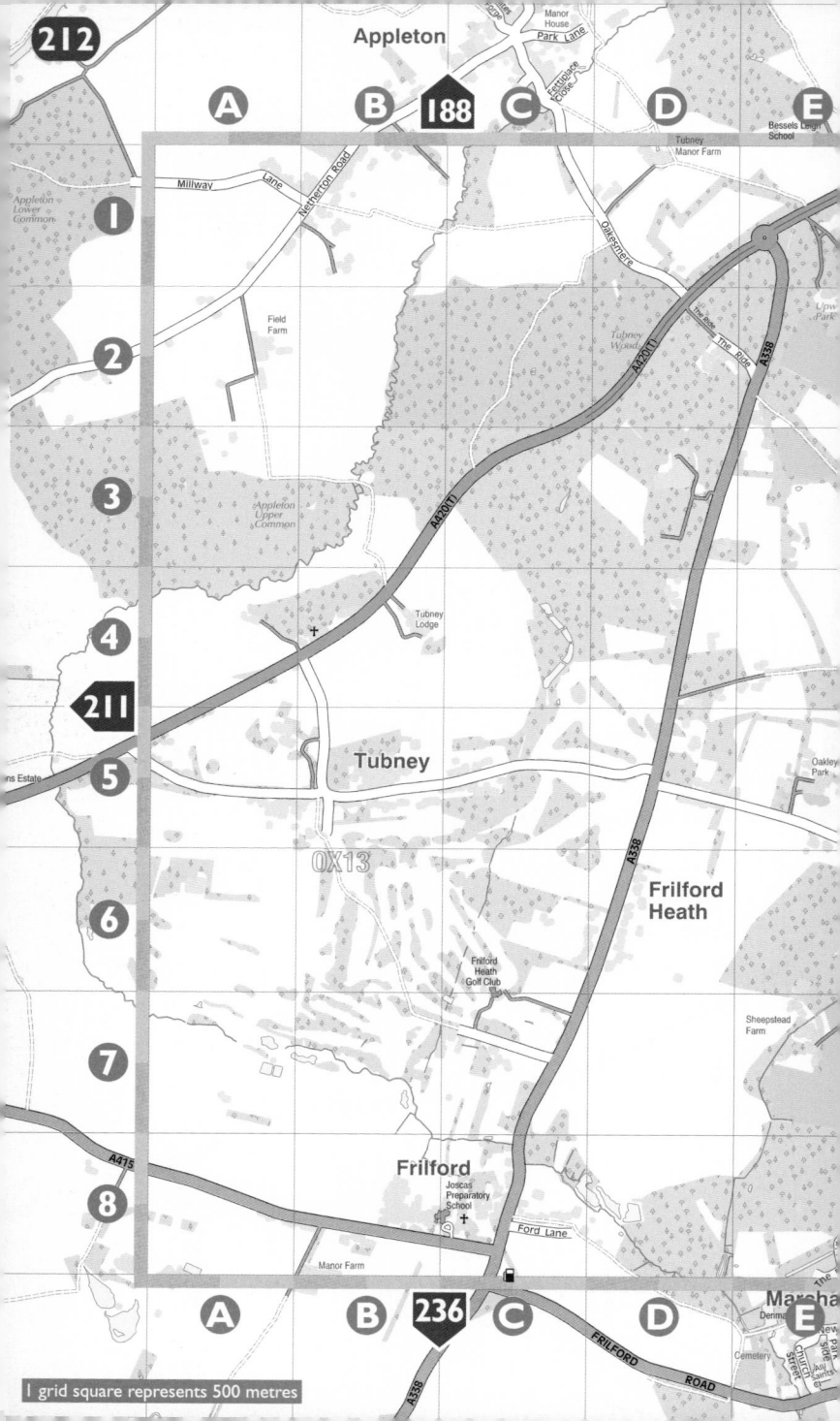

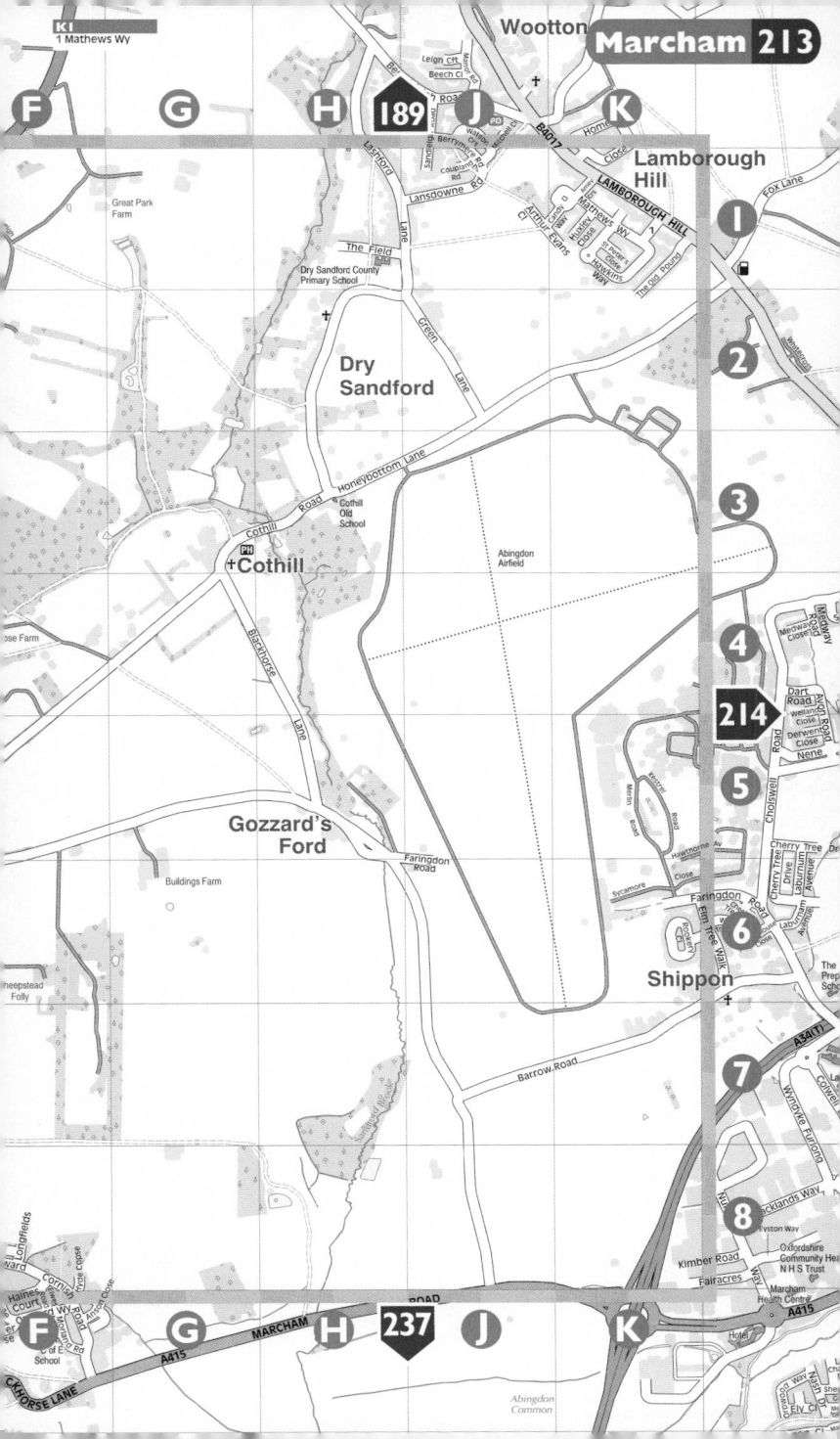

Wootton

Lamborough Hill

F **G** **H** 189 **J** **K**

LAMBOROUGH HILL

I

Fox Lane

K1
1 Mathews Wy

Great Park Farm

Be... Road
Leigh Crt
Beech Cl

Sandling...
Berrymere...
Coupland...
Lansdowne Rd

The Field

Dry Sandford County Primary School

Dry Sandford

Green Lane

Carthur Evans...
Mathews Wy
Hawkes...
Close
Stroner Close
Hewkins Way
The Old Pound

2

Honeybottom Lane

Cothill Old School

Abingdon Airfield

3

Cothill
PH
Cothill

Blackhorse Lane

Cothill Road

Menin Road

Kestrel Road

Hawthorne Av

Sycamore Close

Faringdon Road

Elm Tree Walk

Ferny Close

Shippon

4

214

Dart Road
Medway Road
Wetlands Close
Derwent Close
Nene

Cholswell Road

5

Cherry Tree Dr
Cherry Tree Drive
Laburnum Avenue

Faringdon Road

Laburnum...

6

The Prep Sch

Gozzard's Ford

Faringdon Road

Buildings Farm

Sheepstead Folly

Barrow Road

A34(T)

7

Cumnor Furlong
Wyndoke Green

Oxfordshire Community Heal... N H S Trust

Packlands Way
Lyston Way

8

Kimber Road
Fairacres

Marcham Health Centre

A415

F **G** **H** 237 **J** **K**

MARCHAM ROAD

A415

Longfields...
Haines Court
C of E School

Cornish Wy
Winsmore La
Abbot Close

CKHORSE LANE

Holt...
Ely Cl...

Abingdon Common

F4
1 Bucklers Bury Rd
2 Covent Cl
3 Shrieves Cl

F5
1 Amyce Cl
2 Childrey Wy
3 Henor Mill Cl
4 Lynges Cl
5 Otwell Cl
6 Sandford Cl
7 Thistlecroft Cl
8 Yeld Hall Rd

F

G

H

191

J

K

1

F6
1 Evenlode Pk

2

F7
1 Clarendon Cl
2 Hobbs Cl
3 Kempster Cl
4 Kent Cl
5 Saffron Ct

3

G5
1 Beagle Cl
2 Champs Cl
3 Corn Avill Cl
4 Holywell Cl
5 Penn Cl
6 Rushmead Copse

4

216

Lowe

5

G6
1 Heathcote Pl

6

G7
1 Ferguson Pl
2 Morton Cl

7

J1
1 Sugworth Crs

8

Radley
Park

The Infirmary

Radley
College

Radley C of E
Primary School

Radley

Radley Station

Park Farm

Goose
Acre Farm

Home Farm

Wick Hall

Pumney
Farm

Sugworth
Farm

Sugworth Lane

Sugworth Lane

OXFORD ROAD A4183

A4411

Twelve Acre Drive

Peachcroft Road

Peachcroft
Shopping Centre

Radley Road

Thrupp Road

Thrupp Lane

Barton Lane

Thames Path

Kennington Road

Church Road

White's Lane

Foxborough

Cooseacre

The Copse

Audlett Drive

Sewell Close

Hagland Road

F

G

H

239

J

K

K4
1 Catherine Cl

F   G   H   193   J   K

I

Manor House

Lower Farm

PH

Toot Baldon

2

Baldon Row

3

Gotham F

Marsh Baldon C of E Primary School

4

Marsh Baldon

Queens College

218

ham enay

MaryIands Farm

Baldon Lane

Baldon House

5

B4015   MaryIands Gn

6

Baldon Brook

Little Baldon Farm

7

en Balls

A4074

8

F   G   H   241   J   K

Barrington Cl

Russell Jackson

Fane Dr

Tower Rd

Crutch Furlong

Cherw Road

Everton

Clymer Drive

Burcot Farm

F G H J K

195

I

Belcher's Farm

PO

Gold St

Little Milton School

Little Milton

Ditchend Farm

2

Brook

A329

Coldharbour

4

A329

HAMPTON ROAD

3

Haseley Brook

Cowleaze Copse

Rofford Lane

4

220

hampton

Belcher's Farm

Rofford Hall

5

Newington

CUXHAM ROAD

B480

6

Ascott Farm

7

Hill Farm

Lower End

Brookside Est

High Street

8

Great Holc...e **243**

Little Holcombe

Langley Hall

Chalgrov

F G H J K

NEWINGTON RD

SCHOOL ST

Holcombe La

Mill Lane

Newington

Haseley Brook

I

2

Cornwell
Copse

Stoke
Grange

Lower
Farm

3

Poppets
Hill Farm

4

Stoke
Talmage

222

5

Clare

6

Stoney
Lane

Golden
Manor

7

8

A B 198 C D E

Harlesford
House

Harlesford
Farm

M40

1

A40

M40

Lower
Farm

2

3

Adwell

†

Overcombe Way

4

†

Wheatfield

221

5

Salt Lane

6

South
Weston

Overcombe Way

Rectory La

7

Stokefield Farm

8

Knightsbridge Lane

Knightsbridge Farm

Model
Farm

A B 246 C D E

1 grid square represents 500 metres

G7
1 Barley Cl

K4
1 Aston Gdns

F G H 199 J Kingston
Stert
K

I

Copcourt

Chalford

court

2

ox Tree Lane

Lower Road

Chalford Road

Adwell Farm

3

Postcombe

Kingst

Aston Rowant
C of E
Primary School

4

Aston
Crick

School

Prowder

B40

OX9

224

Church

Aston
Rowant

5

Aston Park Stud

CHINNOR

Woodway Farm

ROA

Nethercote

6

Nethercote Lane

Butts Way

Lewknor
C of E
School

B4009

7

High Street

M40

Lewknor

Junction 6

8

Bean's Way

Watlington
Road

Hill Rd

The Knapp

ROAD

F eld Farm House G H 247 J K

Hill Road

Nature
Reserve

E1
1 Lacemakers
2 Wheelers End

D1
1 Ashridge
2 Hailey Cft
3 Robins Platt

C3
1 Pleck La

A   B   200   C   D   E

Mill Lane County
Primary School

Wellington
Practice

1

Oakley

2

Mill Lane

Oakley Lane

Cowlease

Stoke Way

OAKLEY ROAD

Greenwood Ave

CROWELL ROAD

CHINNOR ROAD

B4009

3

Crowell

Kingston Blount

Steed Lane

Brook Street

Baker's Piece

Chapel Lane

Old Cft Lane

HIGH STREET

Aston Rowant
C of E
Primary School

School Lane

Plowden Park

4

Aston Rowant
Cricket Club

Park Lane

Kingston House

Kingston

5

223

B4009

ROAD

CHINNOR

Swan's Way

6

Woodway Farm

Swan's Way

Kingston
Wood

7

Kingston
Grove

Kingston

Grove
Woods

Aston
Wood

Hill

8

ASTON   HILL

A40

Hill Farm

Gur

A   B   248   C   D   E

Nature
Reserve

Kiln Farm

OXFORD

I grid square represents 500 metres

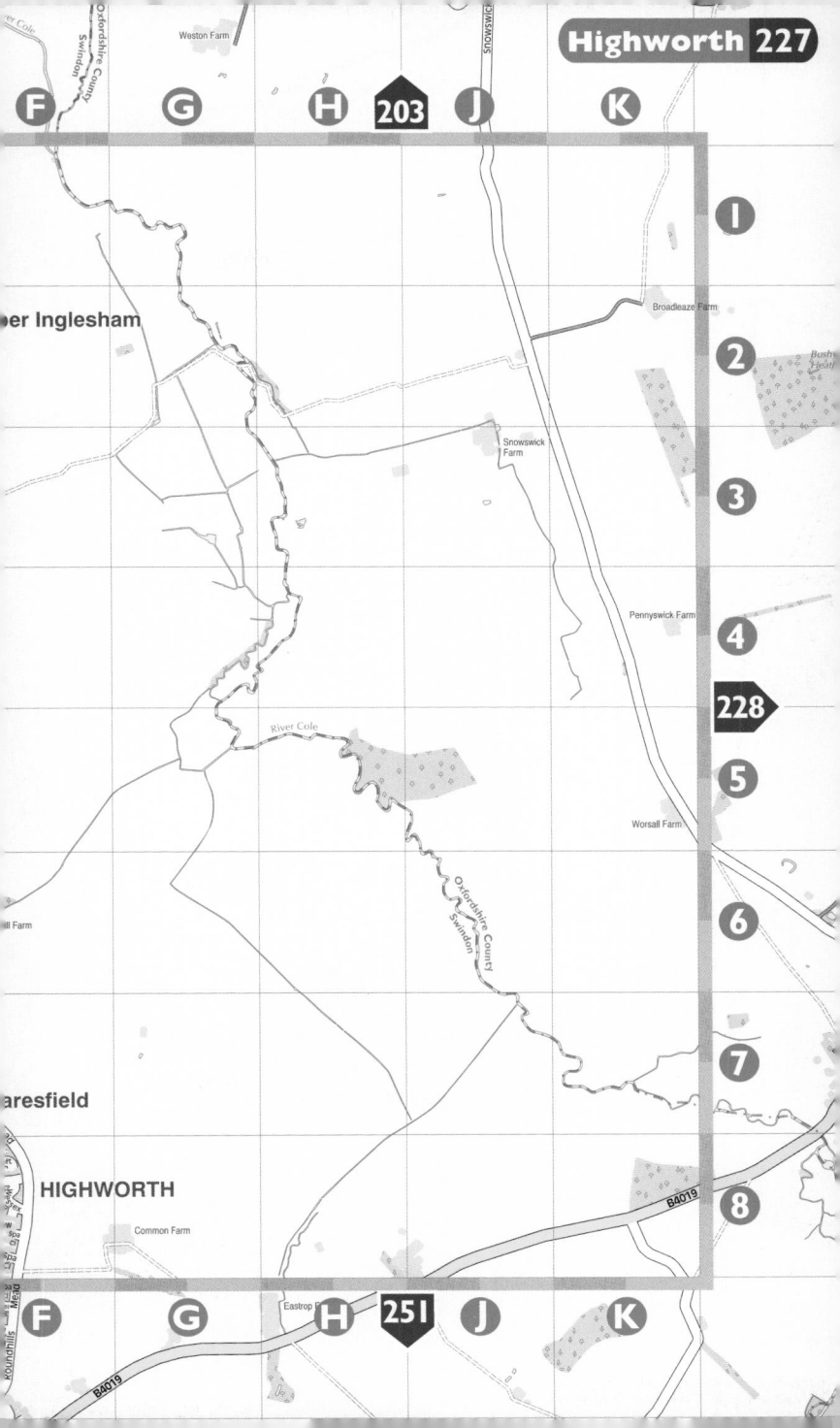

F G H **203** J K

1

2

3

4

228

5

6

7

8

F G H **251** J K

Weston Farm

Broadleaze Farm

Bushy Field

Snowswick Farm

Pennyswick Farm

River Cole

Worsall Farm

Oxfordshire County Swindon

Oxfordshire County Swindon

er Inglesham

aresfield

HIGHWORTH

Common Farm

Eastrop

B4019

B4019

A B 204 C D E

LECHLADE ROAD A417

I

Buscot
Park (NT)

Broadleaze Farm

2
Bushy
Heath

Heath Farm

Oldfield Farm

3

Pennywick Farm

Brimstone Farm

4

227

Middle
Leaze Farm

5

Worsall Farm

6

Colleyn

B4019

School Lane

7
CHURCH LANE

Coleshill

Ashen Copse Farm

8
B4019

A B 252 C D E

I grid square represents 500 metres

Tudor Farm

A B **206** C D E

I

2

Haremoor Farm

London Street

3

A0995
RADCOT ROAD

A4095

Grove Wood

Church Walk
London Street
A420(T)

Woodview
Faringdon Junior School
Faringdon Infant School
Regent Mews
Hotel
GLOUCESTER ST
Police Stn
Canada Lane
Cedar Street
Church Walk
CHURCH ST
Church Street
Coach Lane
Stanford Road
A417

FARINGDON

4

STANFORD ROAD

Ferndale Preparatory Schools
MARLBOROUGH ST
A417

The Pines
Beech Close
Elm Road
The Elms
Marlborough
Faringdon Health Centre
COXWELL ROAD
COXWELL ST
HIGHWORTH ROAD
A1019

Park Road Industrial Est
PARK ROAD A417

5

Westland Road
Coxwell Road
Fernham Road
Folly View Road
Leamington
Marines Drive
Town End Rd
Faringdon School
Faringdon Leisure Centre
Tollington Court

6

A420(T)

7

A420(T)

Cole's Pits

Wickleshamlodge Farm

8 **Little Coxwell**

A B **254** C D E

F

G Littlewor H **207** J K Carswell Golf Club

Ashtree Farm

I

2

Sandy Lane

3

Sandy Lane

4

232

5

Chinham Farm

A417

6

Kitemoor Farm

B4508

7

Stanford in th

Church Street

Shellingford

8

White Horse Business Park

ROAD

F G H **255** J K well Brook

Sands Farm

F G H 209 J K

I

2

3

4

234

5

Charney Ba

6

7

8

Pusey

Lovell's
Court Farm

Pusey
Lodge Farm

Buckland Road

Eastfield Farm

New Road

Chapel

Main Street

The Green

Orchard

Longworth

PO

Brook
PH
Sandpit

Gooseywick Farm

Stanford
Park Farm

Park Lane

Blackacres Farm

mead

Lan

Land Brook

Ⓐ Ⓑ **210** Ⓒ Ⓓ Ⓔ

Lower
Lodge Farm

Newhouse Farm

1

Lovell's
Court Farm

Sheephouse
Farm

2

3

Manor Farm

4

◀ **233**

5

Chapel

The Green

Charney Bassett

Orchard
Cl

Lyford

The Green

6

wick Farm

7

8

Northmead

Lane

Ⓐ Ⓑ **258** Ⓒ Ⓓ Ⓔ

The Meads

Hanney Road

New Road

Longworth Road

Hyde Road

I grid square represents 500 metres

F G H 211 J K

I

2
Garford

3

4

236

5

6

7

8

F G H 259 J K

F G H **213** J K

I

2

3

4

238

5

6

7

8

F G H **261** J K

MARCHAM ROAD

A415

THORSE LANE

Marcham C of E School

Orchard Wy

Cornish Rd

Hyde Copse

Alton Cl

Abingdon Common

River Ock

Meadow Farm House

Marcham Mill

A34(T)

Kimber Road

Fairacres

Oxfordshire Community Health N H S Trust

Marcham Health Centre

A415

Eyston Way

Blackland...

Nash Dr

Ely Cl

Byron Cl

Tennyson

Longfellow

Masefield Crese

DRAYTON ROAD

238

Corneville Road

Lynton Close

ABINGDON ROAD

Byron Wick Lane

Primary School

Crabtree Lane

Gilbourn's Farm

Sutton Wic

Henleys Lane

Fisher Close

Hillsf...

Manor...

Church Lane

Chandli... Close

Gravel Lane

Chilvers Farm

Churc...

Marcham Road

B4017

HIGH STREET

B4016

Drayton

Whitecrofts Way

Lockway

Steventon Road

Doctors Surgery

East Way

STEVENTON ROAD

A34(T)

Drayton

Haywards Road

Drayton Golf Club

B4017

Milton Mill

...nney Road

F G H **215** J K

I

2

3

Warren Farm

High Lodge

Thame Lane

4

Thame Lane

Schola Europaea

OX14

ABINGDON ROAD

Culham Station

Station Road

Parochial School
The Glebe
Croft

Toligate Road

Zouch Farm

Fullamoor

240

5

Abingdon Road

APPLEFORD ROAD B4016

6

Thames Path

Church Mi
Rd

enay

7

Bridge Farm

School Lane

Appleford Station

Chambral Close

Church St

Appleford

8

B4016 MAIN ROAD

orse Lane

F G H **263** J K

LC

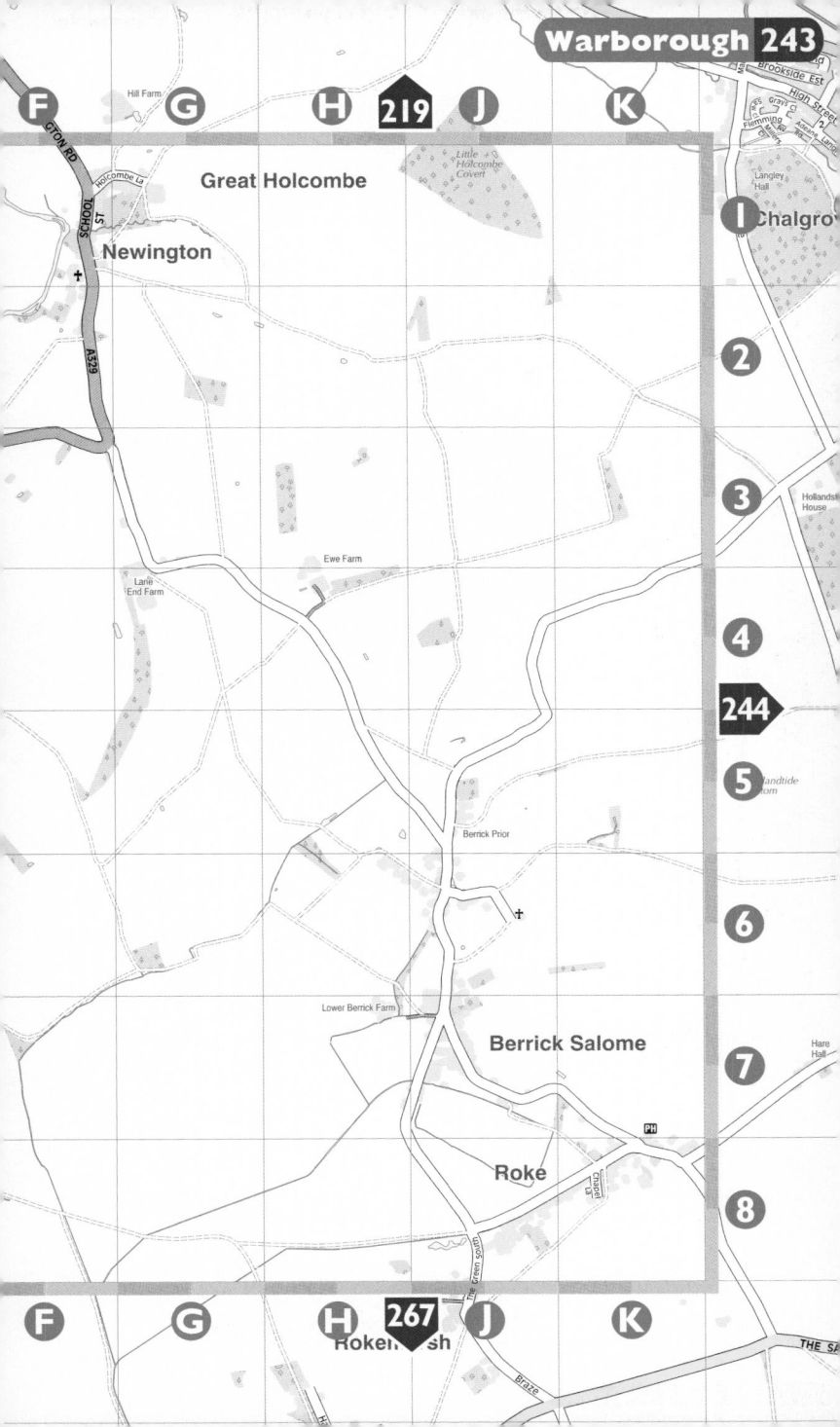

F G H 219 J K

I Chalgro

Hill Farm

Brookside Est
High Street

Langley
Hall

Great Holcombe

Little
Holcombe
Covert

Newington

Hollands
House

A529

Ewe Farm

Lane
End Farm

244

Sandtide
Tom

Berrick Prior

Berrick Salome

Lower Berrick Farm

Hare
Hall

Roke

PH

F G H 267 J K

Roken sh

THE SA

Brase

C I
1 Chiltern Cl
2 Cromwell Cl
B₁
1643 ●

B I
1 Hampden Cl
2 Ireton Cl
3 Mayfield Cl
4 St Mary's Cl

A **B** **220** **C** **D** **E**

Monument
Business Park

Tower End
Brookside Est
High Street
Brittania Rd

The
Surgery

Langley
Hall

Chalgrove

Primary School

Church

Chalgrove
Farm

CUXHAM ROAD B480

Hollandside
House

Cadwell
Covert

Cadwell Farm

I

2

3

4 **243**

Whitehouse Farm

Cadwell Lane

5

Hollandtide
Bottom

6

Rumbolds Farm

7

Hare
Hall

Chapel
La

8

Cottesmore
Lane

A **B** **268** **C** **D** **E**

THE SANDS

B4009 GROVE LANE

I grid square represents 500 metres

F G H **223** J K

The

ROAD

Field Farm House

Hill Farm

Swan's Way

Hill Road

M40

I

Nature
Reserve

2

Upper
Vicar's Farm

3

Cowleaze
Wood

Lydall's
Wood

4

248

5

Beechwood

Swan's Way

Shirburn
Wood

Portobello Farm

6

Shirburn Lodge

Shotridge
Wood

7

Portways

ill Road

Oxfordshire Way

8

Black
Wood

**Christmas
Common**

F G H **271** J K **Northend**

Launder's Farm

Watlington
Park

Queha
Wood

ASTON HILL

A40

E3
1 Studdridge Ct

A

B

224

C   Hill Farm

D

E

Kiln Farm

OXFORD

I

Nature
Reserve

M40

M40

IBSTONE RD

Hailey
Wood

Junction 5

2

Upper
Vicar's Farm

Mill La

Independent
Business
Park

Wallace Hill

Mill Road

3

Lower
Vicar's
Farm

Little Stud

4

Lydall's
Wood

Ibstone Road

247

Wellground Farm

5

Bowley's
Wood

Common
Wood

Wormsley
Park

6

Buckinghamshire County
Oxfordshire County

Hungryhill
Wood

Bla
We

7

Ibstone
Common

8

Blackmoor's
Wood

Hale
Wood

Gray's Lane

North A

B

272

C

D

E

Launder's Farm

1 grid square represents 500 metres

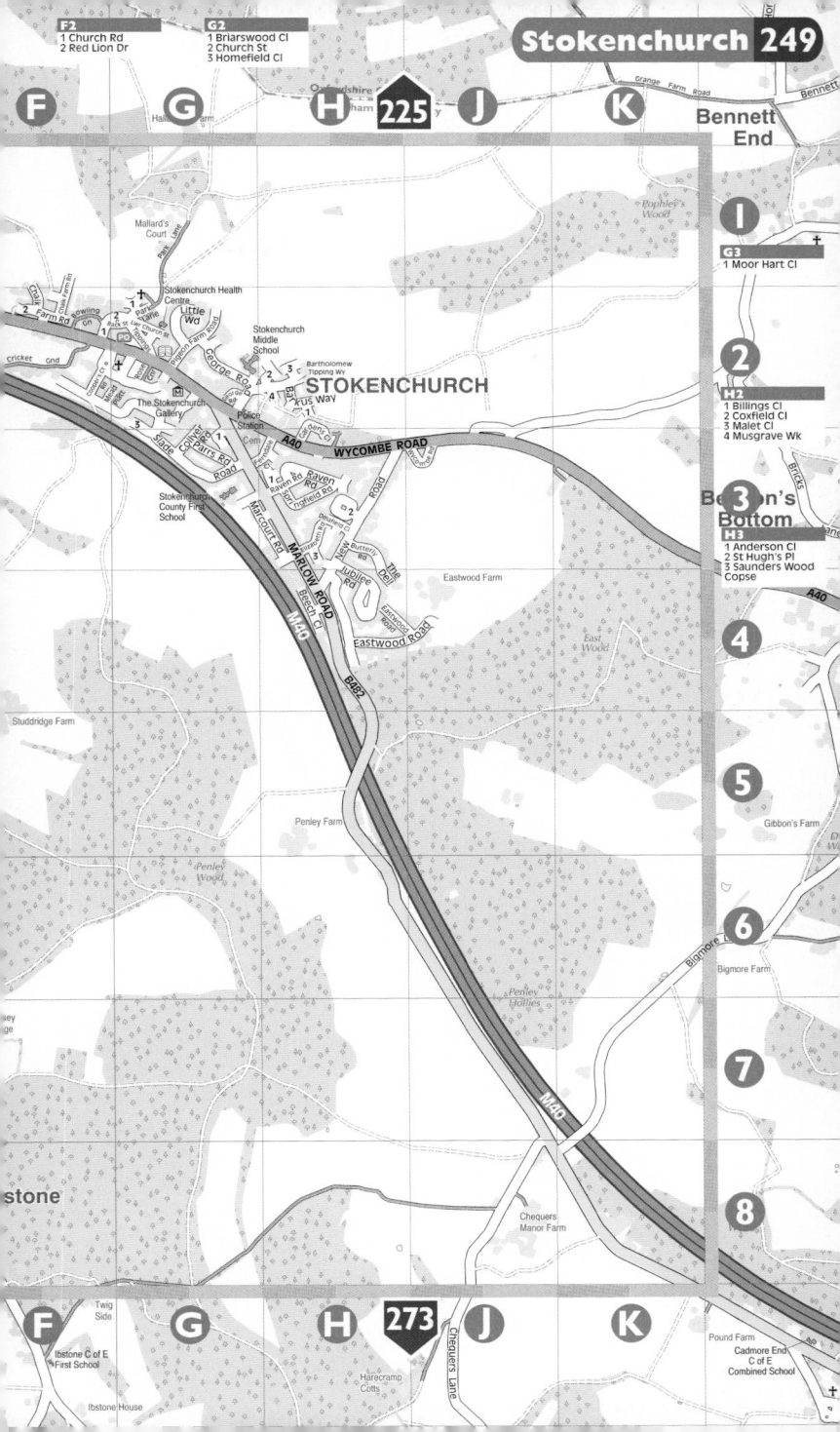

KS
1 Downlands

Little
Coxwell

F   G   H   229   J   K

I
2
3
4
254
5
6
7
8

A420(T)

Field Farm

Tithe Farm

King's Lane

Hughes Cresent

Mallins Lane

Priors Mews

B4508

FERNHAM RD

MAJORS ROAD B4508

Barrington Avenue

Bowls Green

Church Close

SHRIVENHAM ROAD

Longcot

Stone Farm

Cleveland Farm

Bower Brook

Longcot Road

Old Wharf Road

Longcot Road

Old Wharf Road

Broadleaze Farm

Claypit Lane

Cowleaze Farm

F   G   H   277   J   K

eyhern

Stanford Park Farm

Northmead Lane

F G H 233 J K

Park Lane

Blackacres Farm

Land Brook

I

Millaway Farm

Millaway Lane

2

Hyde Road

Cow Lane

Denchworth
Cemetery

Brook Lane

Goosey

Circourt Road

3

Church Farm

Circourt Road

4

Upper
Circourt Farm

258

Farm

5

Woodhill Brook

6

A417

Challow Marsh Farm

Woodhill Brook

Woodhill Lane

7

Garlands Farm

A417

Woodhill Lane

8

F G H 281 J K

Mill Lane

W & G
Industrial
Estate

ROAD

D6
1 Fulmar Pl
2 Hawksworth Cl

D5
1 Shepherds Cl
2 Vestry Cl

C8
1 Canal Ct

A   B   234   C   D   E

D7
1 Barbury Dr
2 De Vitre Pl
3 Farm End
4 Pound Cft

Hyde Farm
Hyde Road
Northn... Lane

1

2

Denchworth
Cemetery
Brook Lane
B3... Cl

3

Circourt Road

4

Upper
Circourt

257

5

Denchworth Road
Cemetery
Grove Wick Farm
Monks Farm

Grove

Howard Close
Denchworth Rd
The Maples

Grove
Primary
School
Oxfor

6

Further
Education
Coll

Millbrook
County
Junior Sch

Vale Av
Vicarage
esterfield

Glebe
Gdns
Harling

Carlton
Close

Wayland Road
Limetree Cl

St Ives Rd

Membury
Cherbury Gn
Sharland
Street

Mays
Flora
Cl
thorn Cl

Woodhill Brook

Woodhill Lane

Stephenson
Road

Euston
Way

Wayland Av
Faraday
Road

Gower
Road

Rider Way

Newlins Drive
White
Horse
Way

Columb
Albert...

Bretton Drive

Boucher
Drive

Cane
La

Laurel Crs

7

Woodhill Lane

8

Downsview Road
Denchworth Road

Mabl...
Mably Gv
Way

A358
GROVE ROAD

A   B   282   C   D   E

Elizabeth Drive

Fitzwaryn
School

St James'

Wilan
Road
Tinkerbu...

Harcourt

F G H **243** J K

I THE SA

Rokemarsh

Braze

Lane

The Green

2

Port Hill
Road

Hale Farm

Hale
Road

Sands

B4009

The Close

Sunbridge

WATLINGTON

RD

Blackland Road

Green

The Cedars

Street

Littleworth

B4009

Oxford
Road

Littleworth
Road

OXFORD ROAD

Benson C of E
Junior School

Mill Stream Surg

High St

3

River Thames

Pensfield

Church Rd

Castle

Benson

St Helen's
Cres

St Helen's Avenue

Coach Wy

Old London Road

Paddock

Benson Airfield

4

268

Clay Lane

RD

Preston
Crowmarsh

Thames Path

Crowmarsh
Battle Farm

Benson La

5

OX10

6

Cemetery

ford
School

7

ck's Lane

WALLINGFORD

The
Surg

Castle
St

Hotel
Street

Chilterns Fine
Art Gallery

Corn Exchange
Theatre

R.A.F. &
Wallingford
Rowing Club

St Leonard's La

The Street

Crowmarsh
Gifford

The Street

Thames
Md

Marsh Lane

Clack's Lane

A4074

8

Coldharbour Farm

Reading Road

St Lucian's La

Crowmarsh
Gifford
C of E Sch

F G H **291** J K

Crowmarsh Hill

WAY

A4074

OX5

CROWMARSH HILL

The
Murren

Newnham Farm

Chilterns

Hamstyles

Britwell
Priory

PH

245

**Britwell
Salome**

Britwell Salome
House

Swyncombe
Downs

270

Lower Farm

Down Farm

RECTORY

Swynco

SWAN'S WAY
RIDGEWAY

Ewelme Downs

RIDGEWAY

SWAN'S
WAY

Ewelme Park

RIDGEWAY

293

A B 246 C D E

I

2

3

4

269

5

6

7

8

A B 294 C D E

Icknield House

HOWE ROAD B480

Dame Alice Farm

The Howe

Howe Wood

Swyncombe Downs

RED LANE B480

Lower Farm

Coates Farm

Coates Copse

Cookley Green

Coates Lane

Church Lane

RECTORY

B481

Swyncombe House

Lane

Ridgeway

Ridgeway

Parkcorner Farm

Priors Wood

1 grid square represents 500 metres

F G H **247** J K

Christmas
Common

Northend
I

Blackmoor
Wood

Launder's Farm

Wallingtons
Park

Queen
Wood

2

Queensboard Way

Greenfield
Copse

3

Hollandridge Farm

Greenfield

4

Lower Greenfield Farm

Hollandridge Lane

272

Greenfield
Wood

Oxfordshire Way

5

Buckinghamshire / Oxfordshire County

6

LANE

Pishill Bottom

B480

Pishill Bank

PH

B480

Pishill

Church Hill

ssell's
Water

7

Holland Lane

B48

Doyley
Wood

8

Greensfield Way

Upper
Maidensgrove

Russell's
Water
Common

F G H **295** J K

PH

Oak Farm

Maidensgrove

Park Lane

Westwood

Sto

A B **248** C D E

Blackmoor
Wood

Northend

Launder's Farm.

1

2

Swain's
Wood

Holloway Lane

3

Blundells

Hollandridge Farm

4

Turville Park

**Turville
Heath**

Turville
Grange

271

5

**Summer
Heath**

Balham's Lane

6

Church Hill

Pishill

Balhams
Farm House

Balham's
Wood

7

Hollandridge Lane

Drovers Lane

B480

8

Whitepond Farm

Stonor House

Stonor
Park

Kimble Far

Cray's Lane

Buckinghamshire County
Oxfordshire County

Holland

Oxfordshire

A B **296** C D E

Park Lane

Hotel

stone

F **G** **H** 249 **J** **K**

Twig Side

Ibstone C of E First School

Pound Wood

Pound End

Pound End C of E Combined School

Cadmore End

Harecramp Cotts

Ibstone House

1

2

or Farm

Ashfield Barn

Hanger Wood

3

Manor Farm

Holloway Lane

Hanger Farm

4

+**Turville**

Fingest +

Fingest Lane

School La PH

PH

Watery Lane

5

n Lane

Dolesden

Poynatts Farm

6

Godda

PH

Skirmett

Shogmoor

7

Elmdown

Shogmoor La

Great Wood

Flint Hall

8

Luxters Farm

Gassetts Wood

F **G** **H** 297 **J** **K**

Dup Lane

The Hyde

Henleyshill Wood

Ⓐ   Ⓑ   256   Ⓒ   Ⓓ   Ⓔ

Broadleaze Farm

Ⓘ   Kingston Common Farm

❷   Cemetery

    Hill View

❸   ✝

Westcot Lane

Westcot Lane

Westcot Lane

Westerry Lane

West St   Pulpit Hill

Sparsholt St   Broadbrook Lane

PH

Sparsholt

Church   Way

✝   Eastmanton Lane

Westcot

❹   B4507

B4507

❺

❻

Lodge Farm

❼   Sincombe Farm

B4001

❽

Ⓐ   Ⓑ   302   Ⓒ   Ⓓ   Ⓔ

Ridgeway

1 grid square represents 500 metres

G3
1 Lawrence Cl

K2
1 Hedge Hill Rd

F G H **257** J K

I

ROAD

Silver Lane

W & G
Industrial
Estate

A417

Orchard Gdns

The scene

**West
Challow**

2

**East
Challow**

Old School La

Field Gdns

Cornhill Farm

East Challow
C of E School

Witham Place

Vicarage

Townsend

Cemetery

3

Church Row

Childrey

B4001

Chapel Way

HIGH ST

Dog Lane

The Ridgeway
C of E Primary
School

West Street

B4507

4

282

Mill

Manor
Field

5

Old Mill
Ct

Court
Rd

Let

Bakery
Sqm

New St

Post Office
Lane

6

Court

Old Stables
Yard

HOLLOW WAY B4001

Cemetery

Blandy's Farm

Bassett Road

Warborough
Road

7

College Farm

8

**Letcombe
Bassett**

Holborn Hill

Knap
Close

Rectory Lane

Bassett Road

F G H **303** J K

282

B2
1 Ogbourne Cl

A6
1 Anvil Paddock

A5
1 Croft End
2 Hamlyn Cl
3 Regis Pl

A **B** **258** **C** **D** **E**

I

C1
1 Wasbrough Av

2

C2
1 Dean Butler Cl
2 Reeds Cl

East Challow
C of E School

East
Challow

Townsend

3

C3
1 Greenacres Dr

ICKLETON   ROAD   B4507

NEWBURY ST

Fitzwaryn
School

Stockham
County
Primary School

Lydsee Gate

Segsbury
Rd

Nalderown

West
Hill

Hamfield

Hamfield

King Alfreds
School West

Priory Orchard

MILL ST

CHALLOW   ROAD

A417

Belmont

Elizabeth Drive

Wilian Way

Barwell

Denchworth

Vale & Downland
Museum & Visitor Cen

Wantage
C of E
Infant Sch

King Alfreds
Grammar
Sch

Wantage
Leisure
Centre

ORMOND
RD

ORMOND RD   B4494

St Andrews
School

Wantage Town
Football &
Social Club.

Wantage
C of E
School

Willow Lane

OX12

GROVE ROAD

A338

B507

4

281

5

D1
1 Bailey Cl
2 Copperfield Cl
3 Donnington Pl
4 Highclere Gdns
5 Liddiard Cl
6 Willow Wk
7 Worthington Wy

Mill
Paddock

Letcombe Regis

Old Mill
Ct

Blandy's Farm

6

Post Office
Lane

Old Stables
Yard

D3
1 Alfred St
2 Church St
3 Market Pl
4 The Cloisters

7

E2
1 Haywards Cl
2 Stirling Cl
3 Suzan Crs

Warborough   Road

Court Hill Road

Manor Farm

A338

MANOR ROAD

8

Warborough Farm

Court Hill Road

Furzewick Farm

A **B** **304** **C** **D** **E**

1 grid square represents 500 metres

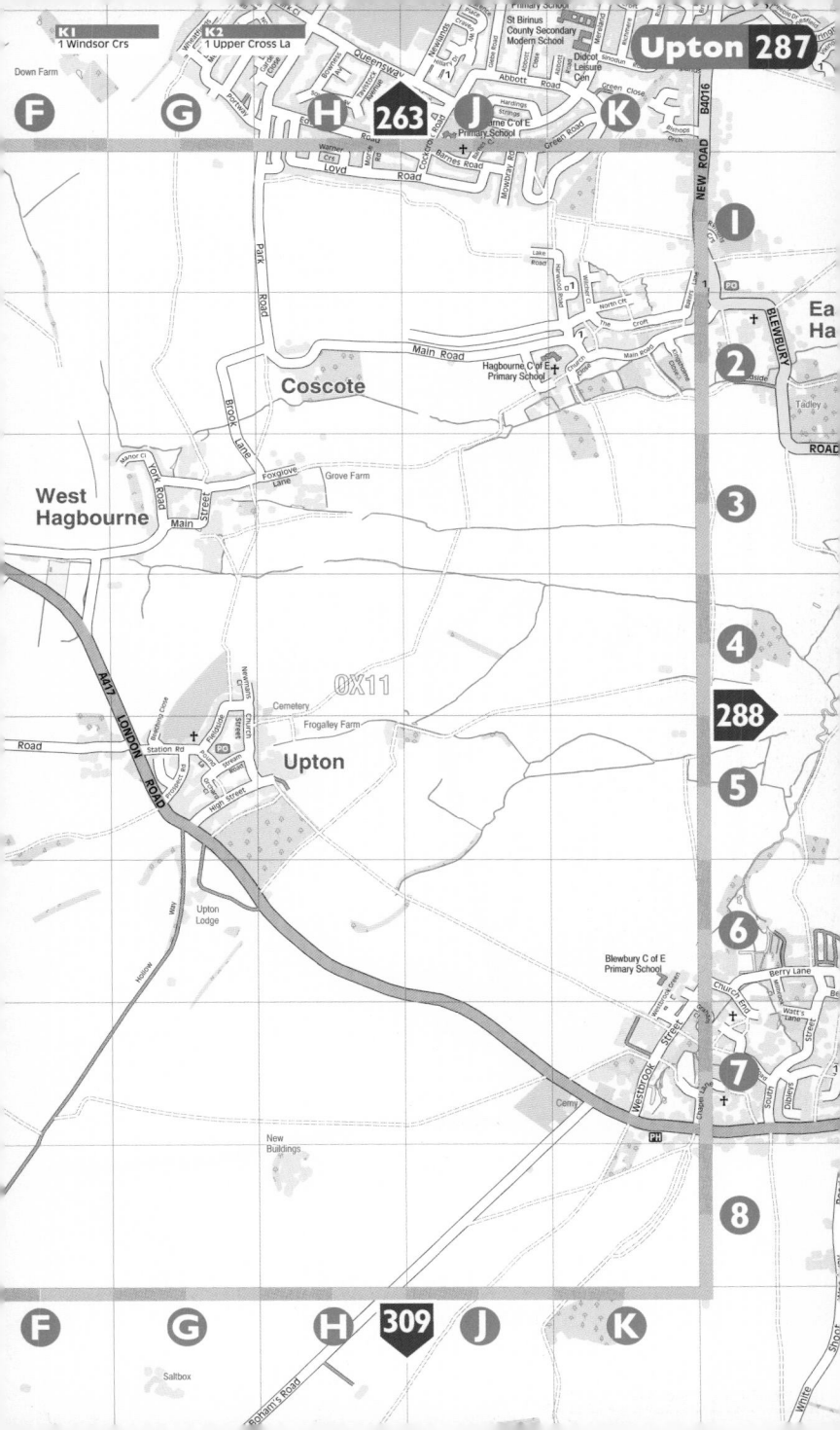

E5
1 Lion Meadow
2 The Old Kiln
3 Pottery Flds

D5
1 The Ridgeway

D4
1 Elms Wy
2 Pearces Meadow

A B **270** C D E

1

Parkcorner Farm

Priors Wood

2

Bramley Road

Park Corner

Digberry Lane

3

Nuffield Place

Huntercombe End Lane

Huntercombe End

A4130

Priest Cl

4

Port Hill

293

Hayden Lane

PORT HILL

Nettlebed

5

Hayden Farm

Doctors' Surgery

HIGH ST

Nettlebed CP School

Joyce Grove

A4130

6

English Farm

7

Howberrywood

Swan Wood

Flg Tree

8

Nott Wood

A B **316** C D E Highm

F G H **271** J K

Doyley Wood

Russell's Water Common

PH

Oak Farm

Maidensgrove

1 Park Lane

Sto

Westwood Manor Farm

2

Nature Reserve

Maidensgrove Scrubs

Pages Farm

Oxfordshire Way

3

Soundness Farm

Soundness House

4

296

Valley End Farm

Oxfordshire Way

5

Crocker End

Catslip

Halfridge Wood

6

Little Bixbottom Farm

Nettlebed Woods

Bix Hall

7

A4130

White Lane

rrimoles

Bix

8

Bix

Westleaze Cottages

er Highmoor

F G H **317** J K

Manor

A4130

Brawns House

F **G** **H** 279 **J** **K**

I

2

3

4

302

5

6

7

8

Kingstone
Warren

Oxfordshire County
West Berkshire

Wellbottom Down

Lambourn Valley Way

Sevenbarrows
House

Postdown Farm

Lambourn Valley Way

e Farm

Maddle Road

B4001

B4001

Wether
Down

F **G** **H** **J** **K**

Newbarn

Upper
Lambourn

Street

ROAD

F G H 281 J K

Letcombe Bassett

Holbo...
Rectory Lane
Crang's Hill
Smith's Hill

1

2
Ridgeway
Smith's Hill Farm
Ridgeway
Segsbury Farm
Hill Fort

3

Flint Farm

4

304

Cockleberry Farm

5

6

Warren Farm

7

8

F G H J K

F G H **285** J K

1

Ridgeway

Chilton Downs

Ridgeway

2

3

Sheep Down

Cow Down

Bury Down

Oxfordshire County West Berkshire

Knollend Down

Folly Farm

4

308

5

West Ilsley

PH

Fir Tree Paddock

The Malting

Churchway

P3

Starveall Farm

6

Catmore Road

Hodcott House

Berkshire Circular Route

7

The Barracks

8

Fore Down

East Hendred Down

Hodcott Buildings

F G H J K

Berkshire Circular Route

Ball Pit F

F G H **289** J K

Lollingdon Farm

Carrimers Farm

Sheephouse Farm

Westfield Road

Halfpenny Lane

1

Breach House

2

Westfield Stables

Cholsey Downs

SHORTLANDS HILL A417

Kingstanding H

3

Moulsford Bottom

Starveall Farm

4

A417

Unhill Bottom

312

Lingley Knoll

5

Moulsford Downs

Well Barn

6

Unhill Wood

Oxfordshire County
West Berkshire

7

Cow Common

Thurle Grange

Ham Wood

Thurle Down

Goring & Streatley Golf Clu

Rectory Road

8

lley en

Warren Farm

F G H J K

Kiddington Cottage

F G H 291 J K

Ipsden

Ipsden House

Barracks Farm

B4009

The

I

Braziers Park

2

Watch Folly

Swan's Way

Swan's Way

Woodcote Road

Icknield Farm

Ivol Barn

Ouseley Barn

3

LANE

A4074

4

314

South Stoke Road

Upper Cadle

5

Grove Farm

South Stoke Road

Broad Street Farm

6

Beech Lane

Beech Farm

Beech Lane

7

Wroxhills Wood

Elmorepark Wood

Icknield Road

8

Elvend

Battle Road

Elvendon Priory

Park Wood

Burntwood

B4

F G H **295** J K

Westleaze Cottages

r Highmoor

Bix Hill

A4130

Bix Manor Farm

1

Brawns House

Lawrence's Farm

Bromsden Farm

Lambridge Wood

2

Rockylane Farm

3 oadplat

atwell

Greys Court (NT)

Shepherd's Green

Satwell Ct

Rocky Lane

4

318

Greys Green

5

Bolt's Cross

Church Ct

6

Rotherfield Greys

Dog Lane

Crosslanes

7 Cowfields Farm

PEPPARD HILL

Church Lane

School

Springwood Lane

Grange Avenue

8

Upper House Farm

Rotherfield Peppard

Lane

Shiplake Hill

F G H **327** J K

Kings Farm Lane

Blounts Court Road

Church Lane

Widmore Lane

Devil's Hill

F5
1 Adwell Sq
2 Baronsmead
3 West La

F6
1 Homelands Wy

Fawley
Court Farm

F **G** **H** **297** **J** **K**

Mi
En

I

F7
1 Cromwell Cl

Temple Island

Remenham Lane

Remenham

2

G6
1 Grove Rd

The
Mount

3

Swiss Farm

Dryleas
Sports
Ground

Remenham
Court

Common
Barn

4

MARLOW ROAD

A4155

Phyllis Ct Drive

NORTHFIELD END

Leicester
Rd

Rupert Ct

Rupert
House
Sch

Kenton
Theatre

Radnor Cl

Remenham
Place

Remenham Lane

Church Lane

River Thames

Henley Reach

Thames Path

Reme

Century
Galleries
Hotel

Thames
Gallery

Police
Stn

NEW ST

BELL ST

Clarence
Rd

The
York
Rd

Bell Surg

Hart Surg

West Street

Market
Pl

Town
Hall

Art Gallery

DUKE ST

Woodlands

PH

A4130

WHITE HILL

5

The Henley
College

Greys
Gallery

Bohun
Gallery

Friday St

Park Place

6

Deanfield Av

Greys Hill

Greys
Rd

Norman Av

Station Rd

Henley-on-Thames Stn

Centenary
Business
Park

The River & Rowing
Museum at Henley

7

Sacred Heart
School

**HENLEY-
ON-THAMES**

St
Mark's

A4155

READING RD

Preparatory
School

Primary
School

Newtown

Fairview Trading
Est

Henley Town
Football Club

WARGRAVE ROAD

Temple
Combe

8

St
Andrew's
Rd

Berkshire Road

Belle Vue Rd

Cromwell Road

Manor Rd

Western Road

Peppard Rd

Harpsden Way

Rotherfield
Road

Football
Club

Mill Lane

Wokingham

Oxfordshire County

River Thames

A321

F **G** **H** **329** **J** **K**

Henley Golf Club

Harpsden

A4155

Lower
Bolney Farm

Sheephouse Farm

A B **299** C D E

1

2

Russley Park

3

Gore
Lane Farm

Peaks
Downs

M4

4

M4

5

North Farm

Baydon Road

6

East
Leaze Farm

7

North
Field Barn

8

Aldbourne Circular Route

A B C D E

Greenhills

I grid square represents 500 metres

F G H **313** J K

Battle Road

Elvendon Priory

Park Wood

I

READING ROAD B4526

Burntwood

2

Great Chalk Wood

Flint Ho

Upper Gatehampton Farm

Stapnall's Farm

Cold Harbour

3

Gatehampton Manor

Thames Path

4

Coombe End Farm

River Thames

Church Farm

324

RG8

29

5

Beech Farm

Lower Basildon

Hartslock Vw

Park Wall Lane

Thames Path

6

Basildon House

Beale Park

Mead Lane

The Ridge

Basildon Park (NT)

Coombe Park

7

Park Farm

SHOOTER'S

Oxfordshire County

West Berkshire

B471

Manor Road

8

HILL

Whitchurch-on-Thames

F G H J K

A329 Hartslock Court

Home Farm

Pangbourne Station

St James

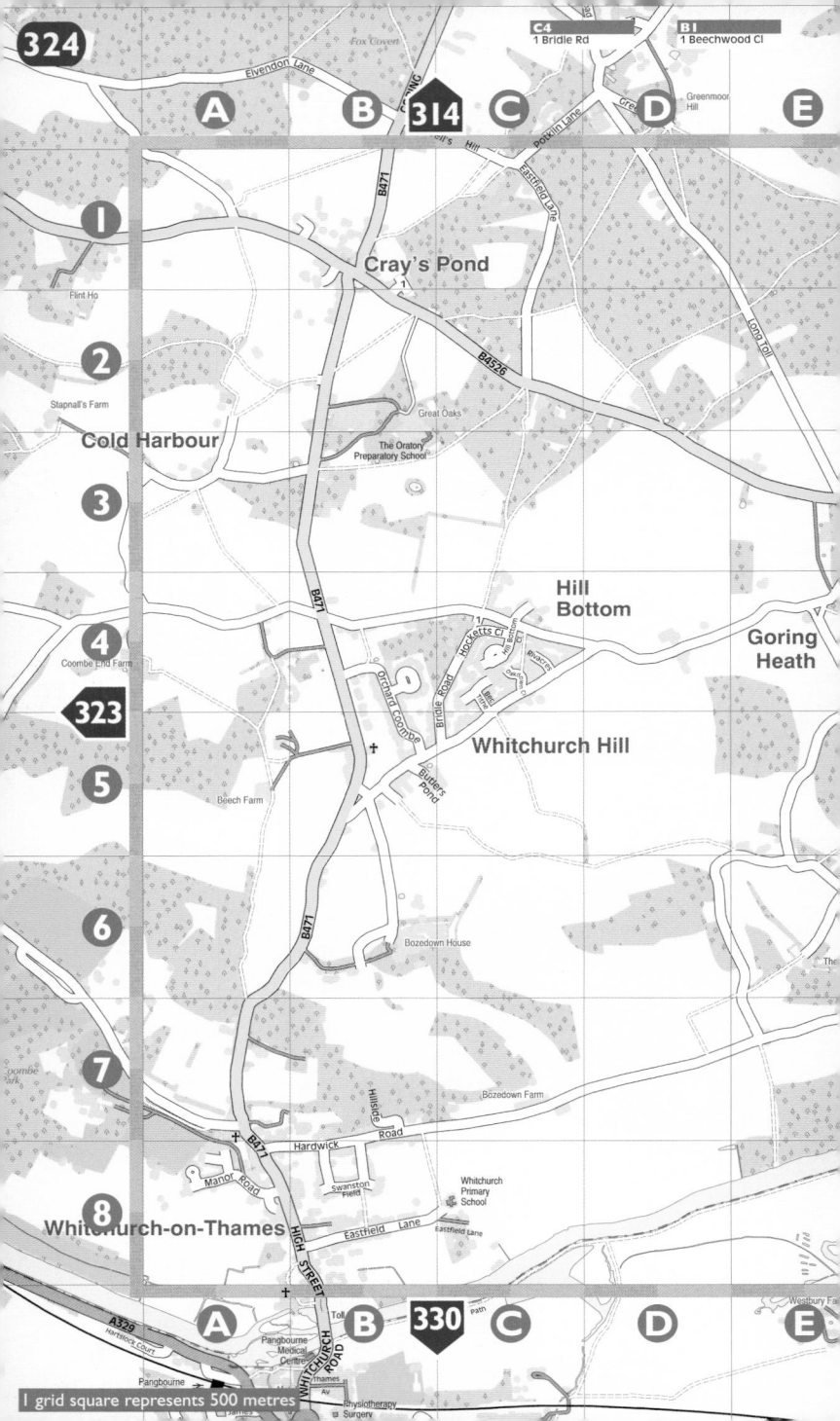

Wyfold

F   G   H   **315**   J   K

1

Park Lane

2

Withy Copse

College or Abbots Wood

Lackmore Wood

DEADMAN'S LANE B4526

A4074

Kempwood

3

Abbotsfield

Alnut's Hospital

Deadman's Lane

Cane End Farm

READING ROAD

Nuney Green

Cane End

4

326

5

Collins End

Lane

Holly Copse

Bottom Wood

Whittles Farm

Cross Lanes

Hodmore Farm

6

7

Tren Gre

Thames

Thames Path

Bottom Farm

Lilley Farm

8

F   G   H   **331**   **Mapledurham**   J   K

Pond Lane

Watermill

Home Farm

Mapledurham House

E2
1 Bramley Crs

E1
1 Appletree Cl

C2
1 Orchard Fld

A   B   316   C   D   E

I

Gallowstree
Common

2

Wyfold

Nippero
Grove

Withy
Copse

New Copse

Woodside
La

Hearns
La

The Hamlet

Horsepond Road

Horsepond Road

Reade's
Lane

Hazelmoor

Wood Lane

Bishopswood Farm

Shiplake
Bottom

SONNI
COMM

Lambourne
Road

Reade's
Lane

Chiltern Edge
Secondary
School

3

READING ROAD

Cane
E 4

325

5

Cane
End Farm

Wood
Lane

Crayleaze

Kidmore

Kidmore End

Kidmore End
Primary School

Cemetery Coopers
Pightle

Highland
Wood

Green
Dean
Wood

oss Lanes

6

Hodmore Farm

Cross Farm

Mill Lane

Tokers

7

Sheepways

Skarries
View

Green

Trench
Green

Pithouse Farm

Lane

Chazey
Heath

Chazey

A4074

Rokeby
Drive

Gaskells End

Bardolph's Cl

Tokers
Green

Rosebery
Rd

Russell
Rd

Beech Rd

Lane

8

Newell's

Lane

Elm
Rd

Tokers Grn Lane

A   B   332   C   D   E

Pond

Lane

Rose Farm

Shepherds Lane

Silverthorne Drive

Sandcroft

1 grid square represents 500 metres

A B 318 C D E

1

Devil's Hill

2

3

327 4

5

6

7

8

Harpsden
Bottom

Mays
Green

Shiplake
Row

Binfield Heath

Dunsden
Green

Littlestead
Green

King's Farm Lane
Old Place
White Hill
Red Hill
Perseverance Hill
Hunt's Farm
Highlands Farm
Henley District
Indoor Sports Centre
Gillotts School
Gillotts Lane
Bellehatch Park
High Wood
Chalk
Bones Lane
PH
Coppid Hall
Home Farm
Heathfield Av
Heathfield Cl
Comp Farm
Gravel Road
Heath Rd
Green Lane
Sandpit
Cork's Farm Lane
Row Lane
Bryant's Farm
Kiln Road
Foxhill
Bint's Farm
Hampstead Farm
Span Hill
Henley
A4155
Road
Spring
Caversham Park
Road
Primary Sch
St Martin's RC Primary School
Queensway
Hemdean
Whitby
Foxhill Lane

1 grid square represents 500 metres

F   G   H   **319**   J   K

1

Henley Golf Club

Harpsden

Lower Bolney Farm

Woodlands Road

Harpsden Wood

2

Clay House

Upper Bolney House

Woodlands Road

Bolney Lane

Bolney Road

Brampton Chase

Thornfield Av

Bolney Trevor Drive

LC

Shiplake Station

Basmore Av

3

Lashbrook Road

Lowes Close

Station Rd

Oaks Rd

Baskerville La

The Crs

The Chestnuts

Crowsley Rd

Bucklers Wy

A4155

4

Lower Shiplake

New Road

Mill Road

New Cross

Mill Lane

Thames Path

5

Shiplake

Avenue

Orchard Cd

Memorial

Shiplake C of E Primary School

Plough

Plowden Wy Lane

Church Lane

Shiplake House

Shiplake College

Thames Path

London Drive

Wargrave Station

Station Road

WARGR

Church St

6

Borough Marsh

The Lynch

Hallsmead Ait

Thames Path

7

The Pigg Church of E School

8

F   G   H   **335**   J   K

St Bridge

Oxfordshire County

Reading

Loddon Park Farm

Loddon Drive

BATH   ROAD   A4(T)

Mapledurham

Tilehurst

A3
1 Bramber Ms
2 Cadogan Cl
3 Chestnut Av

A2
1 Eynsford Cl
2 Framlingham Dr
3 Gifford Cl
4 Montpelier Dr

A1
1 Ilchester Ms
2 Launceston Av
3 Littlestead Cl
4 Melford Gdn

A
B
C
D
E

328

Duften Ben Green

Littlestead Green

Caversham Park

Caversham

A7
1 Riversdale Ct

Primary Sch
St Martins RC Primary School

Foxhill Farm

Play Hatch

Henley Road

Sonnin Eye

B478 PLAYHATCH ROAD

The Gallery

B478

A8
1 Cholmeley Pl
2 Cholmeley Ter

HENLEY ROAD A4155

Reading

Oxfordshire County

C7
1 Shepherd's House La

CP School

Lowfield Farm

Reading Blue Coat School

333

FR HENLEY ROAD

Peel Cl

5

E7
1 Shepherds Hl

Honey Meadow Cl

Amersham

Road Industrial Estate

Marina

Thames Valley Business Park

Lower Caversham

6

David Lloyd Sports Centre

Sonning Meadows

Thames Path

Superstore

P

Oracle Pkwy

River Thames

Thames Path

Trout

SHEPHERDS HILL

LONDON ROAD

BATH ROAD

7

Suttons Avenue

Suttons Business Park

Pk Avenue

Suttons Business Park

LONDON ROAD A4(T)

LONDON ROAD

Delamere Rd

B3350

PITTS LANE

Infant School

Liverpool Rd

Coventry rd

Norton Rd

Filey Road

Kennet Side

Chiltern Crs

The Drive

Erleigh Ct Gdns

CHURCH ROAD

The Bulmershe School

KING'S R

8

Reading College

Food

Swimming Baths

Doctors Surgery

New Town

Palmer Park

Cemetery

The Drive

Whiteknights

Byron Road

Culver

Milton Rd

Blackthorn Cl

Oldfield

Milton Rd

University of Reading

William Gra Infants School

Reading School

A329 WOKINGHAM ROAD

A4

Palmer Park Av

House

Orange Av

A3290

Alfred Sutton Primary School

College

Green Road

CHURCH ROAD

Fairfourt Avenue

Bulmershe Road

A
B
C
D
E

Abingdon	214 C8
Abingdon Bridge	238 C1
Adderbury	38 D4
Adlestrop	65 J5
Adwell	222 C3
Albury	173 F8
Alkerton	17 K5
Alvescot	181 K1
Ambrosden	116 A4
Appleford	239 K7
Appleton	188 B8
Ardington	284 A1
Ardington Wick	260 B7
Ardley	77 H3
Arlescote	10 C1
Ascott	32 D5
Ascott d' Oyley	104 A5
Ascott Earl	103 J6
Ascott-under-Wychwood	103 K5
Ashbury	277 G8
Asthall	140 B4
Asthall Leigh	141 F1
Aston	184 C4
Aston Rowant	223 J5
Aston Sandford	177 F3
Aston Tirrold	288 D7
Aston Upthorpe	288 E5
Astrop	40 A2
Aynho	40 B7
Bainton	79 F4
Baldon Row	217 G2
Balscote	18 B7
Bampton	183 H3
Banbury	3 D2
Barford St John	37 G8
Barford St Michael	55 G1
Barnard Gate	145 F5
Barton	169 F3
Barton Abbey	91 K1
Barton Hartshorn	63 G5
Barton-on-the-Heath	48 A1
Baulking	255 H5
Baydon	321 G7
Baynard's Green	59 J8
Bayworth	190 E8
Beacon's Bottom	249 K3
Beckley	151 H4
Begbroke	128 C6
Belmont	282 D2
Bennett End	225 K8
Benson	267 J3
Berinsfield	241 J2
Berrick Salome	243 J7
Bessels Leigh	189 F7
Bicester	96 E3
Binfield Heath	328 C6
Binsey	166 C3
Bishopstone	298 D3
Bix	295 K8
Blackbird Leys	192 D6
Black Bourton	182 B2
Blackditch	163 G7
Blackthorn	116 C3
Bladon	127 K5
Bledington	83 H6
Bledlow	201 K6
Blenheim	169 J8
Blenheim	193 K5
Bletchingdon	112 A8
Blewbury	288 B7
Bloxham	36 D2
Boars Hill	190 A6
Boarstall	134 E6
Bodicote	28 E7
Borough Marsh	329 J7
Botley	166 A6
Bould	101 H1
Bourton	276 A4
Bow	232 C6
Bridge End	241 J7
Brighthampton	186 B3
Brightwell Baldwin	245 F5
Brightwell-cum-Sotwell	265 J5
Britwell Salome	245 J8
Brize Norton	158 E4
Broadplat	318 A3
Broadwell	64 B3
Broadwell	180 E3
Brookend	86 D7
Brookhampton	218 E6
Broughton	27 J6
Broughton Poggs	180 B3
Bruern Abbey	102 B2
Buckland	208 B7
Buckland Marsh	208 B3

Bucknell	78 A8
Bunkers Hill	110 E7
Burcot	241 F3
Burdrop	25 G7
Burford	138 E3
Buscot	204 A7
Bushey Ground	141 G7
Caldecott	238 C1
Calthorpe	3 D6
Camp Corner	196 D2
Campsfield	128 B5
Cane End	325 K4
Carswell Marsh	207 J5
Carterton	158 C4
Cassington	146 D5
Caulcott	94 A2
Caversfield	78 E8
Caversham	333 F4
Caversham Heights	333 F3
Chacombe	22 D2
Chadlington	87 F7
Chalford	223 H1
Chalgrove	244 A1
Chalkhouse Green	327 C6
Charlbury	106 B4
Charlton	41 F2
Charlton	283 G2
Charlton-on-Otmoor	132 A3
Charney Bassett	234 A5
Charterville Allotments	141 G6
Charvil	335 J2
Chastleton	65 H1
Chawley	189 K1
Chazey Heath	326 C8
Checkendon	315 H4
Chesterton	96 B7
Chetwode	63 H7
Childrey	281 G3
Chilson	104 C4
Chilton	286 B7
Chimney	209 F1
Chimney-end	122 B4
Chinnor	225 F1
Chipping Norton	68 C5
Chipping Warden	14 C1
Chislehampton	218 C5
Cholsey	290 A5
Christmas Common	247 G8
Church End	50 E3
Church End	144 C8
Church End	176 C2
Church Enstone	70 E8
Church Hanborough	145 K1
Churchill	85 G2
Church Westcote	100 D1
Clanfield	182 B7
Clare	221 J6
Clattercote	7 F8
Claydon	6 E6
Cleeve	312 E7
Cleveley	89 G3
Clifton	57 G3
Clifton Hampden	240 C3
Cogges	143 G8
Cold Harbour	323 K3
Coleshill	228 B7
Collins End	325 F5
The Colony	24 C8
Combe	126 B2
Compton Beauchamp	277 J5
Cookley Green	270 D5
Cornwell	66 C4
Coscote	287 H2
Cote	184 E5
Cothill	213 G3
Cottisford	61 F4
Covingham	274 C8
Cowleaze Corner	182 E5
Cowley	192 E2
Cowpasture	33 F5
Crawley	142 C3
Cray's Pond	324 B1
Crocker End	295 F5
Cropredy	13 J5
Cross Lanes	325 J6
Croughton	41 J8
Crowell	224 D3
Crowell Hill	225 F6
Crowmarsh Gifford	267 H8
Crowsley	327 J3
Cuddesdon	194 E4
Culham	238 E5
Cumnor	189 F2
Cumnor Hill	190 A1
Curbridge	159 K1

Cutteslowe	149
Cuxham	245
Daylesford	65
Dean	87
Dean Court	165
Deddington	56
Delly End	124
Denchworth	257
Denton	194
Didcot	263
Dorchester	241
Draycot	172
Drayton	20
Drayton	237
Drayton St Leonard	242
Dry Sandford	213
Ducklington	160
Dunsden Green	328
Duns Tew	74
Dunthrop	69
Duxford	209
Easington	2
Easington	245
East Adderbury	38
East Challow	282
East End	34
East End	38
Eastend	87
East End	125
East Ginge	284
East Hagbourne	288
East Hanney	235
East Hendred	285
Eastleach Martin	155
Eastleach Turville	154
East Lockinge	283
Eaton	188
Eaton Hastings	205
Edgcote	14
Edgehill	9
Elsfield	150
Emmer Green	333
Emmington	200
Enslow	111
Enstone	88
Epwell	25
Evenley	43
Evenlode	64
Ewelme	268
Exlade Street	315
Eynsham	145
Faringdon	229
Farmoor	164
Farnborough	306
Fawler	106
Fawler	279
Fawley	296
Fawley	304
Fawley Bottom	296
Fencott	132
Fernham	254
Fewcott	77
Field Assarts	122
Fifield	101
Filchampstead	164
Filkins	180
Fingest	273
Finmere	45
Finstock	124
Fordwells	122
Forest Hill	170
Forty Green	201
Foscot	83
Foxcombe Hill	190
Freeland	126
Frilford	212
Frilford Heath	212
Fringford	80
Fritwell	58
Fulbrook	120
Fulwell	88
Fyfield	179
Fyfield	211
Gagingwell	89
Gainfield	232
Gallowstree Common	326
Garford	235
Garsington	194
Gawcombe	82
Gibraltar	110
Glympton	90
Godington	81
Golden Balls	216
Goosey	257
Goring	322

...pring Heath ... 324 E4
...osford ... 129 J8
...ozzard's Ford ... 213 G5
...rafton ... 4 C6
...randpont ... 205 J1
...reat Barrington ... 118 B7
...reat Bourton ... 13 F7
...reat Coxwell ... 229 J7
...reat Haseley ... 196 B7
...reat Holcombe ... 243 G1
...reat Milton ... 196 A5
...reat Purston ... 31 H3
...reat Rollright ... 50 E4
...reat Tew ... 53 J8
...reenfield ... 86 D8
...reenlands ... 271 G3
...he Green ... 297 J7
...reys Green ... 56 D8
...rimsbury ... 317 K5
...rove ... 3 F3
...addenham ... 258 D5
...ailey ... 176 C2
...ailey ... 142 E1
...ampton ... 292 B7
...ampton Gay ... 250 B2
...ampton Poyle ... 129 G2
...anwell ... 129 K4
...arcourt Hill ... 20 B2
...ardwick ... 190 C1
...ardwick ... 20 D6
...ardwick ... 60 E7
...aresfield ... 162 A6
...arpsden ... 227 F7
...arpsden Bottom ... 329 G1
...arwell ... 328 E1
...atford ... 262 C8
...eadington ... 232 B5
...eadington Hill ... 168 C3
...eathfield Village ... 5 F3
...empton ... 130 D1
...empton Wainhill ... 55 J3
...enley-on-Thames ... 201 J8
...ensington ... 319 F6
...enton ... 109 K8
...enwood ... 201 G5
...ethe ... 189 H6
...eythrop ... 61 H7
...igh Cogges ... 69 K3
...igh Cogges ... 161 J1
...ighfield ... 96 E4
...ighmoor ... 316 E1
...ighmoor Cross ... 316 C2
...ighworth ... 227 F8
...ill Bottom ... 324 C4
...inton-in-the-Hedges ... 41 K1
...inton Waldrist ... 209 J5
...olly Green ... 201 J4
...olton ... 170 E6
...olwell ... 138 A8
...ook End ... 315 H7
...ook Norton ... 51 K1
...opcroft's Holt ... 74 C8
...orley ... 19 H2
...ornton ... 18 D1
...orspath ... 193 K1
...orton-cum-Studley ... 152 B2
...untercombe End ... 294 B3
...bstone ... 249 F8
...ckford ... 172 E4
...comb ... 82 C5
...dbury ... 101 G3
...dstone ... 299 F2
...ffley ... 191 K3
...lmer ... 177 H7
...nglesham ... 202 E5
...psden ... 292 A8
...slip ... 130 E6
...luniper Hill ... 60 E2
...Kelmscot ... 204 D4
...Kencot ... 181 F1
...Kennington ... 191 J6
...Kiddington ... 90 C5
...Kidlington ... 129 H6
...Kidmore End ... 326 C4
...Kingham ... 84 B3
...King's End ... 96 E5
...Kingsey ... 176 C5
...Kings Sutton ... 39 K3
...Kingston Bagpuize ... 210 E7
...Kingston Blount ... 224 A4
...Kingstone Winslow ... 277 H7
...Kingston Lisle ... 279 J3
...Kingston Stert ... 199 J8
...Kirtlington ... 111 H3

Kitebrook ... 47 J4
Knighton ... 278 A4
Lamborough Hill ... 213 K1
Langford ... 180 E5
Langley ... 121 K4
Latchford ... 197 G8
Launton ... 98 B6
Leafield ... 122 C4
Lechlade ... 203 H3
Ledwell ... 72 D2
Letcombe Bassett ... 281 H8
Letcombe Regis ... 282 A5
Lew ... 159 K6
Lewknor ... 223 G7
Lidstone ... 88 A1
Little Barrington ... 137 F1
Little Bourton ... 21 F3
Little Chesterton ... 114 A2
Little Clanfield ... 181 H8
Little Compton ... 48 C6
Little Coxwell ... 229 K8
Little Faringdon ... 179 K7
Little Haseley ... 220 C1
Little Heath ... 330 E7
Little London ... 191 H6
Little Marsh ... 99 K3
Little Milton ... 219 J1
Little Minster ... 141 F4
Littlemore ... 192 C5
Little Rollright ... 49 H6
Littlestead Green ... 334 A1
Little Tew ... 71 G2
Little Wittenham ... 241 G7
Littleworth ... 170 A7
Littleworth ... 207 G8
Littleworth ... 267 G2
Longcot ... 253 J5
Long Crendon ... 174 B1
Long Hanborough ... 126 D6
Long Wittenham ... 240 C7
Longworth ... 210 C4
Lower Arncott ... 116 B6
Lower Assendon ... 323 F5
Lower Basildon ... 7 K2
Lower Boddington ... 333 K6
Lower Caversham ... 122 D3
Lower End ... 93 G1
Lower Heyford ... 316 E1
Lower Highmoor ... 316 E1
Lower Middleton Cheney ... 23 F7
Lower Oddington ... 64 C7
Lower Radley ... 216 A5
Lower Shiplake ... 329 H4
Lower Tadmarton ... 26 E8
Lower Tysoe ... 8 C8
Lower Wainhill ... 201 H8
Lyford ... 234 C6
Lyneham ... 103 F2
Mackney ... 265 K7
Maidensgrove ... 295 J1
Mapledurham ... 331 J1
Marcham ... 236 E1
Marsh Baldon ... 217 F4
Marsh Gibbon ... 99 H4
Marston ... 167 J1
Mays Green ... 328 D2
Meadside ... 242 A7
Merton ... 114 E7
Middle Assendon ... 296 B7
Middle Aston ... 74 E4
Middle Barton ... 73 G6
Middleton Cheney ... 22 E6
Middleton Stoney ... 95 G4
Middle Tysoe ... 16 B2
Milcombe ... 36 A6
Millend ... 86 E5
Milton ... 37 K4
Milton ... 262 B2
Milton Common ... 197 F4
Milton Heights ... 261 K4
Milton Hill ... 261 K6
Milton under Wychwood ... 102 A6
Minster Lovell ... 141 H5
Mixbury ... 44 B7
Mollington ... 12 B3
Moreton ... 187 G7
Moreton ... 198 D1
Moreton-in-Marsh ... 46 B1
Moulsford ... 312 B3
Mount Skippett ... 123 K3
Murcott ... 133 F3
Neat Enstone ... 88 D2
Neithrop ... 28 B1
Nethercote ... 21 K8
Nethercott ... 111 F1

Netherton ... 211 H4
Nether Westcote ... 100 D2
Nether Worton ... 54 D6
Nettlebed ... 294 D5
New Botley ... 166 C6
Newbottle ... 31 J8
Newbridge ... 186 E7
New Cross ... 329 G5
New Headington ... 168 D6
New Hinksey ... 191 H1
Newington ... 243 F1
Newland ... 143 F7
New Marston ... 5 E1
Newton Morrell ... 62 C8
Newton Purcell ... 62 D5
New Town ... 48 B7
Newtown ... 319 G7
New Town ... 334 A8
New Yatt ... 124 D8
Noke ... 131 H8
North Aston ... 74 E1
Northbrook ... 93 H6
Northcourt ... 214 E5
Northend ... 271 K1
North Hinksey Village ... 166 C8
North Leigh ... 125 G8
Northmoor ... 187 J5
North Moreton ... 265 F8
North Newington ... 27 H3
North Stoke ... 291 F6
North Weston ... 173 K7
Nuffield ... 293 H4
Nuneham Courtenay ... 216 E4
Nuney Green ... 325 J4
Nythe ... 274 A8
Oakley ... 224 D2
Oakley Wood ... 292 D1
Oddington ... 131 J5
Old Chalford ... 69 J7
Old Woodstock ... 109 H7
Osney ... 4 A5
Over Kiddington ... 90 B6
Over Norton ... 68 B2
Overthorpe ... 30 A1
Over Worton ... 55 F8
Oxford ... 4 C2
Park Corner ... 294 C2
Park Town ... 4 B1
Piddington ... 117 H8
Piddington Cow Leys ... 117 F4
Pishill ... 271 K7
Pishill Bank ... 271 H6
The Platt ... 194 C8
Play Hatch ... 334 B2
Poffley End ... 143 G1
Port Hill ... 294 B4
Postcombe ... 223 F3
Poundon ... 81 H8
Preston Crowmarsh ... 267 G5
Purley on Thames ... 330 E3
Pusey ... 233 F1
Pyrton ... 246 B3
Radcot ... 206 B3
Radford ... 90 B3
Radfordbridge ... 89 K4
Radley ... 215 J5
Radley Park ... 215 G3
Radway ... 9 H2
Ramsden ... 124 A4
Ramsden Heath ... 123 J3
Ratley ... 10 A3
Reading ... 333 F7
Redlands ... 250 D4
Remenham ... 319 J2
Risinghurst ... 169 G4
Roke ... 243 J8
Rokemarsh ... 267 H1
Rose Hill ... 192 A3
Rotherfield Greys ... 317 J6
Rotherfield Peppard ... 317 F8
Rousham ... 92 E3
Rowstock ... 261 K8
Ruscote ... 2 A1
Russell's Water ... 271 F7
Salford ... 67 H2
Sandford-on-Thames ... 192 B8
Sandford St Martin ... 72 D5
Sandhills ... 169 H3
Sarsden ... 85 H4
Sarsden Halt ... 84 E1
Satwell ... 317 F3
Scotland End ... 33 J8
Sevenhampton ... 251 F6
Shabbington ... 173 H4
Shalstone ... 45 H1

Shellingford 231 G8
Shenington 17 H5
Shepherd's Green 317 G4
Shifford 185 K6
Shillingford 266 C1
Shilton 157 H2
Shiplake 329 G5
Shiplake Bottom 326 E1
Shiplake Row 328 D5
Shippon 213 K6
Shipton-on-Cherwell 128 E1
Shipton under Wychwood ... 102 D7
Shirburn 246 C3
Shores Green 143 K8
Shorthampton 104 D2
Shotteswell 11 K8
Shrivenham 252 B8
Shutford 26 A2
Sibford Ferris 25 G8
Sibford Gower 24 E6
Signet 138 D6
Signet Hill 138 B4
Skirmett 273 K6
Skittle Green 201 H4
Slade End 266 B5
Somerton 75 J1
Sonning 335 F3
Sonning Common 326 E1
Sonning Eye 334 E2
Souldern 58 C3
Southcoombe 69 G4
Southend 194 B7
Southend 272 E7
South Hinksey 191 G2
South Leigh 162 C2
South Marston 274 C3
Southmoor 210 D6
South Moreton 288 E2
South Newington 35 K8
Southrop 52 A1
Southrop 178 E4
South Stoke 312 C3
South Weston 222 E6
Sparsholt 280 D3
Spelsbury 87 J7
Sprig's Alley 225 G5
Stadhampton 219 F5
Standlake 186 C4
Stanford in the Vale 232 A8
Stanton Harcourt 163 H7
Stanton St John 152 A8
Steeple Aston 74 E7
Steeple Barton 91 J1
Steventon 261 H3
Stoke Lyne 78 C2
Stokenchurch 249 H2
Stoke Row 316 A2
Stoke Talmage 221 J4
Stonesfield 107 J7
Stonor 296 A1
Stratton Audley 79 K6
Streatley 312 C8
Sulham 330 C6

Summer Heath 272 D5
Summerstown 99 K5
Summertown 167 G1
Sunningwell 214 C1
Sunnymead 149 F7
Sutton 163 H6
Sutton Courtenay 238 E7
Sutton Green 163 H5
Sutton Wick 238 A6
Swalcliffe 25 K7
Swanborough 250 B3
Swerford 52 E4
Swerford Heath 53 H3
Swinbrook 140 A2
Swinford 164 D2
Sydenham 199 K7
Tackley 110 E2
Tadmarton 26 C7
Taston 88 B7
Taynton 119 G7
Temple Cowley 192 C1
Tetsworth 198 A7
Thame 175 G6
Thenford 23 J7
Thrupp 129 F3
Thrupp 206 C5
Tiddington 172 E8
Tilehurst 331 J6
Tokers Green 326 D8
Toot Baldon 217 H1
Towersey 176 B8
Townsend 282 A3
Town's End 99 G5
Trench Green 326 A8
Tubney 212 B5
Turners Court 292 C2
Turville 273 H4
Turville Heath 272 C4
Twyford 38 D2
Uffington 254 E7
Upper Arncott 116 B7
Upper Astrop 31 G8
Upper Heyford 75 H7
Upper Inglesham 227 F2
Upper Milton 102 B8
Upper Oddington 64 D8
Upper Rissington 100 A3
Upperton 245 F6
Upper Tysoe 16 C3
Upper Wardington 14 C7
Upper Wolvercote 148 C7
Upton 138 C1
Upton 287 H5
Walcot 105 J3
Wallingford 267 F7
Walton Grounds 40 A5
Walton Manor 4 A1
Wantage 282 E2
Warborough 242 C7
Wardington 14 B5
Warkworth 30 B2
Warmington 11 F3

Warpsgrove 220
Watchfield 252
Water Eaton 149
Waterperry 171
Waterstock 172
Water Stratford 45
Watlington 246
Weald 183
Well Place 292
Wendlebury 114
West Adderbury 38
Westbury 44
West Challow 281
Westcot 280
Westcott Barton 72
Westend 86
West End 187
West End 290
West Ginge 284
West Hagbourne 287
Westhall Hill 138
West Hanney 259
West Hendred 284
West Ilsley 307
West Lockinge 283
Weston-on-the-Green 113
Westwell 137
Wheatley 170
Whichford 32
Whistlow 73
Whitchurch Hill 324
Whitchurch-on-Thames 323
Whiteoak Green 123
Widford 139
Wigginton 35
Wigginton Heath 35
Wildmoor 214
Williamscot 13
Windrush 136
Winterbrook 290
Witheridge Hill 316
Witney 143
Wolvercote 148
Woodcote 314
Woodeaton 150
Woodfield 96
Woodgreen 143
Woodlands 319
Woodley Green 335
Woodleys 108
Woodstock 127
Woodway 310
Woolstone 278
Wootton 109
Wootton 189
Worminghall 172
Worsham 140
Worton 147
Wroxton 19
Wytham 165
Yarnton 147
Yelford 185

USING THE STREET INDEX

Street names are listed alphabetically. Each street name is followed by its postal town or area locality, the Postcode District, the page number, and the reference to the square in which the name is found.

Example: **Abbey Pl** *OX/KTN* OX1 .... **4** B5 ▯

Some entries are followed by a number in a blue box. This number indicates the location of the street within the referenced grid square. The full street name is listed at the side of the map page.

GENERAL ABBREVIATIONS

ACC	ACCESS	BRK	BROOK	CHYD	CHURCHYAR
ALY	ALLEY	BTM	BOTTOM	CIR	CIRCL
AP	APPROACH	BUS	BUSINESS	CIRC	CIRCL
AR	ARCADE	BVD	BOULEVARD	CL	CLOS
ASS	ASSOCIATION	BY	BYPASS	CLFS	CLIFF
AV	AVENUE	CATH	CATHEDRAL	CMP	CAM
BCH	BEACH	CEM	CEMETERY	CNR	CORNE
BLDS	BUILDINGS	CEN	CENTRE	CO	COUNT
BND	BEND	CFT	CROFT	COLL	COLLEG
BNK	BANK	CH	CHURCH	COM	COMMO
BR	BRIDGE	CHA	CHASE	COMM	COMMISSIO

CON — CONVENT	HVN — HAVEN	PRT — PORT
COT — COTTAGE	HWY — HIGHWAY	PT — POINT
COTS — COTTAGES	IMP — IMPERIAL	PTH — PATH
CP — CAPE	IN — INLET	PZ — PIAZZA
CPS — COPSE	IND EST — INDUSTRIAL ESTATE	QD — QUADRANT
CR — CREEK	INF — INFIRMARY	QU — QUEEN
CREM — CREMATORIUM	INFO — INFORMATION	QY — QUAY
CRS — CRESCENT	INT — INTERCHANGE	R — RIVER
CSWY — CAUSEWAY	IS — ISLAND	RBT — ROUNDABOUT
CT — COURT	JCT — JUNCTION	RD — ROAD
CTRL — CENTRAL	JTY — JETTY	RDG — RIDGE
CTS — COURTS	KG — KING	REP — REPUBLIC
CTYD — COURTYARD	KNL — KNOLL	RES — RESERVOIR
CUTT — CUTTINGS	L — LAKE	RFC — RUGBY FOOTBALL CLUB
CV — COVE	LA — LANE	RI — RISE
CYN — CANYON	LDG — LODGE	RP — RAMP
DEPT — DEPARTMENT	LGT — LIGHT	RW — ROW
DL — DALE	LK — LOCK	S — SOUTH
DM — DAM	LKS — LAKES	SCH — SCHOOL
DR — DRIVE	LNDG — LANDING	SE — SOUTH EAST
DRO — DROVE	LTL — LITTLE	SER — SERVICE AREA
DRY — DRIVEWAY	LWR — LOWER	SH — SHORE
DWGS — DWELLINGS	MAG — MAGISTRATE	SHOP — SHOPPING
E — EAST	MAN — MANSIONS	SKWY — SKYWAY
EMB — EMBANKMENT	MD — MEAD	SMT — SUMMIT
EMBY — EMBASSY	MDW — MEADOWS	SOC — SOCIETY
ESP — ESPLANADE	MEM — MEMORIAL	SP — SPUR
EST — ESTATE	MKT — MARKET	SPR — SPRING
EX — EXCHANGE	MKTS — MARKETS	SQ — SQUARE
EXPY — EXPRESSWAY	ML — MALL	ST — STREET
EXT — EXTENSION	ML — MILL	STN — STATION
F/O — FLYOVER	MNR — MANOR	STR — STREAM
FC — FOOTBALL CLUB	MS — MEWS	STRD — STRAND
FK — FORK	MSN — MISSION	SW — SOUTH WEST
FLD — FIELD	MT — MOUNT	TDG — TRADING
FLDS — FIELDS	MTN — MOUNTAIN	TER — TERRACE
FLS — FALLS	MTS — MOUNTAINS	THWY — THROUGHWAY
FLS — FLATS	MUS — MUSEUM	TNL — TUNNEL
FM — FARM	MWY — MOTORWAY	TOLL — TOLLWAY
FT — FORT	N — NORTH	TPK — TURNPIKE
FWY — FREEWAY	NE — NORTH EAST	TR — TRACK
FY — FERRY	NW — NORTH WEST	TRL — TRAIL
GA — GATE	O/P — OVERPASS	TWR — TOWER
GAL — GALLERY	OFF — OFFICE	U/P — UNDERPASS
GDN — GARDEN	ORCH — ORCHARD	UNI — UNIVERSITY
GDNS — GARDENS	OV — OVAL	UPR — UPPER
GLD — GLADE	PAL — PALACE	V — VALE
GLN — GLEN	PAS — PASSAGE	VA — VALLEY
GN — GREEN	PAV — PAVILION	VIAD — VIADUCT
GND — GROUND	PDE — PARADE	VIL — VILLA
GRA — GRANGE	PH — PUBLIC HOUSE	VIS — VISTA
GRG — GARAGE	PK — PARK	VLG — VILLAGE
GT — GREAT	PKWY — PARKWAY	VLS — VILLAS
GTWY — GATEWAY	PL — PLACE	VW — VIEW
GV — GROVE	PLN — PLAIN	W — WEST
HR — HIGHER	PLNS — PLAINS	WD — WOOD
HL — HILL	PLZ — PLAZA	WHF — WHARF
HLS — HILLS	POL — POLICE STATION	WK — WALK
HO — HOUSE	PR — PRINCE	WKS — WALKS
HOL — HOLLOW	PREC — PRECINCT	WLS — WELLS
HOSP — HOSPITAL	PREP — PREPARATORY	WY — WAY
HRB — HARBOUR	PRIM — PRIMARY	YD — YARD
HTH — HEATH	PROM — PROMENADE	YHA — YOUTH HOSTEL
HTS — HEIGHTS	PRS — PRINCESS	

POSTCODE TOWNS AND AREA ABBREVIATIONS

ABGD — Abingdon	HEN — Henley-on-Thames	SHPSTR — Shipston-on-Stour
BAN — Banbury	HGHW — Highworth	SKCH — Stokenchurch
BIC — Bicester	HUNG — Hungerford/Lambourn	STAD — Stadhampton
BRACKY — Brackley	KID — Kidlington	STHM — Southam
BUCK/WIN — Buckingham/Winslow	KSCL — Kingsclere/Rural Newbury	SWDNE — Swindon east
BUR/CRTN — Burford/Carterton	MARL — Marlborough	THAME — Thame
CAV/SC — Caversham/Sonning Common	MCHM/KBPZ — Marcham/Kingston Bagpuize	THLE — Theale/Rural Reading
CHNR — Chinnor	MIM — Moreton-in-Marsh	TLHT — Tilehurst
CHNTN — Chipping Norton	OX/KTN — Oxford/Kennington	WANT — Wantage
CIR — Cirencester	OXN/BOT/CM — Oxford north/Botley/Cumnor	WAR/TWY — Wargrave/Twyford
COTS — Cotswolds	PRRI — Princes Risborough	WDSTK — Woodstock
COW/LTMR — Cowley/Littlemore	RAYLW — Rural Aylesbury west	WGFD — Wallingford
DAV — Daventry	RBANNE — Rural Banbury north & east	WHLY — Wheatley
DID — Didcot	RBANSW — Rural Banbury south & west	WIT/EY — Witney/Eynsham
ERL — Earley	RBICN — Rural Bicester north	WODY — Woodley
FDN — Faringdon	RBICS/W — Rural Bicester south & west	WOO/WRO — Wootton Bassett/Wroughton
GOR/PANG — Goring/Pangbourne	RDGW — Reading west	WTLGN — Watlington
HADM — Haddenham	READ — Reading	
HEAD — Headington	RWWCK/WEL — Rural Warwick/Wellesbourne	

A

Abattoirs Rd READ RG1 .... 333 G7
Abberbury Av COW/LTMR OX4 .... 192 A4
Abberbury Rd COW/LTMR OX4 .... 191 K5
Abbey Cl ABGD OX14 .... 214 D8
Abbey Pl OX/KTN OX1 .... 4 B5 🔢
    WIT/EY OX8 .... 146 A8
Abbey Rd BAN OX16 .... 2 A3
    OXN/BOT/CM OX2 .... 4 A4
    WIT/EY OX8 .... 142 C8
Abbey Sq READ RG1 .... 333 H8
Abbey St READ RG1 .... 333 H7
    WIT/EY OX8 .... 146 A8
Abbey Woods Cl WGFD OX10 .... 241 J2
Abbot Rdg RAYLW HP18 .... 174 D2
Abbots Cl GOR/PANG RG8 .... 314 D7 🔢
Abbots Md WGFD OX10 .... 290 C7
Abbotsmead Pl READ RG1 .... 333 G5
Abbots Wk CIR GL7 .... 203 H3
    READ RG1 .... 333 H7
Abbots Wood (East) HEAD OX3 ...... 168 E7 🔢
Abbots Wood (West) HEAD OX3 ..... 168 E7 🔢
Abbott Cl DID OX11 .... 263 J8
Abbott Rd ABGD OX14 .... 214 D7
    DID OX11 .... 263 J8
Abelwood Rd WIT/EY OX8 .... 126 B6
Aberaman CAV/SC RG4 .... 333 F1
Aberford Cl TLHT RG30 .... 332 C8 🔢
Abingdon Br ABGD OX14 .... 238 D1
Abingdon Rd THAME OX9 .... 175 F1
Abingdon Dr BUR/CRTN OX18 .... 333 J1
Abingdon Rd ABGD OX14 .... 237 J3
    ABGD OX14 .... 239 F5
    ABGD OX14 .... 261 J1
    BUR/CRTN OX18 .... 158 A4
    DID OX11 .... 264 B6
    KSCL RG20 .... 308 C8
    MCHM/KBPZ OX13 .... 261 J2
    OX/KTN OX1 .... 191 H3
    OXN/BOT/CM OX2 .... 189 G3 🔢
    WGFD OX10 .... 241 H9
    WIT/EY OX8 .... 186 B4
Ablett Cl COW/LTMR OX4 .... 168 A7 🔢
Abrahams Rd HEN RG9 .... 318 E4
Acacia Gdns MCHM/KBPZ OX13 ...... 210 D6
Acacia Wk BAN OX16 .... 20 D6
    BIC OX26 .... 97 F2 🔢
Acer Cl BUR/CRTN OX18 .... 138 D8
Ackerman Rd CHNTN OX7 .... 68 C4 🔢
Acland Cl HEAD OX3 .... 168 C6 🔢
Acorn Cl BIC OX26 .... 97 F2 🔢
Acorn Wy BAN OX16 .... 21 H6
Acre End St WIT/EY OX8 .... 145 K8
Acremead Rd WHLY OX33 .... 170 A7
Adam Ct HEN RG9 .... 319 F5
Adderbury Ct RBANNS OX17 .... 38 D3 🔢
Addiscombe Cha CALC RG31 .... 331 F4 🔢
Addison Crs COW/LTMR OX4 .... 191 K1
Addison Dr COW/LTMR OX4 .... 192 C4
Addison Rd BAN OX16 .... 2 C6
    READ RG1 .... 333 G6
Adeane Rd STAD OX44 .... 220 A8
Adelaide St OXN/BOT/CM OX2 .... 4 B2
Adkin Wy WANT OX12 .... 282 D2
Adwell Sq HEN RG9 .... 319 F5 🔢
Akeman Rd RBICS/W OX25 .... 116 A3
Akeman St KID OX5 .... 111 K2 🔢
Akeman St WIT/EY OX8 .... 108 B7
Alan Bullock Cl COW/LTMR OX4 .... 5 F4 🔢
Albany Rd TLHT RG30 .... 332 D8
Albermarle Dr WANT OX12 .... 258 D7
Albert Illsley Cl CALC RG31 .... 331 H7
Albert Rd CAV/SC RG4 .... 333 F3
    HEN RG9 .... 319 G6
Albert St BAN OX16 .... 3 D4
    OXN/BOT/CM OX2 .... 4 B3
Albion Pl OX/KTN OX1 .... 4 C5 🔢
Albion St CHNTN OX7 .... 68 B5
Albury Cl TLHT RG30 .... 332 C6
Albury Vw THAME OX9 .... 196 E1
Alchester Rd BIC OX26 .... 96 A7
Aldbarton Dr HEAD OX3 .... 168 E5
Aldeburgh Cl CAV/SC RG4 .... 327 J7 🔢
Alden Crs HEAD OX3 .... 169 F3
Aldenham Cl CAV/SC RG4 .... 333 J1
Alder Dr RBICS/W OX25 .... 115 K3
Aldergate Rd BIC OX26 .... 96 D6
Alderley Cl BUR/CRTN OX18 .... 157 K6
    WODY RG5 .... 335 H6
Aldrich Rd OXN/BOT/CM OX2 .... 149 F7
Aldridge Cl WGFD OX10 .... 267 J3 🔢
Aldsworth St WIT/EY OX8 .... 142 C7 🔢
Aldworth Av WANT OX12 .... 283 F1
Alesworth Gv HEAD OX3 .... 168 B2 🔢
Alexander Cl ABGD OX14 .... 214 E4
Alexandra Rd OXN/BOT/CM OX2 ..... 166 D6
    READ RG1 .... 333 K8
Alexandra Sq CHNTN OX7 .... 68 A5
Alford Cl TLHT RG30 .... 331 H7 🔢
Alfredston Pl WANT OX12 .... 282 E3
Alfred St OX/KTN OX1 .... 4 C4
    READ RG1 .... 333 F8 🔢

Want OX12 .... 282 D3 🔢
Alfriston Pl BAN OX16 .... 20 C6 🔢
Alice Smith Sq COW/LTMR OX4 ..... 192 C5
Allam St OXN/BOT/CM OX2 .... 4 A2
Allder Cl ABGD OX14 .... 214 D5
Allectus Av RBICS/W OX25 .... 116 A3
Allens La RBICS/W OX25 .... 75 H6
Allens Orch RBANNS OX17 .... 14 D1
All Hallows Rd CAV/SC RG4 .... 333 K4
Allin Cl COW/LTMR OX4 .... 192 D4
Allin's La WANT OX12 .... 261 F8
Allison Gdns GOR/PANG RG8 .... 331 G2
Allnatt Av WGFD OX10 .... 266 E7 🔢
Allnut Cl WTLGN OX49 .... 246 B6
All Saints Cl MCHM/KBPZ OX13 ...... 236 E1
All Saints La ABGD OX14 .... 239 F6
All Saints Rd HEAD OX3 .... 168 C5
Alma Gn HEN RG9 .... 316 A3
Alma Pl COW/LTMR OX4 .... 5 F5
Alma St TLHT RG30 .... 332 C7
Almond Av KID OX5 .... 129 H8
Almond Dr CAV/SC RG4 .... 334 B3
Almond Rd BIC OX26 .... 97 F4
Alpha Av STAD OX44 .... 193 J8
Alphin Brook DID OX11 .... 263 J4
Alvescot Rd BUR/CRTN OX18 .... 157 J6
Alvis Ga BAN OX16 .... 20 B7
Amberley Ct BAN OX16 .... 20 C6 🔢
Amblecote Rd TLHT RG30 .... 332 B8
Ambleside Cl WODY RG5 .... 335 G8
Ambleside Dr HEAD OX3 .... 168 B2
Ambrose Pl READ RG1 .... 333 F8 🔢
Ambrose Ri WHLY OX33 .... 170 E8
Amersham Rd CAV/SC RG4 .... 333 K5
Amey Crs MCHM/KBPZ OX13 .... 213 K1
Amity Rd READ RG1 .... 334 A8
Amity St READ RG1 .... 334 A8
Ammanford CAV/SC RG4 .... 333 F2
Amory La COW/LTMR OX4 .... 192 D4
Ampney Orch BUR/CRTN OX18 .... 183 H4
Amwell Pl WGFD OX10 .... 290 B6
Amyce Cl ABGD OX14 .... 215 F5 🔢
Ancastle Gn HEN RG9 .... 318 E6
Ancholme Cl DID OX11 .... 263 K5 🔢
Anchor La DID OX11 .... 289 F5
Ancil Av BIC OX26 .... 98 A5
Andersey Wy ABGD OX14 .... 238 C3
Anderson Cl SKCH HP14 .... 249 H3 🔢
Andersons Cl KID OX5 .... 129 F7
Andover Cl BIC OX26 .... 97 H3
    CALC RG31 .... 331 H6 🔢
Andover La BUR/CRTN OX18 .... 158 B5 🔢
Andover Rd WGFD OX10 .... 268 B4
Andrew Rd WGFD OX10 .... 266 D6
Andrews Av COW/LTMR OX4 .... 193 F6 🔢
Andromeda Cl COW/LTMR OX4 .... 193 F6 🔢
Anemone Cl COW/LTMR OX4 .... 192 E7 🔢
Angelica Cl COW/LTMR OX4 .... 193 F6
Angle Field Rd CAV/SC RG4 .... 333 J4
Anglers Wy READ RG1 .... 333 K8
Angus Cl BAN OX16 .... 2 A1
Anna Pavlova Cl ABGD OX14 .... 214 B8
Anne Greenwood Cl
    COW/LTMR OX4 .... 192 A2
Annesley Cl KID OX5 .... 111 K7 🔢
Annesley Rd COW/LTMR OX4 .... 192 A3
Ansell Wy CHNTN OX7 .... 102 B6
Anson Av BUR/CRTN OX18 .... 158 A6
Anson Cl MCHM/KBPZ OX13 .... 237 F1
    WHLY OX33 .... 170 E7
Anson Rd WGFD OX10 .... 268 B4
Anson Wy BIC OX26 .... 97 G4
Anstey Rd READ RG1 .... 333 F8
Anthian Cl WODY RG5 .... 335 K7
Anthony Hill Rd WGFD OX10 .... 268 A6
Anvil Cl FGDN SN7 .... 232 C8
Anvil Paddock WANT OX12 .... 282 A6 🔢
Anxey Wy HADM HP17 .... 176 B1
A P Ellis Rd COTS GL54 .... 100 A4
Apley Wy WIT/EY OX8 .... 142 C7
Appleby Cl BAN OX16 .... 20 A8
Appleby Rd TLHT RG30 .... 332 B8 🔢
Apple Cl CALC RG31 .... 331 F3
Appleford Dr ABGD OX14 .... 215 F5
Appleford Rd ABGD OX14 .... 239 F5
Appleton Rd MCHM/KBPZ OX13 ..... 210 C5
    OXN/BOT/CM OX2 .... 189 G7 🔢
Appletree Cl CAV/SC RG4 .... 326 E1 🔢
    COW/LTMR OX4 .... 193 F7 🔢
Appletree Rd RBANNS OX17 .... 14 D1
The Approach BIC OX26 .... 96 E4 🔢
Apsley Rd OXN/BOT/CM OX2 .... 148 E7
Arbury Banks RBANNS OX17 .... 14 D2
Arbury Cl BAN OX16 .... 29 G5
Archery Rd RBANNS OX17 .... 22 E6
Archway Rd READ RG1 .... 333 G5
Arden Cl RBANSW OX15 .... 20 A7
Ardington La WANT OX12 .... 260 A3
Ardler Rd CAV/SC RG4 .... 333 J5
Ardley Rd RBICN OX27 .... 77 K6
    RBICS/W OX25 .... 75 K1
    RBICS/W OX25 .... 95 F3
Argentan Cl ABGD OX14 .... 238 B3

Argosy Cl STAD OX44 .... 244 C
Argosy Rd BUR/CRTN OX18 .... 158 B5
    WGFD OX10 .... 268 E
Argyle Rd READ RG1 .... 332 E
Argyle St COW/LTMR OX4 .... 5 F
    READ RG1 .... 332 E
Aristotle La OXN/BOT/CM OX2 .... 4 A
Arkel Cl BUR/CRTN OX18 .... 120 E
Arkell Av BUR/CRTN OX18 .... 157 K
Arkwright Rd BIC OX26 .... 97 F
Arlington Cl BUR/CRTN OX18 .... 158 A
Arlington Dr HEAD OX3 167
Armour Hl CALC RG31 .... 331 H
Armour Rd CALC RG31 .... 331 H
Armour Wk CALC RG31 .... 331 H6
Armstrong Wy WODY RG5 335
Arncott Rd RBICS/W OX25 .... 117 C
Arncott Wood Rd RBICS/W OX25 .... 134 C
Arndale Beck DID OX11 .... 264 A5
Arnold Rd COW/LTMR OX4 .... 191 k
Arnold's Wy OXN/BOT/CM OX2 ...... 165 k
Arnold Wy THAME OX9 .... 174 E
Arnott's Yd RAYLW HP18 .... 174 D1
Arran Gv BAN OX16 .... 2 C
Arran Wy HGHW SN6 .... 226 C
Arrow Cl RBANNS OX17 .... 22 E
Arthray Rd OXN/BOT/CM OX2 .... 166 A
Arthur Evans Cl
    MCHM/KBPZ OX13 .... 213 .
Arthur Garrard Cl
    OXN/BOT/CM OX2 .... 4 B2
Arthur St OXN/BOT/CM OX2 .... 4 A
Arundel Cl BUR/CRTN OX18 .... 157 J5
    RBANNS OX17 .... 39 .
Arundel Pl BAN OX16 .... 28 E
Arun Ms DID OX11 .... 264 A
Ascot Gv RWWCK/WEL CV35 .... 8 E
Ascott Hl SHPSTR CV36 .... 32 C
Ascott Rd CHNTN OX7 .... 102 E
    SHPSTR CV36 .... 32 E
Ashburton La RBANSW OX15 .... 52 A
Ashbury Dr CALC RG31 .... 331 C
Ashbury Hl HGHW SN6 .... 299 H
Ashby Ct BAN OX16 .... 3 C
Ashby Rd BIC OX26 .... 96 C
Ash Cl FGDN SN7 .... 230 A
    KID OX5 .... 129 H
    WTLGN OX49 .... 246 A
Ashcombe Cl WIT/EY OX8 .... 142 E
Ashcroft Cl CAV/SC RG4 .... 332 E
    OXN/BOT/CM OX2 .... 165 k
Ashcroft Rd BAN OX16 .... 29 F
Ashdene Rd BIC OX26 .... 96 C
Ashenden Cl ABGD OX14 .... 214 C
Ashfield Est BUR/CRTN OX18 .... 157 K
Ashfield Rd BUR/CRTN OX18 .... 157 K
Ashfields Cl WANT OX12 .... 235 .
Ashfields La WANT OX12 .... 235 H
Ashford Av CAV/SC RG4 .... 326 E
Ash Gdns SWDNE SN3 .... 274 C
Ash Gv BIC OX26 .... 96 A
    HEAD OX3 .... 168 C
Ashhurst Wy COW/LTMR OX4 .... 192 A
Ashlade RBANNS OX17 .... 23 F8
Ash La RBICS/W OX25 .... 116 A
Ashlee Wk GOR/PANG RG8 .... 314 C
Ashlong Rd HEAD OX3 .... 168 A
Ashmere Ter TLHT RG30 .... 332 E
Ashmole Pl COW/LTMR OX4 .... 193 F
Ashmole Rd ABGD OX14 .... 238 C
Ashridge CHNR OX39 .... 224 D1
Ashridge Cl BAN OX16 .... 29 F5
Ash Rd TLHT RG30 .... 331 .
Ashsdown Wy WANT OX12 .... 258 C
Ashton Cl CALC RG31 .... 331 C
Ashtrees Rd WODY RG5 .... 335 H
Ashville Wy COW/LTMR OX4 .... 192 E
Aspen Cl BIC OX26 .... 97 F
Aspen Sq COW/LTMR OX4 .... 192 E6
Asquith Rd COW/LTMR OX4 .... 192 B
Astley Av KID OX5 .... 148 D
Astley Rd THAME OX9 .... 175 H
Aston Av CALC RG31 .... 331 F
Aston Cl ABGD OX14 .... 214 D
    BAN OX16 .... 29 C
    GOR/PANG RG8 .... 330 B
    WGFD OX10 .... 266 E
Aston Gdns WTLGN OX49 .... 223 K4
Aston Hl WTLGN OX49 .... 224 B
Aston Rd BUR/CRTN OX18 .... 183 H
    HADM HP17 .... 176 C
    WIT/EY OX8 .... 160 D
    WIT/EY OX8 .... 161 F
    WIT/EY OX8 .... 186 A
Aston St COW/LTMR OX4 .... 5 F
    DID OX11 .... 289 F
Astrop Gdns RBANNS OX17 .... 39 k
Astrop Gra RBANNS OX17 .... 39 J
Astrop Rd RBANNS OX17 .... 22 D
    RBANNS OX17 .... 30 D
    RBANNS OX17 .... 39 k
Atherton Cl TLHT RG30 .... 331 K7
Atkinson Cl HEAD OX3 .... 168 E2
Atkyns Rd HEAD OX3 .... 168 .
Atwell Cl WGFD OX10 .... 266 E7

...twell Pl HEAD OX3 .... 168 D6 🔲
...udlett Dr ABGD OX14 .... 214 E8
...udley St TLHT RG30 .... 332 D7
...ugust End TLHT RG30 .... 332 C7 🔲
...ustin Dr BAN OX16 .... 20 B7
...ustin Pl ABGD OX14 .... 214 C5
...ustin Rd RBANSW OX15 .... 29 G8
...ustin's Wy RBANSW OX15 .... 34 B7
...uton Pl HEN RG9 .... 319 F7
...utumn Cl CAV/SC RG4 .... 327 J8
...venue Four WIT/EY OX8 .... 143 F8
...venue La COW/LTMR OX4 .... 5 F5
...venue Rd BAN OX16 .... 3 E3
    HGHW SN6 .... 276 A4
The Avenue CHNR OX39 .... 225 F1
    CHNTN OX7 .... 53 J7
    OX/KTN OX1 .... 191 J8
    RAYLW HP18 .... 172 C2
    RBANNS OX17 .... 22 E7
    RBANSW OX15 .... 36 E3
    WHLY OX33 .... 170 E8
...vington Cl CALC RG31 .... 331 F7
...vocet Wy BAN OX16 .... 16 B3
    BIC OX26 .... 97 J7
...von Av RWWCK/WEL CV35 .... 16 B3
...von Crs BIC OX26 .... 96 C4
...von Pl READ RG1 .... 333 K7
...von Rd DID OX11 .... 286 A6
    MCHM/KBPZ OX13 .... 214 A4
...von Wy DID OX11 .... 263 K4
    RWWCK/WEL CV35 .... 16 B3
...vro Rd COTS GL54 .... 100 A2
...xis Rd HGHW SN6 .... 252 E6
...xtell Cl KID OX5 .... 129 C6
...ylesbury Rd THAME OX9 .... 175 F6
...ylsham Cl TLHT RG30 .... 331 J7
...ynho Rd RBANNS OX17 .... 38 E3
    RBANNS OX17 .... 39 J7
...yrshire Cl BAN OX16 .... 20 C6
...yrton Senna Rd CALC RG31 .... 331 G8 🔲
...ysgarth Rd KID OX5 .... 147 K1
...zalea Av KID OX5 .... 148 C1

B

...ablock Hythe Rd WIT/EY OX8 .... 188 B2
...ack La BUCK/WIN MK18 .... 63 K1
    BUR/CRTN OX18 .... 184 B4
    MIM GL56 .... 64 D7
    RBANSW OX15 .... 25 K7
    RWWCK/WEL CV35 .... 16 B2
    SHPSTR CV36 .... 49 H1
    WIT/EY OX8 .... 146 A8
    WIT/EY OX8 .... 161 F3
...ack Rw MIM GL56 .... 65 H4
...ackside La RBANSW OX15 .... 24 E6
...ack St SKCH HP14 .... 249 F2
    THAME OX9 .... 198 B7
...ack Wy STAD OX44 .... 196 C2
...ader Dr RBICS/W OX25 .... 76 B8
...adgemore La HEN RG9 .... 319 F4
...adgers Copse ABGD OX14 .... 215 J5
...adgers Farm La RWWCK/WEL CV35.. 8 C8
...adgers Ri CAV/SC RG4 .... 333 G2
...adgers Wk HEN RG9 .... 329 J4
...adger Wy BAN OX16 .... 3 E6
...adswell La MCHM/KBPZ OX13 .... 188 C7
...agley Cl WANT OX12 .... 282 D1 🔲
...agley Wood Rd OX/KTN OX1 .... 191 H5
...ailey Cl WANT OX12 .... 282 D1 🔲
...ailie Cl ABGD OX14 .... 238 C1
...ainton Rd OXN/BOT/CM OX2 .... 166 E2
    RBICN OX27 .... 61 H8
    RBICN OX27 .... 78 B7
...akehouse La RBANNS OX17 .... 11 K7
...aker Cl HEAD OX3 .... 169 F5
    RBICN OX27 .... 79 G8
    WGFD OX10 .... 268 B5
...aker Rd ABGD OX14 .... 238 C2
...akers La COW/LTMR OX4 .... 191 K3
    DID OX11 .... 287 K2
    RBANSW OX15 .... 25 K7
    RBANSW OX15 .... 36 A8
    WGFD OX10 .... 266 B5
...aker's Piece CHNR OX39 .... 225 F1
    WIT/EY OX8 .... 145 F5 🔲
...akers Sq FGDN SN7 .... 254 C5 🔲
...aker St READ RG1 .... 333 F8
    READ RG1 .... 333 F8
...akery La BUR/CRTN OX18 .... 182 A7
    WANT OX12 .... 282 A6
...aldon La STAD OX44 .... 217 F4
...aldons Cl GOR/PANG RG8 .... 314 D7 🔲
...aldwins La RWWCK/WEL CV35 .... 16 B3
...alfour La COW/LTMR OX4 .... 192 C4
...alham's La HEN RG9 .... 272 B7
...allard Cha ABGD OX14 .... 214 E4
...allard Cl CHNTN OX7 .... 73 F6
...allards CHNTN OX7 .... 102 E7 🔲
...alliol Cl KID OX5 .... 111 F1

Balliol Dr DID OX11 .... 264 B7
Balliol Rd BIC OX26 .... 97 G4
    WAR/TWY RG10 .... 332 D4
Ball La KID OX5 .... 110 E1
Balme Cl WAR/TWY RG10 .... 335 K4
Balmoral Av BAN OX16 .... 28 B3
Balmoral Rd DID OX11 .... 264 A7
Balmoral Wy RBANNS OX17 .... 39 J1 🔲
Balmore Dr CAV/SC RG4 .... 333 H5
Balmore Pk CAV/SC RG4 .... 333 G5
Baltic Whf OX/KTN OX1 .... 4 C5 🔲
Bampton Cl COW/LTMR OX4 .... 192 C4
Bampton Rd BUR/CRTN OX18 .... 182 B6
    BUR/CRTN OX18 .... 184 B5
    WIT/EY OX8 .... 159 K2
Banbury Gdns CAV/SC RG4 .... 333 J4 🔲
Banbury Hl CHNTN OX7 .... 88 D4
    CHNTN OX7 .... 106 B3
Banbury La RBANNS OX17 .... 22 A7
    RBANNS OX17 .... 23 G3
    RBANNS OX17 .... 30 B8
Banbury Rd BIC OX26 .... 97 F5
    CHNTN OX7 .... 51 J7
    CHNTN OX7 .... 52 B6
    CHNTN OX7 .... 68 C3
    CHNTN OX7 .... 69 F1
    KID OX5 .... 110 B4
    KID OX5 .... 129 F5
    OXN/BOT/CM OX2 .... 148 E5
    OXN/BOT/CM OX2 .... 167 G2
    RBANNS OX17 .... 11 F4
    RBANNS OX17 .... 14 C2
    RBANNS OX17 .... 21 J4
    RBANNS OX17 .... 38 D1
    RBANNS OX17 .... 40 B8 🔲
    RBANSW OX15 .... 26 B2
    RBANSW OX15 .... 27 J4
    RBANSW OX15 .... 37 F1
    RBANSW OX15 .... 56 C2
    RBICS/W OX25 .... 92 B2
    WDSTK OX20 .... 109 K8

Banbury Road Crossing
    CHNTN OX7 .... 68 C4 🔲
Bandet Wy THAME OX9 .... 199 H1
Banesberie Cl BAN OX16 .... 20 C6
Banjo Rd COW/LTMR OX4 .... 192 C2
Banks Furlong BIC OX26 .... 96 A7
Bankside BAN OX16 .... 3 E5
    BAN OX16 .... 29 G5
    HEAD OX3 .... 168 E4 🔲
    KID OX5 .... 129 F5
    WANT OX12 .... 284 D1
    WIT/EY OX8 .... 127 G6
Banks Rd HADM HP17 .... 176 C1
Bannister Cl COW/LTMR OX4 .... 5 E6
Bannister Rd THAME OX9 .... 175 J8
Barbara's Meadow CALC RG31 .... 331 F5
Barbel Cl EARL RG6 .... 334 C7
Barbrook Cl CALC RG31 .... 331 H4 🔲
Barbury Dr WANT OX12 .... 258 D7 🔲
Barclose Av CAV/SC RG4 .... 333 J4
Barcombe Cl BAN OX16 .... 20 B6
Barcote La FGDN SN7 .... 207 J8
Bardolph's Cl CAV/SC RG4 .... 326 D7
Bardwell Rd OXN/BOT/CM OX2 .... 4 C1
Bardwell Ter BIC OX26 .... 97 G5 🔲
Barefoot Cl CALC RG31 .... 331 F6
Barfleur Cl ABGD OX14 .... 215 F4
Barford Rd RBANSW OX15 .... 37 F5
The Bargeway DID OX11 .... 308 C1
Barksdale Av BRACKY NN13 .... 59 K1
Barkus Wy SKCH HP14 .... 249 H2
Barley Cl RBANSW OX15 .... 24 E7 🔲
    RBANSW OX15 .... 37 F2
    WGFD OX10 .... 290 E1
    WTLGN OX49 .... 223 G7 🔲
Barleycott La OX/KTN OX1 .... 191 J5 🔲
Barley Flds DID OX11 .... 263 C7
Barlow Cl RBANSW OX15 .... 36 B5
    WHLY OX33 .... 170 B7
Barnacre WTLGN OX49 .... 246 B6
Barnard Cl CAV/SC RG4 .... 333 J1
Barnards Wy WANT OX12 .... 283 F2
Barn Cl KID OX5 .... 129 G7
    OXN/BOT/CM OX2 .... 189 K1
    WANT OX12 .... 257 K3
Barncroft SHPSTR CV36 .... 49 G1
    WGFD OX10 .... 266 B7 🔲
Barn End BUR/CRTN OX18 .... 183 C5
Barnes Cl DID OX11 .... 287 J1
Barnes Rd DID OX11 .... 287 J1
Barnet St COW/LTMR OX4 .... 168 A8
Barnett Rd MCHM/KBPZ OX13 .... 261 H2
    RBANNS OX17 .... 22 D7
Barnfield WANT OX12 .... 233 K6
Barnfield Cl RBICN OX27 .... 97 G1
Barn La BUR/CRTN OX18 .... 158 D2
    HEN RG9 .... 318 C3
Barns Hay HEAD OX3 .... 167 K1
Barns La BUR/CRTN OX18 .... 138 E3
Barn's Rd COW/LTMR OX4 .... 192 C3
Barnwood Cl TLHT RG30 .... 332 F2
Baron Ct TLHT RG30 .... 332 E8
Baronshurst Dr STAD OX44 .... 244 B1
Baronsmead HEN RG9 .... 319 F5 🔲

Barracks La COW/LTMR OX4 .... 168 B8
Barra Cl HGHW SN6 .... 250 C1
Barrats Hl SHPSTR CV36 .... 32 B5
Barrett's Cl WIT/EY OX8 .... 107 H8 🔲
Barrett St OXN/BOT/CM OX2 .... 4 A5
Barrett's Wy ABGD OX14 .... 262 D1
Barrington Av HGHW SN6 .... 253 F5
Barrington Cl HEAD OX3 .... 168 C5 🔲
    WGFD OX10 .... 241 J1
    WIT/EY OX8 .... 142 C8
Barrington Rd HGHW SN6 .... 252 D7
Barrow Hill Cl ABGD OX14 .... 215 G5
Barrow La DID OX11 .... 262 C7
Barrow Rd DID OX11 .... 262 C7
    MCHM/KBPZ OX13 .... 213 J7
Barry Av BIC OX26 .... 96 E3
Barry Pl READ RG1 .... 333 G6
Bartholomew Av KID OX5 .... 147 K2
Bartholomew Cl WIT/EY OX8 .... 145 K7
    WIT/EY OX8 .... 161 F5 🔲
Bartholomew Rd COW/LTMR OX4 .... 192 C3
Bartholomew Tipping Wy
    SKCH HP14 .... 249 H2
Bartlemas Cl COW/LTMR OX4 .... 168 A8
Bartlemas Rd COW/LTMR OX4 .... 168 A8
Bartlett Cl WIT/EY OX8 .... 142 E7
Barton Cl RBANNS OX17 .... 39 J1 🔲
Barton La ABGD OX14 .... 215 G8
    HEAD OX3 .... 168 D3
Barton Rd HEAD OX3 .... 168 E2
Barton Village Rd HEAD OX3 .... 168 E2 🔲
Barwell WANT OX12 .... 282 D2
Basil Hill Rd DID OX11 .... 263 H4
Baskerville La HEN RG9 .... 329 J4
Baskerville Rd CAV/SC RG4 .... 326 E2
    SWDNE SN3 .... 274 C8
Basmore La HEN RG9 .... 329 K3
Bassett Av BIC OX26 .... 97 G4
Bassett Rd HEAD OX3 .... 169 F3
    WANT OX12 .... 281 J8
Basset Wy DID OX11 .... 129 J6
Bateman St HEAD OX3 .... 168 C5
Bates La RBICN OX27 .... 58 C4
Bath Pl OX/KTN OX1 .... 5 D4
Bath Rd BAN OX16 .... 2 C4
    CAV/SC RG4 .... 334 E6
Bath St ABGD OX14 .... 214 D8
    COW/LTMR OX4 .... 5 F4
Battle Cl BIC OX26 .... 97 H4
Battle Rd GOR/PANG RG8.. .... 313 H8
    WGFD OX10 .... 268 B5
Battle St READ RG1 .... 333 F7
Baulking La FGDN SN7 .... 255 J6
Baydon Rd HUNG RG17 .... 321 K7
    MARL SN8 .... 320 C5
Bayswater Farm Rd HEAD OX3 .... 169 G3
Bayswater Rd HEAD OX3 .... 169 F2
Beaconsfield Rd BAN OX16 .... 28 E5
Beagle Cl ABGD OX14 .... 215 G5 🔲
Beagles Cl KID OX5 .... 129 K8
Beal's La CALC RG31 .... 330 E8
Beanacre Rd RBANSW OX15 .... 52 A1
Beanfurlong RBANNS OX17 .... 22 C3
Beanhill Rd WIT/EY OX8 .... 160 E2
Bear Cl WDSTK OX20 .... 127 J1
Beargarden Rd BAN OX16 .... 2 C4
Bear La DID OX11 .... 265 G8
    STAD OX44 .... 218 E6
    WGFD OX10 .... 267 F7
Bears Hedge COW/LTMR OX4 .... 192 A3
Beatrice Dr BAN OX16 .... 2 A4
Beatty Dr TLHT RG30 .... 331 J7
Beauchamp La COW/LTMR OX4 .... 192 B3
Beaufield Cl WODY RG5 .... 335 F8
Beaufort Cl BIC OX26 .... 97 H4 🔲
    DID OX11 .... 264 A7
Beaulieu Cl BAN OX16 .... 3 F3
Beaulieu Ms DID OX11 .... 264 A4
Beaumaris Cl BAN OX16 .... 20 B8
Beaumont Buildings OX/KTN OX1 .... 4 B5
Beaumont Cl BAN OX16 .... 20 E6
Beaumont La OX/KTN OX1 .... 4 C3 🔲
Beaumont Pl OX/KTN OX1 .... 4 C3 🔲
Beaumont Rd BAN OX16 .... 2 C1
    HEAD OX3 .... 168 E4
Beaumont St OX/KTN OX1 .... 4 C3 🔲
Beaver Wy WODY RG5 .... 335 K8
Bec Cl WANT OX12 .... 282 B2
Beckdale Cl BIC OX26 .... 96 C4 🔲
Becket St OX/KTN OX1 .... 4 B4
Beckett Av HGHW SN6 .... 252 C8
Beckett Dr HGHW SN6 .... 252 C8
Becketts Cl WIT/EY OX8 .... 126 C6 🔲
Beckley Cl GOR/PANG RG8 .... 314 D7 🔲
Beckley Cl HEAD OX3 .... 151 H5
Becquerel Av DID OX11 .... 285 J3
Bec Tithe GOR/PANG RG8 .... 324 C4
Bedford Cl BAN OX16 .... 20 B7 🔲
Bedford Rd READ RG1 .... 333 F7
Bedford St COW/LTMR OX4 .... 191 K1
Bedwells Heath OX/KTN OX1 .... 190 B6
Beecham Rd TLHT RG30 .... 332 C8
Beech Cl FGDN SN7 .... 230 A4
    MCHM/KBPZ OX13 .... 189 J8
    SKCH HP14 .... 249 H4

WTLGN OX49 .... 246 A5
Beech Crs *KID* OX5 .... 148 C1
Beech Croft Rd *OXN/BOT/CM* OX2 .. 167 F1
The Beeches *CALC* RG31 .... 331 H4
GOR/PANG RG8 .... 322 D2
HEAD OX3 .... 168 E3
RBANSW OX15 .... 56 C5
Beechey Av *HEAD* OX3 .... 5 F1
Beechfield Crs *BAN* OX16 .... 2 C6
Beechgate *WIT/EY* OX8 .... 160 E1
Beech Gv *BUR/CRTN* OX18 .... 139 F1
HGHW SN6 .... 250 D2
Beeching Cl *DID* OX11 .... 287 D2
Beech La *GOR/PANG* RG8 .... 313 H6
GOR/PANG RG8 .... 314 C7
Beech Ri *CAV/SC* RG4 .... 326 E1
Beech Rd *CAV/SC* RG4 .... 326 D8
CHNR OX39 .... 224 E1
GOR/PANG RG8 .... 330 E2
HEAD OX3 .... 168 C4
OXN/BOT/CM OX2 .... 166 B8
THAME OX9 .... 174 D7
WGFD OX10 .... 266 D3
WHLY OX33 .... 170 D8
WIT/EY OX8 .... 142 D7
WIT/EY OX8 .... 146 A7
Beechwood Av *CALC* RG31 .... 331 H7
WODY RG5 .... 335 F8
Beechwood Cl *GOR/PANG* RG8 ... 324 B1
Beef La *OX/KTN* OX1 .... 4 C4
Beesley Rd *BAN* OX16 .... 2 A5
Beeson Cl *GOR/PANG* RG8 .... 314 D7
Begbroke Crs *KID* OX5 .... 128 D6
Beggarsbush HI *WGFD* OX10 .... 268 B6
Beggars Hill Rd *WODY* RG5 .... 335 K6
Beggar's La *MCHM/KBPZ* OX13...... 210 C6
Behoes La *GOR/PANG* RG8 .... 314 B6
Belbroughton Rd
OXN/BOT/CM OX2 .... 167 F2
Belfast Rd *WGFD* OX10 .... 268 B4
Belgrove Cl *KID* OX5 .... 129 G7
Bellamy Cl *MCHM/KBPZ* OX13 .... 210 E6
Bell Cl *WANT* OX12 .... 258 E6
WIT/EY OX8 .... 147 F5
Bellenger Wy *KID* OX5 .... 129 G7
Belle Ter *BUR/CRTN* OX18 .... 157 K6
Belle Vue Rd *HEN* RG9 .... 319 F7
READ RG1 .... 333 F8
Bell Gdns *SWDNE* SN3 .... 274 C3
Bell HI *RBANSW* OX15 .... 34 A8
Bellingham La *HGHW* SN6 .... 250 E5
Bellisle *GOR/PANG* RG8 .... 331 F2
Bell La *BIC* OX26 .... 97 F5
BUR/CRTN OX18 .... 183 C4
CIR GL7 .... 203 C4
HEN RG9 .... 319 C4
THAME OX9 .... 175 F6
WGFD OX10 .... 266 A5
WHLY OX33 .... 170 D7
WIT/EY OX8 .... 147 F5
Bell's La *RBANSW* OX15 .... 34 A8
Bell St *HEN* RG9 .... 319 C5
RBANSW OX15 .... 18 C1
Belmont *WANT* OX12 .... 282 D2
Belmont Rd *TLHT* RG30 .... 332 D8
Belvedere Rd *COW/LTMR* OX4.. 168 A8
Bembridge Pl *READ* RG1 .... 333 J8
Benares Gv *HEN* RG9 .... 316 A5
Ben Cl *KID* OX5 .... 129 H6
Benhams La *HEN* RG9 .... 297 F5
Benmead Rd *KID* OX5 .... 129 H6
Bennett Cl *RBANSW* OX17 .... 22 C3
Bennett Rd *FGDN* SN7 .... 230 B4
Bensgrove Cl *GOR/PANG* RG8 .... 314 D7
Benson Cl *BIC* OX26 .... 97 J4
Benson La *WGFD* OX10 .... 267 H8
Benson Pl *OXN/BOT/CM* OX2.... 5 D1
Benson Rd *ABGD* OX14 .... 214 C5
HEAD OX3 .... 168 D7
Bentley Cl *BAN* OX16 .... 20 B7
Benton Dr *CHNR* OX39 .... 200 E8
Benwells *CHNR* OX39 .... 224 E1
Berens Rd *HGHW* SN6 .... 276 B1
Beresford Rd *TLHT* RG30 .... 332 E7
Bergamont Pl *COW/LTMR* OX4 .... 192 E6
Bergen Av *ABGD* OX14 .... 238 B3
Berins Hl *WGFD* OX10 .... 315 F1
Berkeley Cl *BAN* OX16 .... 20 A8
Berkeley Rd *OX/KTN* OX1 .... 190 C6
THAME OX9 .... 175 C6
Berkshire Circular Route
GOR/PANG RG8 .... 330 B5
KSCL RG20 .... 307 K7
Berkshire Dr *CALC* RG31 .... 331 G7
Berkshire Rd *HEN* RG9 .... 319 F7
Bernard La *KID* OX5 .... 148 A2
Berner's Wy *FGDN* SN7 .... 230 C4
Bernwood Rd *BIC* OX26 .... 97 F5
HEAD OX3 .... 168 E3
Berrick Rd *STAD* OX44 .... 244 B2
Berry Cl *COW/LTMR* OX4.. .... 193 F4
Berry Cft *ABGD* OX14 .... 214 C6
Berrycroft *HGHW* SN6 .... 277 G8
Berry Hill Rd *RBANSW* OX17 .... 38 C5
Berrylands Rd *CAV/SC* RG4 .... 333 H4

Berry La *DID* OX11 .... 288 A6
WANT OX12 .... 259 H1
Berrymere Rd *MCHM/KBPZ* OX13 .. 189 J8
Berrymoor Rd *BAN* OX16 .... 2 B4
Bertie Pl *OX/KTN* OX1 .... 191 H2
Bertie Rd *OXN/BOT/CM* OX2 .... 189 H2
Besbury La *CHNTN* OX7 .... 85 C1
Bessels Lea Rd *DID* OX11 .... 288 A6
Besselsleigh Rd
MCHM/KBPZ OX13 .... 189 C7
Bessel's Wy *DID* OX11 .... 288 B6
Bessemer Cl *BIC* OX26 .... 97 H5
Betam Rd *READ* RG1 .... 333 K8
Betony Wy *BIC* OX26.. .... 97 F3
Bettina Crs *BAN* OX16 .... 20 C5
Betty La *OX/KTN* OX1 .... 191 C4
Between Towns Rd
COW/LTMR OX4 .... 192 C2
Beverley Cl *ABGD* OX14 .... 214 C6
STAD OX44 .... 244 C1
Beverley Crs *BUR/CRTN* OX18 .... 158 A3
Beverley Gdns *BIC* OX26 .... 97 H3
Beverley Rd *CALC* RG31 .... 331 H6
Beverly Cl *WGFD* OX10 .... 268 B4
Bevington Rd *OXN/BOT/CM* OX2 ...... 4 B2
Bhandari Cl *COW/LTMR* OX4 .... 192 B1
Bibury Cl *WIT/EY* OX8 .... 142 B7
Bicester Hl *BRACKY* NN13 .... 43 C5
Bicester Rd *BIC* OX26 .... 97 K5
CHNTN OX7 .... 88 E1
KID OX5 .... 129 J8
RAYLW HP18 .... 174 C1
RBICN OX27 .... 78 A8
RBICN OX27 .... 95 C4
RBICS/W OX25 .... 95 C4
Bickerton Rd *HEAD* OX3 .... 168 C5
Biddel Springs *HGHW* SN6 .... 251 F1
Biddlesden Rd *BRACKY* NN13 .... 44 D2
Bigmore La *SKCH* HP14 .... 249 K6
Bignell Park Barns *BIC* OX26 .... 95 J6
Bignolds Cl *RBANSW* OX17 .... 7 F7
Billings Cl *SKCH* HP14 .... 249 H2
Billwell *RAYLW* HP18 .... 174 C1
Bingley Gv *WODY* RG5 .... 335 H6
Binsey La *OXN/BOT/CM* OX2 .... 166 C5
Binswood Av *HEAD* OX3 .... 168 E5
Birch Av *TLHT* RG30 .... 332 A7
Birch Cl *CAV/SC* RG4 .... 327 F3
Birch Dr *BUR/CRTN* OX18 .... 138 C8
Birchen Cl *GOR/PANG* RG8 .... 314 D7
Birchfield Cl *COW/LTMR* OX4.. .... 192 E5
Birch Rd *RBICS/W* OX25 .... 115 K3
STAD OX44 .... 195 K5
Birchwood *BAN* OX16 .... 29 F5
BUR/CRTN OX18 .... 158 A5
Birchwood Cl *CAV/SC* RG4 .... 333 J1
Birchwood Dr *KID* OX5 .... 128 E1
The Birchwoods *CALC* RG31 .... 331 F7
Bird Cl *BAN* OX16 .... 2 B3
Birdlip Cl *WIT/EY* OX8 .... 142 B6
Birds La *RBANSW* OX15 .... 24 E1
Bird Wood Ct *CAV/SC* RG4 .... 327 C3
Biscoe Ct *WHLY* OX33 .... 170 E7
Bishop Kirk Pl *OXN/BOT/CM* OX2 .. 148 C3
Bishops Cl *RBANSW* OX15 .... 55 F1
Bishops Orch *DID* OX11 .... 263 K8
Bisley Cl *BIC* OX26 .... 97 H4
Bitham Rd *WANT* OX12 .... 283 J8
Bitterell *WIT/EY* OX8 .... 146 A8
Bix Hl *WIT/EY* OX8 .... 296 A8
Blackberry La *STAD* OX44.. .... 195 C7
Blackbird Assarts La *WIT/EY* OX8.. 124 A6
Blackbird Leys *COW/LTMR* OX4.. 192 E5
Black Bourton Rd
BUR/CRTN OX18 .... 158 A5
BUR/CRTN OX18 .... 182 A5
Black Cft *WANT* OX12 .... 282 D1
Blackditch *WIT/EY* OX8 .... 163 F7
Blackfriars Rd *OX/KTN* OX1 .... 4 C5
Blackhall Rd *OX/KTN* OX1 .... 4 C3
Blackhorse La *MCHM/KBPZ* OX13... 213 C4
Blacklands Rd *WGFD* OX10 .... 267 J2
Blacklands Wy *ABGD* OX14 .... 214 A8
Blacklocks Hl *RBANSW* OX17 .... 21 K7
Blackman Cl *OX/KTN* OX1 .... 191 J5
Blackmore Cl *SWDNE* SN3 .... 274 C8
Blackmore La *CAV/SC* RG4 .... 327 C2
Blacknall Rd *ABGD* OX14 .... 238 C1
Blacksmiths Hl *RBANSW* OX17 .... 40 B8
Blacksmiths La *KID* OX5 .... 132 B3
Blacksmiths Meadow
COW/LTMR OX4 .... 193 F6
Blackstock Cl *HEAD* OX3.. .... 168 E8
Blackstone Rd *WGFD* OX10 .... 266 E6
Blackthorn Cl *CALC* RG31 .... 331 F5
EARL RG6 .... 334 C8
HEAD OX3 .... 168 D3
RBICS/W OX25 .... 116 C4
Blackthorn Rd *BIC* OX26 .... 98 A6
Blackwater Cl *CAV/SC* RG4 .... 334 A3
Blackwater Wy *DID* OX11 .... 264 A4
Blackwood Pl *RBANSW* OX15 .... 29 H7
Blackworth *HGHW* SN6 .... 226 E7
Bladon Cl *OXN/BOT/CM* OX2 .... 148 D7
Bladon Rd *WDSTK* OX20 .... 128 A3

Blaenavon *CAV/SC* RG4 .... 333 F7
Blagrave Cl *ABGD* OX11 .... 263 J6
Blagrave Farm La *CAV/SC* RG4 .... 332 C7
Blagrave La *CAV/SC* RG4 .... 332 C4
Blagrave St *READ* RG1 .... 333 H4
Blake Crs *SWDNE* SN3 .... 274 A4
Blakehope Burn *DID* OX11 .... 263 K4
Blake Rd *BIC* OX26.. .... 97 F7
Blakes Av *WIT/EY* OX8 .... 143 H1
Blakes Cottages *READ* RG1 .... 333 J8
Blake's Fld *DID* OX11 .... 263 H4
Blake Wy *THAME* OX9 .... 175 C4
Blanchard Cl *WODY* RG5.. .... 335 K1
Blandford Aly *HGHW* SN6 .... 250 E2
Blandford Av *OXN/BOT/CM* OX2..... 148 B6
Blandford Rd *KID* OX5 .... 129 C7
Blandy Av *MCHM/KBPZ* OX13 .... 210 E8
Blandy Rd *HEN* RG9 .... 319 F7
Blankstone Cl *WIT/EY* OX8 .... 145 K4
Blay Cl *COW/LTMR* OX4.. .... 192 E5
Bleache Pl *COW/LTMR* OX4 .... 192 D3
Blencowe Cl *RBICN* OX27 .... 97 C5
Blenheim *BRACKY* NN13 .... 41 C2
Blenheim Cl *DID* OX11 .... 263 J2
Blenheim Cft *BRACKY* NN13 .... 43 C5
Blenheim Dr *BIC* OX26 .... 96 D7
BIC OX26 .... 98 A4
OXN/BOT/CM OX2 .... 148 E4
WIT/EY OX8 .... 142 C8
Blenheim Gdns *WANT* OX12 .... 258 D7
Blenheim Hl *DID* OX11 .... 262 D8
Blenheim La *WIT/EY* OX8 .... 145 C7
Blenheim Orch *WANT* OX12 .... 259 H4
Blenheim Pl *WGFD* OX10 .... 268 B6
Blenheim Ri *RBANSW* OX17 .... 39 J1
Blenheim Rd *BAN* OX16 .... 29 C7
CAV/SC RG4 .... 333 C7
KID OX5 .... 129 J1
READ RG1 .... 333 K5
STAD OX44 .... 219 J3
WHLY OX33 .... 169 J1
WTLGN OX49 .... 246 E7
Blenheim Wy
MCHM/KBPZ OX13 .... 210 D6
WHLY OX33 .... 169 J3
Bletchingdon Rd *KID* OX5 .... 111 K6
KID OX5 .... 129 K7
KID OX5 .... 130 C7
Blewbury Dr *CALC* RG31 .... 331 F7
Blewbury Hl *DID* OX11 .... 288 C5
Blewbury Rd *DID* OX11 .... 288 A4
Blomfield Pl *OXN/BOT/CM* OX2 .... 4 B2
Blossoms Gld *ABGD* OX14.. .... 215 J2
Blounts Court Rd *CAV/SC* RG4.. .... 327 C7
The Blowings *WIT/EY* OX8 .... 126 B8
Blowingstone Hl *WANT* OX12 .... 279 J7
Bloxham Br *RBANNS* OX17.. .... 38 B8
Bloxham Grove Rd *RBANSW* OX15 ... 37 C7
Bloxham Rd *BAN* OX16 .... 2 B6
BAN OX16 .... 28 C5
RBANSW OX15 .... 36 C1
RBANSW OX15 .... 37 F7
Bluebell Ct *COW/LTMR* OX4 .... 193 F6
Bluebell Ride *ABGD* OX14 .... 191 J8
Blue Boar St *OX/KTN* OX1 .... 4 C4
Blundells Rd *TLHT* RG30 .... 331 J1
Blunts Hay *CIR* GL7 .... 154 D8
Blythe Pl *BIC* OX26 .... 96 C6
Bobby Fryer Cl *COW/LTMR* OX4 .. 192 E5
Boddington La *WIT/EY* OX8.. .... 125 H4
Boddington Rd *RBANNS* OX17 .... 7 F6
Bodley Rd *COW/LTMR* OX4 .... 192 C2
Body Rd *READ* RG1 .... 333 C8
Boham's Rd *DID* OX11 .... 309 C6
Bolney La *HEN* RG9 .... 329 J2
Bolney Rd *HEN* RG9 .... 329 K3
Bolney Trevor Dr *HEN* RG9 .... 329 J3
Bolsover Cl *WIT/EY* OX8 .... 126 B6
Bolton Rd *BAN* OX16 .... 2 C3
Bolton's La *WIT/EY* OX8 .... 126 D4
Bonar Rd *HEAD* OX3 .... 168 E6
Bonds End La *RBANSW* OX15.. .... 24 E2
Bones La *HEN* RG9.. .... 328 C2
Bonham Pl *BUR/CRTN* OX18 .... 157 K3
Boot St *WIT/EY* OX8 .... 107 H8
Boreford Rd *ABGD* OX14 .... 215 F5
Borough Av *WGFD* OX10 .... 266 E8
Borough Rd *BRACKY* NN13 .... 43 C2
Borough Wk *ABGD* OX14 .... 214 C6
Borrowmead Rd *HEAD* OX3.. .... 168 B2
Bosley Crs *WGFD* OX10 .... 267 F8
Bosley's Orch *DID* OX11 .... 263 J6
WANT OX12 .... 258 E6
Bostock Rd *ABGD* OX14 .... 214 B8
Boston Rd *BIC* OX26 .... 97 H4
HEN RG9 .... 319 C3
Boswell Rd *COW/LTMR* OX4.. .... 192 C3
Botany *HGHW* SN6 .... 250 C2
The Bothy *RBANNS* OX17 .... 40 C8
Botley Rd *OXN/BOT/CM* OX2.. .... 4 A4
Bottom La *GOR/PANG* RG8 .... 314 E3
Boucher Cl *WANT* OX12 .... 258 D7
The Boulevard *KID* OX5 .... 128 E1
Boulter Dr *ABGD* OX14 .... 214 E6
Boulter St *HEAD* OX3 .... 5 E4

Boults Cl HEAD OX3................ 167 K2
Boults La HEAD OX3................ 167 K2
Boult St READ RG1 .... 333 J8
Boundary Brook Rd
   COW/LTMR OX4 .... 192 A1 🔲
Boundary Cl WDSTK OX20 .... 127 J1
Boundary La CAV/SC RG4 .... 332 E4
Boundary Rd BRACKY NN13 .... 43 H1
Bourlon Wd ABGD OX14 .... 214 B6
Bourne Cl BIC OX26 .... 96 E6 🔲
   OXN/BOT/CM OX2 .... 149 F6
Bourne La RBANSW OX15 .... 33 K7
Bourne Rd GOR/PANG RG8 .... 330 C2
Bourne-Stevens La READ RG1 ... 333 H8 🔲
Bourne St DID OX11 .... 263 K7
The Bourne RBANSW OX15 .... 33 K8
Bourton Cl BUR/CRTN OX18 .... 182 B6
   TLHT RG30 .... 331 K8
   WIT/EY OX8 .... 142 C7
Bovewell RBICN OX27 .... 58 D4
Bovingdon Rd BUR/CRTN OX18 .... 158 A4
Bowbank MCHM/KBPZ OX13 .... 210 C4
Bowbank Cl MCHM/KBPZ OX13 .... 210 C4
Bow Br WHLY OX33 .... 172 A7
Bower End STAD OX44 .... 220 A8
Bower Gn HCHW SN6 .... 253 F6
Bowerman Cl KID OX5 .... 129 G7 🔲
Bowfell Cl CALC RG31 .... 331 G5 🔲
Bowgrave Copse ABGD OX14 ...... 215 G6
Bowling Cl HEN RG9 .... 318 E4
Bowling Gn SKCH HP14 .... 249 F2
Bowling Green Cl BUR/CRTN OX18.. 183 H5
Bowling Green La GOR/PANG RG8 .. 331 F2
Bowman Cl RBANSW OX17 .... 22 E7
Bowmen's Lea RBANSW OX17 ...... 40 B8
Bowness Av DID OX11 .... 263 H8
   HEAD OX3 .... 168 A3
Bow Rd FGDN SN7 .... 232 C7
Bowyer Rd ABGD OX14 .... 214 D7
Boxhedge Rd BAN OX16 .... 2 B3
Boxhedge Rd West BAN OX16 ..... 2 B3
Boxhedge Sq BAN OX16 .... 2 B5 🔲
Boxhill Rd ABGD OX14 .... 214 D7
Boxhill Wk ABGD OX14 .... 214 C7
Box Tree La THAME OX9 .... 223 F3
Boxwell Cl ABGD OX14 .... 215 F5
Bracegirdle Rd HEAD OX3 .... 168 E6
Bracken Cl BUR/CRTN OX18 .... 157 K3
   CALC RG31 .... 331 G6 🔲
Brackley Rd BRACKY NN13 .... 41 J7
   BRACKY NN13 .... 44 D2
Brackstone Cl CAV/SC RG4 .... 333 J5
The Bradburys RBICN OX27 .... 80 A7
Braddons Furlong RAYLW HP18 .. 174 C1 🔲
Bradford Cl RBANSW OX15 .... 36 E5 🔲
Brading Wy GOR/PANG RG8 .... 331 H2
Bradley Rd HEN RG9 .... 293 K2
Bradley's St GOR/PANG RG8 ..... 315 F3
Bradmore Rd OXN/BOT/CM OX2 ... 4 C1
Bradshaw Cl RBICS/W OX25 .... 74 D7
Bradshaw Rd TLHT RG30 .... 332 A6
Bramshaw Rd TLHT RG30 .... 332 A6
Bramwell Pl COW/LTMR OX4 ...... 5 F5
Bran Cl TLHT RG30 .... 331 J7
Brandon Av RLYW RG5 .... 335 J6
Brandon Cl KID OX5 .... 129 G7
Brans La MIM GL56 .... 64 D7
Brantwood Ri BAN OX16 .... 2 A5
Brasenose Driftway
   COW/LTMR OX4 .... 192 E1
Brasenose Dr KID OX5 .... 129 J6 🔲
Brasenose La OX/KTN OX1 .... 4 C4 🔲
Brasenose Rd DID OX11 .... 263 G6
Brashfield Rd BIC OX26 .... 97 F3
Brassey Cl CHNTN OX7 .... 68 C3
Braybrooke Cl CHNTN OX7 .... 88 E2
Braze La WGFD OX10 .... 267 J1
Braziers La GOR/PANG RG8 ...... 314 C2
Brecon Cl WODY RG5 .... 335 H7
Breedons Hl GOR/PANG RG8 ..... 330 A2
Brenda Cl BAN OX16 .... 2 B5 🔲
Brendon Cl DID OX11 .... 263 G5
   TLHT RG30 .... 331 J6 🔲
Brent Av DID OX11 .... 263 K3
Brentford Cl WGFD OX10 .... 290 A6
Brereton Dr WANT OX12 .... 258 D7

Bretch Hl BAN OX16 .... 2 A5
   BAN OX16 .... 20 A8
   BAN OX16 .... 28 B2
Brett Cl THAME OX9 .... 175 H7
Brewer Ct ABGD OX14 .... 238 D1 🔲
Brewer St OX/KTN OX1 .... 4 C5 🔲
Brewery La RBANSW OX15 .... 33 J8
Brewery St WANT OX12 .... 250 E2
Briant's Av CAV/SC RG4 .... 333 J5
Briar Cl BAN OX16 .... 29 F5 🔲
   CAV/SC RG4 .... 333 G3
   KID OX5 .... 129 F5
Briar End KID OX5 .... 129 F5
Briars La GOR/PANG RG8 .... 330 C2
Briarswood Cl SKCH HP14 .... 249 G2 🔲
Briar Thicket WDSTK OX20 ...... 127 K1
Briar Wy COW/LTMR OX4 .... 193 F5
Briary Rd CIR GL7 .... 203 H1
Brice Rd RBICS/W OX25 .... 76 E7 🔲
Brick Hl RBANSW OX15 .... 52 A1
Brickle La RBANSW OX15 .... 37 F2
Bridens Wy HAM HP17 .... 176 B1
Bridewell Cl WIT/EY OX8 .... 125 F8
Bridge Cl DID OX11 .... 264 A8
Bridge End WGFD OX10 .... 241 K7
Bridge Farm Cl WANT OX12 ...... 258 D8
Bridge Rd RAYLW HP18 .... 172 D5
Bridges Cl ABGD OX14 .... 238 A2
Bridge St ABGD OX14 .... 238 D7
   BAN OX16 .... 43 F1
   BRACKY NN13 .... 43 G4
   BUR/CRTN OX18 .... 185 G5
   KID OX5 .... 130 E7
   OXN/BOT/CM OX2 .... 4 A4
   READ RG1 .... 333 G8
   READ RG1 .... 333 G5
   WIT/EY OX8 .... 143 F6
Bridgewater Cl TLHT RG30 ...... 332 C7 🔲
   TLHT RG30 .... 332 C6 🔲
Bridle Cl BAN OX16 .... 3 F6
Bridle Pth GOR/PANG RG8 .... 314 C7
   WANT OX12 .... 233 K6
Bridle Rd GOR/PANG RG8 .... 324 C4
Bridus Md DID OX11 .... 288 B6
Brierley Pl CALC RG31 .... 331 G3 🔲
Briggs Cl BAN OX16 .... 28 B3
Brigham Rd READ RG1 .... 333 G6
Brightwell St WGFD OX10 .... 265 K5
Brill Cl CAV/SC RG4 .... 333 G3
Brill Rd WHLY OX33 .... 152 E2
Brinds Cl CAV/SC RG4 .... 327 F2
Brinkburn Gv BAN OX16 .... 3 F1
Brinkinfield Rd STAD OX44 ..... 220 A8
Brisbane Rd TLHT RG30 .... 332 B7
Bristol Rd BIC OX26 .... 97 H4
   COTS GL54 .... 100 A3
Britannia Cl BUR/CRTN OX18 .... 158 A3
Britannia Rd BAN OX16 .... 3 D4
Britwell Rd DID OX11 .... 263 J6
   WGFD OX10 .... 268 D3
   WTLGN OX49 .... 246 A6
Brixton Hl WGFD OX10 .... 292 D3
Brize Norton Rd BUR/CRTN OX18. 158 A5
   WIT/EY OX8 .... 141 F7
Broad Bridges WIT/EY OX8 ...... 186 E5
Broadbrook La WANT OX12 .... 280 D3
Broad Cl KID OX5 .... 129 G7
   OXN/BOT/CM OX2 .... 165 K6
   RBANSW OX15 .... 55 F1
Broad End RBANSW OX15 .... 29 G6 🔲
Broadfields COW/LTMR OX4 ..... 192 D5 🔲
Broad Gap RBANSW OX15 .... 29 G6
Broadhead Pl HEAD OX3 .... 168 B2 🔲
Broadhurst Gdns COW/LTMR OX4 . 192 A6
Broad La BRACKY NN13 .... 38 A7
Broadmarsh Cl WANT OX12 ...... 258 D7
Broad Marsh La WIT/EY OX8 .... 145 G1 🔲
Broadmoor La CAV/SC RG4 ...... 335 G3
Broadmoor Rd SWDNE SN3 .... 250 B8
Broad Oak HEAD OX3 .... 168 E7
Broad St ABGD OX14 .... 214 D8 🔲
   BAN OX16 .... 3 D4
   BUR/CRTN OX18 .... 185 G4
   FGDN SN7 .... 254 E8
   KSCL RG20 .... 308 C8
   OX/KTN OX1 .... 4 C4 🔲
   READ RG1 .... 333 H8
   SHPSTR CV36 .... 49 G1
Broadwaters Av THAME OX9 ..... 175 F8
Broad Wy FGDN SN7 .... 278 E3
Broadway DID OX11 .... 263 J7
   DID OX11 .... 264 A6
   DID OX11 .... 286 C1
   KID OX5 .... 148 D1 🔲
Broadway Cl DID OX11 .... 286 C1
   WIT/EY OX8 .... 142 B6
The Broadway KID OX5 .... 132 B5
Broadwell Cl BIC OX26 .... 96 E5
Broadwell Rd CIR GL7 .... 180 D4
   MIM GL56 .... 64 E6
Brock Gdns TLHT RG30 .... 332 C7
Brocklesby Rd COW/LTMR OX4 ... 192 A5
Brockley Cl TLHT RG30 .... 332 A7
Brocks Wy HEN RG9 .... 329 J4

Brode Cl ABGD OX14 .... 215 F5
Brogden Cl OXN/BOT/CM OX2 .... 166 C7
Brome Pl HEAD OX3 .... 168 E3
Bromeswell Cl RBICS/W OX25 ... 93 H1
Bromsgrove FGDN SN7 .... 230 B4 🔲
Brooke Rd BAN OX16 .... 2 A6
Brookfield HGHW SN6 .... 226 D8
Brookfield Cl CHNTN OX7 .... 102 B6
   WGFD OX10 .... 290 E2 🔲
Brookfield Crs HEAD OX3 .... 168 A2
Brookhampton Cl STAD OX44 .... 218 E6 🔲
Brook Hl WDSTK OX20 .... 127 J1
Brook La DID OX11 .... 287 G2
   THAME OX9 .... 174 E7
   WANT OX12 .... 258 A3
Brooklime Wk COW/LTMR OX4 ... 192 E6 🔲
Brooklyn Dr CAV/SC RG4 .... 327 H8
Brookmead Dr WGFD OX10 ...... 266 E8 🔲
   WGFD OX10 .... 290 E1 🔲
Brook Rd BAN OX26 .... 96 D4
   CHNTN OX7 .... 53 J8
Brooksby Rd CALC RG31 .... 331 H5
Brookside ABGD OX14 .... 214 D6
   CHNTN OX7 .... 53 J7
   DID OX11 .... 262 C8 🔲
   HEAD OX3 .... 168 C5
   RBANSW OX15 .... 33 K8
   THAME OX9 .... 175 F6
   WANT OX12 .... 259 G1
   WGFD OX10 .... 290 B6
   WTLGN OX49 .... 246 B5
Brookside Cl THAME OX9 .... 172 D8
Brookside Est STAD OX44 .... 220 A8
Brookside Wy RBANSW OX15 ..... 36 D4
Brook St ABGD OX14 .... 238 E7
   CHNR OX39 .... 224 B3
   OX/KTN OX1 .... 4 C6
   WGFD OX10 .... 267 J3
   WTLGN OX49 .... 246 B6
Brook Vw COW/LTMR OX4 .... 193 G5
Brook Wy WIT/EY OX8 .... 126 C6 🔲
Broome Wy BAN OX16 .... 3 E2
Broomfield Rd TLHT RG30 .... 331 K7
Broughton Cl TLHT RG30 .... 332 C6 🔲
Broughton Rd BAN OX16 .... 2 B4
   BAN OX16 .... 28 A4
Broughtons Cl HEAD OX3 .... 167 K2 🔲
Browning Dr BIC OX26 .... 96 D3
Browning Rd BAN OX16 .... 2 A6
Brownlow Rd READ RG1 .... 332 E8
Browns Cl OXN/BOT/CM OX2 .... 165 J7 🔲
Brown's La CHNTN OX7 .... 106 A4
   WDSTK OX20 .... 127 H1 🔲
Bruce Rd WODY RG5 .... 335 F8
Bruern Rd CHNTN OX7 .... 102 B4
Brumcombe La OX/KTN OX1 ...... 190 D6
Brunel Crs WANT OX12 .... 258 D6
Brunel Dr WODY RG5 .... 335 H6
Brunel Rd DID OX11 .... 263 G7
Brunstock Beck DID OX11 .... 263 K4
Brunswick Hl READ RG1 .... 332 E8
Brunswick Pl BAN OX16 .... 3 E5
Bryant Pl GOR/PANG RG8 .... 331 F2 🔲
Bryan Wy WANT OX12 .... 283 F1
Bryony Cl COW/LTMR OX4 .... 193 G5
Bryworth La CIR GL7 .... 202 E1
Buccaneer Cl WODY RG5 .... 335 K7 🔲
Buchanan Rd RBICS/W OX25 .... 134 B1
Buchan Rd BIC OX26 .... 96 D3
Buckingham Cl DID OX11 .... 264 A7
Buckingham Crs BIC OX26 ...... 97 G4
Buckingham Dr CAV/SC RG4 .... 333 H2
Buckingham Rd BIC OX26 .... 97 F4
Buckingham St OX/KTN OX1 ..... 4 C5
Buckland Rd BUR/CRTN OX18 ... 183 H4
   FGDN SN7 .... 208 C7
   FGDN SN7 .... 208 A3
   FGDN SN7 .... 232 E3
Buckler Pl COW/LTMR OX4 ...... 192 A6 🔲
Buckler Rd OXN/BOT/CM OX2 ... 149 F7
Bucklers Bury Rd ABGD OX14 ... 215 F4 🔲
Bucknell Av GOR/PANG RG8 ..... 330 C2
Bucknell Rd BIC OX26 .... 96 C2
Buckner's Cl WGFD OX10 .... 267 H5
Buck Side READ RG1 .... 333 G5
Buckthorn La WGFD OX10 .... 290 B6
Budds Cl WDSTK OX20 .... 109 K8
Bulan Rd HEAD OX3 .... 168 D7
Bull Baulk RBANNS OX17 .... 22 E7
Bull Hl CHNTN OX7 .... 86 E7
Bullingdon Av WGFD OX10 ...... 241 H2
Bullingdon Rd COW/LTMR OX4 ... 5 F6
The Bull Meadow GOR/PANG RG8 . 322 C1
Bullockspits La MCHM/KBPZ OX13. 210 C7
Bull Ring RBANSW OX15 .... 56 C3 🔲
   RBANNS OX17 .... 9 J2
Bullsmead MCHM/KBPZ OX13 .... 214 C2
Bullstake Cl OXN/BOT/CM OX2 .. 166 D6
Bull St BUR/CRTN OX18 .... 184 C5
Bulrush Rd COW/LTMR OX4 ...... 193 F5
Bunce's La GOR/PANG RG8 ...... 324 E5
Bungalow Cl HEAD OX3 .... 151 J5
Bunkers Hl KID OX5 .... 110 D7
The Buntings SWDNE SN3 .... 274 B8 🔲

Bunyan Rd *BIC* OX26 .... 96 D3
Burbush Rd *COW/LTMR* OX4 .... 192 E2 🔲
Burchester Av *HEAD* OX3 .... 168 E3
Burchester Pl *BAN* OX16 .... 3 F2 🔲
Burcombe Wy *CAV/SC* RG4 .... 333 H3
Burcot La *WGFD* OX10 .... 241 K3
Burcot Pk *ABGD* OX14 .... 241 F3
Burdell Av *HEAD* OX3 .... 169 G3
Burden Cl *SWDNE* SN3 .... 274 A6
Burditch Bank *WDSTK* OX20 .... 109 G2
Bure Pl *BIC* OX26 .... 97 F5
Burford Rd *BUR/CRTN* OX18 .... 139 K6
BUR/CRTN OX18 .... 140 C6
BUR/CRTN OX18 .... 157 K4
BUR/CRTN OX18 .... 158 B1
CHNTN OX7 .... 68 B5
WIT/EY OX8 .... 141 J5
Burford St *CIR* GL7 .... 203 C3
Burgan Cl *COW/LTMR* OX4 ...... 192 D3 🔲
Burleigh Ms *CAV/SC* RG4 .... 333 J1 🔲
Burlington Crs *HEAD* OX3 .... 169 G4 🔲
Burlington Gdns *BAN* OX16 .... 3 F2 🔲
Burlington Rd *TLHT* RG30 .... 331 H8
Burnham Ri *CAV/SC* RG4 .... 327 J8
The Burnhams *RAYLW* HP18 ...... 173 H4
Burns Crs *BIC* OX26 .... 96 D4
Burns Rd *BAN* OX16 .... 2 A5
Burra Cl *COW/LTMR* OX4 .... 192 A8
Burr Cl *WIT/EY* OX8 .... 163 H6
Burrows Hl *HEAD* OX3 .... 168 D4 🔲
Burrows Hl *WGFD* OX10 .... 268 D4
Burr St *DID* OX11 .... 262 C8
Bursill Cl *HEAD* OX3 .... 169 G5
Burswin Rd *BUR/CRTN* OX18 .... 157 K3
Burton Cl *ABGD* OX14 .... 238 C1
Burton Pl *COW/LTMR* OX4 .... 192 E1
Burt's La *RAYLW* HP18 .... 174 D1
Burwell Cl *WIT/EY* OX8 .... 142 C8
Burwell Dr *WIT/EY* OX8 .... 142 C8
Burwell Meadow *WIT/EY* OX8 .. 160 D1
Bury Croft Rd *RBANSW* OX15 ...... 51 K1
The Burycroft *ABGD* OX14 .... 238 E3
Bury Md *WIT/EY* OX8 .... 163 G7
Busby Cl *WIT/EY* OX8 .... 107 J8
Busby's Cl *BUR/CRTN* OX18 .... 182 A7
Buscot Dr *ABGD* OX14 .... 214 E5
Busgrove La *GOR/PANG* RG8 .... 315 K4
Bushey Cl *OXN/BOT/CM* OX2 .. 165 K6
Bushey Leys Cl *HEAD* OX3 .... 168 E2
Bushey Rw *BUR/CRTN* OX18 .... 183 H3
Bush Furlong *DID* OX11 .... 264 B5
The Bush *HADM* HP17 .... 176 B2
Butcher's La *CHNTN* OX7 .... 71 H1
Butcher's Rw *BAN* OX16 .... 3 D3
Bute Cl *HGHW* SN6 .... 226 D8
Butler Cl *RBANSW* OX15 .... 37 F1
WHLY OX33 .... 193 K1
Butlers Cl *SHPSRTE* SV36 .... 49 H1
Butlers Dr *BUR/CRTN* OX18 ...... 157 K6
Butler's Fld *CIR* GL7 .... 203 G2
Butlers La *SHPSRTE* SV36 .... 49 G2
Butlers Orch *SHPSRTE* SV36 ...... 326 D4
Butlers Pond *GOR/PANG* RG8 .... 324 B5
Butlers Rd *SHPSRTE* SV36 .... 49 H2
Buttercup Sq *COW/LTMR* OX4 .. 193 F6 🔲
Butterfly Rd *SKCH* HP14 .... 249 H3
Butter Market *READ* RG1 .... 333 H8
THAME OX9 .... 175 F7 🔲
Buttermilk La *WIT/EY* OX8 .... 122 C6
Butterwort Cl *COW/LTMR* OX4 . 193 F6 🔲
Butterwyke Pl *OX/KTN* OX1 .... 4 C5 🔲
Buttfurlong *HADM* HP17 .... 176 C1
Butts Cl *RBANNS* OX17 .... 40 B8
Butts Hill Rd *WODY* RG5 .... 335 C6
Butts La *HEAD* OX3 .... 167 K1
Butts Rd *FGDN* SN7 .... 230 B5
WHLY OX33 .... 193 J1
The Butts *RBANNS* OX17 .... 40 C8
RBICS/W OX25 .... 114 E7
WIT/EY OX8 .... 186 D4
Butts Wy *WTLGN* OX49 .... 225 J6
Buxton Av *CAV/SC* RG4 .... 333 F3
Buzzards Cl *RBANNS* OX17 .... 21 F2 🔲
Bydemill Gdns *HGHW* SN6 ...... 250 C2
The Byeway *BAN* OX16 .... 3 F2 🔲
Byfield Rd *RBANNS* OX17 .... 14 D1
Byron Cl *ABGD* OX14 .... 238 A2
Byron Ct *SWDNE* SN3 .... 274 C2 🔲
Byron Rd *BAN* OX16 .... 2 A6
EARL RG6 .... 334 C8
Byron Wy *BIC* OX26 .... 96 D4

C

Cadogan Cl *CAV/SC* RG4 .... 334 A3 🔲
TLHT RG30 .... 331 J8 🔲
Cadogan Pk *WDSTK* OX20 .... 127 J3
Cadwell La *STAD* OX44 .... 244 C2
WTLGN OX49 .... 244 E4
Caernarvon Wy *BAN* OX16 .... 28 B1
Caesars Ga *BRACKY* NN13 .... 43 H1 🔲
Calais Dene *BUR/CRTN* OX18 .... 183 H3

Calais Rd *WIT/EY* OX8 .... 185 J1
Calcot Cl *HEAD* OX3 .... 168 E6
Calcroft La *BUR/CRTN* OX18 .... 181 G5
Caldecott La *ABGD* OX14 .... 238 B1
Caldecott Rd *ABGD* OX14 .... 238 B1
Calder Cl *BAN* OX16 .... 3 F2
TLHT RG30 .... 331 K7
Calder Wy *DID* OX11 .... 264 B5
Caldicott Cl *WGFD* OX10 .... 266 D1 🔲
Caleta Cl *CAV/SC* RG4 .... 333 K5 🔲
Calthorpe Rd *BAN* OX16 .... 2 C5
Calthorpe St *BAN* OX16 .... 2 C4
Calves Cl *KID* OX5 .... 129 G7
Cambridge St *READ* RG1 .... 332 E7
Cam Cl *DID* OX11 .... 263 K6
Camden Cl *MIM* GL56 .... 48 A2
The Camellias *BAN* OX16 .... 20 D6
Cameron Av *ABGD* OX14 .... 215 G6
Campbell Cl *BIC* OX26 .... 97 F5
Campbell Rd *COW/LTMR* OX4 .. 192 A2
Campbells Cl *WDSTK* OX20 ...... 127 K1 🔲
Campden Cl *WIT/EY* OX8 .... 142 C6 🔲
Campion Cl *BUR/CRTN* OX18 .. 158 A6 🔲
Campion Hall Dr *DID* OX11 ...... 264 B7
Campion Pl *BIC* OX26 .... 96 E2
Campion Rd *ABGD* OX14 .... 215 F7
Camp La *RBANSW* OX15 .... 10 E3
Camp Rd *RBICS/W* OX25 .... 75 J7
Canada La *FGDN* SN7 .... 230 A4
Canal Ct *WANT* OX12 .... 258 C8 🔲
Canal La *RBANNS* OX17 .... 29 H6
Canal Rd *KID* OX5 .... 128 E3
Canal St *BAN* OX16 .... 3 D4
OXN/BOT/CM OX2 .... 4 A3
Canal Wy *READ* RG1 .... 333 K8
WANT OX12 .... 282 A2
Candy Wy *MCHM/KBPZ* OX13 .. 213 K1
Cane La *WANT* OX12 .... 258 D7
Canning Crs *OX/KTN* OX1 .... 191 H2
Cannons Fld *HEAD* OX3 .... 167 K1
Cannon St *READ* RG1 .... 332 E7
Canon Hill's Gdns *HGHW* SN6 .. 276 C1 🔲
Canterbury Cl *BAN* OX16 .... 21 J8 🔲
Canterbury Rd *OXN/BOT/CM* OX2 .... 4 B1
Capel Cl *OXN/BOT/CM* OX2 ...... 148 E7
Capitol Cl *SWDN* SN3 .... 274 B6
Caps La *WGFD* OX10 .... 290 D4
Cardiff Rd *READ* RG1 .... 332 E6
Cardigan St *OXN/BOT/CM* OX2 .. 4 B2 🔲
READ RG1 .... 333 H5
Cardinal Cl *COW/LTMR* OX4 .... 192 B4
READ RG1 .... 333 H5
Cardwell Crs *HEAD* OX3 .... 168 B5
Carew Cl *CALC* RG31 .... 331 F3 🔲
Carey Cl *OXN/BOT/CM* OX2 .... 148 D6
Carey St *READ* RG1 .... 333 F8
Carisbrooke Cl *CAV/SC* RG4 .... 333 J1 🔲
Carling Rd *CAV/SC* RG4 .... 326 E1
Carlisle Rd *CALC* RG31 .... 331 J4
Carlton Cl *WANT* OX12 .... 258 C6
Carlton Rd *CAV/SC* RG4 .... 332 D2
OXN/BOT/CM OX2 .... 149 F6
Carnarvon Rd *READ* RG1 .... 334 A8
Caroline St *READ* RG1 .... 333 F7 🔲
Carpenter Cl *COW/LTMR* OX4 .. 192 C5 🔲
Carr Av *BUR/CRTN* OX18 .... 157 J5
Carrick Gdns *WODY* RG5 .... 334 E8
Carron Cl *TLHT* RG30 .... 332 A8
Carse Cl *ABGD* OX14 .... 215 F4
Carswell Cl *RBICS/W* OX25 .... 76 E8 🔲
Carswell Crs *RBICS/W* OX25 ...... 76 B7 🔲
Carswell La *FGDN* SN7 .... 207 J6
Carter Cl *HEAD* OX3 .... 169 F5
Carter Crs *FGDN* SN7 .... 230 A5
Carters Cl *BUR/CRTN* OX18 ...... 157 K5
Carterton Rd *BUR/CRTN* OX18 .. 158 B4
Cartwright Gdns *RBANNS* OX17 .. 40 E2
Cartwright Rd *RBANNS* OX17 .... 40 E2
Cassington Rd *KID* OX5 .... 147 J3
WIT/EY OX8 .... 146 B7
Castle Cl *RBICN* OX27 .... 79 G8 🔲
RBICN OX27 .... 99 K4
WGFD OX10 .... 267 H3
Castle Flds *RBICN* OX27 .... 77 G3
Castle La *WGFD* OX10 .... 267 F7
Castle Mt *BRACKY* NN13 .... 43 F2
Castle Rd *WDSTK* OX20 .... 109 G2
WTLGN OX49 .... 246 D3
Castle Sq *WGFD* OX10 .... 267 H3 🔲
Castle St *BAN* OX16 .... 3 D3
MCHM/KBPZ OX13 .... 261 H4
OX/KTN OX1 .... 4 C4 🔲
RBANSW OX15 .... 99 K4
RBICN OX27 .... 99 K4
READ RG1 .... 333 G8
WGFD OX10 .... 267 F7
Castle View Rd *SWDNE* SN3 .... 274 A6
Caswell La *WIT/EY* OX8 .... 159 H1
Catalina Cl *WODY* RG5 .... 335 K8
Catherine Cl *ABGD* OX14 .... 215 K4 🔲
HGHW SN6 .... 276 C1
Catherine St *COW/LTMR* OX4 ...... 5 F6
TLHT RG30 .... 332 D7
Cat La *STAD* OX44 .... 219 F5
WGFD OX10 .... 268 D3

Catmore Cl *WANT* OX12 .... 258 C3
Catmore Rd *KSCL* RG20 .... 306 E5
KSCL RG20 .... 307 G6
Catsham La *CHNTN* OX7 .... 86 E3
CHNTN OX7 .... 105 F3
Catslip *HEN* RG9 .... 295 H4
Cat St *WANT* OX12 .... 285 F1
Cattle Market *CHNTN* OX7 .... 68 E3
Catwell Cl *COW/LTMR* OX4 ...... 192 E3
Caudwell Cl *ABGD* OX14 .... 237 K4
WANT OX12 .... 258 E2
Causeway *BAN* OX16 .... 3 F2
BIC OX26 .... 97 F5
KID OX5 .... 111 K4
The Causeway *CAV/SC* RG4 ...... 333 K8
MCHM/KBPZ OX13 .... 261 H4
WANT OX12 .... 259 C3
WDSTK OX20 .... 109 H1
Causmans Wy *CALC* RG31 .... 331 C5
Cavalier Rd *THAME* OX9 .... 175 G5
Cavell Rd *COW/LTMR* OX4 ...... 191 K6
Cavendish Dr *HEAD* OX3 .... 167 J4
Cavendish Pl *RBICN* OX27 .... 80 A5
Cavendish Rd *CAV/SC* RG4 ...... 333 F1
OXN/BOT/CM OX2 .... 149 F7
Caversham Br *READ* RG1 .... 333 G5
Caversham Park Dr *CAV/SC* RG4 .. 333 J2
Caversham Park Rd *CAV/SC* RG4 .. 333 K2
Caversham Rd *READ* RG1 .... 333 G5
Cave St *COW/LTMR* OX4 .... 5 F6
Cawley Rd *RBANNS* OX17 .... 38 E2
Cawsam Gdns *CAV/SC* RG4 ...... 333 G2
Caxton Cl *TLHT* RG30 .... 332 C4
Cecil Aldin Dr *CALC* RG31 .... 331 F3
Cecil Sharpe Cl *HEAD* OX3 .... 168 C8
Cedar Cl *BAN* OX16 .... 29 F7
Cedar Crs *THAME* OX9 .... 174 D2
Cedar Dr *BIC* OX26 .... 97 C4
GOR/PANG RG8 .... 330 A8
Cedar Rd *FGDN* SN7 .... 230 A4
OXN/BOT/CM OX2 .... 166 A2
The Cedars *CALC* RG31 .... 331 H3
WGFD OX10 .... 267 J3
Cedar Wood Crs *CAV/SC* RG4 .. 333 H4
Celandine Pl *COW/LTMR* OX4 .. 193 F6
Celsea Pl *WGFD* OX10 .... 290 C6
Cemetery Rd *ABGD* OX14 .... 214 D4
BIC OX26 .... 97 F3
Centaury Pl *COW/LTMR* OX4 .... 193 C2
Centre Ri *WHLY* OX33 .... 193 K4
Centre St *BAN* OX16 .... 3 E1
Centurion Wy *SWDNE* SN3 ...... 274 A7
Chacombe Rd *RBANNS* OX17 .... 22 D1
Chadlington Rd *CHNTN* OX7 ...... 87 H1
OXN/BOT/CM OX2 .... 167 C4
Chaffinch Cl *CALC* RG31 .... 331 F8
Chaffinch Wk *COW/LTMR* OX4 . 193 F6
Chainhill Rd *WANT* OX12 .... 283 F3
Chain St *READ* RG1 .... 333 C4
Chalcraft Cl *HEN* RG9 .... 318 E2
Chalfont Rd *OXN/BOT/CM* OX2 .. 167 K4
Chalford Cl *CHNTN* OX7 .... 68 C4
Chalford Rd *THAME* OX9 .... 223 C4
Chalgrove Rd *THAME* OX9 .... 175 C5
Chalgrove Wy *CAV/SC* RG4 ...... 333 H4
Chalk Farm Rd *SKCH* HP14 ...... 249 F6
Chalk Hl *DID* OX11 .... 289 F2
HEN RG9 .... 289 F7
Chalkhouse Green La *CAV/SC* RG4 .. 327 K5
Chalkhouse Green Rd *CAV/SC* RG4 .. 326 D2
Challenor Cl *ABGD* OX14 .... 238 C1
Challow Rd *WANT* OX12 .... 282 A7
Chalmore Gdns *WGFD* OX10 .... 291 F5
Chalvey Cl *BIC* OX26 .... 96 E6
Chalvey Rd *BIC* OX26 .... 96 E7
Chamberlain Pl *KID* OX5 .... 129 F6
Chambrai Cl *ABGD* OX14 .... 239 K4
Champion Rd *CAV/SC* RG4 .... 333 J1
Champion Wy *COW/LTMR* OX4 . 192 E1
Champs Cl *ABGD* OX14 .... 215 G5
Chancel Wy *CIR* GL7 .... 203 C3
MCHM/KBPZ OX13 .... 212 E1
Chandler Cl *BUR/CRTN* OX18 .. 183 F4
Chandlers Cl *ABGD* OX14 .... 215 C1
WANT OX12 .... 282 E2
Chapel Cl *GOR/PANG* RG8 .... 312 E4
RBANSW OX15 .... 57 H1
WIT/EY OX8 .... 122 E3
Chapel Dr *RBICS/W* OX25 .... 115 J1
Chapel End *BRACKY* NN13 .... 41 H7
CHNTN OX7 .... 50 D4
Chapel Hl *BUR/CRTN* OX18 ...... 158 C1
CALC RG31 .... 331 F8
CHNTN OX7 .... 52 B1
HGHW SN6 .... 252 C2
Chapel La *ABGD* OX14 .... 238 E3
CHNTN OX7 .... 67 C1
CHNTN OX7 .... 71 J2
CHNTN OX7 .... 84 A3
CHNTN OX7 .... 87 G1
CHNTN OX7 .... 102 E3
COW/LTMR OX4 .... 192 E3
DID OX11 .... 288 D2
FGDN SN7 .... 254 D3

FGDN SN7 .... 254 C3
HEN RG9 .... 294 E5
PRRI HP27 .... 201 K4
RBANNS OX17 .... 13 H5
RBANNS OX17 .... 21 F2
RBANNS OX17 .... 38 D3
RBANSW OX15 .... 10 A3
RBANSW OX15 .... 29 C7
RBANSW OX15 .... 37 J4
STAD OX44 .... 244 B1
SWDNE SN3 .... 274 C3
WANT OX12 .... 313 D1
WGFD OX10 .... 243 K8
WGFD OX10 .... 267 H5
WIT/EY OX8 .... 143 F2
WIT/EY OX8 .... 186 D4
WIT/EY OX8 .... 187 H3
hapel Rd FGDN SN7 .... 232 C7
HADM HP17 .... 177 J1
HGHW SN6 .... 277 C8
WIT/EY OX8 .... 162 B1
hapel Sq WANT OX12 .... 285 F1
hapel St BIC OX26 .... 97 F6
CHNTN OX7 .... 83 H5
COW/LTMR OX4 .... 5 F5 ⧉
MIM GL56 .... 64 A4
RBANNS OX17 .... 11 G3
RBANSW OX15 .... 34 A8
RBANSW OX15 .... 37 F3
WTLGN OX49 .... 246 B5
hapel Wy OXN/BOT/CM OX2 .... 166 B6 ⧉
WANT OX12 .... 281 C3
hapelwick Cl HGHW SN6 .... 276 B1
hapmans La RBANSW OX15 .... 56 C4
hapmans Piece BUR/CRTN OX18 138 E2
harbridge La BIC OX26 .... 97 K6
harlbury Cl KID OX5 .... 129 C5
harlbury Rd CHNTN OX7 .... 124 B1
HGHW SN6 .... 276 B1
OXN/BOT/CM OX2 .... 106 B3
harles Dr THAME OX9 .... 175 G6 ⧉
harles Evans Wy CAV/SC RG4 . 333 K5
harles Rd WGFD OX10 .... 290 C7
harles St COW/LTMR OX4 .... 191 K1
READ RG1 .... 333 F7
hariton Pk WANT OX12 .... 283 F2
hariton Rd RBANNS OX17 .... 40 B8
WANT OX12 .... 282 E3
hariton Village Rd WANT OX12 . 283 F2
harney Av ABGD OX14 .... 215 F5
harterville Cl WIT/EY OX8 ...... 141 C5
harter Wy WGFD OX10 .... 266 E8
hartwell Dr CHNTN OX7 .... 106 B3
harvil House Rd WAR/TWY RG10 . 335 J2
harvil La CAV/SC RG4 .... 335 C3
harvil Meadow Rd
WAR/TWY RG10 .... 335 K2
hatham Rd OX/KTN OX1 .... 191 H2
hatham St READ RG1 .... 333 F7
hatsworth Cl CAV/SC RG4 ...... 333 J1
hatsworth Dr BAN OX16 .... 3 E6
BAN OX16 .... 29 G5
hatterpiece La WIT/EY OX8 .... 126 K2
haucer Cl BIC OX26 .... 96 C3
CAV/SC RG4 .... 333 G2
haucer Ct WGFD OX10 .... 268 D3
haundy Rd KID OX5 .... 111 F2
haunterell Wy ABGD OX14 ...... 238 A1
hawley La OXN/BOT/CM OX2 ... 189 H1
hazey Cl CAV/SC RG4 .... 326 C7
hazey Rd CAV/SC RG4 .... 332 D3
heapside RBANNS OX18 .... 183 G4
READ RG1 .... 333 C7
heatle Cl BUR/CRTN OX18 ..... 138 E3
hecker Wk ABGD OX14 .... 214 D8 ⧉
hedworth Dr WIT/EY OX8 .... 142 C7 ⧉
WIT/EY OX8 .... 142 C6 ⧉
heers Farm ABGD OX14 .... 238 A6
helmscot Rw RBANNS OX17 .... 14 D7
helsea Cl TLHT RG30 .... 331 K6
heney La HEAD OX3 .... 168 A6
heney Rd BAN OX16 .... 3 F2
hepstow Gdns BAN OX16 .... 28 B2 ⧉
hepstow Rd CALC RG31 .... 331 G5
hequers La SKCH HP14 .... 273 J1
hequers Pl HEAD OX3 .... 168 E4 ⧉
WGFD OX10 .... 290 B5
hequers Wy WODY RG5 .... 334 E8
herbury Gn WANT OX12 .... 258 D7
heriton Pl CAV/SC RG4 .... 327 F2 ⧉
herry Cl CAV/SC RG4 .... 327 J7
COW/LTMR OX4 .... 193 F6
KID OX5 .... 129 H8 ⧉
RBICN OX27 .... 80 A6
WGFD OX10 .... 242 C8
herry Orch HGHW SN6 .... 250 E1
herry Rd BAN OX16 .... 2 A1
herrys Cl RBANSW OX15 .... 36 E4
herry St RBICN OX27 .... 80 A6
herry Tree Cl HEN RG9 .... 316 A2 ⧉
MCHM/KBPZ OX13 .... 210 D7
WANT OX12 .... 258 E7
herry Tree Dr MCHM/KBPZ OX13 . 214 A6
herry Tree Rd CHNR OX39 ...... 200 E8
herwell Av KID OX5 .... 129 K7

Cherwell Bank RBICS/W OX25 .. 93 H1
Cherwell Banks RBANNS OX17 . 39 K1
Cherwell Cl ABGD OX14 .... 215 F6
BIC OX26 .... 96 E6 ⧉
DID OX11 .... 263 K3 ⧉
WGFD OX10 .... 267 F8 ⧉
Cherwell Dr HEAD OX3 .... 167 K2
Cherwell Rd CAV/SC RG4 .... 333 G1
WGFD OX10 .... 241 J1
Cherwell St BAN OX16 .... 3 D5
HEAD OX3 .... 5 F4
Cheshire Dr RBICS/W OX25 ..... 76 A7
Cheshire Rd THAME OX9 .... 175 H8
Chester St CAV/SC RG4 .... 333 G5
COW/LTMR OX4 .... 5 F6
TLHT RG30 .... 332 D7
Chester Wy BAN OX16 .... 28 B1
Chestnut Av ABGD OX14 .... 215 J3
CAV/SC RG4 .... 334 A3 ⧉
FGDN SN7 .... 230 A4
HEAD OX3 .... 168 D3
THAME OX9 .... 174 D7
Chestnut Cl BIC OX26 .... 96 E8 ⧉
BIC OX26 .... 98 A6
BUR/CRTN OX18 .... 158 E4
HEN RG9 .... 296 B7 ⧉
WIT/EY OX8 .... 143 F5
Chestnut Dr CHNTN OX7 .... 103 J5
Chestnut End BIC OX26 .... 97 F3 ⧉
Chestnut Gv GOR/PANG RG8 .... 331 H2
Chestnut Pl WTLGN OX49 .... 246 B6
Chestnut Rd OXN/BOT/CM OX2 . 166 B8
The Chestnuts ABGD OX14 ...... 215 G6
HEN RG9 .... 329 J4
WANT OX12 .... 283 F2 ⧉
Chestnut Tree Cl
MCHM/KBPZ OX13 .... 214 A6
Chetwode BAN OX16 .... 2 A1
Chetwyn Md BUR/CRTN OX18 .. 183 H4
Cheviot Dr WAR/TWY RG10 ..... 335 K3
Cheviot Wy BAN OX16 .... 20 B6
Cheyney Wk ABGD OX14 .... 214 C6
Chibnall Cl STAD OX44 .... 244 B1
Chichester Cl BIC OX26 .... 97 F5 ⧉
Chichester Pl BUR/CRTN OX18 . 158 E4
Chichester Rd TLHT RG30 .... 331 J7
Chichester Wk BAN OX16 .... 20 B6
Chiers Dr ABGD OX14 .... 238 A6
Chieveley Cl CALC RG31 .... 331 G7
Chilbridge Rd WIT/EY OX8 ...... 145 J8
Childrey Wy ABGD OX14 .... 215 F5 ⧉
CALC RG31 .... 331 F7
Chilgrove Dr RBICN OX27 .... 76 D7
Chillbrook DID OX11 .... 262 C8
Chillingworth Crs HEAD OX3 ... 168 E7
Chilswell La OX/KTN OX1 .... 190 D4
Chilswell Rd OX/KTN OX1 .... 4 C6
Chiltern Cl HEN RG9 .... 318 D7
STAD OX44 .... 244 C1 ⧉
WGFD OX10 .... 241 J2
WGFD OX10 .... 267 H2
Chiltern Ct CAV/SC RG4 .... 333 H1
Chiltern Crs EARL RG6 .... 334 C8
WGFD OX10 .... 266 D7
Chiltern Dr WAR/TWY RG10 .... 335 K3
Chiltern Gdns WTLGN OX49 .... 246 C6
Chiltern Gv THAME OX9 .... 175 G8
Chiltern Rdg SKCH HP14 .... 248 E3
Chiltern Rd CAV/SC RG4 .... 333 J3
HEN RG9 .... 316 E8
Chiltern Vw GOR/PANG RG8 .... 331 H2
STAD OX44 .... 195 H8 ⧉
THAME OX9 .... 198 D7
Chilton Cl ABGD OX14 .... 215 F6
Chilton Rd DID OX11 .... 286 E5
Chilworth Rd STAD OX44 .... 196 A4
Chinalls Cl BUCK/WIN MK18 ... 63 G1
Chinnock Brook DID OX11 .... 263 J4
Chinnor Hl CHNR OX39 .... 225 F5
Chinnor Rd CHNR OX39 .... 224 C3
CHNR OX39 .... 225 J4
PRRI HP27 .... 201 J5
THAME OX9 .... 199 J1
WTLGN OX49 .... 223 K5
Chipmunk Rd WGFD OX10 ...... 268 B4
Chipperfield Park Rd
RBANSW OX15 .... 37 F1
Chipping Norton Rd CHNTN OX7 . 86 D4
RBANSW OX15 .... 51 J1
Choicehill Rd CHNTN OX7 .... 68 B1
Cholmeley Pl READ RG1 .... 334 A8 ⧉
Cholmeley Rd READ RG1 .... 334 A7
Cholmeley Ter READ RG1 .... 334 A8 ⧉
Cholsey Cl COW/LTMR OX4 ..... 192 C3
Cholswell Rd MCHM/KBPZ OX13 . 214 A5
Choswell Spring
COW/LTMR OX4 .... 192 E6 ⧉
Chowns Cl THAME OX9 .... 175 G8
Christchurch Ct BAN OX16 ...... 3 D4
Church Av RBANNS OX17 .... 39 J2 ⧉
Church Cl BUR/CRTN OX18 ...... 182 B2
CHNTN OX7 .... 103 K5
CHNTN OX7 .... 106 A4 ⧉

DID OX11 .... 287 K2
FGDN SN7 .... 253 J5
HEN RG9 .... 317 K6
KID OX5 .... 130 D6
OXN/BOT/CM OX2 .... 164 D5
RBANNS OX17 .... 13 F7
RBANNS OX17 .... 14 C6 ⧉
RBANNS OX17 .... 38 D4 ⧉
RBICN OX27 .... 62 A8
RBICS/W OX25 .... 112 E6
RBICS/W OX25 .... 114 E7
STAD OX44 .... 194 D4
WGFD OX10 .... 267 H5
Church Cowley Rd
COW/LTMR OX4 .... 192 D3
Church End BRACKY NN13 .... 41 J7 ⧉
CHNTN OX7 .... 50 E4 ⧉
DID OX11 .... 288 A6
PRRI HP27 .... 201 K6
WIT/EY OX8 .... 162 C1
WIT/EY OX8 .... 186 D3
Church End La TLHT RG30 .... 331 K8
Church Farm Ct RWWCK/WEL CV35 16 C1
Church Farm La SWDNE SN3 ... 274 C3 ⧉
Churchfield HEN RG9 .... 293 H4 ⧉
Churchfield La WGFD OX10 ...... 267 G3
Church Flds WIT/EY OX8 .... 107 H8
Church Gn FGDN SN7 .... 232 C7
Church Gnd SWDNE SN3 .... 274 D3 ⧉
Church Hl DID OX11 .... 286 B7
HEN RG9 .... 271 K7
KID OX5 .... 110 D2
RBANNS OX17 .... 11 F4
STAD OX44 .... 196 C7
STAD OX44 .... 219 H1
Churchhill Rd CHNTN OX7 .... 68 A6
Church Hill Rd COW/LTMR OX4 . 192 B3
Churchill Cl DID OX11 .... 263 G6
WDSTK OX20 .... 109 J8
Churchill Crs CAV/SC RG4 .... 327 F1
THAME OX9 .... 175 H7
Churchill Dr HEAD OX3 .... 168 C6
Churchill Ga WDSTK OX20 ...... 127 K2
Churchill Pl OXN/BOT/CM OX2 . 148 D7
Churchill Rd BIC OX26 .... 97 G4
CHNTN OX7 .... 68 B7
DID OX11 .... 263 G6
KID OX5 .... 129 H8
Churchill Wy BRACKY NN13 ..... 43 G1
WIT/EY OX8 .... 126 C7
Church La ABGD OX14 .... 238 A6
BIC OX26 .... 97 F6 ⧉
BRACKY NN13 .... 41 J7
BRACKY NN13 .... 43 F4
BRACKY NN13 .... 44 B7
BUR/CRTN OX18 .... 120 A8
BUR/CRTN OX18 .... 136 C1
BUR/CRTN OX18 .... 138 E2
BUR/CRTN OX18 .... 157 H2
CHNR OX39 .... 225 F1
CHNTN OX7 .... 68 B4
CHNTN OX7 .... 73 H8
CHNTN OX7 .... 83 J5
CHNTN OX7 .... 87 J7
CHNTN OX7 .... 106 A4
CIR GL7 .... 180 D5
DID OX11 .... 262 C8
DID OX11 .... 289 F2
FGDN SN7 .... 210 B4
FGDN SN7 .... 254 C3
HEAD OX3 .... 149 K8
HEAD OX3 .... 152 B1
HEN RG9 .... 270 B6
HEN RG9 .... 317 F7
HEN RG9 .... 329 H6
HGHW SN6 .... 228 A7
HGHW SN6 .... 298 C3
KID OX5 .... 111 K4
KID OX5 .... 129 K3
KID OX5 .... 130 E6
KID OX5 .... 132 B3
KID OX5 .... 147 K3
MCHM/KBPZ OX13 .... 261 G4
MIM GL56 .... 64 D1
RBANNS OX17 .... 12 C4
RBANNS OX17 .... 13 H5
RBANNS OX17 .... 20 A3
RBANNS OX17 .... 22 D6
RBANNS OX17 .... 22 C3
RBANNS OX17 .... 38 D4
RBANSW OX15 .... 18 C1
RBANSW OX15 .... 36 B5
RBICN OX27 .... 62 A8
RBICS/W OX25 .... 91 J1
RBICS/W OX25 .... 93 F1
RBICS/W OX25 .... 113 F6
RBICS/W OX25 .... 114 C8
STAD OX44 .... 244 B1
THAME OX9 .... 176 B8
WGFD OX10 .... 242 D2
WGFD OX10 .... 266 A5
WGFD OX10 .... 267 F8
WGFD OX10 .... 268 E5
WGFD OX10 .... 291 F6
WHLY OX33 .... 152 C2

WIT/EY OX8 ... 142 E1
WIT/EY OX8 ... 143 G7
WIT/EY OX8 ... 146 E5
WTLGN OX49 ... 223 K4
WTLGN OX49 ... 246 B3
Churchlea RBANNS OX17 ... 12 C4
Church Leys BRACKY NN13 ... 43 F4
Church Meadow CHNTN OX7 ... 102 B5
Churchmere Rd ABGD OX14 ... 238 E6
Church Ms GOR/PANG RG8 ... 331 H2 🅑
　WODY RG5 ... 335 H7
Church Mill Cl WIT/EY OX8 ... 186 C2
Church Mill Rd ABGD OX14 ... 239 F7
Church Pth FGDN SN7 ... 232 C8
Church Pl MIM GL56 ... 65 F7
Church Ri CHNTN OX7 ... 124 A1
Church Rd ABGD OX14 ... 215 J4
　CHNR OX39 ... 225 F1
　CHNTN OX7 ... 86 E6
　CHNTN OX7 ... 102 B5
　COW/LTMR OX4 ... 192 A7
　DID OX11 ... 288 A7
　FGDN SN7 ... 209 K4
　MCHM/KBPZ OX13 ... 188 C7
　MIM GL56 ... 65 F7
　RBICN OX27 ... 77 H4
　RBICS/W OX25 ... 113 F5
　SKCH HP14 ... 249 F2 🅑
　STAD OX44 ... 195 K6
　THAME OX9 ... 174 E6
　WGFD OX10 ... 267 G3
　WGFD OX10 ... 290 A3
　WHLY OX33 ... 170 D7
　WHLY OX33 ... 193 J1
　WIT/EY OX8 ... 125 G8
　WIT/EY OX8 ... 126 C7
　WODY RG5 ... 335 H7
　WTLGN OX49 ... 223 H7
Church Rw WANT OX12 ... 281 F3
　WOO/WRO SN4 ... 298 A4
Church St ABGD OX14 ... 238 E6
　ABGD OX14 ... 239 K7
　BIC OX26 ... 97 F6
　BUR/CRTN OX18 ... 183 G4
　CAV/SC RG4 ... 333 G5
　CHNTN OX7 ... 68 B4
　CHNTN OX7 ... 85 H5
　CHNTN OX7 ... 84 B3
　CHNTN OX7 ... 101 G5
　CHNTN OX7 ... 102 E7
　CHNTN OX7 ... 106 A4
　DID OX11 ... 263 K7
　DID OX11 ... 287 G4
　FGDN SN7 ... 230 B3
　FGDN SN7 ... 231 H7
　HEAD OX3 ... 151 G3
　HEN RG9 ... 319 F6
　KID OX5 ... 129 J6
　MCHM/KBPZ OX13 ... 236 E1
　RAYLW HP18 ... 135 K7
　RBANSW OX15 ... 19 G7
　RBANSW OX15 ... 29 G7
　RBANSW OX15 ... 36 E3
　RBANSW OX15 ... 55 F1
　RBANSW OX15 ... 56 E3
　RBICN OX27 ... 99 J4
　RBICS/W OX25 ... 75 J1
　SKCH HP14 ... 249 G2 🅑
　WANT OX12 ... 258 E1
　WANT OX12 ... 282 D3 🅑
　WANT OX12 ... 284 A2
　WANT OX12 ... 285 F1
　WDSTK OX20 ... 109 G3
　WDSTK OX20 ... 127 J5
　WIT/EY OX8 ... 125 H1
　WIT/EY OX8 ... 146 A8 🅑
　WIT/EY OX8 ... 161 F3
　WTLGN OX49 ... 246 B3
Church Vw BAN OX16 ... 2 B5
　BUR/CRTN OX18 ... 158 A5
　BUR/CRTN OX18 ... 183 G4
　CHNTN OX7 ... 103 J5
　HEN RG9 ... 315 K2 🅑
　KID OX5 ... 132 B3
　WIT/EY OX8 ... 126 B8
Church View Rd WIT/EY OX8 ... 142 D8
Church Wk CHNTN OX7 ... 102 E6
　FGDN SN7 ... 230 C3
　HGHW SN6 ... 252 C8 🅑
　HGHW SN6 ... 298 C3
　OXN/BOT/CM OX2 ... 4 B1 🅑
　RBICS/W OX25 ... 75 H7
　WIT/EY OX8 ... 126 B3
Churchward Cl WANT OX12 ... 258 D5
Church Wy COW/LTMR OX4 ... 191 K4 🅑
　OXN/BOT/CM OX2 ... 166 B6
　WANT OX12 ... 280 C4
Churchway HADM HP17 ... 176 C2
　KSCL RG20 ... 307 J6
The Chure KID OX5 ... 132 E3
Churnet Cl DID OX11 ... 264 A5
Churn Rd KSCL RG20 ... 309 G8
Cinnaminta Rd HEAD OX3 ... 168 E7 🅑
Cinnamon Cl STAD OX44 ... 220 A8 🅑
Circourt Rd WANT OX12 ... 257 K4

Circular Rd RBICS/W OX25 ... 115 F1
Circus St COW/LTMR OX4 ... 5 E5
City Rd CALC RG31 ... 331 G8
Clack's La WGFD OX10 ... 267 J8
Clanfield Crs CALC RG31 ... 331 G5
Clanfield Rd BUR/CRTN OX18 ... 183 F5
Clapcot Wy WGFD OX10 ... 266 E7
Clarence Pl DID OX11 ... 263 J7
Clarence Rd HEN RG9 ... 319 F5
Clarendon Cl ABGD OX14 ... 215 F7 🅑
Clarendon Dr THAME OX9 ... 175 G6
Clare Ter BUR/CRTN OX18 ... 157 K7
Clarks La SHPSTR CV36 ... 49 H2
Clarkston Rd BUR/CRTN OX18 ... 157 K6
Clay Bank RBANSW OX15 ... 33 K8
Clay Cl CALC RG31 ... 331 F6
Claydon Rd RBANNS OX17 ... 13 G1
Clayhill Cl CHNTN OX7 ... 88 D1
Clay La WGFD OX10 ... 268 A5
Claymond Rd HEAD OX3 ... 169 F3
Claypit La FGDN SN7 ... 253 K8
Claypits La HGHW SN6 ... 252 C8
Cleavers CHNR OX39 ... 224 D1
Cleavers Sq COW/LTMR OX4 ... 192 E6 🅑
The Cleave DID OX11 ... 262 C8
Cleeve Down GOR/PANG RG8 ... 313 F8
Cleeve Rd GOR/PANG RG8 ... 312 D8
Cleeves Av CHNTN OX7 ... 68 C3
Cleeves Cnr CHNTN OX7 ... 68 B2
Clematis Pl COW/LTMR OX4 ... 193 F5
Clements Cl WANT OX12 ... 283 F1
Clements La RBICN OX27 ... 99 J5
Clements Md CALC RG31 ... 331 F7
Clements Rd HEN RG9 ... 318 E4
Clevedon Rd CALC RG31 ... 331 J4
Cleveland WAR/TWY RG10 ... 335 K3 🅑
Cleveland Cl KID OX5 ... 129 K8
Cleveland Dr COW/LTMR OX4 ... 192 C2
Clevelands ABGD OX14 ... 214 E6
Cleveley Rd CHNTN OX7 ... 88 E2
Clevemede GOR/PANG RG8 ... 312 E8 🅑
Cleycourt Rd HGHW SN6 ... 276 A1
Clifden Rd RAYLW HP18 ... 172 C2
Clifford Pl OXN/BOT/CM OX2 ... 148 B7 🅑
Clifton Dr ABGD OX14 ... 214 D7
Clifton Park Rd CAV/SC RG4 ... 333 F4
Clifton Rd RBANSW OX15 ... 56 C5
Clifton St READ RG1 ... 333 F8
Clinton Cl COW/LTMR OX4 ... 191 K4
Clissard Wy BUR/CRTN OX18 ... 156 C1 🅑
Clive Rd COW/LTMR OX4 ... 192 C2
Clock Tower Ct CAV/SC RG4 ... 333 G4
　WANT OX12 ... 282 D5 🅑
The Cloisters CIR GL7 ... 203 G2 🅑
　GOR/PANG RG8 ... 314 D7 🅑
　HEN RG9 ... 319 F7
　RBANNS OX17 ... 14 D1
　WGFD OX10 ... 267 H2
　WIT/EY OX8 ... 163 G7 🅑
Clover Cl OXN/BOT/CM OX2 ... 189 K1
Clover Pl COW/LTMR OX4 ... 193 F5
　WIT/EY OX8 ... 145 K8
Clumber Park Rd RWWCK/WEL CV35 ... 8 E1
Coach La FGDN SN7 ... 230 C3
Coach Wy WGFD OX10 ... 267 H3
Coalport Wy TLHT RG30 ... 331 J6
Coates La HEN RG9 ... 270 C5
Cobden Crs OX/KTN OX1 ... 4 C5 🅑
Cobham Rd WODY RG5 ... 335 H8
Cochrane Rd WGFD OX10 ... 268 B6
Cockcroft Rd DID OX11 ... 287 J1
Cockington Gn BAN OX16 ... 3 E2 🅑
Cockpit Cl WDSTK OX20 ... 127 H1
Cockshoot Cl WIT/EY OX8 ... 107 H8 🅑
Cocks La WHLY OX33 ... 151 K8
Cody Cl WODY RG5 ... 335 K7
Cogges Hill Rd WIT/EY OX8 ... 143 G8
Coghill KID OX5 ... 111 K7
Colbourne Rd DID OX11 ... 263 H7
Coldharbour Cl HEN RG9 ... 318 E7
Coldharbour Rd WANT OX12 ... 284 B7
Coldicutt St CAV/SC RG4 ... 333 J6
Cole Ct DID OX11 ... 263 K4
Colegrave Rd RBANSW OX15 ... 37 F2
Colemans Hl HEAD OX3 ... 168 E4 🅑
Colemans Moor Rd WODY RG5 ... 335 K8
Coleridge Cl BIC OX26 ... 96 D3 🅑
　COW/LTMR OX4 ... 192 D2 🅑
Coleridge Dr ABGD OX14 ... 238 B2
Colerne Rd BUR/CRTN OX18 ... 158 A4
Colesbourne Rd RBANSW OX15 ... 36 D4
Coles La STAD OX44 ... 220 B8
Colgrove Down
　OXN/BOT/CM OX2 ... 189 J1
Collcutt Cl WHLY OX33 ... 193 J1
College Cl WGFD OX10 ... 290 B6
College Farm CHNTN OX7 ... 86 E6
College La COW/LTMR OX4 ... 192 B5
College Wy WHLY OX33 ... 193 H1
Collett DID OX11 ... 263 J5
Collett Wy WANT OX12 ... 258 D6

Colley Wd OX/KTN OX1 ... 191 F7
Collice St KID OX5 ... 130 E1
Collier's La FGDN SN7 ... 230 C3
　HEN RG9 ... 316 E7
Colliers Wy TLHT RG30 ... 332 E7
Collingwood Cl ABGD OX14 ... 214 C7
Collingwood Rd DID OX11 ... 263 G5
Collinsmith Dr WANT OX12 ... 258 E7
Collins St COW/LTMR OX4 ... 5 F5
Collinwood Cl HEAD OX3 ... 169 F1
Collinwood Rd HEAD OX3 ... 169 F1
Collyer Rd SKCH HP14 ... 249 C7
Colmore La HEN RG9 ... 316 B2
Colne Cl BIC OX26 ... 96 E3
　WANT OX12 ... 258 C7
Colne Dr DID OX11 ... 264 A5
　WGFD OX10 ... 241 K7
Coln Rd DID OX11 ... 285 K1
Colony Rd RBANSW OX15 ... 24 E3
Colterne Cl HEAD OX3 ... 168 A2
Coltman Av RAYLW HP18 ... 174 C2
Colton Rd HEN RG9 ... 276 A6
Coltsfoot Sq COW/LTMR OX4 ... 193 F5
Columbia Wy WANT OX12 ... 258 C7
Colvile Cl BUR/CRTN OX18 ... 183 H5
Colville Wk BAN OX16 ... 3 E2
Colwell Dr ABGD OX14 ... 214 A7
　HEAD OX3 ... 169 G1
　WIT/EY OX8 ... 160 C2
Colwell Rd WGFD OX10 ... 241 J7
Colyton Wy GOR/PANG RG8 ... 331 G8
Combe Ga WIT/EY OX8 ... 126 B8
Combe Rd OXN/BOT/CM OX2 ... 4 A3 🅑
　TLHT RG30 ... 331 K7
　WIT/EY OX8 ... 107 G8
Combewell STAD OX44 ... 193 K8
Comet Wy WODY RG5 ... 335 J8
Comfrey Rd COW/LTMR OX4 ... 193 F5
Common Cl HGHW SN6 ... 252 C8
　WIT/EY OX8 ... 144 B1 🅑
Common La CHNTN OX7 ... 67 K2
Common Rd HEAD OX3 ... 151 F1
　WIT/EY OX8 ... 144 B1
Compass Cl COW/LTMR OX4 ... 192 C3
Compton Av CALC RG31 ... 331 F7
Compton Dr ABGD OX14 ... 215 F7
Concorde Wy WODY RG5 ... 335 J8
Condor Cl CALC RG31 ... 331 G8
Conduit Hill Ri THAME OX9 ... 174 E6
Conduit Rd ABGD OX14 ... 214 C7
Conifer Cl OXN/BOT/CM OX2 ... 166 A6
Conifer Dr BIC OX26 ... 97 F5
　CALC RG31 ... 331 F7
Conigre CHNR OX39 ... 224 D2
Conisboro Av CAV/SC RG4 ... 332 E3
Conisboro Wy CAV/SC RG4 ... 332 E3
Coniston Av HEAD OX3 ... 168 A3
Coniston Dr TLHT RG30 ... 331 K6
Connaught Cl TLHT RG30 ... 332 D8
Connaught Rd TLHT RG30 ... 332 D8
Connolly Dr BUR/CRTN OX18 ... 157 K6
Constable Cl WODY RG5 ... 335 K7
Constable's Cft RBICS/W OX25 ... 116 E2
Constantine Cl SWDNE SN3 ... 274 B7
Constitution Hl WGFD OX10 ... 291 C1
Constitution Rd TLHT RG30 ... 332 B7
Conway Dr BAN OX16 ... 28 B5
Conway Rd MCHM/KBPZ OX13 ... 214 B7
Conyer Cl KID OX5 ... 130 D6
Conyger Cl KID OX5 ... 130 D6
Cook La WGFD OX10 ... 291 C1
Cook's Hl RBANSW OX15 ... 26 B5
Cooks La CHNTN OX7 ... 67 C2
Coolidge Cl HEAD OX3 ... 168 C4
Coombe Hill Crs THAME OX9 ... 174 E6
Coombes Cl CHNTN OX7 ... 102 E6
The Coombe GOR/PANG RG8 ... 322 E3
　CHNTN OX7 ... 68 C3
Cooper Pl HEAD OX3 ... 169 F4
Cooper Rd HEN RG9 ... 318 E4
Cooper's Court Rd SKCH HP14 ... 249 F2
Coopers Ga ABGD OX14 ... 3 D2
Coopers Gn BIC OX26 ... 97 G5
Coopers La WANT OX12 ... 283 F1
Coopers Piece WGFD OX10 ... 266 E7
Coopers Pightle CAV/SC RG4 ... 326 D1
Cope Cl OXN/BOT/CM OX2 ... 166 B6
Copenhagen Dr ABGD OX14 ... 214 B7
Cope Rd BAN OX16 ... 2 C3
Copperage Rd WANT OX12 ... 306 A1
Copper Beeches HGHW SN6 ... 250 D2
Copperfield Cl WANT OX12 ... 282 D1
Coppice Cl BAN OX16 ... 3 E2
Coppock Cl HEAD OX3 ... 168 E5
Copse Av CAV/SC RG4 ... 333 K4
Copse Cl CALC RG31 ... 331 H8
Copse La HEAD OX3 ... 168 A4
Copse Md WODY RG5 ... 335 J8
The Copse ABGD OX14 ... 215 G6
Copson La STAD OX44 ... 218 E3
Copthorne Rd KID OX5 ... 129 K4
Corbett Gdns WODY RG5 ... 335 J8
Corbett Rd BUR/CRTN OX18 ... 157 K6
Corby Cl WODY RG5 ... 335 K7
Cordrey Gn COW/LTMR OX4 ... 191 K6

Corfe Ms CAV/SC RG4 .... 334 A3
Coriander Wy COW/LTMR OX4 ...... 193 F6
Corinium Wy SWDNE SN3 .... 274 A7 ☑
Corn Bar WIT/EY OX8 .... 142 D7
Corndel Gdns WIT/EY OX8 .... 142 E7
Corneville Rd ABGD OX14 .... 237 K5
Cornfield Cl WIT/EY OX8 .... 142 C8 ☑
Cornfield Rd WODY RG5 .... 335 J7
Cornish Rd CHNTN OX7 .... 68 A6
Cornmarket THAME OX9 .... 175 F7
Cornmarket St OX/KTN OX1 .... 4 C4 ☑
Cornmarsh Wy SWDNE SN3 .... 274 C8
Corn St WIT/EY OX8 .... 142 E7
Cornwallis Rd COW/LTMR OX4 .... 192 C5
Coromandel ABGD OX14 .... 238 B3
Corunna Crs COW/LTMR OX4 .... 192 E1 ☑
Corwen Rd TLHT RG30 .... 331 H7
Cosin Cl COW/LTMR OX4 .... 168 A7 ☑
Costar Cl COW/LTMR OX4 .... 192 D4
Cote Rd BUR/CRTN OX18 .... 184 C4
Cothill Rd MCHM/KBPZ OX13 .... 213 G3
Cotman Cl ABGD OX14 .... 238 C2
Cotmore Cl THAME OX9 .... 175 H8
Cotmore Gdns THAME OX9 .... 175 H8
Cotshill Gdns CHNTN OX7 .... 68 C4
Cotsmore Cl RBANSW OX15 .... 25 F8 ☑
    WIT/EY OX8 .... 141 C5
Cotswold Cnr CHNTN OX7 .... 50 D4 ☑
Cotswold Cl CHNTN OX7 .... 68 B6
    HEAD OX3 .... 167 J2
Cotswold Mdw MIM GL56 .... 46 A2
Cotswold Meadow WIT/EY OX8 .... 142 B8
Cotswold Pk DID OX11 .... 263 G5 ☑
Cotswold Rd OXN/BOT/CM OX2 ..... 189 K1
Cotswold Vw CHNTN OX7 .... 105 J3
Cotswold Vw BUR/CRTN OX18 .... 157 K3
Cotswold Wy BUR/CRTN OX18 ..... 157 K3
    CALC RG31 .... 331 G5
Cottage Rd FGDN SN7 .... 232 B7
Cottesmore La WGFD OX10 .... 244 B8
Cottesmore Rd COW/LTMR OX4 .... 192 A5
Cotton Grass Cl COW/LTMR OX4 .. 192 E6 ☑
Couching St WDSTK OX49 .... 246 B6
Coulings Cl WANT OX12 .... 261 F8
County Vw RBANSW OX15 .... 57 G5
Coupland Rd MCHM/KBPZ OX13... 213 J1
Court Cl CHNTN OX7 .... 102 E3
    KID OX5 .... 129 G2
    RBANSW OX17 .... 11 G3
Court Close Rd THAME OX9 .... 176 A8
Court Dr WGFD OX10 .... 266 D2
Courtenay Cl ABGD OX14 .... 238 E8
Courtenay Dr CAV/SC RG4 .... 327 H8
Courtenay Rd WANT OX12 .... 282 E2
Court Farm Rd COW/LTMR OX4 ..... 191 K4
Courtfield Rd WHLY OX33 .... 152 A8
Court Hill Rd WANT OX12 .... 282 A6
Courtiers Gn ABGD OX14 .... 240 D2
Courtington La RBANSW OX15 ..... 36 E3
Courtland Rd COW/LTMR OX4 ..... 192 A5
Courtlands Hi GOR/PANG RG8 ..... 330 A3
Courtlands Rd CHNTN OX7 .... 102 E7
Court Place Gdns COW/LTMR OX4 .. 191 K4
Court Rd WANT OX12 .... 282 E2
Courts Gdns WIT/EY OX8 .... 143 H6
Court Sudbury FGDN SN7 .... 230 C3
The Court ABGD OX14 .... 215 F4 ☑
Covent Cl ABGD OX14 .... 215 F4 ☑
Coventry Rd READ RG1 .... 334 A1
Coverley Rd HEAD OX3 .... 168 D8
The Covert WDSTK OX20 .... 127 K2
Covingham Dr SWDNE SN3 .... 274 A7
Cowderoy Pl FGDN SN7 .... 232 C8 ☑
Cow La DID OX11 .... 262 D7
    DID OX11 .... 263 K6
    DID OX11 .... 264 B4
    FGDN SN7 .... 257 H3
    GOR/PANG RG8 .... 312 B4
    KSCL RG20 .... 308 C8
    MCHM/KBPZ OX13 .... 210 C4
    OX/KTN OX1 .... 191 J6
    RBICS OX25 .... 74 E4
    READ RG1 .... 332 E6
    TLHT RG30 .... 332 E7
    WANT OX12 .... 258 E4
Cowleaze CHNR OX39 .... 224 D1
Cowleaze Cl HGHW SN6 .... 276 B2
Cowley Pl OX/KTN OX1 .... 5 E5
Cowley Rd COW/LTMR OX4 .... 168 A8
    COW/LTMR OX4 .... 192 C5
Cowper Cl BIC OX26 .... 96 D5 ☑
Coxfield Cl SKCH HP14 .... 249 H2 ☑
Cox La CHNTN OX7 .... 67 J5
Coxmoor Cl CHNTN OX7 .... 84 A7
Cox's La HEN RG9 .... 315 K2
    WGFD OX10 .... 291 J1
Cox's Wk HGHW SN6 .... 276 B1
Coxwell Gdns FGDN SN7 .... 230 B4 ☑
Coxwell Rd FGDN SN7 .... 230 A6
Coxwell St FGDN SN7 .... 230 B4
Cozens La CHNTN OX7 .... 84 A3
Crabhill La WANT OX12 .... 283 G1
Crabtree Cnr WGFD OX10 .... 292 B3
Crabtree La ABGD OX14 .... 237 K5

Crabtree Pl ABGD OX14 .... 215 F8
Crabtree Rd HADM HP17 .... 176 C2
    OXN/BOT/CM OX2 .... 166 B7
Crafts End DID OX11 .... 286 C7
Craig Av TLHT RG30 .... 332 B7
Cranbourne Gdns TLHT RG30 ..... 331 K5
Cranbrook Dr OX/KTN OX1 .... 191 J8
Cranbury Rd TLHT RG30 .... 332 D8
Crane Furlong HGHW SN6 .... 226 E8
Cranesbill Dr BIC OX26 .... 96 E2
Cranesbill Wy COW/LTMR OX4 .... 192 E6
Crane Whf READ RG1 .... 333 H8
Cranham St OXN/BOT/CM OX2 ...... 4 B2
Cranham Ter OXN/BOT/CM OX2 ..... 4 B2 ☑
Cranleigh Cl BAN OX16 .... 2 A5
Cranley Rd HEAD OX3 .... 169 F3
Cranmer Cl CALC RG31 .... 331 F4
Cranmer Rd COW/LTMR OX4 .... 192 E1
Cranwell Av BUR/CRTN OX18 ..... 158 B5
Cratlands Cl STAD OX44 .... 218 C5
Craufurd Rd COW/LTMR OX4 .... 192 E1
Craven Common FGDN SN7 .... 255 F8
Craven Wy DID OX11 .... 263 J8
Crawborough Rd CHNTN OX7 ..... 106 A4
Crawley Rd WIT/EY OX8 .... 142 E5
Crawshay Dr CAV/SC RG4 .... 327 H8
Cray Ct DID OX11 .... 263 K3
Craysleaze CAV/SC RG4 .... 326 D4
Creampot Cl RBANSW OX17 .... 13 H5
Creampot Crs RBANSW OX17 ..... 13 H5
Creampot La RBANSW OX17 .... 13 H5
Crecy Wk WDSTK OX20 .... 127 K2
Cremyll Rd READ RG1 .... 333 F6
Crescent Cl COW/LTMR OX4 .... 192 D1
Crescent Rd CALC RG31 .... 331 H6
    COW/LTMR OX4 .... 192 C1
The Crescent BIC OX26 .... 96 E4 ☑
    BUR/CRTN OX18 .... 157 J7
    COW/LTMR OX4 .... 192 D7
    HEN RG9 .... 329 K3
    RBANSW OX17 .... 38 D2
    RBICS/W OX25 .... 74 E8 ☑
    WIT/EY OX8 .... 145 G5
Crescent Wy WGFD OX10 .... 290 B6
Cress Hill Pl HEAD OX3 .... 169 F3 ☑
Cricket Gnd SKCH HP14 .... 249 F2
Cricket Rd COW/LTMR OX4 .... 168 A8
Cricklade Rd HGHW SN6 .... 250 D2
Crick Rd OXN/BOT/CM OX2 .... 4 C1
Cripley Pl OXN/BOT/CM OX2 .... 4 A4 ☑
Cripley Rd OXN/BOT/CM OX2 ...... 4 A4
Crispin Cl CAV/SC RG4 .... 332 D2
Crispin Pl WGFD OX10 .... 267 F8 ☑
Crisp Rd HEN RG9 .... 318 E4
Croasdell Cl ABGD OX14 .... 238 C3
Crockwell Cl BIC OX26 .... 97 F5 ☑
Croft Av KID OX5 .... 129 J7
Croft Cl HEAD OX3 .... 5 F1
    THAME OX9 .... 175 G7
Croft End WANT OX12 .... 282 A5 ☑
Croft Holm MIM GL56 .... 46 B2
Croft La RBANSW OX17 .... 38 D3
    WIT/EY OX8 .... 186 B5
Croft Rd GOR/PANG RG8 .... 322 E1
    HEAD OX3 .... 5 F1
    THAME OX9 .... 175 G8
    WGFD OX10 .... 266 E8
Croft's La RBANSW OX15 .... 51 K1
The Crofts WIT/EY OX8 .... 142 E8
The Croft DID OX11 .... 262 C7
    DID OX11 .... 263 K7
    DID OX11 .... 287 K2
    DID OX11 .... 289 F6
    HADM HP17 .... 176 B2
    HEAD OX3 .... 168 C4
    WANT OX12 .... 259 F1
Croft Wy GOR/PANG RG8 .... 314 D7
Cromer Cl CALC RG31 .... 331 G6 ☑
Cromwell Av THAME OX9 .... 175 G6
Cromwell Cl FGDN SN7 .... 230 C4 ☑
    HEAD OX3 .... 5 E1
    HEN RG9 .... 319 F7 ☑
    STAD OX44 .... 244 C7 ☑
Cromwell Ct BAN OX16 .... 2 B2 ☑
Cromwell Dr DID OX11 .... 264 A8 ☑
Cromwell Rd BAN OX16 .... 2 A2
    CAV/SC RG4 .... 333 H5
    HEN RG9 .... 319 G7
Cromwell Wy KID OX5 .... 148 D1
Cronshaw Cl DID OX11 .... 263 J6
Crookdale Beck DID OX11 .... 264 A4 ☑
Cross Av WGFD OX10 .... 268 B5
Cross Cl WGFD OX10 .... 268 B5
Cross Hill Rd RBANSW OX17 .... 38 C4
Cross Keys Rd GOR/PANG RG8 ..... 312 E4
Crossland Rd READ RG1 .... 333 H8
Crosslands ABGD OX14 .... 214 B6
Crosslands Dr ABGD OX14 .... 214 B6
Cross Leys CHNTN OX7 .... 68 A5
Cross Rd WGFD OX10 .... 290 B5
Cross's La CHNTN OX7 .... 86 B6
Cross St COW/LTMR OX4 .... 5 F5
    READ RG1 .... 333 H8
Cross Tree La CIR GL7 .... 180 B1
Crossville Crs DID OX11 .... 263 H5

Crossway CHNTN OX7 .... 73 G7 ☑
Crotch Crs HEAD OX3 .... 168 A3
Crouch Hill Rd BAN OX16 .... 2 A5 ☑
Crouch St BAN OX16 .... 2 C4
Croughton Rd RBANNS OX17 ..... 40 C8
Crowberry Rd COW/LTMR OX4 .... 193 F5
Crowcastle La KID OX5 .... 111 J2
Crowell Rd CHNR OX39 .... 224 D2
    COW/LTMR OX4 .... 192 C5
Crow La RBANNS OX17 .... 13 F8
    WDSTK OX20 .... 90 D8
Crowmarsh Hl WGFD OX10 .... 267 J8
    WGFD OX10 .... 291 J1 ☑
Crown La DID OX11 .... 289 G2
    WGFD OX10 .... 241 K6
    WGFD OX10 .... 267 H3
Crown Ms ABGD OX14 .... 214 C8 ☑
Crown Rd KID OX5 .... 129 G7
    WHLY OX33 .... 170 D7
Crown St COW/LTMR OX4 .... 5 F5
Crowsley Rd HEN RG9 .... 329 J3
Crowsley Wy CAV/SC RG4 .... 326 E2
Croxford Gdns KID OX5 .... 148 C1
Crozier Cl OXN/BOT/CM OX2 ...... 166 B7
Crumps Butts BIC OX26 .... 97 F5 ☑
Crutch Furlong WGFD OX10 .... 241 H1
Ctyd Cft HADM HP17 .... 176 B2 ☑
Cuckamus La WIT/EY OX8 .... 144 B1 ☑
Cuckoo Cl RBICN OX27 .... 97 G1 ☑
Cuckoo La WIT/EY OX8 .... 145 F1
Cuddesdon Cl GOR/PANG RG8 ..... 314 D7 ☑
Cuddesdon Rd WHLY OX33 .... 194 A2
Cuddesdon Wy COW/LTMR OX4 .. 192 E5
Culham Cl ABGD OX14 .... 214 E6
Cullerne Cl ABGD OX14 .... 214 E4 ☑
Cullerne Rd SWDNE SN3 .... 274 A6
The Cullerns HGHW SN6 .... 250 E1
Cullum Rd WHLY OX33 .... 170 E7
Culworth Rd RBANNS OX17 .... 14 E1
Cumberford ABGD OX14 .... 36 E4 ☑
Cumberford Cl RBANSW OX15 ..... 36 E3
Cumberland Rd COW/LTMR OX4... 168 B8
    READ RG1 .... 333 K7
Cumberlege Cl HEAD OX3 .... 149 J8
Cummings Cl HEAD OX3 .... 168 E5
Cunnor Hl OXN/BOT/CM OX2 ...... 189 H2
Cumnor Rise Rd
    OXN/BOT/CM OX2 .... 166 A7
Cumnor Rd OX/KTN OX1 .... 189 J6
    OXN/BOT/CM OX2 .... 164 E6
Cunetio Rd SWDNE SN3 .... 274 A7
Cunliffe Cl OXN/BOT/CM OX2 ..... 167 F2
Cup And Saucer RBANNS OX17 .. 13 H5
Curbridge Rd WIT/EY OX8 .... 160 B1
Curie Av DID OX11 .... 285 K4
The Cursus CIR GL7 .... 203 G2
Curtis Av ABGD OX14 .... 215 F8
Curtis Rd HGHW SN6 .... 276 A1
    KID OX5 .... 129 H6 ☑
Curtiss Cl BIC OX26 .... 97 H2
Curtyn Cl ABGD OX14 .... 214 D7
Curzon St TLHT RG30 .... 332 D7
Cuthwine Pl CIR GL7 .... 203 G2
Cuxham Rd STAD OX44 .... 244 C1
    WTLGN OX49 .... 246 A5
Cwmcarn CAV/SC RG4 .... 333 F1
Cygnet Cl THAME OX9 .... 198 B7 ☑
Cypress Gdns BIC OX26 .... 97 G2

D

Dacey Dr RBICS/W OX25............ 76 A7
Dacre Av CAV/SC RG4 .... 334 A3
The Daedings RBANSW OX15....... 56 B3
Dagdale Dr DID OX11 .... 263 K4
Daimler Av BAN OX16 .... 20 B7 ☑
Dairy Gnd RBANNS OX17 .... 39 K1
The Dairyground RBANSW OX15 ... 26 A2
Dairy La HEN RG9 .... 297 K6
Dairy Meadow MCHM/KBPZ OX13... 235 J3
Daisy Bank ABGD OX14............ 215 F7
Dale Cl OX/KTN OX1 .... 4 B5
Dale Wk WIT/EY OX8............... 160 E2
Dalton Av DID OX11 .... 285 J5
Dalton Cl TLHT RG30 .... 331 J7 ☑
Damar Gdns HEN RG9............. 319 G7
Damson Trees HGHW SN6 .... 252 A8
Dancers Hl CHNTN OX7 .... 106 A4
Dandis Cl RBANNS OX17 .... 22 E7
Dands Dr RBANNS OX17 .... 22 E7
Danesmoor BAN OX16 .... 2 A1
Danes Rd BIC OX26 .... 96 D5
Danvers Cl RBANSW OX15 .... 27 J6
Danvers Rd COW/LTMR OX4 .... 192 A4
    RBANSW OX15.................... 27 J5
Darcey Lode DID OX11 .... 264 B5 ☑
Darell Rd CAV/SC RG4 .... 333 F4
Dark La CALC RG31 .... 331 F5
    MCHM/KBPZ OX13 .... 214 C2
    RBANSW OX15 .... 19 G7
    WIT/EY OX8 .... 142 E6
Dart Dr DID OX11 .... 263 J4

Dart Rd *MCHM/KBPZ* OX13 .... 214 A4
Dashwood Av *KID* OX5 .... 147 K2
Dashwood Ms *KID* OX5 .... 111 J5 🄳
Dashwood Rd *RBICS/W* OX25 .... 74 A1
Dashwood Rd *BAN* OX16 .... 2 C4
  COW/LTMR OX4 .... 192 A4
Dasset Rd *RBANNS* OX17 .... 6 A7
Datchet Gn *WODY* OX10 .... 266 B5
Daubeny Rd *COW/LTMR* OX4 .... 191 K1
Daubigny Md *BUR/CRTN* OX18 ... 158 E5 🄳
Davenant Rd *OXN/BOT/CM* OX2 .... 148 E7
Davenport Rd *WIT/EY* OX8 .... 142 D6
Daventry Rd *BAN* OX16 .... 3 F2
  RBANNS OX17 .... 21 H5
David Nicholls Cl *COW/LTMR* OX4 ... 192 B5
David Walter Cl *OXN/BOT/CM* OX2.. 149 F6
Davies Rd *MIM* GL56 .... 46 B1
Davis Cl *BUR/CRTN* OX18 .... 158 A5
Davis Gdns *RBICN* OX27 .... 79 G8
Dawes Cl *CIR* GL7 .... 178 D4
Dawls Cl *CHNTN* OX7 .... 103 J6
Dawson Pl *OXN/BOT/CM* OX2 .... 4 A3 🄳
Dawson St *COW/LTMR* OX4 .... 5 E5 🄳
Days Gnd *HGHW* SN6 .... 252 C8
Deaconfield *GOR/PANG* RG8 .... 312 E4 🄳
Deacon Wy *BAN* OX16 .... 2 A4
  TLHT RG30 .... 332 A5
Deadman's La *GOR/PANG* RG8 .... 325 F4
Dean Butler Cl *WANT* OX12 ...... 282 C2 🄳
Dean Cl *BAN* OX16 .... 3 E1
Dean Court Rd *OXN/BOT/CM* OX2 .. 165 K8
Deanes Cl *MCHM/KBPZ* OX13 ...... 261 H4
Deanfield Av *HEN* RG9 .... 319 F6
Deanfield Rd *HEN* RG9 .... 318 E6
  OXN/BOT/CM OX2 .... 165 K6 🄳
Deans Farm *CAV/SC* RG4 .... 333 K6
Dearlove Cl *ABGD* OX14 .... 214 C5
Deaufort Cl *KID* OX5 .... 129 H6 🄳
De Beauvoir Rd *READ* RG1 .... 334 A8
De Bohun Rd *READ* RG1 .... 333 H6
Deddington Rd *RBANNS* OX17 ...... 38 C8
Deene Cl *RBANNS* OX17 .... 38 E5
Deepdene Cl *READ* RG1 .... 332 E8
Deerhurst *MIM* GL56 .... 48 A6
Dee Rd *TLHT* RG30 .... 332 A8
Deer Park Rd *WIT/EY* OX8 .... 142 B7
Deers Cl *RBANSW* OX15 .... 29 G7
Deer's Farm *RBANSW* OX15 .... 29 G8
Deer's La *GOR/PANG* RG8 .... 315 G5
Defiant Cl *BIC* OX26 .... 97 H4 🄳
De Havilland Rd *COTS* GL54 .... 100 A2
Delafield Cl *SKCH* HP14 .... 249 H3
Delamere Wy *OXN/BOT/CM* OX2 .... 165 K8
Delamere Rd *EARL* RG6 .... 334 D7
Delaney Cl *TLHT* RG30 .... 331 K7
Delapre Dr *BAN* OX16 .... 3 F2
Delbush Av *HEAD* OX3 .... 169 H3
Delft Cl *TLHT* RG30 .... 331 K7 🄳
Dell Rd *CALC* RG31 .... 331 G5
The Dell *READ* RG1 .... 333 J8
  SKCH HP14 .... 249 H3
Delly Cl *WIT/EY* OX8 .... 123 K8
Delly Hl *WIT/EY* OX8 .... 123 J8
De Mohun Crs *SHPSTR* CV36 .... 32 C5
De Montfort Rd *READ* RG1 .... 333 G6
Denbigh Pl *READ* RG1 .... 333 F6 🄳
Denbigh Cl *BAN* OX16 .... 28 B3 🄳
Denbigh Rd *THAME* OX9 .... 175 G6
Denby Wy *TLHT* RG30 .... 331 K6
Denchfield Rd *BAN* OX16 .... 29 F5
Denchworth Rd *WANT* OX12 .... 258 C8
  WANT OX12 .... 282 C2
Dene Hollow *DID* OX11 .... 286 C7
Dene Ri *WIT/EY* OX8 .... 142 D7
Dene Rd *HEAD* OX3 .... 168 D7
Denman's La *OXN/BOT/CM* OX2 .... 189 G2
Denmark Av *WODY* OX5 .... 335 J6
Denmark Rd *READ* RG1 .... 333 K8
Denmark St *COW/LTMR* OX4 .... 5 F5
Denton Cl *ABGD* OX14 .... 215 F7
  OXN/BOT/CM OX2 .... 165 J7
Denton Hl *STAD* OX44 .... 194 D6
Denton La *STAD* OX44 .... 194 A6
Dents Cl *HEAD* OX3 .... 168 A2
Derby Rd *CAV/SC* RG4 .... 333 H4
Derby St *READ* RG1 .... 333 F7 🄳
Derwent Av *DID* OX11 .... 264 A6
  HEAD OX3 .... 168 A3
Derwent Cl *MCHM/KBPZ* OX13 .... 214 A5
Derwent Rd *BIC* OX26 .... 96 C4
Desborough Crs *COW/LTMR* OX4 .. 191 K4
Desmesne Furze *HEAD* OX3 .. 168 C6 🄳
Deva Cl *SWDNE* SN3 .... 274 B7
Devereux Pl *COW/LTMR* OX4 .. 192 A4 🄳
Deveron Dr *TLHT* RG30 .... 332 A7
Devil's Hl *HEN* RG9 .... 327 K1
De Vitre Pl *WANT* OX12 .... 258 D7 🄳
Devon Cl *WGFD* OX10 .... 268 B4
Devon Dr *CAV/SC* RG4 .... 334 A3
Devon Pl *BUR/CRTN* OX18 .... 158 B5
Devonshire Gdns *CALC* RG31 ...... 331 F3
Devon Wy *BAN* OX16 .... 20 B7
Dexter Cl *BAN* OX16 .... 3 F1
Diamond Pl *OXN/BOT/CM* OX2 .... 167 F1 🄳
Dibleys *DID* OX11 .... 288 A7

Dickens Cl *BIC* OX26 .... 96 D4
  CAV/SC RG4 .... 333 K5
Dickenson Ct *CHNTN* OX7 .... 68 B4 🄳
The Dickredge *RBICS/W* OX25 ...... 74 E7
Didcot Rd *ABGD* OX14 .... 240 D7
  DID OX11 .... 262 D8
  WGFD OX10 .... 265 J4
Dido Rd *DID* OX11 .... 285 H7
Digberry La *HEN* RG9 .... 294 B2
Digby Cl *THAME* OX9 .... 175 H6 🄳
Digging La *MCHM/KBPZ* OX13 .... 211 J5
Dirac Pl *DID* OX11 .... 264 A7 🄳
Diston's La *CHNTN* OX7 .... 68 B4
Ditch Acre *RBANSW* OX15 .... 24 E7
Ditchedge La *RBANSW* OX15 ...... 24 C6
Ditchley Rd *CHNTN* OX7 .... 106 B3
Divinity Rd *COW/LTMR* OX4 ...... 168 A7
Dobbin Cl *SWDNE* SN3 .... 274 C8
Dobbins Cl *RBANNS* OX17 .... 39 K2 🄳
Dobsons La *HEN* RG9 .... 296 E6
Dodd Dr *COTS* GL54 .... 100 A3
Dodgson Rd *COW/LTMR* OX4 ...... 192 C5
Dodson Ct *ABGD* OX14 .... 214 D8
Doe Lea *DID* OX11 .... 263 K4 🄳
Dog Cl *RBANNS* OX17 .... 38 C4
Dog Kennel La *CHNTN* OX7 .... 102 C8
Dogkennel La *FGDN* SN7 .... 231 H8
Dog La *HEN* RG9 .... 317 G7
  WANT OX12 .... 281 F4
Doily Cl *RBANSW* OX15 .... 33 K8 🄳
Dolesden La *HEN* RG9 .... 275 F6
Dolphin La *BUR/CRTN* OX18 ...... 139 F1 🄳
Donaldson Wy *WODY* RG5 .... 335 J7
Don Bosco Cl *COW/LTMR* OX4 ... 192 D1 🄳
Don Cl *DID* OX11 .... 264 A4
  TLHT RG30 .... 332 A7
Donegal Cl *CAV/SC* RG4 .... 333 J4
Donkin Hl *CAV/SC* RG4 .... 333 J4
Donnington Bridge Rd
  COW/LTMR OX4 .... 191 K2
Donnington Cl *WIT/EY* OX8 .... 142 B8 🄳
Donnington Pl *WANT* OX12 ...... 282 D1 🄳
Donnington Rd *READ* RG1 .... 333 K8
Don Stuart Pl *COW/LTMR* OX4 .. 168 B5
Dora Carr Cl *HEAD* OX3 .... 168 A2
Dorcas Rd *BAN* OX16 .... 29 J1
Dorchester Cl *HEAD* OX3 .... 169 F6
Dorchester Crs *ABGD* OX14 .... 214 C6
Dorchester Gv *BAN* OX16 .... 28 B3
Dorchester Pl *THAME* OX9 .... 175 F7
Dorchester Rd *WGFD* OX10 .... 242 C2
Doris Field Cl *HEAD* OX3 .... 5 F2
Dormer Rd *THAME* OX9 .... 199 H1
The Dormers *HGHW* SN6 .... 250 E1
Dorn Cl *CHNTN* OX7 .... 73 G7
Dornford La *WDSTK* OX20 .... 92 A7
Dorn Vw *WDSTK* OX20 .... 109 H3
Dorset St *TLHT* RG30 .... 332 C7
Douglas Rd *CAV/SC* RG4 .... 333 J5
Dovecote Rd *HADM* HP17 .... 176 B1
Dovecote Cl *HADM* HP17 .... 176 B1
Dove Ct *BUR/CRTN* OX18 .... 158 A3
Dovedale Cl *CAV/SC* RG4 .... 333 F4
Dove Gn *BIC* OX26 .... 96 C4
Dove House Cl
  OXN/BOT/CM OX2 .... 148 D7 🄳
Dovehouse Cl *WIT/EY* OX8........ 146 B7
Dove La *HEN* RG9 .... 316 D7
Doveleat *CHNR* OX39 .... 201 F8
Dover Av *BAN* OX16 .... 28 B1
Dovetrees *BUR/CRTN* OX18........ 157 K4
  SWDNE SN3 .... 274 B8 🄳
Dowding Cl *WODY* RG5 .... 335 J8 🄳
Down End *RBANSW* OX15 .... 34 A8
Downhill La *WIT/EY* OX8 .... 143 F3
Downing Rd *CALC* RG31 .... 331 G5
Downlands *FGDN* SN7 .... 253 K5 🄳
Downs Cl *DID* OX11 .... 286 B1
Downside *DID* OX11 .... 286 A6
Downside End *HEAD* OX3............ 169 G4
Downside Rd *HEAD* OX3.............. 169 F4
Downsmead *MARL* SN8 .... 320 E7
Downs Rd *DID* OX11 .... 263 H8
  WIT/EY OX8 .... 141 K7
  WIT/EY OX8 .... 186 A1
The Downs *WIT/EY* OX8 .... 186 B1
Downs Vw *HGHW* SN6 .... 250 E1
Downsview Rd *WANT* OX12........ 258 B8
Downs Wy *CALC* RG31 .... 331 G5
  DID OX11 .... 285 H7
Dow St *RBICS/W* OX25 .... 76 B7
Doyley Rd *OXN/BOT/CM* OX2 .... 4 A5
  WGFD OX10 .... 266 E6
Dragon Hill Rd *FGDN* SN7 .... 278 C6
Drake Av *DID* OX11 .... 263 H7
Drakes Dr *RAYLW* HP18 .... 174 D5
Drakes Farm *RAYLW* HP18.......... 174 E2
Draycott Rd *MCHM/KBPZ* OX13 .. 210 D6
Draymans' Cft *BIC* OX26 .... 97 F5 🄳
Dray's La *HEN* RG9 .... 317 J5
Drayton East Wy *ABGD* OX14 ...... 238 A7
Drayton Rd *ABGD* OX14 .... 238 A4
  TLHT RG30 .... 332 B7
  WGFD OX10 .... 241 K5
Dresden Wy *TLHT* RG30 .... 331 K6 🄳

Drewitts Cnr *DID* OX11 .... 262 🄳
Drift Acre *RBANSW* OX15 .... 26 🄳
Drivers La *MIM* GL56 .... 48 🄳
The Drive *CHNTN* OX7 .... 88 🄳
  EARL RG6 .... 334 🄳
  SWDNE SN3 .... 274 🄳
Drove Acre Rd *COW/LTMR* OX4 .. 168 A8
Drovers La *HEN* RG9 .... 272 🄳
Droveside *WGFD* OX10 .... 290 🄳
Druce Wy *COW/LTMR* OX4 .... 193 🄳
Druids Wk *CHNR* OX39 .... 224 🄳
Dryden Av *BIC* OX26 .... 96 🄳
Drylands Rd *WIT/EY* OX8 .... 141 🄳
Dry La *WIT/EY* OX8 .... 142 🄳
Drymen Rd *RWWCK/WEL* CV35 ...... 8 🄳
Drysdale Cl *ABGD* OX14 .... 215 🄳
Duck End *BRACKY* NN13 .... 42 🄳
Duck End La *WIT/EY* OX8 .... 163 🄳
Ducklington La *WIT/EY* OX8 .... 142 🄳
Duck Sq *CHNR* OX39 .... 224 🄳
Dudgeon Dr *COW/LTMR* OX4 ...... 192 🄳
Dudley Cl *CALC* RG31 .... 331 🄳
Dudley La *HEN* RG9 .... 297 🄳
Dudley Ms *CALC* RG31 .... 331 J6
Duffield Cl *ABGD* OX14 .... 215 🄳
Duffield Pl *MCHM/KBPZ* OX13 .... 212 🄳
Duffield Rd *WODY* RG5 .... 335 🄳
Duke of York Av *ABGD* OX14 ...... 262 🄳
Dukes Cl *RAYLW* HP18 .... 173 🄳
Dukes Rd *KID* OX5 .... 129 🄳
Duke St *BAN* OX16 .... 3 🄳
  HEN RG9 .... 319 🄳
  OXN/BOT/CM OX2 .... 166 🄳
  READ RG1 .... 333 🄳
Dulas Cl *DID* OX11 .... 263 K5
Dulnan Cl *TLHT* RG30 .... 332 🄳
Dulverton Rd *MIM* GL56 .... 46 🄳
Dumas Cl *BIC* OX26 .... 96 🄳
Dumbarton Wy *CAV/SC* RG4 ...... 334 🄳
Dunbar Dr *THAME* OX9 .... 175 G6
Duncan Cl *WIT/EY* OX8 .... 145 K7
Duncan Gdns *GOR/PANG* RG8 .. 331 G3
Dundas Cl *ABGD* OX14 .... 215 🄳
Dunlin Ct *BAN* OX16 .... 3 E6
Dunluce Gdns *GOR/PANG* RG8 .. 330 C2
Dunmore Rd *ABGD* OX14 .... 214 🄳
Dunnock Wy *COW/LTMR* OX4 ...... 192 🄳
Dunsden Cl *DID* OX11 .... 263 🄳
Dunsfold Rd *TLHT* RG30 .... 331 🄳
Dunsomer Hl *DID* OX11 .... 289 🄳
Dunstall Cl *CALC* RG31 .... 331 H7
Dunstan Av *CHNTN* OX7 .... 68 🄳
Dunstan Rd *HEAD* OX3 .... 168 🄳
Dunster Cl *CAV/SC* RG4 .... 333 🄳
Durant Wy *CALC* RG31 .... 331 🄳
Duxford Cl *BIC* OX26 .... 97 🄳
  BUR/CRTN OX18 .... 158 🄳
Dyer's Hl *CHNTN* OX7 .... 105 🄳
Dynham Pl *HEAD* OX3 .... 168 🄳
Dysonswood La *CAV/SC* RG4 ...... 326 🄳

E

Eady Rd *RBICS/W* OX25 .... 76 A7
Eagle Cl *SWDNE* SN3 .... 274 C8
Eagle La *HGHW* SN6 .... 252 C
Eagles *FGDN* SN7 .... 230 E
Earley Pl *READ* RG1 .... 333 H8
Earlsfield Cl *CAV/SC* RG4 .... 334 A
Earl's La *RBANSW* OX15 .... 56 C
Earlstoke Cl *BAN* OX16 .... 3 E
Earl St *OXN/BOT/CM* OX2 .... 166 D
Early Rd *WIT/EY* OX8.................. 143 C
Easington Gdns *BAN* OX16............ 2 C
Easington Rd *BAN* OX16 .... 2 C
Eason Dr *ABGD* OX14 .... 215 J
East Av *COW/LTMR* OX4 .... 168 A7
Eastbrook Cl *RBICS/W* OX25 ...... 117 H
Eastbury Av *CALC* RG31 .... 331 F
Eastchurch *COW/LTMR* OX4 ...... 191 K4
East Cl *BAN* OX16........................ 3 E
East End *RBANSW* OX15 .... 34 A
Easterfield *WANT* OX12 .... 258 E
Eastern Av *COW/LTMR* OX4 ...... 192 B
  READ RG1 .... 334 A
Eastern By-Pass Rd
  COW/LTMR OX4 .... 192 E
  COW/LTMR OX4 .... 169 F
Eastfield *DID* OX11 .... 288 D
East Field Cl *COW/LTMR* OX4 .... 168 D
Eastfield La *GOR/PANG* RG8 ...... 324 B
  GOR/PANG RG8 .... 324 C
Eastfield Rd *WIT/EY* OX8 .... 143 F
Eastgate *RBANSW* OX15 .... 10 C
East Hawthorn Av *RBICS/W* OX25 .. 116 A
Eastmanton La *WANT* OX12........ 280 D
East Park Farm Dr
  WAR/TWY RG10 .... 335 K
Eastrop *HGHW* SN6 .... 251 F
East Saint Helen St *ABGD* OX14 .. 214 D8
East St *BAN* OX16........................ 3 E
  BIC OX26 .... 96 E

DID OX11 .... 264 A7
MIM GL56 .... 46 A2
OXN/BOT/CM OX2 .... 4 A4
RBANSW OX15 .... 29 G7
RBICN OX27 .... 76 E1
READ RG1 .... 333 H8
SHPSTR CV36 .... 49 G1
THAME OX9 .... 175 G7
ast Wy ABGD OX14 .... 237 K7
astwood Rd SKCH HP14 .... 249 H4
WIT/EY OX8 .... 142 A6
aton Pl READ RG1 .... 333 F7
aton Rd MCHM/KBPZ OX13 .... 188 D5
obes La WANT OX12 .... 235 H7
ccles Cl CAV/SC RG4 .... 333 J5
den Ct DID OX11 .... 264 A6
den Cft ABGD OX14 .... 214 E5
dencroft HGHW SN6 .... 227 F8
den Dr HEAD OX3 .... 168 A3
denhall Cl CALC RG31 .... 331 H4
den Wy BIC OX26 .... 96 C5
dgar Milward Cl TLHT RG30 .... 332 A6
dgecombe Rd HEAD OX3 .... 168 E3
dgehill THAME OX9 .... 175 F5
dgeway Rd HEAD OX3 .... 168 A3
dgeworth Dr BUR/CRTN OX18 .... 157 J5
dinburgh Cl BAN OX16 .... 28 A1
dinburgh Dr DID OX11 .... 263 K6
KID OX5 .... 129 K7
dinburgh Rd TLHT RG30 .... 332 D8
dinburgh Wy BAN OX16 .... 28 A1
dington Rd WIT/EY OX8 .... 142 B7
dmonds Cl DID OX11 .... 263 H7
dmund Halley Rd COW/LTMR OX4 .... 192 B6
dmund Rd COW/LTMR OX4 .... 192 C2
dmunds Rd BAN OX16 .... 28 C2
dward Rd OX/KTN OX1 .... 191 J6
dward Rd WAR/TWY RG10 .... 335 K2
dward Stone Ri CHNTN OX7 .... 68 B6
dward St ABGD OX14 .... 214 B8
BAN OX16 .... 3 F3
dwin Rd DID OX11 .... 263 H8
gerton Rd COW/LTMR OX4 .... 192 A6
WGFD OX10 .... 266 E8
ghteenth St DID OX11 .... 285 J4
ghth Av HEAD OX3 .... 169 F7
ghth St DID OX11 .... 285 K3
an Cl TLHT RG30 .... 331 K8
bourne DID OX11 .... 263 G7
dart Cl TLHT RG30 .... 332 B8
derdene CHNR OX39 .... 201 F7
derfield Crs CHNR OX39 .... 286 B7
derfield Rd RBICN OX27 .... 79 G8
der Wy COW/LTMR OX4 .... 193 F6
don Pl READ RG1 .... 333 J8
don Rd READ RG1 .... 333 J8
don Sq READ RG1 .... 333 J8
don St READ RG1 .... 333 K8
don Ter READ RG1 .... 333 J8
dridge Cl ABGD OX14 .... 214 D5
eanor Cl COW/LTMR OX4 .... 192 B3
ectric Av OXN/BOT/CM OX2 .... 4 A5
eventh St DID OX11 .... 285 K5
ot Cl CAV/SC RG4 .... 333 G3
zabeth Av ABGD OX14 .... 215 G5
zabeth Cl HEN RG9 .... 318 C6
zabeth Dr WANT OX12 .... 282 D1
zabeth Rd BAN OX16 .... 2 B5
zabeth Rd HEN RG9 .... 318 D7
SKCH HP14 .... 249 H3
esmere Cl CAV/SC RG4 .... 333 H4
esmere Rd COW/LTMR OX4 .... 192 A3
iots Wy READ RG1 .... 333 H6
's La RBANSW OX15 .... 27 J8
n Cl BIC OX26 .... 97 F3
RBICS/W OX25 .... 115 K3
THAME OX9 .... 198 B7
WHLY OX33 .... 170 E8
WIT/EY OX8 .... 142 C7
n Ct CAV/SC RG4 .... 327 F3
n Crs CHNTN OX7 .... 106 B3
ncroft GOR/PANG RG8 .... 322 E2
n Dr CHNR OX39 .... 224 D7
STAD OX44 .... 193 J5
n Gv CHNTN OX7 .... 102 C6
KID OX5 .... 148 D1
nhurst Rd GOR/PANG RG8 .... 312 E8
n La RBICS/W OX25 .... 115 K4
nleigh Ct CAV/SC RG4 .... 333 J5
n Lodge Av TLHT RG30 .... 332 D7
n Park Rd TLHT RG30 .... 332 D8
n Rd CAV/SC RG4 .... 326 D8
DID OX11 .... 265 G7
FGDN SN7 .... 230 A4
WANT OX12 .... 283 F1
nscote Rd BAN OX16 .... 28 E5
ns Dr HEAD OX3 .... 167 K2
ns Pde OXN/BOT/CM OX2 .... 166 B6
ns Rd OXN/BOT/CM OX2 .... 166 A6
THAME OX9 .... 175 G7
WIT/EY OX8 .... 146 E5

The Elms CIR GL7 .... 180 C5
HGHW SN6 .... 250 E2
Elmstone Dr CALC RG31 .... 331 G6
Elms Wy HEN RG9 .... 294 D4
Elmthorpe Rd OXN/BOT/CM OX2 .... 148 C7
Elm Tree Cl COW/LTMR OX4 .... 192 B4
Elm Tree Wk MCHM/KBPZ OX13 .... 213 K6
Elsfield Cl HEAD OX3 .... 167 K1
Elsfield Wy OXN/BOT/CM OX2 .... 149 F6
Elsley Rd CALC RG31 .... 331 H4
Elstow Av CAV/SC RG4 .... 333 J1
Elstree Cl CALC RG31 .... 331 H5
Elswith Cl WANT OX12 .... 258 A4
Eltham Av CAV/SC RG4 .... 334 A2
Elton Crs WHLY OX33 .... 170 E8
Elton Rd BAN OX16 .... 29 F5
Elvaston Wy TLHT RG30 .... 331 K8
Elvendon La GOR/PANG RG8 .... 314 A8
Elvendon Rd GOR/PANG RG8 .... 313 F8
Elwes Cl ABGD OX14 .... 215 F7
Elwes Rd MCHM/KBPZ OX13 .... 213 F8
Ely Cl ABGD OX14 .... 258 A1
BUR/CRTN OX18 .... 158 A4
Emberton Dr CALC RG31 .... 331 F2
Embrook MIM GL56 .... 64 D7
Emmens Cl GOR/PANG RG8 .... 315 H4
Emmens La GOR/PANG RG8 .... 315 J5
Emmer Green Cl CAV/SC RG4 .... 333 J2
Emperor Gdns COW/LTMR OX4 .... 192 E6
Enborne Rd CALC RG31 .... 331 G7
Eney Cl ABGD OX14 .... 215 G5
English La HEN RG9 .... 293 J6
Enstone Rd CHNTN OX7 .... 71 F2
CHNTN OX7 .... 72 D8
CHNTN OX7 .... 106 A3
WODY RG5 .... 335 J7
Epping Cl READ RG1 .... 333 H5
Epwell Rd RBANSW OX15 .... 25 K2
RWWCK/WEL CV35 .... 16 B3
Erica Cl BAN OX16 .... 20 C6
COW/LTMR OX4 .... 193 F5
Eric Av CAV/SC RG4 .... 333 G1
Erleigh Court Dr EARL RG6 .... 334 C8
Erleigh Court Gdns EARL RG6 .... 334 C8
Erleigh Rd READ RG1 .... 335 K8
Ermin Cl MARL SN8 .... 521 F7
Ermin St SWDNE SN3 .... 274 A6
Ermont Wy BAN OX16 .... 3 F2
Ernest Rd DID OX11 .... 263 J7
Ernicote Cl RBICS/W OX25 .... 116 B3
Errington Rd GL56 .... 46 B2
Eskin Cl TLHT RG30 .... 332 A8
Essex Rd THAME OX9 .... 175 H8
Essex St COW/LTMR OX4 .... 168 A8
Essex Wy CAV/SC RG4 .... 327 G4
Ester Carling La HEN RG9 .... 316 D7
Estover Wy CHNR OX39 .... 224 D1
Ethelred Ct HEAD OX3 .... 168 C3
Eton Cl WIT/EY OX8 .... 143 H8
Euston Wy WANT OX12 .... 258 A7
Evans Cl WIT/EY OX8 .... 146 A7
Evans Ct KID OX5 .... 129 J7
Evans La KID OX5 .... 129 J7
Evans Rd WIT/EY OX8 .... 146 A8
Evelin Rd ABGD OX14 .... 214 C6
Evelyn Cl OXN/BOT/CM OX2 .... 165 K7
Evenley Rd BRACKY NN13 .... 44 A6
Evenlode Cl BAN OX16 .... 2 B2
Evenlode Crs KID OX5 .... 128 D5
Evenlode Dr DID OX11 .... 263 K5
WGFD OX10 .... 241 J1
WIT/EY OX8 .... 126 B6
Evenlode Gdns MIM GL56 .... 46 B2
Evenlode Pk ABGD OX14 .... 215 F6
Evenlode Rd MIM GL56 .... 46 B2
Everard Cl HEAD OX3 .... 168 D6
Evergreens Cl SWDNE SN3 .... 274 A6
Eversley Cl CHNTN OX7 .... 86 E6
Evesham Rd CAV/SC RG4 .... 333 H2
Ewart Cl BIC OX26 .... 96 E4
Ewert Pl OXN/BOT/CM OX2 .... 167 F1
Ewin Cl HEAD OX3 .... 167 K2
Exbourne Rd ABGD OX14 .... 214 B8
Exe Cl DID OX11 .... 263 K6
Exeter Ct DID OX11 .... 264 B7
Exeter Rd KID OX5 .... 129 H6
Eynsford Cl CAV/SC RG4 .... 334 A2
Eynsham Rd WODY RG5 .... 335 G2
Eynsham Rd OXN/BOT/CM OX2 .... 165 F5
WIT/EY OX8 .... 146 E6
Eyot Pl COW/LTMR OX4 .... 5 F6
Eyres Rd WGFD OX10 .... 268 B2
Eyre's La WGFD OX10 .... 268 C2
Eyston Wy ABGD OX14 .... 214 A8

F

Faber Cl COW/LTMR OX4 .... 192 C5
Fairacres ABGD OX14 .... 213 K8

Fairacres Rd COW/LTMR OX4 .... 191 K1
DID OX11 .... 263 J7
Fair Cl BIC OX26 .... 97 G3
Fairfax Av HEAD OX3 .... 5 E1
Fairfax Cl BAN OX16 .... 2 A4
CAV/SC RG4 .... 333 H5
THAME OX9 .... 175 G7
Fairfax Rd COW/LTMR OX4 .... 192 E1
KID OX5 .... 148 D1
STAD OX44 .... 244 B1
Fairfield WGFD OX10 .... 290 A6
Fairfield Cl WANT OX12 .... 258 D7
Fairfield Dr WIT/EY OX8 .... 142 D8
Fairfield Pl ABGD OX14 .... 214 D7
Fairfield Rd GOR/PANG RG8 .... 313 F8
Fairford Rd CALC RG31 .... 331 G5
Fairford Wy BIC OX26 .... 97 H3
Fairhaven Rd RBICN OX27 .... 79 G8
Fairlawn End OXN/BOT/CM OX2 .... 148 D7
Fairlie Rd COW/LTMR OX4 .... 192 B4
Fair Mile HEN RG9 .... 318 D2
Fairspear Rd WIT/EY OX8 .... 122 B3
Fairsted Cl TLHT RG30 .... 332 A7
Fairthorne Wy HGHW SN6 .... 276 B1
Fair Vw HEAD OX3 .... 168 D8
Fairview Rd BAN OX16 .... 3 D5
Fairway Dr WAR/TWY RG10 .... 335 J2
The Fairway BAN OX16 .... 2 A2
Falcon Cl BAN OX16 .... 28 B3
BUR/CRTN OX18 .... 157 J4
COW/LTMR OX4 .... 192 D5
Falcon Md BIC OX26 .... 97 H6
Falconscroft SWDNE SN3 .... 274 A7
Falkner's Cl RBANSW OX17 .... 38 D5
Fallowfield Cl CAV/SC RG4 .... 333 H3
Fallowfields BIC OX26 .... 97 G5
Fallow Wy BAN OX16 .... 29 F5
Falstaff Cl WIT/EY OX8 .... 145 K7
Fane Cl BIC OX26 .... 96 E4
Fane Dr WGFD OX10 .... 241 J2
Fane Rd HEAD OX3 .... 167 J2
Fanshawe Pl COW/LTMR OX4 .... 192 E2
Fanshawe Rd THAME OX9 .... 175 H7
Faraday Av DID OX11 .... 285 J5
Faraday Rd WANT OX12 .... 258 A7
Faringdon Rd ABGD OX14 .... 214 C7
FGDN SN7 .... 232 B8
HGHW SN6 .... 252 C8
MCHM/KBPZ OX13 .... 210 C6
MCHM/KBPZ OX13 .... 213 H6
OXN/BOT/CM OX2 .... 189 G4
Farleigh Ms CAV/SC RG4 .... 334 A2
Farleigh Rd HGHW SN6 .... 276 A1
Farley Cl WIT/EY OX8 .... 107 H7
Farman Cl WODY RG5 .... 335 K7
Farm Cl BUR/CRTN OX18 .... 184 C5
COW/LTMR OX4 .... 193 F6
GOR/PANG RG8 .... 331 G2
KID OX5 .... 129 H6
KID OX5 .... 131 K5
RAYLW HP18 .... 172 D4
STAD OX44 .... 244 C1
Farm Close La WHLY OX33 .... 170 D7
Farm Close Rd WHLY OX33 .... 170 D7
Farm End WANT OX12 .... 258 D7
Farmer Pl HEAD OX3 .... 5 F1
Farmers Cl WIT/EY OX8 .... 143 F5
Farmers End WAR/TWY RG10 .... 335 K3
Farmfield Rd BAN OX16 .... 2 C6
Farmhouse Cl WIT/EY OX8 .... 163 G7
Farmhouse Meadow WIT/EY OX8 .... 142 C8
Farmington Dr WIT/EY OX8 .... 142 C7
Farm La WIT/EY OX8 .... 142 B2
Farm Mill La WIT/EY OX8 .... 143 F8
Farmoor Ct OXN/BOT/CM OX2 .... 164 E5
Farm Rd ABGD OX14 .... 214 D5
GOR/PANG RG8 .... 322 E1
Farmstead Cl WANT OX12 .... 258 D6
Farm Wy BAN OX16 .... 3 E6
Farndon Rd OXN/BOT/CM OX2 .... 4 B1
Farnham Dr CAV/SC RG4 .... 334 A3
Farriers Cl RBICN OX27 .... 79 K1
WODY RG5 .... 335 G8
Farriers La KSCL RG20 .... 308 C8
Farrier's Md RBICS/W OX25 .... 114 B3
Farriers Rd CHNTN OX7 .... 73 F7
The Farriers CIR GL7 .... 178 D3
Far Rd HEN RG9 .... 319 H7
Farthinghoe Rd RBANNS OX17 .... 40 E2
The Farthings MCHM/KBPZ OX13 .... 236 E1
Fatherson Rd READ RG1 .... 333 K8
Faulder Av BUR/CRTN OX18 .... 157 J4
Faulkner St OX/KTN OX1 .... 4 C5
Fawler La CHNTN OX7 .... 106 C8
Fawler Rd CHNTN OX7 .... 106 A5
FGDN SN7 .... 255 G8
Fawley Bottom La HEN RG9 .... 296 C7
Fawley Ct WANT OX12 .... 282 D1
Featherbed La BRACKY NN13 .... 61 K3
HGHW SN6 .... 298 E1
WANT OX12 .... 261 J6
Feilden Cl WIT/EY OX8 .... 161 F3
Feilden Gv HEAD OX3 .... 168 A4
Fells Cl RAYLW HP18 .... 174 D1

Felton Wy CALC RG31 .... 331 G7
Feltwell Cl BUR/CRTN OX18 ...... 158 A4 ⚄
Fencott Rd KID OX5 .... 132 B3
Fenlock Rd WIT/EY OX8 .... 127 G6
Fennel Wy ABGD OX14 .... 215 G7
Ferguson Pl ABGD OX14 .... 215 G7 ⚄
Fergusson Rd BAN OX16 .... 3 E2
Fermi Av DID OX11 .... 285 J6
Fernbrook Rd CAV/SC RG4 .... 332 D2
Ferndale Cl CALC RG31 .... 331 J4 ⚄
    SKCH HP14 .... 249 G3
Ferndale Rd BAN OX16 .... 20 B8
Ferndale St FGDN SN7 .... 230 B4
Ferne Cl GOR/PANG RG8 .... 312 E8 ⚄
Fern Gln CALC RG31 .... 331 G6 ⚄
Fernham Rd FGDN SN7 .... 230 A6
    FGDN SN7 .... 253 J5
Fernhill Cl KID OX5 .... 129 G7 ⚄
    RBANSW OX15 .... 36 B5
    THAME OX9 .... 196 E1
Fern Hill Rd COW/LTMR OX4 .... 192 D2
Fernhill Rd KID OX5 .... 128 D7
Fern La HADM HP17 .... 176 C1
Ferny Cl ABGD OX14 .... 215 J4
Ferriston BAN OX16 .... 20 D4
Ferry Hinksey Rd OXN/BOT/CM OX2 ..... 4 A4
Ferry La GOR/PANG RG8 .... 312 D3
Ferry Pool Rd OXN/BOT/CM OX2 .... 167 F1
Ferry Rd GOR/PANG RG8 .... 312 E3
    HEAD OX3 .... 5 E2
Ferry Wk ABGD OX14 .... 238 D2
Fetti Pl WANT OX12 .... 283 F2
Fettiplace Cl MCHM/KBPZ OX13 ...... 188 C8
Fettiplace Rd HEAD OX3 .... 168 E2
    MCHM/KBPZ OX13 .... 213 F8
    WIT/EY OX8 .... 142 C6 ⚄
Fewcott Rd RBICN OX27 .... 58 C8
Fidler's La KSCL RG20 .... 308 C8
Field Av COW/LTMR OX4 .... 193 F6
Field Cl KID OX5 .... 129 J7
    KID OX5 .... 147 K1
    RAYLW HP18 .... 172 E4
    WIT/EY OX8 .... 107 H7
Fielden Cl WGFD OX10 .... 268 B5
Fielden Rd WGFD OX10 .... 268 B5
Fieldfare SWDNE SN3 .... 274 B8
Fieldfare Rd COW/LTMR OX4 .... 192 E7
Field Gdns MCHM/KBPZ OX13 .... 261 J2
    WANT OX12 .... 281 K2
Field House Dr OXN/BOT/CM OX2 .. 148 E7
Fieldmere Cl WIT/EY OX8 .... 142 C7
Field Rd CHNTN OX7 .... 84 A4
Fieldside ABGD OX14 .... 214 B6
    ABGD OX14 .... 240 C7
    DID OX11 .... 287 G5
Fields Talbot Rd BUR/CRTN OX18 ... 183 J4
Field St BIC OX26 .... 97 F5
The Field MCHM/KBPZ OX13 .... 213 H1
Field Vw CAV/SC RG4 .... 333 H4
Fiennes Cl BAN OX16 .... 28 B2
    COW/LTMR OX4 .... 192 A4
Fifteenth St DID OX11 .... 285 J5
Fifth Av BRACKY NN13 .... 41 K8
Fifth St BRACKY NN13 .... 41 K8
Fifth St East BRACKY NN13 .... 41 K8
Filbert Dr CALC RG31 .... 331 G7
Filey Rd READ RG1 .... 334 A8
Filkins Rd CIR GL7 .... 180 C4
Finch Cl HEAD OX3 .... 168 C5
Finchdale SWDNE SN3 .... 274 B7
Finchdale Cl BUR/CRTN OX18 .... 157 K4 ⚄
Finches La MARL SN8 .... 321 F5
Finchley La BIC OX26 .... 96 E6 ⚄
Fingest La HEN RG9 .... 273 K4
Finmore Cl ABGD OX14 .... 214 C7
Finmore Rd OXN/BOT/CM OX2 ...... 166 D7
Finsbury Pl CHNTN OX7 .... 68 B4
Fir Cl WGFD OX10 .... 292 B8 ⚄
Fircroft BIC OX26 .... 97 G2 ⚄
Fircroft Cl CALC RG31 .... 331 G6
Firebrass Hl WGFD OX10 .... 268 D5
Fir La RBICS/W OX25 .... 74 E6
Firs Cl CHNTN OX7 .... 83 J5
Firs Meadow COW/LTMR OX4 ...... 192 E7
First Av DID OX11 .... 263 H5
    HEAD OX3 .... 169 F7
The Firs RBANSW OX15 .... 19 G7
First St BRACKY NN13 .... 59 K1
    DID OX11 .... 286 A5
First Turn OXN/BOT/CM OX2 .... 148 D7
Firtree Cl BAN OX16 .... 20 B6
Fir Tree Cl MCHM/KBPZ OX13 ...... 210 E6
Fir Tree Paddock KSCL RG20 .... 307 J5
Fir Trees OX/KTN OX1 .... 191 J8
Fisher Cl ABGD OX14 .... 237 J6
Fishers Cl WIT/EY OX8 .... 142 E1
Fishers Ct CAV/SC RG4 .... 333 J1
Fisher's La CHNTN OX7 .... 106 A4
Fitzcount Wy WGFD OX10 .... 267 F6
Fitzharry's Rd ABGD OX14 .... 214 D7
Fitzherbert Cl COW/LTMR OX4 ... 191 K3 ⚄
Fitzmaurice Cl SWDNE SN3 .... 274 B8

Five Acre CALC RG31 .... 331 F6
Fiveacres KID OX5 .... 133 F3
Five Mile Dr OXN/BOT/CM OX2 ... 148 E6
Flambards CAV/SC RG4 .... 333 J5
Flatford Pl KID OX5 .... 129 F5
Flaxfield Rd COW/LTMR OX4 .... 193 F5
Fleet Wy DID OX11 .... 264 A7
Fleetwood Wy THAME OX9 .... 175 F5
Fleming Cl BIC OX26 .... 96 D3 ⚄
Fleming Dr CHNTN OX7 .... 73 C7
Flemings Rd WOSTK OX20 .... 127 K1
Flemming Av STAD OX44 .... 220 A8
Fletcher Cl FGDN SN7 .... 230 C4 ⚄
    KID OX5 .... 147 K2
Fletcher Rd COW/LTMR OX4 .... 192 E1
Flexney Pl HEAD OX3 .... 168 D6
Flexneys Paddock WIT/EY OX8 .... 163 G7 ⚄
Flint Hollow CHNR OX39 .... 224 D1
Flint St HADM HP17 .... 176 B2
Floral Cl WANT OX12 .... 258 E7
Florence Cl KID OX5 .... 129 H7
Florence Park Rd COW/LTMR OX4 .. 192 B2
Florence Wk READ RG1 .... 333 K8
Florey's Cl WIT/EY OX8 .... 142 E1 ⚄
Flower's Hl GOR/PANG RG8 .... 330 A3
Fludger Cl WGFD OX10 .... 266 E8 ⚄
Fobney St READ RG1 .... 333 G8
Fogwell Rd OXN/BOT/CM OX2 ..... 165 J7
Foliat Cl WANT OX12 .... 282 E2
Foliat Dr WANT OX12 .... 282 E2
Folly Br OX/KTN OX1 .... 4 C5
Folly Cl RBANSW OX15 .... 25 G8
Folly Crs HGHW SN6 .... 226 E8 ⚄
    HGHW SN6 .... 252 D6
Folly Dr HGHW SN6 .... 226 E8
Folly Gn GOR/PANG RG8 .... 314 C7
Folly Orchard Rd GOR/PANG RG8 .. 314 C7
Folly View Crs FGDN SN7 .... 230 A5
Folly View Rd FGDN SN7 .... 230 A5
Folly Wy HGHW SN6 .... 226 E8 ⚄
Forbury Rd READ RG1 .... 333 H7
The Forbury READ RG1 .... 333 H7
Ford La MCHM/KBPZ OX13 .... 212 C8
    RBICS/W OX25 .... 73 G4
    WGFD OX10 .... 242 D1
Fords Cl WHLY OX33 .... 193 J1
Fordy La WANT OX12 .... 285 F1
Forest Cl CHNTN OX7 .... 102 C6
Foresters CHNR OX39 .... 224 D1
    RAYLW HP18 .... 135 G8
Forest Hl WANT OX12 .... 331 K5
Forest Rd CHNTN OX7 .... 105 J4
    HEAD OX3 .... 169 F4
Forest Side OX/KTN OX1 .... 191 H4
Forge Cl CAV/SC RG4 .... 333 J6
    RBICN OX27 .... 99 J4
    RBICS/W OX25 .... 114 E7
    WGFD OX10 .... 267 H3 ⚄
Forge Pl RBICN OX27 .... 58 E8
Forget-me-not Wy
    COW/LTMR OX4 .... 192 E6 ⚄
Forgeway BAN OX16 .... 2 A1
Forrest Cl HGHW SN6 .... 276 A1
Forsey Cl SWDNE SN3 .... 274 C8 ⚄
Forster La OXN/BOT/CM OX2 .... 189 G3
Forsythia Cl BIC OX26 .... 97 F2
Fortescue Dr BIC OX26 .... 96 A8 ⚄
The Forties STAD OX44 .... 195 J5
Fortnam Cl HEAD OX3 .... 168 B4
Forty Gn PRRI HP27 .... 201 H4
The Forty WGFD OX10 .... 290 B5
Forum Cl SWDNE SN3 .... 274 A7
Foscote Ri BAN OX16 .... 3 E5
Fosseway Cl MIM GL56 .... 46 A3
Fosseway Dr MIM GL56 .... 46 A3
The Fosseway BUR/CRTN OX18 ... 158 E4
Foster Rd ABGD OX14 .... 214 D4
Fothergill Pl THAME OX9 .... 175 F7
Foudry Cl DID OX11 .... 264 A5
Foundry St BAN OX16 .... 2 C3
Fourth Av BRACKY NN13 .... 59 K1
    HEAD OX3 .... 169 F7
Fourth St BRACKY NN13 .... 59 K1
    DID OX11 .... 285 K4
Fowler Rd BAN OX16 .... 3 E2
Fowler's Rd CHNTN OX7 .... 84 B3
Foxborough Rd ABGD OX14 .... 215 J5
Foxbridge SWDNE SN3 .... 274 B8
Foxburrow La WIT/EY OX8 .... 163 G6
Foxburrow La WIT/EY OX8 .... 142 C2
Fox Cl BUR/CRTN OX18 .... 183 H3
    CHNTN OX7 .... 68 B5
    STAD OX44 .... 193 K5
    WIT/EY OX8 .... 142 E3
Foxcombe Dr CALC RG31 .... 331 G8
Foxcombe La OX/KTN OX1 .... 190 E6
Foxcombe Rd OX/KTN OX1 .... 190 E5
Fox Cover CHNR OX59 .... 224 E1
Fox Crs OX/KTN OX1 .... 191 J2
Foxcroft Dr BUR/CRTN OX18 .... 157 K5
Foxden Wy RBANNS OX17 .... 13 F8
Foxdown Cl KID OX5 .... 129 H6
Foxes Wk MAR/TWY RG10 .... 335 J4
Foxfield CHNTN OX7 .... 68 C5
Fox Furlong COW/LTMR OX4 ...... 192 A6 ⚄

Foxglove Cl BIC OX26 .... 97 F3
    COW/LTMR OX4 .... 192 E6
Foxglove La DID OX11 .... 287 J ▢
Foxglove Rd KID OX5 .... 128 J
Foxhall Rd DID OX11 .... 263 J
Foxhill Cl CAV/SC RG4 .... 334 ▢
Foxhill La CAV/SC RG4 .... 327 J
    RBICN OX27 .... 58 J
Fox La BIC OX26 .... 96 J
    BRACKY NN13 .... 43 J
    CHNTN OX7 .... 73 J
    MCHM/KBPZ OX13 .... 214 J
    RBICN OX27 .... 58 J
Foxton Cl OXN/BOT/CM OX2 .... 148 J
Foxwell Dr HEAD OX3 .... 168 ▢
Foxwood BUR/CRTN OX18 .... 184 J
Foxwood Cl BAN OX16 .... 28 J
Framlingham Dr CAV/SC RG4 ... 334 A2 ▢
Frampton Cl WODY RG5 .... 335 ▢
Frances Rd CHNTN OX7 .... 73 J
Francis Little Dr ABGD OX14 .... 238 J
Franklin Cl KID OX5 .... 129 J
    STAD OX44 .... 244 ▢
Franklin Rd HEAD OX3 .... 168 J
Franklin St READ RG1 .... 333 J
Franklyn Cl ABGD OX14 .... 214 J
Fraser Av CAV/SC RG4 .... 333 J
Fraser Cl BAN OX16 .... 3 J
Fraser Gdns WGFD OX10 .... 290 E ▢
Frax Cl MCHM/KBPZ OX13 .... 211 J
Frederick Rd COW/LTMR OX4 ..... 192 J
Freeborn Cl KID OX5 .... 129 J
Freehold St RBICS/W OX25 .... 93 J
Freelands Rd COW/LTMR OX4 ..... 191 J
Freeman Rd DID OX11 .... 263 J
Freemans Rd RBANSW OX15 .... 29 J
Frenchay Rd OXN/BOT/CM OX2 ... 166 J
French Cl WIT/EY OX8 .... 142 D8 ▢
French Laurence Wy STAD OX44 .. 244 J
Frensham Cl BAN OX16 .... 20 J
Freshwater Rd READ RG1 .... 334 J
Frethern Cl BUR/CRTN OX18 .... 138 J
Friars Cl HGHW SN6 .... 276 J
Friar's Ct BUR/CRTN OX18 .... 206 J
Friar St READ RG1 .... 333 J
Friars Whf OX/KTN OX1 .... 4 J
Friday La WHLY OX33 .... 170 J
Friday St HEN RG9 .... 319 J
Friends' Cl WIT/EY OX8 .... 107 H6 J
Frilford Rd MCHM/KBPZ OX13 .... 236 ▢
Frilsham St ABGD OX14 .... 238 J
Frimley Cl WODY RG5 .... 335 F7 ▢
Fritwell Rd RBICN OX27 .... 77 J
Frog La CHNTN OX7 .... 102 J
    RBANSW OX15 .... 36 J
Frogmore La FGDN SN7 .... 232 ▢
    RAYLW HP18 .... 174 J
Frome Rd DID OX11 .... 285 J
Fruitlands WIT/EY OX8 .... 145 J
Frys Hl COW/LTMR OX4 .... 192 J
Fullbrook Crs CALC RG31 .... 331 ▢
Fullers Fld STAD OX44 .... 196 J
Fullers Rd DID OX11 .... 288 J
Fullwell Cl ABGD OX14 .... 214 J
Fullwell Rd BUCK/WIN MK18 .... 45 J
Fulmar Cl BIC OX26 .... 97 J3 ▢
Fulmar Pl WANT OX12 .... 258 D6 ▢
Fulmead Rd TLHT RG30 .... 332 J
Fulton Rd COTS GL54 .... 100 J
Fulwell Rd BRACKY NN13 .... 44 J
Furlong Cl COW/LTMR OX4 .... 192 J
Furlong Rw BUR/CRTN OX18 ... 183 A7 ▢
The Furlong WIT/EY OX8 .... 186 J
Fyfield Cl WANT OX12 .... 283 J
Fyfield Rd OXN/BOT/CM OX2 .... 4 J

G

The Gables HADM HP17 .... 176 J
Gadge Cl THAME OX9 .... 174 J
Gainsborough Crs HEN RG9 .... 318 J
Gainsborough Gn ABGD OX14 ...... 238 J
Gainsborough Hl HEN RG9 .... 319 J
Gainsborough Rd HEN RG9 .... 318 J
Gairn Cl TLHT RG30 .... 332 J
Gaisford Rd COW/LTMR OX4 .... 192 J
Gall Cl ABGD OX14 .... 215 J
Galley Fld ABGD OX14 .... 215 J
Gallows Br WANT OX12 .... 235 J
Galpin Cl COW/LTMR OX4 .... 168 A8 J
Galsworthy Dr CAV/SC RG4 .... 333 J
Gangsdown Hl HEN RG9 .... 293 J
The Gap MCHM/KBPZ OX13 .... 236 J
Gap Wy GOR/PANG RG8 .... 314 ▢
Garden Cl BAN OX16 .... 2 J
    DID OX11 .... 263 J
Gardens Cl SKCH HP14 .... 249 J
The Gardens ABGD OX14 .... 215 J
    GOR/PANG RG8 .... 312 J
Garde Rd CAV/SC RG4 .... 335 J
Gardiner Cl ABGD OX14 .... 215 J
    WHLY OX35 .... 170 J

ardiner St *HEAD* OX3 .... 168 D5
arford Cl *ABCD* OX14 .... 215 F5
arford Rd *OXN/BOT/CM* OX2 ...... 167 G2
arner's La *BUR/CRTN* OX18 .... 120 A8
arrard St *READ* RG1 .... 333 G7
arsington Rd *COW/LTMR* OX4 .... 192 D2
arston Cl *WANT* OX12 .... 282 E2
arston La *WANT* OX12 .... 282 E2
arth Rd *DID* OX11 .... 263 J6
he Garth *KID* OX5 .... 147 K2
   OXN/BOT/CM OX2 .... 166 B7 ▣
ascoigne Wy *RBANSW* OX15 .... 37 F5
askells End *CAV/SC* RG4 .... 326 D7
as La *CHNTN* OX7 .... 102 E7
assons Rd *CIR* GL7 .... 203 G2
as Works Rd *READ* RG1 .... 333 J8
atehampton Rd *GOR/PANG* RG8 .. 322 E1
athorne Rd *HEAD* OX3 .... 168 D5
aunflets Cl *RBANSW* OX15 .... 37 F2
aveston Gdns *RBANSW* OX15 .... 56 B3
aveston Rd *DID* OX11 .... 262 B8
avray Dr *BIC* OX26 .... 97 H6
aydon Ct *BUR/CRTN* OX18 .... 158 A4
aydon Wk *BIC* OX26 .... 97 H3 ▣
ayhurst Cl *CAV/SC* RG4 .... 333 K1
elt Burn *DID* OX11 .... 264 B5
entian Cl *COW/LTMR* OX4 .... 193 F5
eoffrey Barbour Rd *ABCD* OX14 .. 214 D7
eoffreyson Rd *CAV/SC* RG4 .... 332 D2 ▣
eoffrey Tuttle Dr *WGFD* OX10 ..... 267 K5
eorge Moore Cl *COW/LTMR* OX4 . 192 A1
eorge Rd *SKCH* HP14 .... 249 G2
eorge St *BAN* OX16 .... 3 D4
   BIC OX26 .... 96 E4
   OX/KTN OX1 .... 4 C4 ▣
   READ RG1 .... 333 F8
eorge Street Ms *OX/KTN* OX1 .... 4 B4
erard Pl *COW/LTMR* OX4 .... 192 C5 ▣
ermander Wy *BIC* OX26 .... 96 E2
errard St *COTS* GL54 .... 100 A4
ibbs Cl *SWDNE* SN3 .... 274 C8
ibbs Crs *OXN/BOT/CM* OX2 .... 4 A5
ibbs Rd *BAN* OX16 .... 3 E2
ibson Cl *ABCD* OX14 .... 214 E4
ibson Dr *RBICS/W* OX25 .... 76 A8
ibson La *HADM* HP17 .... 176 B2
idley Wy *WHLY* OX33 .... 170 A4
iernalls Rd *WIT/EY* OX8 .... 142 E1
ifford Cl *RBICS/W* OX25 .... 116 A3
   WGFD OX10 .... 312 B2
ilbe Cl *RBICS/W* OX25 .... 74 A2
ilbe Gdns *CAV/SC* RG4 .... 335 G4
   WANT OX12 .... 258 E6
ilebelands *BUR/CRTN* OX18 ...... 183 C3
   DID OX11 .... 168 D7
ilbe La *CAV/SC* RG4 .... 335 G4
ilbe Ride *GOR/PANG* RG8 .... 322 D1
ilbe Ri *RBANNS* OX17 .... 39 K2
ilbe St *COW/LTMR* OX4 .... 5 F4
he Glebe *ABGD* OX14 .... 239 F4
   HEN RG9 .... 316 E2
   OXN/BOT/CM OX2 .... 189 G2
   RBANNS OX17 .... 40 C8
   RBANSW OX15 .... 34 A7
   WANT OX12 .... 281 H2
   WHLY OX33 .... 170 D7
   WIT/EY OX8 .... 186 C3
len Cl *RBICN* OX27 .... 80 A6
lendevon Rd *WODY* RG5 .... 335 H7
lenham Rd *THAME* OX9 .... 175 H6
lenmore Rd *BUR/CRTN* OX18 .... 157 K2
lenrhondda *CAV/SC* RG4 .... 333 F2
lenrosa Rd *TLHT* RG30 .... 331 K7
levum Rd *SWDNE* SN5 .... 273 K8
limbers Gv *CHNR* OX39 .... 224 E1
loucester Pl *WIT/EY* OX8 .... 143 F6

Gloucester Rd *TLHT* RG30 .... 332 D8
Gloucester St *FGDN* SN7 .... 230 B3
   OX/KTN OX1 .... 4 C4 ▣
Glovers Cl *CHNTN* OX7 .... 68 B5
   WDSTK OX20 .... 127 K1
Glovers La *RBANNS* OX17 .... 22 D6
Glyme Cl *ABGD* OX14 .... 215 F6
   WDSTK OX20 .... 109 J8
Glyme Dr *WGFD* OX10 .... 241 K1
Glyme Wy *WIT/EY* OX8 .... 128 C7
Glympton Rd *WDSTK* OX20 .... 109 F1
Glyn Av *DID* OX11 .... 263 H6
Glyncastle *CAV/SC* RG4 .... 333 F2
Glyndebourne Gdns *BAN* OX16 .... 20 C6
Glyn Rd *WGFD* OX10 .... 267 F6
Glynswood *CHNR* OX39 .... 224 E1
Goddards La *CHNTN* OX7 .... 68 B3 ▣
Godfrey Cl *ABGD* OX14 .... 238 C1
Godfreys Cl *WANT* OX12 .... 258 E6
Godstow Cl *ABGD* OX14 .... 214 E4
Godstow Rd *OXN/BOT/CM* OX2 .. 148 A8
Godwyn Cl *ABGD* OX14 .... 214 C7
Goffe Rd *THAME* OX9 .... 175 G7
The Goggs *WTLON* OX49 .... 246 A6
Golafre Rd *ABGD* OX14 .... 238 C2
Goldcrest Wy *BIC* OX26 .... 97 G8
Golden Hills *CHNR* OX39 .... 225 F1
Golden La *CHNTN* OX7 .... 67 H2
Golden Rd *COW/LTMR* OX4 .... 168 A8
Golden Villa Cl *BAN* OX16 .... 2 A4 ▣
Golder's Cl *RAYLW* HP18 .... 172 D4
Goldfinch La *WGFD* OX10 .... 290 B4
Goldsmid Rd *READ* RG1 .... 333 F8
Goldsmith Cl *BIC* OX26 .... 96 D3 ▣
Goldsmith's La *WGFD* OX10 .... 267 F8
Gold St *STAD* OX44 .... 219 H1
Goodlake Av *FGDN* SN7 .... 230 C4
Goodliffe Gdns *CALC* RG31 .... 331 C3 ▣
Goodrich Cl *CAV/SC* RG4 .... 334 A2
Goodrington Cl *BAN* OX16 .... 2 B3
Goor La *MARL* SN8 .... 320 D3
Goosacre *BRACKY* NN13 .... 43 F1 ▣
   RBANSW OX15 .... 56 C4 ▣
Goose La *RBANSW* OX15 .... 29 F7
Goose Wk *RBANSW* OX15 .... 36 E3 ▣
Goosey La *FGDN* SN7 .... 256 E4
Gordon La *HEAD* OX3 .... 167 K2
Gordon Dr *ABGD* OX14 .... 215 G6
Gordon Pl *TLHT* RG30 .... 332 C7
Gordon Rd *RBICS/W* OX25 .... 76 A7
Gordon St *OX/KTN* OX1 .... 191 G1
Goring Rd *GOR/PANG* RG8 .... 314 B8
Gorse Dr *WODY* RG5 .... 335 J7 ▣
Gorselands *CAV/SC* RG4 .... 334 A8
Gorse Leas *HEAD* OX3 .... 168 B2 ▣
Gorwell *WTLON* OX49 .... 246 B6
Gosbrook Rd *CAV/SC* RG4 .... 333 J5 ▣
   READ RG1 .... 333 H5
Gosford Cl *KID* OX5 .... 148 D1
Goslyn Cl *HEAD* OX3 .... 168 D6 ▣
Gott Cl *RBICN* OX27 .... 97 H1
Gouldland Gdns *HEAD* OX3 .... 168 B3
Goulds Vls *BAN* OX16 .... 2 A4
Gower Rd *WANT* OX12 .... 258 A7
Gower St *READ* RG1 .... 332 E8
Grafton Orch *CHNR* OX39 .... 201 F8
Grafton Rd *TLHT* RG30 .... 331 H8
Graham Cl *DID* OX11 .... 287 K7
Grahame Av *GOR/PANG* RG8 ..... 330 B2
Graham Rd *BIC* OX26 .... 96 E4
Gramp's Hl *WANT* OX12 .... 303 H3
Granby Ct *READ* RG1 .... 334 A8
Granby Gdns *EARL* RG6 .... 334 A8
Grand Br *WDSTK* OX20 .... 127 G2
Grange Av *HEN* RG9 .... 317 G7
Grange Beck *DID* OX11 .... 264 A4 ▣
Grange Cl *GOR/PANG* RG8 .... 322 D2
   HGHW SN6 .... 250 E2
   RBANSW OX15 .... 9 K3
Grange Ct *OXN/BOT/CM* OX2 .... 165 K6
Grange Farm *SKCH* HP14 .... 225 J7
Grange La *RBANSW* OX15 .... 25 H8
Grange Pk *RBICS/W* OX25 .... 74 D6
Grange Rd *BAN* OX16 .... 28 E5
   COW/LTMR OX4 .... 192 B5
   HEN RG9 .... 319 G6
The Grange *CHNTN* OX7 .... 84 A3
Grants Ms *COW/LTMR* OX4 .... 5 F5
Granville Wy *BIC* OX26 .... 97 H5
Grasmere Av *TLHT* RG30 .... 331 K5
Grass Hl *CAV/SC* RG4 .... 332 A5
The Grates *COW/LTMR* OX4 .... 192 C3
Gratwicke Rd *TLHT* RG30 .... 331 J7
Gravel Cl *WGFD* OX10 .... 267 H3
Gravel Hl *CAV/SC* RG4 .... 332 E1
   HEN RG9 .... 327 F1
Gravel Hill Crs *HEN* RG9 .... 327 F1
Gravel La *ABGD* OX14 .... 237 K6
   WGFD OX10 .... 242 D8
Gravel Pits La *KID* OX5 .... 147 K1
Gravel Rd *CAV/SC* RG4 .... 328 B6
Gravel Wk *FGDN* SN7 .... 230 B3
Graveney Dr *CAV/SC* RG4 .... 332 E4
Gravenhill Rd North *RBICS/W* OX25 . 97 G8

Gravett Cl *HEN* RG9 .... 318 E7
Grays Cl *STAD* OX44 .... 220 A8
Grays Crs *WODY* RG5 .... 334 E7
Gray's La *MIM* GL56 .... 46 A2
   SKCH HP14 .... 248 E8
Grays Rd *HEAD* OX3 .... 168 B5
Great Clarendon St
   OXN/BOT/CM OX2 .... 4 B3
Great Close Rd *KID* OX5 .... 147 K2
Great Knollys St *READ* RG1 .... 333 F7
Great Md *OXN/BOT/CM* OX2 .... 4 B5 ▣
Great Western Dr *DID* OX11 .... 263 H5
Grebe Cl *ABGD* OX14 .... 238 D2
Grebe Rd *BAN* OX16 .... 3 E6
Green Acre Mt *TLHT* RG30 .... 331 H7 ▣
Greenacres *ABGD* OX14 .... 237 K5
Greenacres Dr *WANT* OX12 .... 282 C3 ▣
Greenacres La *BUR/CRTN* OX18 . 184 B4
Green Cl *BIC* OX26 .... 97 G5
   DID OX11 .... 263 K8
   MCHM/KBPZ OX13 .... 261 H2
   OXN/BOT/CM OX2 .... 266 E8 ▣
   WGFD OX10 .... 267 J2
Green Close Goose
   OXN/BOT/CM OX2 .... 148 C7 ▣
Green Dean Hl *CAV/SC* RG4 ...... 326 B5
Green Farm *RBANNS* OX17 .... 38 D5 ▣
Greenfield Crs *WGFD* OX10 .... 266 D8
   WIT/EY OX8 .... 107 J8
Greenfield Rd *WIT/EY* OX8 .... 107 J8
Greenfields *RBICS/W* OX25 .... 116 A8
   SWDNE SN5 .... 274 C2
Greenfinch Cl *COW/LTMR* OX4 .. 193 F6
Green Furlong *WGFD* OX10 .... 241 J2
Greenheart Wy
   MCHM/KBPZ OX13 .... 210 E6
Green Hl *COW/LTMR* OX4 .... 193 G5
Greenhills Pk *RBANSW* OX15 ...... 36 E3
Green Hitchings *STAD* OX44 ...... 196 A5
Green La *BAN* OX16 .... 3 D5
   BIC OX26 .... 96 A8
   CAV/SC RG4 .... 327 F2
   CHNTN OX7 .... 70 A1
   CHNTN OX7 .... 102 C6
   GOR/PANG RG8 .... 314 D8
   GOR/PANG RG8 .... 330 A2
   HEN RG9 .... 319 F7
   MCHM/KBPZ OX13 .... 210 C5
   MCHM/KBPZ OX13 .... 213 J2
   MIM GL56 .... 46 D8
   OXN/BOT/CM OX2 .... 165 J7
   RBANNS OX17 .... 40 D2
   RBANSW OX15 .... 26 A7
   RBANSW OX15 .... 36 A8
   RBICS/W OX25 .... 116 D8
   SKCH HP14 .... 248 E2
   WDSTK OX20 .... 109 J8
   WGFD OX10 .... 242 C7
   WGFD OX10 .... 268 B3
   WIT/EY OX8 .... 124 E8
Greenleas Av *CAV/SC* RG4 .... 327 H8
Greenmere *WGFD* OX10 .... 266 A4
Greenmoor *GOR/PANG* RG8 ...... 314 D7
The Green North *WGFD* OX10 ... 242 E7
Green Pl *OX/KTN* OX1 .... 191 H1
Green Ridges *HEAD* OX3 .... 169 G3
Green Rd *DID* OX11 .... 263 J8
   HEAD OX3 .... 169 F4
   KID OX5 .... 129 H7
   WGFD OX10 .... 266 D3
Greens Garth *RBANSW* OX15 ..... 37 G2 ▣
The Green South *WGFD* OX10 ... 242 E7
   WGFD OX10 .... 243 J8
Green's Rd *WIT/EY* OX8 .... 146 A7
Green St *COW/LTMR* OX4 .... 168 A7
The Greensward *RBANNS* OX17 .. 14 C6
The Green *BIC* OX26 .... 98 B5
   CHNTN OX7 .... 50 D4 ▣
   CHNTN OX7 .... 67 H2
   CHNTN OX7 .... 68 B5
   CHNTN OX7 .... 84 B2
   CHNTN OX7 .... 103 K5
   CHNTN OX7 .... 106 B3
   FGDN SN7 .... 254 E7
   FGDN SN7 .... 254 C3 ▣
   HGHW SN6 .... 250 E2 ▣
   HGHW SN6 .... 276 B1 ▣
   KID OX5 .... 110 E2
   MIM GL56 .... 46 A1 ▣
   RBANNS OX17 .... 13 F8
   RBANSW OX15 .... 18 C1
   RBANSW OX15 .... 34 A8 ▣
   RBANSW OX15 .... 36 A5
   STAD OX44 .... 194 D4
   STAD OX44 .... 194 A6
   STAD OX44 .... 195 K5
   STAD OX44 .... 244 B1
   WANT OX12 .... 234 A5
   WANT OX12 .... 234 C6
   WDSTK OX20 .... 127 J5 ▣
   WHLY OX33 .... 152 C2
   WIT/EY OX8 .... 125 J5
   WIT/EY OX8 .... 146 E5
   WIT/EY OX8 .... 163 G7
Greenway *HADM* HP17 .... 176 B2

RBICS/W OX25 .... 93 K3
THAME OX9 .... 175 F6
The Greenway WANT OX12 .... 260 D8
Greenwich La WIT/EY OX8 .... 122 E4
Greenwood Av CHNR OX39 .... 224 E2
Greenwood Dr BIC OX26 .... 96 C4
Greenwood Meadow CHNR OX39 .. 224 E1
Grenoble Rd COW/LTMR OX4 ...... 192 B7
Grenville Wy THAME OX9 .... 175 H6
Gresham Wy TLHT RG30 .... 332 A5
Greyfriars Rd READ RG1 .... 333 G7
Greygoose La MIM GL56 .... 66 C1
Greyhound La THAME OX9 .... 175 F6
Greys Cl BAN OX16 .... 28 B1
Greys Ct READ RG1 .... 333 J8
Greys Hl HEN RG9 .... 319 F6
Greys Rd HEN RG9 .... 318 E7
Greystoke Rd CAV/SC RG4 .... 333 J3
Greystones Cl KID OX5 .... 129 G6
Griffin Rd THAME OX9 .... 175 H7
Griffiths Cl WIT/EY OX8 .... 187 J4 🔢
Griffiths Gdns RBICN OX27 .... 79 G8
Grimmer Wy GOR/PANG RG8 .... 314 D7
Grimsbury Dr BAN OX16 .... 3 E2
Grimsbury Gn BAN OX16 .... 3 D1
Grimsbury Sq BAN OX16 .... 3 E2
Grosvenor Rd BAN OX16 .... 3 D4 🔢
CAV/SC RG4 .... 333 J4
OXN/BOT/CM OX2 .... 190 C1
Ground CHNTN OX7 .... 101 H5 🔢
Grove Ct RBANSW OX15 .... 56 C5 🔢
Grove Hl CAV/SC RG4 .... 333 G3
HGHW SN6 .... 226 E8
Groveland Pl TLHT RG30 .... 332 B7 🔢
Grovelands KID OX5 .... 129 G7 🔢
Grovelands Rd HEAD OX3 .... 169 G5
TLHT RG30 .... 332 B7
Grove La CHNTN OX7 .... 87 H7
WGFD OX10 .... 268 D1
Grove Orch HGHW SN6 .... 226 D8
Grove Park Dr WANT OX12 .... 259 G4
Grove Rd CAV/SC RG4 .... 327 F2
CAV/SC RG4 .... 333 H2
DID OX11 .... 262 A2
HEN RG9 .... 319 G6 🔢
WANT OX12 .... 282 E1
WDSTK OX20 .... 127 K4
Grove St BAN OX16 .... 3 D4
OXN/BOT/CM OX2 .... 149 K4
WANT OX12 .... 282 D5
The Grove ABGD OX14 .... 215 F5
HGHW SN6 .... 276 A5
MIM GL56 .... 46 B2 🔢
RBANSW OX15 .... 56 C3
READ RG1 .... 333 J8
Grundy Cl ABGD OX14 .... 215 F7
Grundy Crs OX/KTN OX1 .... 191 J7
Grunsell Cl HEAD OX3 .... 168 A2
Guernsey Wy BAN OX16 .... 20 B6
Guildenford BUR/CRTN OX18 ...... 138 E2 🔢
Gullicott La RBANNS OX17 .... 20 A3
Gulliver's Cl RBANSW OX15 .... 19 H3
Gun St READ RG1 .... 333 G8
Gurden Pl HEAD OX3 .... 168 E3 🔢
Gurl Cl HEAD OX3 .... 168 E3 🔢
Gurney Cl CAV/SC RG4 .... 332 D2
Gurney Dr CAV/SC RG4 .... 332 D3 🔢
Gwyneth Rd COW/LTMR OX4 .... 192 A5
Gwynne Cl CALC RG31 .... 331 H4

H

Hackers La CHNTN OX7 .... 85 F3
Haddenham Rd WHAM HP17 .... 176 C5
Hadden Hl DID OX11 .... 264 D6
Haddon Dr WODY RG5 .... 335 G7
Hadland Rd ABGD OX14 .... 215 G7
Hadleigh Ri CAV/SC RG4 .... 334 A2
Hadow Rd HEAD OX3 .... 168 A3
Hadrians Cl SWDNE SN3 .... 274 A6
Hafod CAV/SC RG4 .... 333 F1
Hagbourne Cl GOR/PANG RG8 ..... 314 D7 🔢
Hagbourne Rd DID OX11 .... 264 A6 🔢
DID OX11 .... 288 C5
Hailey Av THAME OX9 .... 68 A6
Hailey Crs CHNTN OX7 .... 68 B6 🔢
Hailey Cft CHNR OX39 .... 224 D1 🔢
Hailey Rd CHNTN OX7 .... 68 A6
WIT/EY OX8 .... 142 E1
Haines Ct MCHM/KBPZ OX13 ...... 237 F1
Halcyon Ter TLHT RG30 .... 331 J7 🔢
Haldane Rd CAV/SC RG4 .... 332 E2
COW/LTMR OX4 .... 193 F4 🔢
Hale Rd WGFD OX10 .... 267 H1
Halfpenny La WGFD OX10 .... 312 A2
Halifax Rd BIC OX26 .... 97 H4
Hall Cl WTLGN OX49 .... 246 B3
The Hall Cl RBICS/W OX25 .... 74 E1
Hallett Cl WANT OX12 .... 282 E1
Halliday Hl HEAD OX3 .... 168 B2
Halls Cl ABGD OX14 .... 238 A6

OXN/BOT/CM OX2 .... 166 A8
Hall's La BRACKY NN13 .... 43 F1
WANT OX12 .... 235 H8
Halse Water DID OX11 .... 264 A5
Halstead Cl WODY RG5 .... 335 G8
Halton Rd BUR/CRTN OX18 .... 158 B5
Hambleden Dr WGFD OX10 .... 266 D7
Hamble Dr ABGD OX14 .... 215 F6
Hamble Rd DID OX11 .... 264 A6
Hambleside BIC OX26 .... 96 C5
Hambridge La CIR GL7 .... 203 G2
Hamels La OX/KTN OX1 .... 190 D6
The Hamel OX/KTN OX1 .... 4 E4 🔢
Hamfield WANT OX12 .... 282 C3
Hamilton Av HEN RG9 .... 319 G6
Hamilton Rd OXN/BOT/CM OX2 ... 149 F8
THAME OX9 .... 175 G6
Ham La BUR/CRTN OX18 .... 184 C6
The Hamlet CAV/SC RG4 .... 326 B2
Hamlyn Rd WANT OX12 .... 282 A5 🔢
Hammer La WGFD OX10 .... 242 C6
Hammersmith Bottom CIR GL7 ... 178 A2
Hampden Av THAME OX9 .... 175 F8
Hampden Cl BAN OX16 .... 28 B2
BIC OX26 .... 97 H4
STAD OX44 .... 244 B1 🔢
Hampden Dr KID OX5 .... 148 D1
Hampden Rd CAV/SC RG4 .... 333 H5
COW/LTMR OX4 .... 192 C3
WANT OX12 .... 282 E2
Hampden Wy WGFD OX10 .... 268 D3
Hampton Dr RBANNS OX17 .... 39 J1
Ham Rd WANT OX12 .... 282 C3
Hamstyles WTLGN OX49 .... 245 J8
Hanborough Cl WIT/EY OX8 .... 146 A7
Hanborough Rd WIT/EY OX8 .... 146 A7
Handlo Pl HEAD OX3 .... 169 F3 🔢
Hanney Rd MCHM/KBPZ OX13 ..... 210 D8
WANT OX12 .... 236 B8
Hannis Rd CHNTN OX7 .... 68 A6
Hanover Gdns BIC OX26 .... 97 F6
Hans Av WANT OX12 .... 282 E2
Hanson Rd ABGD OX14 .... 214 D4
Hanwood Cl WODY RG5 .... 334 E7
Harberton Md HEAD OX3 .... 5 F2
Harbord Rd OXN/BOT/CM OX2 ..... 148 E5
Harborne Rd KID OX5 .... 111 F2
Harcourt Cl HEN RG9 .... 318 E6
Harcourt Gn WANT OX12 .... 283 F2
Harcourt Hl OXN/BOT/CM OX2 .... 190 B2
Harcourt Rd WANT OX12 .... 282 E2
Harcourt Ter HEAD OX3 .... 168 B5
Harcourt Wy ABGD OX14 .... 214 D6
WANT OX12 .... 282 E1
Harding Cl FGDN SN7 .... 230 C4
Harding Rd ABGD OX14 .... 214 B7
WODY RG5 .... 334 E7
Hardings STAD OX44 .... 244 B1
Hardings Cl COW/LTMR OX4 .... 192 B4 🔢
Hardings Strings DID OX11 .... 263 J8
Hardwell Cl WANT OX12 .... 258 D6
Hardwick Av KID OX5 .... 129 H8
Hardwick Pk BAN OX16 .... 20 B6
Hardwick Rd GOR/PANG RG8 ...... 324 B8
RBICN OX27 .... 61 G8
TLHT RG30 .... 331 K8
Hardy Cl CAV/SC RG4 .... 333 J5
Harebell Rd COW/LTMR OX4 .... 193 F5
Harecourt WANT OX12 .... 283 F2
Harefields OXN/BOT/CM OX2 ...... 149 F6
Harewood Rd BAN OX16 .... 29 G5 🔢
Harlech Av CAV/SC RG4 .... 334 A2
Harlech Cl BAN OX16 .... 28 B2
Harlequin Wy BAN OX16 .... 20 D6
Harley Rd OXN/BOT/CM OX2 ...... 166 D6
READ RG1 .... 333 H5
Harlington Av WANT OX12 .... 258 E6
Harlow Wy HEAD OX3 .... 149 K8
Harmon Cl RBICN OX27 .... 97 H1 🔢
Harolde Cl HEAD OX3 .... 168 D3
Harold Hicks Pl COW/LTMR OX4 .. 191 K1 🔢
Harolds Cl WIT/EY OX8 .... 142 E1
Harold White Cl HEAD OX3 .... 169 F5 🔢
Harper Cl RBICS/W OX25 .... 116 A8
Harpes Rd OXN/BOT/CM OX2 ...... 149 F7
Harpsden Rd HEN RG9 .... 319 G7
Harpsden Wy HEN RG9 .... 319 G8
Harpsichord Pl COW/LTMR OX4 ... 5 F4 🔢
Harrier Pk DID OX11 .... 263 H4
The Harriers SWDNE SN3 .... 274 A8
Harriers Vw BAN OX16 .... 2 C5
Harrier Wy BIC OX26 .... 97 H3
Harris Cl WODY RG5 .... 335 K7
Harrison Pl THAME OX9 .... 175 H6 🔢
Harrison's La WDSTK OX20 .... 127 H1 🔢
Harris Rd RBICS/W OX25 .... 76 A8
Harris's La MCHM/KBPZ OX13 ..... 210 C5
Harrisville RBICS/W OX25 .... 74 E7
Harroell RAYLW HP18 .... 174 D1
Harrogate Rd CAV/SC RG4 .... 332 E3
Harrowby Rd BAN OX16 .... 29 F5
Harrow Rd COW/LTMR OX4 .... 193 F4
Hart Av FGDN SN7 .... 230 B4 🔢
Hart Cl ABGD OX14 .... 215 G7
Hartigan Pl WODY RG5 .... 335 J7 🔢

Hartley Cl WGFD OX10 .... 266 D7
Hart Pl BIC OX26 .... 97 F3
Harts Cl KID OX5 .... 129 G6
Hartslock Vw GOR/PANG RG8 ..... 323 G3
Hartslock Wy CALC RG31 .... 331 G5
Harts Rd HADM HP17 .... 176 D5
Hart St OXN/BOT/CM OX2 .... 4 B1 🔢
WGFD OX10 .... 267 F8
Harvard Cl WODY RG5 .... 335 K8
Harwell Cl ABGD OX14 .... 214 E6
Harwell Rd ABGD OX14 .... 262 D1
Harwood Rd DID OX11 .... 237 H4
Haseley Rd STAD OX44 .... 219 H7
Haslemere Wy BAN OX16 .... 2 E5
Hastings Dr BUR/CRTN OX18 .... 158 E1
Hastings Hl CHNTN OX7 .... 85 F7
Hastings Rd BAN OX16 .... 20 E1
Hatch Cl KID OX5 .... 111 G4
Hatch End KID OX5 .... 111 G5
Hatchet Hl WOO/WRO SN4 .... 298 A8
Hatching La WIT/EY OX8 .... 122 C1
Hatch Wy KID OX5 .... 111 G5
Hatfield Pits La WIT/EY OX8 .... 143 G2
Hathaways WHLY OX33 .... 170 D7
Hatherhall Cl SWDNE SN3 .... 274 A8
Havelock Rd COW/LTMR OX4 .... 192 C6
Haven Cl WGFD OX10 .... 241 K6
Havers Av ABGD OX14 .... 262 E5
Hawke La RBANSW OX15 .... 36 E3
Hawker Sq COTS CL54 .... 100 A5
Hawkes La RBANSW OX15 .... 25 F5
Hawkins St COW/LTMR OX4 .... 5 F6 🔢
Hawkins Wy MCHM/KBPZ OX13 ... 213 J7
Hawksmead BIC OX26 .... 97 H7
Hawksmoor Rd OXN/BOT/CM OX2 ... 149 F2 🔢
Hawkswell Gdns
    OXN/BOT/CM OX2 .... 149 G4
Hawkswood SWDNE SN3 .... 274 A8
Hawksworth DID OX11 .... 263 H6
Hawksworth Cl WANT OX12 .... 258 D6 🔢
Hawthorn Av HEAD OX3 .... 168 C5
    THAME OX9 .... 174 E8
Hawthorn Cl WGFD OX10 .... 266 E7
Hawthorn Crs WANT OX12 .... 258 E7
Hawthorn Dr BUR/CRTN OX18 ..... 138 E7
Hawthorne Av MCHM/KBPZ OX13 ... 213 J7
Hawthorne Cl
    OXN/BOT/CM OX2 .... 166 B7
Hawthorne Rd CAV/SC RG4 .... 334 A3
Hawthornes CALC RG31 .... 331 F5 🔢
Hawthorn Gv BUR/CRTN OX18 ..... 157 K6
Hawthorn Rd FGDN SN7 .... 230 A4 🔢
    WIT/EY OX8 .... 146 A4
The Hawthorns BAN OX16 .... 3 D4 🔢
    WAR/TWY RG10 .... 335 J8 🔢
Hawthorn Wy CAV/SC RG4 .... 335 J8
    KID OX5 .... 129 H8 🔢
Hayden La HEN RG9 .... 294 B1
Haydon La KSCL RG20 .... 308 C6
Haydon Rd DID OX11 .... 263 K6
Hayes Av MCHM/KBPZ OX13 .... 210 C1
Hayes Cl HEAD OX3 .... 5 F2
Hayfield Cl CALC RG31 .... 331 G3
Hayfield Rd OXN/BOT/CM OX2 ..... 167 F1 🔢
Haynes Rd HEAD OX3 .... 167 H4
Hay Pool RBANNS OX17 .... 6 E4 🔢
Hay's Br RBANNS OX17 .... 14 E1
Hayward Dr BUR/CRTN OX18 ...... 157 K6
Hayward Rd OXN/BOT/CM OX2 .... 148 E5
Haywards Cl HEN RG9 .... 318 E6
    WANT OX12 .... 282 E2 🔢
Haywards Rd ABGD OX14 .... 237 F5
Haywood Ct EARL RG6 .... 334 E8
Hazel Av THAME OX9 .... 174 E8
Hazelbury Crs SWDNE SN3 .... 274 A8
Hazel Crs KID OX5 .... 148 C5
Hazeldene Gdns BAN OX16 .... 3 D4 🔢
Hazel Gdns CAV/SC RG4 .... 327 F4
Hazel Gv BIC OX26 .... 97 G2
    WGFD OX10 .... 266 E8 🔢
Hazells La CIR GL7 .... 180 D7
    HGHW SN6 .... 276 C2
Hazelmoor La CAV/SC RG4 .... 326 C1
Hazelnut Pth ABGD OX14 .... 191 J8 🔢
Hazelrig Cl THAME OX9 .... 175 G5 🔢
Hazel Rd CALC RG31 .... 331 G2
    OXN/BOT/CM OX2 .... 166 A7
Hazelton Cl THAME OX9 .... 174 E7 🔢
Hazelwood Cl CALC RG31 .... 331 G6
Headington Rd HEAD OX3 .... 5 J7
Headley Cl WODY RG5 .... 335 J7
Headley Rd WODY RG5 .... 335 J7
Headley Rd East WODY RG5 .... 335 J7
Headley Wy HEAD OX3 .... 168 E5
Healey Cl ABGD OX14 .... 238 C6
Hean Cl ABGD OX14 .... 215 J6
Hearns La CAV/SC RG4 .... 326 A6
Hearthway BAN OX16 .... 2 E3
Heath Br RBICN OX27 .... 117 K7
Heath Cl HEAD OX3 .... 168 D4
    RBANSW OX15 .... 36 E3
Heathcote Av BAN OX16 .... 29 G6
Heathcote Pl ABGD OX14 .... 215 G6
Heath Dr CAV/SC RG4 .... 328 E8
Heather Cl BUR/CRTN OX18 .... 158 C2

CAV/SC RG4 ... 327 F2
leather Pl HEAD OX3 ... 5 F1
leather Rd BIC OX26 ... 97 F2
leathfield Av HEN RG9 ... 328 D5
TLHT RG30 ... 331 H8
leathfield Cl HEN RG9 ... 328 D5
leath La WDSTK OX20 ... 127 J5
leathway CALC RG31 ... 331 G7 ☑
ledge End WDSTK OX20 ... 127 K2
ledgerley CHNR OX39 ... 224 D1
he Hedges RBANSW OX15 ... 18 B7
lelen Rd OXN/BOT/CM OX2 ... 166 D6
len's Wy WCFD OX10 ... 267 H4
lelmsdale Cl TLHT RG30 ... 332 B7
lelwys Pl KID OX5 ... 129 G5
lemdean Hl CAV/SC RG4 ... 333 G4
lemdean Ri CAV/SC RG4 ... 333 G4
lemdean Rd CAV/SC RG4 ... 333 G3
lemingway Dr BIC OX26 ... 96 D5
lempton Rd RBANSW OX15 ... 56 B3
lendon Pl BIC OX26 ... 97 H3 ☑
lendred St COW/LTMR OX4 ... 192 B2
lendred Wy ABGD OX14 ... 215 F6
lengest Ga DID OX11 ... 262 C8
lengrove Cl HEAD OX3 ... 168 D3
lenley Av CAV/SC RG4 ... 192 A2
lenley Dr HGHW SN6 ... 226 E8
lenley Rd CAV/SC RG4 ... 333 H4
COW/LTMR OX4 ... 192 B7
HEN RG9 ... 328 E7
WCFD OX10 ... 241 K7
lenleys La ABGD OX14 ... 237 K6
lenley St COW/LTMR OX4 ... 5 F6
lennef Wy BAN OX16 ... 3 E1
lenor Mill Cl ABGD OX14 ... 215 F5 ☑
lenrietta Rd THAME OX9 ... 175 G6
lenry OXN/BOT/CM OX2 ... 4 A4
lenry Taunt Cl HEAD OX3 ... 168 E2
lensington Cl WDSTK OX20 ... 127 K1
lensington Rd WDSTK OX20 ... 127 J1
lenwood Dr OX/KTN OX1 ... 189 J6
lerald Wy BIC OX26 ... 97 H3
lerbert Cl COW/LTMR OX4 ... 168 B8
lereford Wy BAN OX16 ... 20 B6
leritage La CHNTN OX7 ... 103 J5
lerman Cl ABGD OX14 ... 215 F7
lermitage Rd ABGD OX14 ... 238 D1
lernes Rd OXN/BOT/CM OX2 ... 149 F7
leron Cl BUR/CRTN OX18 ... 157 J4
leron Cl ABGD OX14 ... 238 D3
BIC OX26 ... 97 J6 ☑
leron Dr BIC OX26 ... 97 J6
leron Island CAV/SC RG4 ... 333 J6
leron Rd CAV/SC RG4 ... 268 B4
leronscroft SWDNE SN3 ... 274 B8
leron Shaw GOR/PANG RG8 ... 312 E8 ☑
leron's Wk ABGD OX14 ... 214 D6
leron Wy BAN OX16 ... 2 A5
lerriefs Farm Rd BRACKY NN13 ... 43 C2
lerringcote WCFD OX10 ... 241 K5 ☑
lerschel Crs COW/LTMR OX4 ... 192 C4
lertford Cl BIC OX26 ... 97 G4
CAV/SC RG4 ... 333 K1
lertford St COW/LTMR OX4 ... 168 A8
lethe Rd BRACKY NN13 ... 61 H4
RBICN OX27 ... 60 E7
lewett Av CAV/SC RG4 ... 332 D3
lewett Cl CAV/SC RG4 ... 332 D3
lewetts Cl WIT/EY OX8 ... 122 D4
lewetts Cl WIT/EY OX8 ... 122 D4
leycroft WIT/EY OX8 ... 146 A8
leydons Terr RBANSW OX17 ... 6 A7
leyford Cl WIT/EY OX8 ... 186 C2
leyford La COW/LTMR OX4 ... 191 K5
leyford Md KID OX5 ... 129 G6 ☑
leyford Rd KID OX5 ... 111 J3
RBICS/W OX25 ... 74 E7
RBICS/W OX25 ... 95 F3
licks Cl WIT/EY OX8 ... 142 E1 ☑
lid's Copse Rd OXN/BOT/CM OX2 ... 165 J8
ligh Acres BAN OX16 ... 3 E5
lighbridge Cl CAV/SC RG4 ... 334 A2
lighbridge Whf READ RG1 ... 333 H8 ☑
lighbury Rd CALC RG31 ... 330 E8
lighclere Gdns BAN OX16 ... 28 A1
WANT OX12 ... 282 D1 ☑
lighcliffe Vw WODY RG5 ... 335 H6
ligh Cross Wy HEAD OX3 ... 168 E2 ☑
lighdown Av CAV/SC RG4 ... 333 F5
lighdown Hill Rd CAV/SC RG4 ... 327 G8
lighfield RAYLW HP18 ... 174 C1
lighfield Av HEAD OX3 ... 168 C5
lighfield Cl THAME OX9 ... 174 C7
lighfield Cl BRACKY NN13 ... 43 F1 ☑
lighfield Rd CALC RG31 ... 331 F3
ligh Furlong BAN OX16 ... 2 B1
ligh House Cl BUR/CRTN OX18 ... 182 A7
ligh Land Cl RAYLW HP18 ... 135 K6
lighlands BAN OX16 ... 20 B6
lighlands La HEN RG9 ... 318 C8
ligh Meadow CAV/SC RG4 ... 332 D4

RBANSW OX15 ... 24 E6
Highmoor Rd CAV/SC RG4 ... 333 F4
High Rd WGFD OX10 ... 266 A4
High St ABGD OX14 ... 214 D8
ABGD OX14 ... 238 E8
ABGD OX14 ... 238 A6
ABGD OX14 ... 240 C4
ABGD OX14 ... 262 A3
BAN OX16 ... 2 C4
BRACKY NN13 ... 41 H7
BRACKY NN13 ... 43 G1
BUR/CRTN OX18 ... 183 H4
BUR/CRTN OX18 ... 184 B5
CAV/SC RG4 ... 335 F4
CHNR OX39 ... 201 F8
CHNR OX39 ... 224 C4
CHNTN OX7 ... 50 D4
CHNTN OX7 ... 68 B4
CHNTN OX7 ... 101 G5
CHNTN OX7 ... 102 E7
CHNTN OX7 ... 102 B7
CHNTN OX7 ... 102 E2
CHNTN OX7 ... 103 K5
CHNTN OX7 ... 123 K4
CIR GL7 ... 203 G4
DID OX11 ... 263 K7
DID OX11 ... 265 G8
DID OX11 ... 286 C1
DID OX11 ... 287 G5
FGDN SN7 ... 209 K5
FGDN SN7 ... 232 C8
FGDN SN7 ... 255 F8
GOR/PANG RG8 ... 322 C1
GOR/PANG RG8 ... 324 C8
HADM HP17 ... 176 B1
HADM HP17 ... 178 E1
HEAD OX3 ... 151 G4
HEN RG9 ... 294 D5
HGHW SN6 ... 250 E2
HGHW SN6 ... 252 D7
HGHW SN6 ... 276 B1
HGHW SN6 ... 277 G8
HGHW SN6 ... 298 D3
KID OX5 ... 129 H6
KID OX5 ... 130 E6
KID OX5 ... 132 B5
OX/KTN OX1 ... 5 D4
OXN/BOT/CM OX2 ... 189 F2
RAYLW HP18 ... 135 K7
RAYLW HP18 ... 174 D1
RBANNS OX17 ... 13 H5
RBANNS OX17 ... 22 D7
RBANNS OX17 ... 38 D3
RBANSW OX15 ... 10 A4
RBANSW OX15 ... 26 A2
RBANSW OX15 ... 33 K8
RBANSW OX15 ... 36 A8
RBANSW OX15 ... 37 F5
RBANSW OX15 ... 55 G2
RBANSW OX15 ... 56 C3
RBICN OX27 ... 58 D3
RBICS/W OX25 ... 75 J7
STAD OX44 ... 194 D5
STAD OX44 ... 220 A8
THAME OX9 ... 174 E6
THAME OX9 ... 198 B7
WANT OX12 ... 281 J5
WANT OX12 ... 284 A2
WANT OX12 ... 285 F1
WDSTK OX20 ... 109 G3
WDSTK OX20 ... 127 H1
WGFD OX10 ... 241 K6
WGFD OX10 ... 242 D2
WGFD OX10 ... 267 F8
WGFD OX10 ... 267 H3
WGFD OX10 ... 268 C3
WHLY OX33 ... 170 C7
WIT/EY OX8 ... 107 H8
WIT/EY OX8 ... 143 F7
WIT/EY OX8 ... 146 A8
WIT/EY OX8 ... 186 C5
WTLGN OX49 ... 223 H7
WTLGN OX49 ... 246 B5
Hightown Gdns BAN OX16 ... 3 D5
Hightown Leyes BAN OX16 ... 3 D6
Hightown Rd BAN OX16 ... 3 D5
High Vw WANT OX12 ... 282 A1
Highworth Pl WIT/EY OX8 ... 142 E8
Highworth Wy FGDN SN7 ... 230 A5
HGHW SN6 ... 250 A8
HGHW SN6 ... 250 B6
HGHW SN6 ... 251 J5
HGHW SN6 ... 252 A7
SWDNE SN3 ... 250 B8
Highworth Wy CALC RG31 ... 331 F5
Hilcot Rd TLHT RG30 ... 332 D7
Hildens Dr CALC RG31 ... 331 G8
Hillary Dr DID OX11 ... 263 J8
Hillary Wy WHLY OX33 ... 170 E8
Hill Bottom Cl GOR/PANG RG8 ... 324 C4
Hill Cl CHNTN OX7 ... 68 B6
CHNTN OX7 ... 106 B4
WANT OX12 ... 282 A3
Hillcraft Rd WHLY OX33 ... 151 K8
Hill Crs CHNTN OX7 ... 124 B2

Hillcrest La HEN RG9 ... 317 F8
Hill Farm Ct CHNR OX39 ... 225 F1
Hill Farm La RBICS/W OX25 ... 74 A1
Hill Gdns GOR/PANG RG8 ... 322 C1
Hilliat Flds ABGD OX14 ... 237 K6
Hilliers Cl ABGD OX14 ... 238 D7
Hill Piece DID OX11 ... 286 C8
Hill Ri CHNTN OX7 ... 50 D4
WDSTK OX20 ... 109 H7
WHLY OX33 ... 193 K1
Hill Rd CHNR OX39 ... 225 F1
HGHW SN6 ... 252 D6
WTLGN OX49 ... 223 G8
WTLGN OX49 ... 246 C6
WTLGN OX49 ... 247 J1
Hillsborough Rd COW/LTMR OX4 ... 192 B3
Hillside DID OX11 ... 285 J4
GOR/PANG RG8 ... 324 B7
OXN/BOT/CM OX2 ... 189 J1
Hillside Cl BAN OX16 ... 3 E6
RBICS/W OX25 ... 116 D8
Hillside Rd CHNTN OX7 ... 73 F6
The Hill HGHW SN6 ... 276 A4
STAD OX44 ... 194 A6
Hilltop RAYLW HP18 ... 174 D2
Hilltop Gdns KID OX5 ... 130 E6
Hill Top La CHNR OX39 ... 225 H3
Hill Top Rd COW/LTMR OX4 ... 168 B3
Hilltop Rd CAV/SC RG4 ... 332 D2
EARL RG6 ... 334 D7
Hill Vw BUR/CRTN OX18 ... 157 K5
FGDN SN7 ... 254 E8 ☑
HEAD OX3 ... 169 G3
WANT OX12 ... 279 K5
Hillview Cl CALC RG31 ... 331 F5
Hill View Crs BAN OX16 ... 20 B8
Hill View La MCHM/KBPZ OX13 ... 189 J7
Hillview Rd ABGD OX14 ... 214 D5
OXN/BOT/CM OX2 ... 4 A4
Hill View Rd SWDNE SN3 ... 274 A6 ☑
Hilton Rd BAN OX16 ... 2 B3
Hinksey Hl OX/KTN OX1 ... 191 F4
Hinton Hl WOO/WRO SN4 ... 298 A4
Hinton Rd BRACKY NN13 ... 43 F1
FGDN SN7 ... 210 A5
Hinton Springs HGHW SN6 ... 298 B3
Hirstwood TLHT RG30 ... 331 J6 ☑
Hiskins WANT OX12 ... 282 B2
Hithercroft Rd WGFD OX10 ... 266 C8
WGFD OX10 ... 289 K1
Hixet Wd CHNTN OX7 ... 106 A4
Hobbs Cl ABGD OX14 ... 215 F7 ☑
Hobby Ct COW/LTMR OX4 ... 193 F6 ☑
Hobbyhorse La ABGD OX14 ... 239 F8
Hobson Rd OXN/BOT/CM OX2 ... 149 F8
Hocketts Cl GOR/PANG RG8 ... 324 C4
Hockmore St COW/LTMR OX4 ... 192 C5
Hodges Ct OX/KTN OX1 ... 4 C6 ☑
Hodgson Cl RBICN OX27 ... 58 E8
Hodsoll Rd READ RG1 ... 333 F7
Hogarth Pl ABGD OX14 ... 238 C2
Hogg End RBANNS OX17 ... 14 D1
RBANSW OX15 ... 37 F3
Hogg La RBANNS OX17 ... 40 E2
Holborn Hl WANT OX12 ... 281 H8
Holcombe La WGFD OX10 ... 243 F1
Holford Cl CALC RG31 ... 331 G2 ☑
Holford Rd WIT/EY OX8 ... 142 D8
Holkam Cl TLHT RG30 ... 331 K6 ☑
Holland Cl CHNR OX39 ... 201 F7 ☑
Holland Pl HEAD OX3 ... 168 E7 ☑
Hollandridge La HEN RG9 ... 271 K4
Holland Ri RBANNS OX17 ... 39 J3
Holland Rd TLHT RG30 ... 331 H8
Holley Crs HEAD OX3 ... 168 D4
Hollicombe Cl TLHT RG30 ... 331 J8 ☑
Holliers Cl CHNR OX39 ... 199 K7
THAME OX9 ... 174 E7
Holliers Crs CHNTN OX7 ... 73 G7
Hollington RAYLW HP18 ... 174 B1
Hollis Cl WIT/EY OX8 ... 143 H8
Holloway La HEN RG9 ... 272 C2
Holloway Rd WHLY OX33 ... 170 D7
WIT/EY OX8 ... 142 E7
The Holloway Rd FGDN SN7 ... 229 H8
The Holloway DID OX11 ... 286 C1
RBANNS OX17 ... 12 C4
Hollow Furlong WIT/EY OX8 ... 146 E5
Hollow Wy COW/LTMR OX4 ... 192 D1 ☑
DID OX11 ... 287 G6
RBANNS OX17 ... 40 B8
WANT OX12 ... 281 G5
Hollybush Rd BUR/CRTN OX18 ... 157 K5 ☑
RBANSW OX15 ... 34 A7
Hollybush Rw OX/KTN OX1 ... 4 B4
Holly Cl BIC OX26 ... 97 G2 ☑
HEN RG9 ... 316 E2
Holly Green La PRRI HP27 ... 201 J4
Holmemoor Dr CAV/SC RG4 ... 335 F5
Holme Park Farm La CAV/SC RG4 ... 334 E5
Holmlea Rd GOR/PANG RG8 ... 322 E2
Holm Wy BIC OX26 ... 97 G2
The Holt ABGD OX14 ... 214 D7
RBANNS OX17 ... 12 B4

Holy Cl *KID* OX5 .... 129 H8
Holyoake Rd *HEAD* OX3 .... 168 D4
Holyrood Cl *CAV/SC* RG4 .... 333 K1
Holywell Cl *ABGD* OX14 .... 215 G5 ▣
Holywell St *OX/KTN* OX1 .... 5 D3
Home Cl *BUR/CRTN* OX18 .... 157 K5
   KID OX5 .... 129 H6
   MCHM/KBPZ OX15 .... 189 H8
   MCHM/KBPZ OX15 .... 213 K1
   MIM GL56 .... 64 C6
   OXN/BOT/CM OX2 .... 148 B7
   RBANNS OX17 .... 23 F7
Home Cft *CALC* RG31 .... 331 F6
Homefarm *HGHW* SN6 .... 250 D1
Homelands Wy *HEN* RG9 .... 319 F6 ▣
Home Farm *WGFD* OX10 .... 267 H8 ▣
Home Farm Ct *CHNTN* OX7 .... 102 E8
   RBICS/W OX25 .... 115 K3
   WANT OX12 .... 261 F8
Home Farm Ct *RBANNS* OX17 .... 38 E3
Homefield Cl *SKCH* HP14 .... 249 G2 ▣
Homelands Wy *HEN* RG9 .... 319 F6 ▣
Homeleaze Rd *HGHW* SN6 .... 252 E7
Homestall Cl *OXN/BOT/CM* OX2 ..... 165 K6
Homestead Rd *BAN* OX16 .... 29 G5 ▣
   WDSTK OX20 .... 127 K4
The Homestead *KID* OX5 .... 129 G7 ▣
   WDSTK OX20 .... 127 K4
Honeybottom La
   MCHM/KBPZ OX13 .... 213 H3
Honeyham Cl *BUR/CRTN* OX18 .... 158 E4
Honey La *WGFD* OX10 .... 290 B6
Honey Meadow Cl *CAV/SC* RG4 .... 334 A5
Honeysuckle Cl *BIC* OX26 .... 97 G2 ▣
Honeysuckle Gv
   COW/LTMR OX4 .... 193 G5 ▣
Honor Cl *KID* OX5 .... 129 J7
Hookend La *GOR/PANG* RG8 .... 315 H6
Hook End La *GOR/PANG* RG8 .... 322 A5
Hook Norton Rd *CHNTN* OX7 .... 50 D4
   RBANSW OX25 .... 25 F8
Hooks Cl *CIR* GL7 .... 180 E6
Hopcraft Cl *RBICS/W* OX25 .... 116 A8
Hopcraft La *RBANSW* OX15 .... 56 C4
Hop Gdns *HEN* RG9 .... 319 F5
Hopton Rd *THAME* OX9 .... 175 G6
Hordern Cl *HADM* HP17 .... 199 E5 ▣
Horley Path Rd *RBANSW* OX15 .... 19 H7
Hornbeam Cl *BAN* OX16 .... 2 B4 ▣
   GOR/PANG RG8 .... 331 G2 ▣
Hornbeam Dr *COW/LTMR* OX4 .... 193 G5 ▣
Hornbeam Rd *BIC* OX26 .... 97 G2
Horne *RBICN* OX27 .... 79 H8
Horn Hl *RBANSW* OX15 .... 55 G1
Horn Hill Rd *RBANSW* OX17 .... 38 C4
Horn La *MIM* GL56 .... 64 E1
   WANT OX12 .... 285 F2
Hornsea Cl *TLHT* RG30 .... 331 J6 ▣
Horse Close Cottages *STAD* OX44... 196 B7
The Horse Cl *CAV/SC* RG4 .... 335 J3
Horsecroft *FGDN* SN7 .... 232 C8
Horse Fair *BAN* OX16 .... 2 B4 ▣
   CHNTN OX7 .... 68 B4
   RBANSW OX15 .... 56 C3
Horseman Cl *HEAD* OX3 .... 167 K2
Horsemere La *WIT/EY* OX8 .... 147 F5
Horsepond Rd *CAV/SC* RG4 .... 326 B2
Horse Shoe La *CHNTN* OX7 .... 86 E7
Horseshoe Pk *GOR/PANG* RG8 ...... 330 B2
Horseshoe Rd *GOR/PANG* RG8 ...... 330 B2
Horseshoes Cl *WGFD* OX10 .... 267 H3
Horseshoes Pl *THAME* OX9 .... 175 C8 ▣
Horsham Cl *BAN* OX16 .... 20 B6
Horspath Driftway *HEAD* OX3 .... 168 E8
Horspath Rd *COW/LTMR* OX4 .... 193 F1
Horton Av *THAME* OX9 .... 175 G8
Horton Cl *RBANNS* OX17 .... 22 E8
Horton Crs *RBANNS* OX17 .... 22 E7 ▣
Horton Dr *RBANNS* OX17 .... 22 E7
Horton La *RBANSW* OX15 .... 36 B5
Horton Rd *RBANNS* OX17 .... 22 E8
Horton Vw *BAN* OX16 .... 2 C6
Horwood Cl *HEAD* OX3 .... 168 C4 ▣
Hosier St *READ* RG1 .... 333 G8
Hosker Cl *HEAD* OX3 .... 169 G3
Hound Cl *ABGD* OX14 .... 215 G5
Howard Av *WANT* OX12 .... 258 E6
Howard Cl *RBANNS* OX17 .... 22 E8
Howard Cornish Rd
   MCHM/KBPZ OX13 .... 213 F8
Howard Rd *BAN* OX16 .... 3 F3
Howard St *COW/LTMR* OX4 .... 191 K1
   READ RG1 .... 333 H7
Howbery Farm *WGFD* OX10 ...... 267 H8 ▣
Howe Cl *WHLY* OX33 .... 170 C7
Howe Rd *WTLGN* OX49 .... 270 D1
Howland Rd *THAME* OX9 .... 199 H1
Howth Dr *WODY* RG5 .... 335 F8
Hoyle Cl *WIT/EY* OX8 .... 142 E4
Huckleberry Cl *GOR/PANG* RG8 .. 331 G3 ▣
Hudleston Av *WGFD* OX10 .... 268 B6
Hudson Cl *RBANSW* OX15 .... 56 C3 ▣
Hudson St *BIC* OX26 .... 96 E4
   RBANSW OX15 .... 56 C3
Hugh Allen Crs *HEAD* OX3 .... 5 F2
Hughes Cl *CHNTN* OX7 .... 106 B5
Hughes Crs *FGDN* SN7 .... 253 J4

Humber Cl *DID* OX11 .... 264 A6
   WANT OX12 .... 282 E2
Humber St *RBANSW* OX15 .... 37 F3 ▣
Humber Wk *BAN* OX16 .... 20 B7
Humfrey Rd *HEAD* OX3 .... 169 F3
Humphries Cl *BUR/CRTN* OX18 ... 158 A4 ▣
Hundred Acres Cl *HEAD* OX3 .... 168 E8
Hunsdon Rd *COW/LTMR* OX4.... 192 A3
Hunt Cl *BIC* OX26 .... 97 F5
Hunter Cl *ABGD* OX14 .... 215 F4
   COW/LTMR OX4 .... 192 E1
Huntercombe End La *HEN* RG9 ... 294 A3
Hunters Cha *CAV/SC* RG4 .... 333 F2
Hunters Cl *WANT* OX12 .... 258 C6
Hunters Fld *FGDN* SN7 .... 232 C8
Hunters Piece *HGHW* SN6 .... 276 A5
Hunters Point *CHNR* OX39 .... 224 D1
Hunt Rd *THAME* OX9 .... 175 H8
Hunts Cl *BUR/CRTN* OX18 .... 138 D3
   WIT/EY OX8 .... 107 H8 ▣
Hunts Ri *SWDNE* SN3 .... 250 A8
Hurdeswell *WIT/EY* OX8 .... 126 C6 ▣
Hurdlers Gn *WTLGN* OX49 .... 246 A5
Hurricane Wy *WODY* RG5 .... 335 J8
Hursley Cl *TLHT* RG30 .... 331 J8 ▣
Hurst Cl *WGFD* OX10 .... 290 E1
Hurst La *OXN/BOT/CM* OX2 .... 189 K1
   WIT/EY OX8 .... 145 G1
Hurst Rise Rd *OXN/BOT/CM* OX2 .. 166 A7
Hurst St *COW/LTMR* OX4 .... 5 F6
Huscarle Wy *CALC* RG31 .... 331 G5 ▣
Hutchcombe Farm Cl
   OXN/BOT/CM OX2 .... 166 A8 ▣
Hutchcomb Rd *OXN/BOT/CM* OX2 .. 166 A7
Huxley Cl *BIC* OX26 .... 96 D4 ▣
   MCHM/KBPZ OX15 .... 213 K1
Hyacinth Wk *COW/LTMR* OX4 .... 192 E7 ▣
Hyde Copse *MCHM/KBPZ* OX13 .. 237 F1
Hyde Gv *RBANSW* OX15 .... 36 D4
Hyde Rd *WANT* OX12 .... 258 A2
The Hydes *CALC* RG31 .... 331 G5 ▣
The Hyde *ABGD* OX14 .... 238 B2
Hythe Bridge St *OX/KTN* OX1 .... 4 B4

Ian Mikardo Wy *CAV/SC* RG4 ...... 333 K5
Ibstock Cl *TLHT* RG30 .... 332 B8
Ibstone Av *CAV/SC* RG4 .... 334 A2
Ibstone Rd *SKCH* HP14 .... 248 E4
Ickford Rd *RAYLW* HP18 .... 172 C1
   RAYLW HP18 .... 173 G5
   THAME OX9 .... 172 D7
Ickleton Rd *WANT* OX12 .... 282 A3
Icknield Cl *CHNR* OX39 .... 224 B3
   DID OX11 .... 263 G6
Icknield La *WANT* OX12 .... 282 E3
Icknield Pl *GOR/PANG* RG8 .... 313 H7
Icknield Rd *GOR/PANG* RG8 .... 313 F7
Icknield Wy *HGHW* SN6 .... 298 C3
Icknieldway *PRRI* HP27 .... 201 K8
Idbury Cl *WIT/EY* OX8 .... 142 B8
Idstone Av *HGHW* SN6 .... 299 C2
Idstone Rd *HGHW* SN6 .... 299 C1
Iffley Rd *COW/LTMR* OX4 .... 5 F6
Iffley Turn *COW/LTMR* OX4 .... 192 A2
Ilchester Ms *CAV/SC* RG4 .... 334 A1 ▣
Ilex Cl *CAV/SC* RG4 .... 327 F3
Ilges La *WGFD* OX10 .... 290 B5
Ilkley Rd *CAV/SC* RG4 .... 332 E4
Illingworth Av *CAV/SC* RG4 .... 334 A1
Ilsley Cl *CAV/SC* RG4 .... 327 F2 ▣
Ilsley Rd *HEAD* OX3 .... 168 A5
Ingham La *WTLGN* OX49 .... 246 B6
Ingle Cl *HEAD* OX3 .... 168 B3
Inglewood Cl *CAV/SC* RG4 .... 327 F2
Ingrebourne Wy *DID* OX11 .... 263 K4
Inkerman Cl *ABGD* OX14 .... 214 B6
Innsworth Rd *BUR/CRTN* OX18 ... 158 A4
Inott Furze *HEAD* OX3 .... 168 D8
Insall Rd *CHNTN* OX7 .... 68 B3
Ireton Cl *STAD* OX44 .... 244 B1 ▣
Ireton Ct *THAME* OX9 .... 175 F6
Iron Down Hl *RBANSW* OX15 .... 54 A4
Ironstone *BAN* OX16 .... 2 A1
Ironstone Hollow *RBANSW* OX15 .. 34 B7
Isis Av *BIC* OX26 .... 96 B5
Isis Cl *ABGD* OX14 .... 215 H4
   WIT/EY OX8 .... 126 C7
Islay Crs *HGHW* SN6 .... 250 D1
Islip Rd *KID* OX5 .... 111 K7
   OXN/BOT/CM OX2 .... 149 F7
Itchen Cl *DID* OX11 .... 264 A4
Ivybank *CALC* RG31 .... 331 G6
Ivydene Rd *TLHT* RG30 .... 332 C5
Ivy La *RBANNS* OX17 .... 12 C4
   RBANSW OX15 .... 26 B2

Jack Argent Cl *COW/LTMR* OX4 .... 193 F6
Jackdaw La *COW/LTMR* OX4 .... 5 E
Jackies La *WHLY* OX33 .... 170 E
Jackman Cl *ABGD* OX14 .... 214 B
Jackson Cl *BUR/CRTN* OX18 .... 157 K
Jackson Dr *OX/KTN* OX1 .... 191 F
Jackson Rd *CHNTN* OX7 83
   OXN/BOT/CM OX2 .... 149 F
Jacksons La *CAV/SC* RG4 .... 332 A
Jack Straw's La *HEAD* OX3 .... 168 A
Jacobs Cl *WIT/EY* OX8 .... 143 F6
Jacobs Yd *CHNTN* OX7 .... 73 C
James St *COW/LTMR* OX4 .... 5 F
   READ RG1 .... 333 F8
James Wolfe Rd *COW/LTMR* OX4 ... 168 E
Janaway Pl *COW/LTMR* OX4 .... 192 A
Japonica Cl *BIC* OX26 .... 97 C
Jarn Wy *OX/KTN* OX1 .... 190 E
Jarvis' La *BIC* OX26 97
Jasmine Cl *COW/LTMR* OX4 .... 193 F5
Jasmine Pl *BIC* OX26 .... 97 G2
Javelin Wv *WGFD* OX10 268
Jay Cl *BIC* OX26 96
Jaynes Cl *BAN* OX16 .... 29 F
Jefferson Cl *CAV/SC* RG4 327
Jeffersons Piece *CHNTN* OX7 .... 106 B3
Jefferson Wy *THAME* OX9 .... 199 C
Jeffs Cl *RWWCK/WEL* CV55 .... 16 E
Jemmetts Cl *WGFD* OX10 .... 241 K6
Jenner Wk *CALC* RG31 .... 330 E8
Jennings La *DID* OX11 .... 262 C
Jericho St *OXN/BOT/CM* OX2 .... 4 E
Jerome Wy *KID* OX5 .... 128 E
Jersey Dr *BAN* OX16 .... 20 E
Jersey Rd *COW/LTMR* OX4 .... 192 A
Jervis Cl *CHNTN* OX7 .... 73 C
Jespers Hl *FGDN* SN7 .... 230 C4
Jesse's La *RAYLW* HP18 .... 174 C
Jesse Ter *READ* RG1 .... 333 F
Jethro Tull Gdns *WGFD* OX10 ... 267 G8
The Jetty *RBANNS* OX17 .... 14 C
Jeune St *COW/LTMR* OX4 .... 5 F
Joan Lawrence Pl *HEAD* OX3 ...... 168 E6
Job's La *BUR/CRTN* OX18 .... 138 C
John Buchan Rd *HEAD* OX3 .... 168 C
John Garne Wy *HEAD* OX3 .... 5 F
John Lopes Rd *WIT/EY* OX8 .... 146 A8
John Mason Rd *ABGD* OX14 .... 214 E
John Morris Rd *ABGD* OX14 .... 238 C
John Snow Pl *HEAD* OX3 .... 168 E
Johnston's Wy *CHNTN* OX7 ...... 68 B5
John Towle Cl *OX/KTN* OX1 .... 191 H
Jordan Cl *CAV/SC* RG4 .... 334 A
   DID OX11 .... 264 A5
Jordan Hl *OXN/BOT/CM* OX2 ...... 148 A
Josey Cl *CAV/SC* RG4 .... 327 F1
Jourdain Rd *COW/LTMR* OX4 .... 193 G
Jowett Wk *OX/KTN* OX1 .... 5 C
Joyce's Rd *FGDN* SN7 .... 232 E
Jubilee Cl *RBICS/W* OX25 .... 74 C
Jubilee La *CHNTN* OX7 .... 102 E
Jubilee Rd *SKCH* HP14 .... 249 H
Jubilee Wy *DID* OX11 .... 264 A
Judd's Cl *WIT/EY* OX8 .... 143 H
Judges Cl *KID* OX5 .... 129 C
Judges Rd *GOR/PANG* RG8........ 315 F
Junction Rd *BAN* OX16 .... 3 E3
   CHNTN OX7 .... 85 F
   COW/LTMR OX4 .... 192 D
Juniper Cl *BAN* OX16 .... 20 D
Juniper Dr *COW/LTMR* OX4 .... 193 F
Juniper Gdns *BIC* OX26 .... 97 C
Juniper Wy *CALC* RG31 .... 331 H
Jurassic Wy *BAN* OX16 .... 3 F
   RBANNS OX17 .... 14 E
   RBANNS OX17 .... 30 A
Juxon St *OXN/BOT/CM* OX2......... 4 A

Kames Cl *COW/LTMR* OX4 .... 192 E
Katchside *ABGD* OX14 .... 262 D
Katherine's Wk *CIR* GL7 .... 203 H
Keane Cl *WODY* RG5 .... 335 C
Keats Cl *BIC* OX26 .... 96 D3
Keats Rd *BAN* OX16 .... 2 A
Keble Cl *CIR* GL7 .... 203 H2
   SWDNE SN5 .... 274 A
Keble Rd *BIC* OX26....................... 97 C
   MIM GL56 .... 64 C
   OX/KTN OX1 .... 4 C
Kedleston Ri *BAN* OX16 .... 29 C
Keene Cl *COW/LTMR* OX4 .... 192 E
Keens La *CHNR* OX39 .... 225 E
Keeys Cl *RBICN* OX27 .... 77 H3
Kelburne Rd *COW/LTMR* OX4 .... 192 E
Kelham Hall Dr *WHLY* OX33 .... 170 C
Kelly's Rd *WHLY* OX33................ 170 E

Kelmscott Cl CAV/SC RG4 .... 332 E4
Kelvedon Wy CAV/SC RG4 .... 332 E2
Kempson Crs COW/LTMR OX4 ...... 192 A5
Kemps Rd RBANNS OX17 .... 38 C1
Kempster Cl ABGD OX14 .... 215 F7 🖽
Kenavon Dr READ RG1 .... 333 J7
Kendal Av CAV/SC RG4 .... 333 K2
Kendall Crs OXN/BOT/CM OX2 ...... 149 F6
Kendal Piece CHNTN OX7 .... 106 B3
Kenhill Rd RBANSW OX15 .... 17 J5
Kenilworth Av COW/LTMR OX4 .... 168 B8
Kenilworth Rd
    OXN/BOT/CM OX2 .... 189 G3 🖽
Kenilworth Wy BAN OX16 .... 28 B2
Kenley Av BUR/CRTN OX18 .... 158 A4
Kennedy Av COW/LTMR OX4 .... 168 B8
Kennedy Crs WGFD OX10 .... 290 B6
Kennedy Dr GOR/PANG RG8 .... 330 B2
Kennedy Rd BIC OX26 .... 96 D6
Kennel La CHNTN OX7 .... 67 J5
    MCHM/KBPZ OX13 .... 261 K3
Kennet Cl BIC OX26 .... 96 E6 🖽
    WANT OX12 .... 258 D6
    WGFD OX10 .... 241 J3
Kennet Rd ABGD OX14 .... 215 F6
    DID OX11 .... 286 A6
Kennet Side READ RG1 .... 333 J8
Kennet St READ RG1 .... 333 J8
Kennett Rd HEAD OX3 .... 168 C4
Kennington Rd ABGD OX14 .... 215 J3
    OX/KTN OX1 .... 191 J5
Kennylands Rd CAV/SC RG4 .... 327 F3
Kensington Cl ABGD OX14 .... 238 C3
    RBANNS OX17 .... 39 J1 🖽
Kensington Rd TLHT RG30 .... 332 D8
Kent Cl ABGD OX14 .... 215 F7 🖽
    COW/LTMR OX4 .... 192 E4
Kent Rd TLHT RG30 .... 332 D8
Kentwood Cl TLHT RG30 .... 331 H6
    WGFD OX10 .... 290 B6
Kentwood Hl CALC RG31 .... 331 H5
    TLHT RG30 .... 331 J6
Kenville Rd OX/KTN OX1 .... 191 H5
Kernham Dr CALC RG31 .... 331 F5 🖽
Kerry Cl BAN OX16 .... 20 C6 🖽
Kersington Crs COW/LTMR OX4 ... 192 D4
Kerwood Cl WDSTK OX20 .... 109 J8
Keston Cl CAV/SC RG4 .... 333 J4
Kestrel Cl BUR/CRTN OX18 .... 157 K4
Kestrel Crs COW/LTMR OX4 .... 192 D5
Kestrel Pl COW/LTMR OX4 .... 192 D5 🖽
Kestrel Rd MCHM/KBPZ OX13 ..... 213 K1
The Kestrels WANT OX12 .... 258 D5
Kestrel Wy BIC OX26 .... 97 H8
Keswick Cl TLHT RG30 .... 331 H8
Ketchmere Cl RAYLW HP18 .... 174 C1
Kew Win DID OX11 .... 264 A5 🖽
Keydale Cl BIC OX26 .... 97 G3
Keyser Rd RBANSW OX15 .... 29 G3
Keyte's Cl RBANNS OX17 .... 38 D3
Kibble Cl DID OX11 .... 264 A7
Kiddington Dr WDSTK OX20 .... 89 K7
Kiddington Rd CHNTN OX7 .... 75 F7
Kidlington Rd KID OX5 .... 130 D6
Kidmore End Rd CAV/SC RG4 ...... 327 J5
Kidmore La CAV/SC RG4 .... 326 D4
Kidmore Rd CAV/SC RG4 .... 332 E1
Kilbale Crs BAN OX16 .... 3 D5
Kildare Gdns CAV/SC RG4 .... 333 J4
Kilda Rd HGHW SN6 .... 226 D8
Kilkenny La BUR/CRTN OX18 .... 158 A1
Kiln Cl BUR/CRTN OX18 .... 184 B4
    COW/LTMR OX4 .... 192 B7
Kiln La CALC RG31 .... 330 E7
    HEAD OX3 .... 169 F5
    HEN RG9 .... 328 E5
    STAD OX44 .... 193 J6
    WHLY OX33 .... 170 C7
Kiln Rd CAV/SC RG4 .... 327 J8
Kilowna Cl WAR/TWY RG10 .... 335 J3
Kimbells St RAYLW HP18 .... 173 H5
Kimber Cl WHLY OX33 .... 170 C7
Kimber Rd ABGD OX14 .... 214 E3
Kinecroft WGFD OX10 .... 267 F8 🖽
Kineton Rd OX/KTN OX1 .... 4 C6
King Alfred Dr DID OX11 .... 263 K6
King Edward St OX/KTN OX1 ...... 5 D4 🖽
Kingfisher Cl ABGD OX14 .... 238 D3
Kingfisher Dr BAN OX16 .... 3 E6
    SWDNE SN3 .... 274 B8
Kingfisher Gn COW/LTMR OX4 .... 193 H6
Kingfisher Pl READ RG1 .... 333 H7
Kingfishers WANT OX12 .... 258 E2
Kingfisher Wy BIC OX26 .... 97 H7
Kingham Dr BUR/CRTN OX18 ...... 157 K5
Kingham Rd CHNTN OX7 .... 84 E2
King James Wy HEN RG9 .... 318 E7
Kings Av BIC OX26 .... 96 E6
    HGHW SN6 .... 250 E2
    MCHM/KBPZ OX13 .... 212 E8
Kingsclere Rd BIC OX26 .... 96 E5
Kings Cl RAYLW HP18 .... 172 B2
    THAME OX9 .... 175 F7
King's Cross Rd OXN/BOT/CM OX2 .. 149 F6
King's End BIC OX26 .... 96 E6

Kingsey Rd THAME OX9 .... 175 H7
Kings Farm La HEN RG9 .... 327 K1
Kingsfield Crs WIT/EY OX8 .... 143 G7
Kingsgate St READ RG1 .... 333 K8
King's Head La KID OX5 .... 130 E6
Kingsholme Cl DID OX11 .... 287 K2
Kings La CIR GL7 .... 180 D2
    DID OX11 .... 262 C8
    FGDN SN7 .... 253 H5
Kingsley Cl WAR/TWY RG10 .... 335 J2
Kingsley Rd BIC OX26 .... 96 D3 🖽
Kingsmead CIR GL7 .... 205 G2
King's Meadow Rd READ RG1 ...... 333 H7
King's Mill La HEAD OX3 .... 5 F3
King's Orch WGFD OX10 .... 266 A4
King's Rd BAN OX16 .... 2 B3
    CAV/SC RG4 .... 333 H5
    HEN RG9 .... 319 F5
    HEN RG9 .... 319 F5
    RBANSW OX15 .... 36 E3
    READ RG1 .... 333 K8
    THAME OX9 .... 175 G7
Kings Stile RBANNS OX17 .... 22 D6
Kingston Cl ABGD OX14 .... 214 D7 🖽
    RBANNS OX17 .... 22 E8 🖽
Kingston Hts WIT/EY OX8 .... 125 G8 🖽
Kingston Hl CHNR OX39 .... 224 C7
Kingston Rd OXN/BOT/CM OX2 ...... 4 B1
King St OXN/BOT/CM OX2 .... 4 B2
Kingsway BAN OX16 .... 2 B4
    CAV/SC RG4 .... 334 A1
Kings Way Dr KID OX5 .... 129 K7
Kinson Rd TLHT RG30 .... 332 A6
Kipling Cl BIC OX26 .... 96 D5
Kirby Cl CHNTN OX7 .... 75 G7
Kirby Pl COW/LTMR OX4 .... 192 D2 🖽
Kirby Rd COTS GL54 .... 100 A4
Kirk Cl OX/KTN OX1 .... 191 J7
    OXN/BOT/CM OX2 .... 148 E6
Kirkfell Cl CALC RG31 .... 331 G5
Kirkham Cl CAV/SC RG4 .... 334 A1
Kirtlington Rd RBICS/W OX25 .... 75 K8
Kirton Cl TLHT RG30 .... 332 B8
Kit La GOR/PANG RG8 .... 315 H1
Kittiwake Cl WODY RG5 .... 335 K8
Knapp Cl ABGD OX14 .... 214 B7
Knapton's Cft RBICS/W OX25 ..... 93 G1 🖽
Knighton Cl CAV/SC RG4 .... 333 G4
Knighton Rd HGHW SN6 .... 278 A5
Knightsbridge La THAME OX9 ...... 222 A8
Knights Rd COW/LTMR OX4 .... 192 D5
Knights Wy CAV/SC RG4 .... 333 H2
The Knob RBANNS OX17 .... 39 K2
Knoll Cl WANT OX12 .... 281 J8
Knolles Rd COW/LTMR OX4 .... 192 C2
The Knoll CALC RG31 .... 331 F5 🖽
Knollys Cl ABGD OX14 .... 214 E4
Knott Oaks WIT/EY OX8 .... 126 A2
Knowlands HGHW SN6 .... 226 E8
Knowle Cl CALC RG31 .... 332 D3
Knowle La RBICS/W OX25 .... 113 F6
Knowsley Rd CALC RG31 .... 331 F4
Kybald St OX/KTN OX1 .... 5 D4 🖽
Kyetts Cnr RBANNS OX17 .... 13 H5
Kynaston Rd DID OX11 .... 263 K7
Kysbie Cl ABGD OX14 .... 214 D5

L

Laburnam Av MCHM/KBPZ OX13 .. 214 A6
Laburnum Av MCHM/KBPZ OX13 .. 214 A6
Laburnum Cl RBICS/W OX25 .... 115 K4
Laburnum Crs KID OX5 .... 148 C1
Laburnum Gv BAN OX16 .... 29 F5
    DID OX11 .... 263 K7
Laburnum Rd OXN/BOT/CM OX2 .. 166 B8
Lacemakers CHNR OX39 .... 224 E1 🖽
Lacey Dr THAME OX9 .... 175 H8 🖽
Lackmore Gdns GOR/PANG RG8 .. 314 D7
Ladburn La BUR/CRTN OX18 ...... 157 J2
Ladder Hl WHLY OX33 .... 170 C8
Ladenham Rd COW/LTMR OX4 ... 192 E4 🖽
Lady Gv DID OX11 .... 264 B2
Ladygrove Paddock
    ABGD OX14 .... 238 B1 🖽
Lady Jane Ct CAV/SC RG4 .... 333 H4
Ladywell St WIT/EY OX8 .... 144 C1
Laggots Cl FGDN SN7 .... 209 K5 🖽
Lakefield Rd COW/LTMR OX4 ...... 192 B6
Lake Rd DID OX11 .... 287 J1
    HGHW SN6 .... 252 C8
Lakeside OXN/BOT/CM OX2 .... 148 D5
Lakesmere Cl KID OX5 .... 129 F5
Lake St OX/KTN OX1 .... 191 G1
Lake Wk RBANNS OX17 .... 38 E3
Lamarsh Rd OXN/BOT/CM OX2 ... 166 C6
Lambe Av ABGD OX14 .... 262 A5
Lambert Wk THAME OX9 .... 175 F6
Lambeth Ct TLHT RG30 .... 331 K8 🖽
Lamb La WDSTK OX20 .... 127 J5

Lamborough Hl
    MCHM/KBPZ OX13 .... 213 K1
Lambourne Cl CALC RG31 .... 331 H7 🖽
Lambourne Crs BIC OX26 .... 97 G6 🖽
Lambourne Rd CAV/SC RG4 .... 326 E2
Lambourne Wy RBANNS OX17 ...... 38 E3
Lambourn Rd COW/LTMR OX4 .... 192 A4
Lambourn Valley Wy FGDN SN7 .. 278 C6
Lambrick Wy ABGD OX14 .... 238 C3
Lambridge La HEN RG9 .... 318 D4
Lambridge Wood Rd HEN RG9 .... 318 D3
Lambs Cl KID OX5 .... 129 H5
Lamb's Crs BAN OX16 .... 3 D5
Lamb's La WDSTK OX20 .... 109 C3
Lambton Cl COW/LTMR OX4 .... 168 E8
Lammas Cl ABGD OX14 .... 214 D6
Lamorna Crs CALC RG31 .... 331 G6
Lampitts Gn RBANSW OX15 .... 19 G7
Lancaster Av WGFD OX10 .... 268 B4
Lancaster Cl BIC OX26 .... 97 H5
Lancaster Ms SWDNE SN3 .... 274 A1
Lancaster Pl BUR/CRTN OX18 ... 158 A6 🖽
    SWDNE SN3 .... 274 A1
Lanchester Dr BAN OX16 .... 20 B7
Lancing Cl TLHT RG30 .... 332 D8
Lancott La WIT/EY OX8 .... 186 B4
Lancut Rd WIT/EY OX8 .... 142 C6
Landells Rd BUR/CRTN OX18 ...... 183 G4
Landscape Cl RBICS/W OX25 .... 113 F2
Landscape Rd RBICS/W OX25 ...... 112 E2
Landsend La WODY RG5 .... 335 K5
Lane Cl KID OX5 .... 129 G7
    RBANSW OX15 .... 19 H5
Lane End WGFD OX10 .... 267 J8 🖽
Lanes End BIC OX26 .... 98 A5
The Lanes BUR/CRTN OX18 .... 183 G4
The Lane CHNTN OX7 .... 53 H8
    DID OX11 .... 286 C7
    MIM GL56 .... 47 J8
    RBANSW OX15 .... 55 H3
    RBICN OX27 .... 58 D8
    RBICS/W OX25 .... 93 G1
    STAD OX44 .... 194 D5
Langdale Ga WIT/EY OX8 .... 143 F7
Langdale Rd THAME OX9 .... 175 G7
Langford Cl CAV/SC RG4 .... 333 J2
Langford Gdns BIC OX26 .... 96 D5
Langford La KID OX5 .... 128 D5
    RBICS/W OX25 .... 114 E4
Langley Cl HEAD OX3 .... 168 D5
Langley La BUR/CRTN OX18 .... 205 K2
Langley Rd ABGD OX14 .... 214 D5
    STAD OX44 .... 220 A8
Langley's La WIT/EY OX8 .... 186 C6
Langston Cl CHNTN OX7 .... 85 F2
Langton Av RBICS/W OX25 .... 116 A3
Lanham Wy COW/LTMR OX4 ...... 192 B5
Lansdown Cl BAN OX16 .... 2 B6
Lansdowne Rd
    MCHM/KBPZ OX13 .... 213 J1
    TLHT RG30 .... 331 H8
Lansdown Rd FGDN SN7 .... 230 C4
Lapwing Cl BIC OX26 .... 97 H7 🖽
Lapwing La WGFD OX10 .... 290 C6
Larch Cl BIC OX26 .... 97 G3
    MCHM/KBPZ OX13 .... 210 E6
Larch End STAD OX44 .... 193 K5
The Larches BUR/CRTN OX18 ..... 157 K5
    HEAD OX3 .... 169 G4
Larissa Cl CALC RG31 .... 331 J6 🖽
Larkdown WANT OX12 .... 283 F3
Larkfield WGFD OX10 .... 290 B6
Larkfields HEAD OX3 .... 168 E5
Lark Hl WANT OX12 .... 283 F3
Larkhill Pl ABGD OX14 .... 214 B6
Larkhill Rd ABGD OX14 .... 214 C7
Larkins La HEAD OX3 .... 168 D3
Larksfield SWDNE SN3 .... 274 A7
Larksfield Cl BUR/CRTN OX18 ..... 157 J7
Larksfield Rd BAN OX16 .... 29 F5
Larkswood Cl CALC RG31 .... 331 H4 🖽
Larsen Rd RBICS/W OX25 .... 76 C7
Lashbrook Rd HEN RG9 .... 329 K3
Lashford La MCHM/KBPZ OX13... 189 H8
Lashlake Rd THAME OX9 .... 175 F6
Latchford La STAD OX44 .... 196 D8
Lathbury Rd OXN/BOT/CM OX2 ... 167 F2
Latimer Rd BUR/CRTN OX18 .... 158 A5
    HEAD OX3 .... 168 C5
Latton Cl DID OX11 .... 286 C7
    MCHM/KBPZ OX13 .... 210 D6
Laud's Cl HEN RG9 .... 318 E6
Laughton Hl WIT/EY OX8 .... 107 H8
Launceston Av CAV/SC RG4 ...... 334 A1 🖽
Laundry La BUR/CRTN OX18 ...... 184 B4
Launton Rd BIC OX26 .... 97 G6
    RBICN OX27 .... 80 A7
Laurel Cl BAN OX16 .... 29 F5
    STAD OX44 .... 220 B8
Laurel Crs WANT OX12 .... 258 E7
Laurel Dr CALC RG31 .... 331 F7
    MCHM/KBPZ OX13 .... 210 E6
Laurel Farm Cl HEAD OX3 .... 168 C3 🖽
The Laurels FGDN SN7 .... 229 H7
    GOR/PANG RG8 .... 330 B2 🖽

STAD OX44	218 E5 ◨
THAME OX9	198 B7
Lavender Cl BAN OX16	20 D6
Lavender Pl BUR/CRTN OX18	157 J5
Lavenham Dr WODY RG5	335 H7
Lawn Hill Ct CHNTN OX7	68 B4 ◨
The Lawns RAYLW HP18	135 K6
Lawrence Cl WANT OX12	281 G3 ◨
Lawrence Flds RBICS/W OX25	74 E7
Lawrence La BUR/CRTN OX18	138 E2
Lawrence Leys RBANSW OX15	37 F2
Lawrence Rd COW/LTMR OX4	192 C2 ◨
TLHT RG30	332 A7
Lawrence Wy BIC OX26	96 C5
Lawson Dr CAV/SC RG4	332 E2
Lawson La DID OX11	286 B7
Lawton Av BUR/CRTN OX18	157 K5
Lawyers Cl BRACKY NN13	43 F5
Lay Av WGFD OX10	241 J1
Laytom Ri CALC RG31	331 G4
Leabrook Cl BAN OX16	28 E5
Leach Rd BIC OX26	96 D5
WGFD OX10	241 K2
Leafield Rd CHNTN OX7	103 F8
COW/LTMR OX4	192 C1
WIT/EY OX8	121 K2
WIT/EY OX8	123 H8
WIT/EY OX8	142 B2
Lea Gv DID OX11	263 K5
Leamington Dr FGDN SN7	230 A5
Lea Rd CAV/SC RG4	327 F3
Leaver Rd HEN RG9	318 E6
Lechlade Rd CIR GL7	178 D4
CIR GL7	180 C5
FGDN SN7	203 J6
HGHW SN6	226 E1
HGHW SN6	250 E1
Leckford Pl OXN/BOT/CM OX2	4 B2 ◨
Leckford Rd OXN/BOT/CM OX2	4 B2
Ledbury Cl TLHT RG30	332 C7 ◨
Ledgers Cl COW/LTMR OX4	192 C5
Ledwell Rd CHNTN OX7	72 C5
Lee Av ABGD OX14	215 F5
Lee Cl CHNTN OX7	106 B4
KID OX5	129 G5
Lee Ct THAME OX9	175 F7
Lees Hts CHNTN OX7	68 B5
The Lees FGDN SN7	230 B4 ◨
Leicester Cl HEN RG9	319 F4
Leiden Rd HEAD OX3	168 D1
Leigh Cl WIT/EY OX8	144 B2
Leigh Cft MCHM/KBPZ OX13	189 J8
Leigh Gv BAN OX16	2 B5
Lemart Cl TLHT RG30	331 J7 ◨
Lennox Gdns BAN OX16	2 A5
Lenthal KID OX5	111 K8
Lenthall Rd ABGD OX14	214 C7
COW/LTMR OX4	191 K4
Lenton Rd BAN OX16	29 F5
Leon Cl COW/LTMR OX4	5 F5
Leopold St COW/LTMR OX4	5 F6
Lerwick Cft BIC OX26	97 H3
Lester Cl RBANNS OX17	38 D1
Lester Wy WGFD OX10	266 D8
Letcombe Av ABGD OX14	214 C7
Letcombe St READ RG1	333 H8 ◨
The Level RBANSW OX15	17 J5
Levenot Cl BAN OX16	3 F3
Levery Cl ABGD OX14	215 F7
Lewell Av HEAD OX3	5 F1
Lewin Cl COW/LTMR OX4	192 C5 ◨
Lewington Cl STAD OX44	196 B7 ◨
Lewis Cl HEAD OX3	169 G5
Lewis Rd CHNTN OX7	68 A5
Lexton Gdns RBANNS OX17	23 F7 ◨
Leyburn Cl WODY RG5	335 J7
Leyburne Gdns CHNR OX39	200 E8
The Leyes RBANSW OX15	56 C5
Leys Ap CHNTN OX7	68 B5
Leys Cl RBANSW OX15	19 G7
Leyshon Rd WHLY OX33	170 E8
Leys Pl COW/LTMR OX4	168 A8
Leys Rd OXN/BOT/CM OX2	188 D2
The Leys CHNTN OX7	68 A5
RBANNS OX17	38 C4
The Ley WDSTK OX20	127 K1
Library Av DID OX11	286 A5
Liddell Rd COW/LTMR OX4	192 C3
Lidden Rd STAD OX44	220 B8
Lidderdale Rd COTS GL54	100 A4
Liddiard Cl OX/KTN OX1	191 J7
WANT OX12	282 D1 ◨
Lido Rd DID OX11	285 H7
Lidsey Rd BAN OX16	2 A4
Lilac Cl GOR/PANG RG8	331 H2 ◨
Limborough Rd WANT OX12	282 D2
Lime Av BAN OX16	3 E5
Lime Crs BIC OX26	97 G2
Lime Gv CHNR OX39	225 F1
MCHM/KBPZ OX13	210 D6
Lime Kiln Rd KID OX5	111 F2
Lime Rd OXN/BOT/CM OX2	166 B8
The Limes RBICN OX27	80 A6
WGFD OX10	241 K5
WGFD OX10	267 H8 ◨

Limes Wy RAYLW HP18	173 H4
Lime Tree Cl BUR/CRTN OX18	157 K4 ◨
Limetree Cl WANT OX12	258 D6
Limetree Rd GOR/PANG RG8	322 D1
Limetrees DID OX11	286 C6
Lime Wk HEAD OX3	168 C5
Linacre Cl DID OX11	264 B7
Lince La KID OX5	111 G6
Lincoln Cl BAN OX16	2 A4
BIC OX26	97 H3
WIT/EY OX8	186 D3
Lincoln Pl THAME OX9	175 F7
Lincoln Rd OX/KTN OX1	191 H2
Lincombe La OX/KTN OX1	190 C8
Lincon Gdns DID OX11	264 B7
Lincraft Cl KID OX5	129 H8 ◨
Lindberg Wy WODY RG5	335 K6 ◨
Linden Crs WANT OX12	259 F6
Linden Ga DID OX11	262 C8
Linden Rd BIC OX26	97 G5
Lindsay Dr ABGD OX14	215 F5
Links Dr TLHT RG30	332 A7 ◨
Linkside Av OXN/BOT/CM OX2	148 D5
Links Rd OX/KTN OX1	191 J7
The Link BAN OX16	2 A2
HEAD OX3	5 E1
HEAD OX3	169 F4
Linkwood Rd WIT/EY OX8	142 A6
Linnet Cl COW/LTMR OX4	192 D5
Linnetsdene SWDNE SN3	274 A7 ◨
SWDNE SN3	274 B7 ◨
Linton Rd OXN/BOT/CM OX2	167 G2
Lion Meadow HEN RG9	294 E5 ◨
Lipscombe Pl BUR/CRTN OX18	157 K3
Liskeard Rd RWWCK/WEL CV35	8 E1
Lismore Rd HGHW SN6	250 C1
Lister Cl GOR/PANG RG8	331 G2
Litchfield Cl CHNTN OX7	88 E2 ◨
Lithgow Rd COTS GL54	100 A4
Little Acreage HEAD OX3	167 K1
Little Blenheim KID OX5	147 J3
Little Brewery St COW/LTMR OX4	5 F4
Little Bridge Rd RBANSW OX15	36 E2
Littlebrook Meadow CHNTN OX7	102 E6
Little Bury COW/LTMR OX4	193 G5
Little Clarendon St OX/KTN OX1	4 B3
Little Croft Rd GOR/PANG RG8	322 E2
Little Glebe CAV/SC RG4	335 G4
Little Gn RBANSW OX15	36 E3
Littlehay Rd COW/LTMR OX4	192 B2
Little Heath Rd CALC RG31	330 E8
Little Howe Cl ABGD OX14	215 J4
Little John's La TLHT RG30	332 C7 ◨
Littlejohn's La TLHT RG30	332 D6
Little La RBANNS OX17	40 B8
Little Langlands DID OX11	263 K8
Little Lees CHNTN OX7	106 B4
Little Marsh Rd RBICN OX27	99 K4
Littlemore Rd COW/LTMR OX4	192 C4
Little Oak Dr CALC RG31	331 G7 ◨
Little Paddock RBICN OX27	79 K1
Littlestead Cl CAV/SC RG4	334 A1 ◨
Little St READ RG1	332 E7
Little Wittenham Rd ABGD OX14	240 E6
Little Wd SKCH HP14	249 G2
Littleworth Hl WANT OX12	282 C2
Littleworth Rd WGFD OX10	267 G3
WHLY OX33	170 B7
Liverpool Rd READ RG1	334 A7
Livery Cl READ RG1	333 H8
Lobelia Rd COW/LTMR OX4	193 F5
Lock Crs KID OX5	148 C1
Lockhart Crs COW/LTMR OX4	192 D3
Lockheed Cl BAN OX16	2 C1
Lockinge Cl DID OX11	263 J8 ◨
Lock Pl READ RG1	333 K8
Locks La WANT OX12	282 C3
Lockstile Md GOR/PANG RG8	312 E8
Lockstile Wy GOR/PANG RG8	322 E1
Lockway ABGD OX14	237 J6
Locombe Hl CIR GL7	155 F7
Lodden Av WGFD OX10	241 J2
Loddon Cl ABGD OX14	215 F6
Loddon Dr DID OX11	264 B6
WAR/TWY RG10	329 K6
WAR/TWY RG10	335 K1
Loder Rd DID OX11	262 C8
Lodersfield CIR GL7	203 G3
Lodge Cl BAN OX16	3 D5
BIC OX26	97 F2
HEAD OX3	149 K8
Lodge Rd WDSTK OX20	127 G6
Logan Cl TLHT RG30	331 K8 ◨
Lombard St ABGD OX14	214 D8 ◨
Lombard Wy BAN OX16	29 J1
Lomond Av CAV/SC RG4	334 A2
London La CHNTN OX7	103 K5
London Rd BIC OX26	97 G7
CHNTN OX7	68 D4
DID OX11	287 G5
EARL RG6	334 E7
HEAD OX3	168 C4
HEAD OX3	169 F4
MIM GL56	46 A1
THAME OX9	196 D3

WHLY OX33	170 D2
London St FGDN SN7	230 C8
READ RG1	333 H7
Long Barrow RBANNS OX17	14 C
Longburges RBANNS OX17	23 F
Long Cl HEAD OX3	168 E
OXN/BOT/CM OX2	165 K
Longcot Rd FGDN SN7	253 H
HGHW SN6	276 E
Long Crendon Rd RAYLW HP18	173 H
Longelandes Cl BAN OX16	2 A
Longelandes Wy BAN OX16	2 A
Longfellow Cl BIC OX26	96 D4
Longfellow Dr ABGD OX14	238 A
Longfellow Rd BAN OX16	2 A
Longfields BIC OX26	97 C
MCHM/KBPZ OX13	213 F
Long Ford Cl OX/KTN OX1	4 C
Longford Wy DID OX11	263 K
Long Furlong HADM HP17	176 B
Long Furlong Rd	
MCHM/KBPZ OX13	214 E
Long Gnd COW/LTMR OX4	192 C
Longhurst Cl CAV/SC RG4	333
Longlands Rd COW/LTMR OX4	192 E4
Long La CALC RG31	331 F
COW/LTMR OX4	192 C
Longleat Cl BAN OX16	3 E
Longleat Dr CALC RG31	331 F4
Longmead ABGD OX14	214 C
Longmore Av COTS GL54	100 A
Longore WIT/EY OX8	107 H
Longridge Cl TLHT RG30	332 BB
Long Toll GOR/PANG RG8	324 E
Long Tow MCHM/KBPZ OX13	214 E
Longwall COW/LTMR OX4	192 E
Long Wall HADM HP17	176 E
Longwall St OX/KTN OX1	5 D4
Long Wittenham Rd DID OX11	265 F
Longworth Av CALC RG31	331 H
Longworth Cl BAN OX16	3 E
Longworth Rd OXN/BOT/CM OX2	4 A
WANT OX12	234 A
Lonsdale Rd OXN/BOT/CM OX2	149 F
Lord Cl BUR/CRTN OX18	157 K
Lords Piece Rd CHNTN OX7	68 E
Lorne Pl READ RG1	332 E
Lorne St READ RG1	332 E
Lostock Pl DID OX11	263 K
Lovatt Cl BUR/CRTN OX18	157 H
CALC RG31	331 F
Lovegrove's La GOR/PANG RG8	315 C
Lovelace Cl ABGD OX14	214 A
Lovelace Dr KID OX5	129 K
Lovelace Rd OXN/BOT/CM OX2	148 E
Love La WTLGN OX49	246 E
Lovell Cl HEN RG9	318 E
SWDNE SN3	274 A
WIT/EY OX8	141 C
WIT/EY OX8	161 H
Loverock Rd TLHT RG30	332 C
Lowell Pl WIT/EY OX8	142 E
Lower Armour Rd CALC RG31	331 H
Lower Cherwell St BAN OX16	3 C
Lower Church St SKCH HP14	249 C
Lower Cl RBANSW OX15	29 C
Lower Common FGDN SN7	255 H
Lower Crs WIT/EY OX8	141 C
Lower Elmstone Dr CALC RG31	331 C
Lower End CHNTN OX7	67 C
RBANSW OX15	26 E
RBICS/W OX25	72 C
STAD OX44	195 H
Lower Farm Cl RAYLW HP18	173 H
Lower Farm La COW/LTMR OX4	216 E
RBANNS OX17	12 E
Lower Hades Rd KID OX5	110 E
Lower Henley Rd CAV/SC RG4	333 C
Lower Heyford Rd RBICS/W OX25	94 A
Lower Icknield Wy CHNR OX39	201 F8
Lower Rd CHNR OX39	200 B
DID OX11	286 E
RBICS/W OX25	116 C
THAME OX9	223 F
WDSTK OX20	127 C
Lower St KID OX5	130 E
RBANSW OX15	55 C
Lower Whf WGFD OX10	267 F
Lower Whitley Rd	
OXN/BOT/CM OX2	164 E
Lowes Cl HEN RG9	329 H
SKCH HP14	248 E
Lowfield Gn CAV/SC RG4	334 A
Lowfield Rd CAV/SC RG4	333 K
Loyd Cl ABGD OX14	214 E
Loyd Rd DID OX11	287 H
Lucca Dr ABGD OX14	238 C
Lucerne Av BIC OX26	96 E
Lucerne Dr STAD OX44	218 E5
Lucerne Rd OXN/BOT/CM OX2	149 C
Lucey Cl CALC RG31	331 F4
Lucky La BAN OX16	2 E
Ludgershall Rd RBICS/W OX25	117 C
Ludlow Dr BAN OX16	20 D
THAME OX9	175 C

Ludsden Gv *THAME* OX9 .... 175 G7
Luker Av *HEN* RG9 .... 318 E4
Lumberd Rd *ABGD* OX14 .... 215 F5
Lunds Farm Rd *WODY* RG5 .... 335 J7
Lundy La *TLHT* RG30 .... 332 C8
Lune Cl *DID* OX11 .... 264 A6
Lupton Rd *THAME* OX9 .... 199 G1
  WCFD OX10 .... 290 D1
Luscombe Cl *CAV/SC* RG4 .... 333 K5
Luther Ct *OX/KTN* OX1 .... 4 C5
Lych Gate La *STAD* OX44 .... 195 K5
Lycroft La *GOR/PANG* RG8 .... 312 E8
Lydalls Cl *DID* OX11 .... 263 J6
Lydalls Rd *DID* OX11 .... 263 J6
Lydia Cl *HEAD* OX3 .... 169 F5
Lydsee Ga *WANT* OX12 .... 282 B2
Lyefield Ct *CAV/SC* RG4 .... 333 H1
Lye Va *HEAD* OX3 .... 168 D8
Lyford Cl *ABGD* OX14 .... 237 K5
Lyford Wy *ABGD* OX14 .... 215 F5
Lymbrook Cl *WIT/EY* OX8 .... 162 C2
Lyme Gv *CALC* RG31 .... 331 H6
Lymington Ga *CAV/SC* RG4 .... 332 E2
The Lynch *WANT* OX12 .... 285 F2
Lyndene Rd *DID* OX11 .... 263 H4
Lyndhurst Rd *GOR/PANG* RG8 .... 322 E1
  TLHT RG30 .... 331 K6
Lyndworth Cl *HEAD* OX3 .... 168 E3
Lyneham Cl *BUR/CRTN* OX18 .... 158 A4
  WIT/EY OX8 .... 142 C6
Lyneham Rd *BIC* OX26 .... 97 H4
  CHNTN OX7 .... 102 C5
Lyne Rd *KID* OX5 .... 129 F6
Lynges Cl *ABGD* OX14 .... 215 F5
Lynmouth Rd *DID* OX11 .... 263 J7
  READ RG1 .... 333 G6
Lynn Cl *HEAD* OX3 .... 5 F1
Lynton La *WIT/EY* OX8 .... 147 F5
Lynt Rd *HGHW* SN6 .... 226 E2
Lyon Cl *ABGD* OX14 .... 214 E6
Lyon Sq *TLHT* RG30 .... 332 A8
Lysander Cl *BIC* OX26 .... 97 H4
  WODY RG5 .... 335 J7
Lytham Rd *BUR/CRTN* OX18 .... 158 A4
Lytham Rd *WODY* RG5 .... 335 G8
Lytton Rd *COW/LTMR* OX4 .... 192 A2

M

Maberley Cl *ABGD* OX14 .... 238 A2
Mably Gv *WANT* OX12 .... 282 D1
Mably Wy *WANT* OX12 .... 258 D8
Macaulay Cl *BIC* OX26 .... 96 D4
Macdonald Cl *DID* OX11 .... 263 H6
Mackenzie Av *ABGD* OX14 .... 262 B4
Mackenzie Cl *BIC* OX26 .... 96 D4
Mackley Cl *RBANSW* OX15 .... 56 B3
Mackney La *WCFD* OX10 .... 266 A5
Macmillan Wy *MIM* GL56 .... 65 G5
  RBANNS OX17 .... 6 D7
  RBANNS OX17 .... 14 C1
  RBANSW OX15 .... 10 E4
  RBANSW OX15 .... 24 D2
  SHPSTR CV36 .... 32 B6
  SHPSTR CV36 .... 33 F5
Macray Rd *WIT/EY* OX8 .... 161 F3
Maddle Rd *HUNG* RG17 .... 301 F8
Mafeking Rw *WTLGN* OX49 .... 246 E3
Magdalen Br *OX/KTN* OX1 .... 5 E4
Magdalen Cl *BIC* OX26 .... 97 G4
Magdalen Ct *DID* OX11 .... 264 B7
Magdalen Rd *COW/LTMR* OX4 .... 5 F6
Magdalen Rd *BUR/CRTN* OX18 .... 157 K5
Magdalen St *OX/KTN* OX1 .... 4 C4
Magnette Cl *ABGD* OX14 .... 214 D8
Magnolia Cl *KID* OX5 .... 129 H8
The Magnolias *BAN* OX16 .... 20 D6
  BIC OX26 .... 97 G2
Magpie La *BRACKY* NN13 .... 43 F1
  OX/KTN OX1 .... 5 D4
Maidcroft Rd *COW/LTMR* OX4 .... 192 C3
Maiden's Cl *HGHW* SN6 .... 252 D6
Maidley Cl *WIT/EY* OX8 .... 143 G5
Main Av *COW/LTMR* OX4 .... 192 C3
Main Rd *ABGD* OX14 .... 239 K8
  DID OX11 .... 287 J2
  MCHM/KBPZ OX13 .... 211 J5
  RBANNS OX17 .... 22 E3
  RBANSW OX15 .... 27 H6
  WANT OX12 .... 258 E1
  WIT/EY OX8 .... 126 C6
  WIT/EY OX8 .... 159 K1
Main St *BRACKY* NN13 .... 44 D2
  BUCK/WIN MK18 .... 45 H2
  BUR/CRTN OX18 .... 182 A8
  CHNTN OX7 .... 88 C2
  CHNTN OX7 .... 83 J5
  CHNTN OX7 .... 106 C8
  DID OX11 .... 286 B7
  DID OX11 .... 287 C3
  MIM GL56 .... 65 H4
  RBANNS OX17 .... 12 B4

Rbanns OX17 .... 20 A3
Rbanns OX17 .... 40 E3
Rbansw OX15 .... 19 G7
Rbansw OX15 .... 24 E7
Rbansw OX15 .... 25 C7
Rbansw OX15 .... 26 C7
Rbansw OX15 .... 27 H3
Rbicn OX27 .... 61 H7
Rbicn OX27 .... 79 K1
Rbicn OX27 .... 81 J8
Rbics/w OX25 .... 73 K2
Rwwck/wel CV35 .... 16 C2
  WANT OX12 .... 233 K5
  WANT OX12 .... 258 E7
  WANT OX12 .... 259 H1
  WANT OX12 .... 282 A5
Maitland Rd *READ* RG1 .... 332 E5
Maiwand Gdns *TLHT* RG30 .... 331 H8
Majors Rd *FGDN* SN7 .... 253 F5
  HGHW SN6 .... 252 D5
Makins Rd *HEN* RG9 .... 318 E7
Malet Cl *SKCH* HP14 .... 249 H2
Malford Rd *HEAD* OX3 .... 169 F3
Mallard Cl *COW/LTMR* OX4 .... 192 D5
Mallards Wy *BIC* OX26 .... 97 H6
  WANT OX12 .... 258 C6
Mallins La *FGDN* SN7 .... 253 J5
Mallory Av *CAV/SC* RG4 .... 333 J1
The Mall *HGHW* SN6 .... 252 D8
Maltfield Rd *HEAD* OX3 .... 168 A2
Malthouse *HGHW* SN6 .... 277 G8
Malthouse Cl *HGHW* SN6 .... 277 H8
Malthouse La *RBANSW* OX15 .... 26 A2
  RBANSW OX15 .... 29 F7
  READ RG1 .... 333 F7
  SHPSTR CV36 .... 49 G1
  WGFD OX10 .... 241 K6
Malthouse Paddock *FGDN* SN7 .... 208 C7
Maltings Cl *RBANSW* OX15 .... 36 E3
Maltings Pl *READ* RG1 .... 333 G8
The Maltings *KSCL* RG20 .... 307 J5
Maltsters *WIT/EY* OX8 .... 107 H8
Malvern Cl *BAN* OX16 .... 29 F5
  DID OX11 .... 263 G5
Malyns Cl *CHNR* OX39 .... 200 E8
Managua Cl *CAV/SC* RG4 .... 333 K5
Manchester Rd *READ* RG1 .... 334 A7
Mandarin Pl *WANT* OX12 .... 258 C6
Mandeville Cl *ABGD* OX14 .... 214 C5
Mandhill Cl *WANT* OX12 .... 258 E7
Manners Rd *WODY* RG5 .... 335 F8
Manning Cl *RBANSW* OX15 .... 36 E5
Mannock Wy *WODY* RG5 .... 335 K7
Manor Cl *ABGD* OX14 .... 237 K6
  BUR/CRTN OX18 .... 184 C5
  DID OX11 .... 286 C6
  DID OX11 .... 287 G3
  HGHW SN6 .... 252 B8
  RBANNS OX17 .... 12 E7
  RBANNS OX17 .... 23 F7
  WIT/EY OX8 .... 146 E5
Manor Ct *ABGD* OX14 .... 238 C1
  BAN OX16 .... 3 E2
  CHNTN OX7 .... 87 F6
Manor Crs *DID* OX11 .... 263 H7
  FGDN SN7 .... 232 C8
  WIT/EY OX8 .... 186 D4
Manor Dr *WHLY* OX33 .... 193 J1
Manor Farm Cl *CHNTN* OX7 .... 84 A2
  RBICS/W OX25 .... 114 E7
Manor Farm Ct *WDSTK* OX20 .... 109 G3
Manor Farm La *GOR/PANG* RG8 ..... 330 A5
Manor Farm Rd *WGFD* OX10 .... 241 K6
  WHLY OX33 .... 193 J1
Manor Fld *WANT* OX12 .... 282 A5
Manor Gn *DID* OX11 .... 262 C8
Manor Gv *OX/KTN* OX1 .... 191 J8
Manor La *HGHW* SN6 .... 276 B1
  MARL SN8 .... 321 F7
  WANT OX12 .... 284 D1
Manor Orch *RBANSW* OX15 .... 19 H3
Manor Pk *RBANNS* OX17 .... 7 F6
  SWDNE SN5 .... 274 C3
Manor Pl *OX/KTN* OX1 .... 5 E3
Manor Rd *BAN* OX16 .... 3 E1
  BUR/CRTN OX18 .... 157 K2
  BUR/CRTN OX18 .... 158 D3
  CHNTN OX7 .... 72 D5
  DID OX11 .... 263 H6
  GOR/PANG RG8 .... 322 D1
  GOR/PANG RG8 .... 324 A8
  HEN RG9 .... 319 F7
  MCHM/KBPZ OX13 .... 189 J8
  OX/KTN OX1 .... 5 E3
  OX/KTN OX1 .... 191 F2
  RBANNS OX17 .... 38 B4
  RBICN OX27 .... 62 A8
  THAME OX9 .... 176 B8
  THAME OX9 .... 200 D1
  WANT OX12 .... 284 D1
  WDSTK OX20 .... 109 H8
  WDSTK OX20 .... 127 J6
  WIT/EY OX8 .... 143 G8
  WIT/EY OX8 .... 160 E3

Manorsfield Rd *BIC* OX26 .... 97 F5
Manor Wy *KID* OX5 .... 129 H5
Manor Wood Ga *HEN* RG9 .... 329 J3
Mansell Cl *WIT/EY* OX8 .... 145 J1
Mansfield Gdns *DID* OX11 .... 264 B7
Mansfield Rd *OX/KTN* OX1 .... 5 D3
Mansion Hl *RBANNS* OX17 .... 22 D7
Mansmoor Rd *RBICS/W* OX25 .... 114 A8
Manston Cl *BIC* OX26 .... 97 J4
Manzel Rd *RBICN* OX27 .... 97 G1
Manzil Wy *COW/LTMR* OX4 .... 168 A7
Maple Av *KID* OX5 .... 129 H8
Maple Cl *BAN* OX16 .... 29 F6
  CAV/SC RG4 .... 327 G5
  OXN/BOT/CM OX2 .... 166 B7
Maple Ct *GOR/PANG* RG8 .... 322 D1
Mapledene *CAV/SC* RG4 .... 332 E4
Mapledurham Dr *GOR/PANG* RG8 .. 331 G2
Mapledurham Vw *CALC* RG31 .... 331 H5
Maple Rd *BIC* OX26 .... 97 G5
  FGDN SN7 .... 230 A4
  THAME OX9 .... 174 D7
The Maples *BUR/CRTN* OX18 .... 157 J6
  WANT OX12 .... 258 D5
Maple Wy *CHNTN* OX7 .... 103 J5
Maplewell *WIT/EY* OX8 .... 107 H8
Marathon Cl *WODY* RG5 .... 335 K7
Marcham Rd *ABGD* OX14 .... 237 J6
  MCHM/KBPZ OX13 .... 237 C1
March Rd *RBANNS* OX17 .... 11 J3
Marchwood Av *CAV/SC* RG4 .... 327 J7
Marcourt Rd *SKCH* HP14 .... 249 G3
Margaret Cl *BAN* OX16 .... 2 A4
  BIC OX26 .... 96 E3
Margaret Rd *HEAD* OX3 .... 168 D5
  RBANNS OX17 .... 38 E2
Maria Crs *WANT* OX12 .... 282 E2
Marigold Cl *COW/LTMR* OX4 .... 193 F6
Marigold Wk *BIC* OX26 .... 97 F2
Marines Dr *FGDN* SN7 .... 230 B5
Marjoram Cl *COW/LTMR* OX4 .... 193 G5
Market End Wy *BIC* OX26 .... 96 D4
Market Pl *BAN* OX16 .... 3 D3
  BRACKY NN13 .... 43 F1
  HEN RG9 .... 319 F5
  RBANSW OX15 .... 56 C3
  READ RG1 .... 333 H8
  WANT OX12 .... 282 D3
  WDSTK OX20 .... 127 H1
  WGFD OX10 .... 267 F8
Market Sq *BIC* OX26 .... 97 G6
Market St *CHNTN* OX7 .... 68 B4
  CHNTN OX7 .... 106 A3
  OX/KTN OX1 .... 4 C4
Mark Rd *HEAD* OX3 .... 168 E5
Marlborough Av *KID* OX5 .... 129 G5
Marlborough Cl
  BUR/CRTN OX18 .... 158 A6
  COW/LTMR OX4 .... 192 B5
  FGDN SN7 .... 230 B4
  RBANNS OX17 .... 39 J1
  WIT/EY OX8 .... 146 A7
Marlborough Ct
  OXN/BOT/CM OX2 .... 166 D6
Marlborough Crs *WDSTK* OX20 ..... 109 H8
  WIT/EY OX8 .... 126 B7
Marlborough Cft *BRACKY* NN13 ...... 43 G1
Marlborough Dr *WIT/EY* OX8 .... 146 E6
Marlborough Gdns *FGDN* SN7 .... 230 A5
Marlborough La *FGDN* SN7 .... 232 C8
  WIT/EY OX8 .... 143 F7
Marlborough Pl *BAN* OX16 .... 3 D4
  CHNTN OX7 .... 106 A4
  FGDN SN7 .... 230 A5
  WIT/EY OX8 .... 146 A7
Marlborough Rd *BAN* OX16 .... 2 C4
  CHNTN OX7 .... 68 C4
  OX/KTN OX1 .... 4 C6
Marlborough St *FGDN* SN7 .... 230 B4
Marley La *STAD* OX44 .... 220 A8
Marley Wy *BAN* OX16 .... 2 C2
Marling Cl *CALC* RG31 .... 331 G5
Marlow Cl *WGFD* OX10 .... 266 D7
Marlowe Cl *BAN* OX16 .... 28 B1
Marlow Rd *HEN* RG9 .... 319 G4
  SKCH HP14 .... 249 H3
Marmion Rd *HEN* RG9 .... 319 G7
Marriott Cl *OXN/BOT/CM* OX2 .... 149 F6
Marriott's Cl *HADM* HP17 .... 176 B1
Marriott's La *HADM* HP17 .... 176 B1
Marriott's Wy *HADM* HP17 .... 176 B1
Marsack St *CAV/SC* RG4 .... 333 J5
Marshall Cl *CHNTN* OX7 .... 68 B6
  GOR/PANG RG8 .... 331 H3
Marshall Crs *CHNTN* OX7 .... 73 F6
Marshall Rd *COW/LTMR* OX4 .... 192 D1
Marshalls Cl *RBANSW* OX15 .... 17 J5
Marsh Cl *KID* OX5 .... 148 A2
Marsh Ct *ABGD* OX14 .... 214 D7
Marsh End *THAME* OX9 .... 198 A6
Marshland Sq *CAV/SC* RG4 .... 333 H2
Marsh La *BUR/CRTN* OX18 .... 182 B8
  HEAD OX3 .... 168 A2
  MCHM/KBPZ OX13 .... 211 H3
  WGFD OX10 .... 267 J7

Marsh Rd COW/LTMR OX4 .... 192 C1
 RAYLW HP18 .... 173 G4
Marsh Wy FGDN SN7 .... 278 C1
Marston Ferry Rd
 OXN/BOT/CM OX2 .... 167 G1
Marston Rd HEAD OX3 .... 5 F3
 HEAD OX3 .... 168 A3 🔟
 THAME OX9 .... 175 G6
Marston St COW/LTMR OX4 .... 5 F5
Marten Ga BAN OX16 .... 3 D6 🔟
Marten Pl CALC RG31 .... 331 F4
Martens Cl HGHW SN6 .... 276 A1 🔟
Martens Rd HGHW SN6 .... 276 B1
Martin Cl BIC OX26 .... 97 C7
Martinfield SWDNE SN3 .... 274 B8
Martin's La WCFD OX10 .... 241 K5
Martyn's Wy WGFD OX10 .... 268 D3
Maryfield WANT OX12 .... 282 E3
Marylands Gn STAD OX44 .... 217 K5
Marymead AVFD OX10 .... 290 B5
Mary Whipple Ct WANT OX12 .... 282 B5
Mascall Av HEAD OX3 .... 168 E8
Mascord Cl BAN OX16 .... 2 A4
Mascord Rd BAN OX16 .... 2 A4
Masefield Cl BIC OX26 .... 96 D4 🔟
Masefield Crs ABGD OX14 .... 238 A2
Masefield Rd BAN OX16 .... 2 A5
Masey Cl HEAD OX3 .... 168 D6
Masons Rd HEAD OX3 .... 168 E6
Mason St READ RG1 .... 332 E7
Master Cl WODY RG5 .... 335 K7
Mather Rd HEAD OX3 .... 169 F7
Mathews Wy
 MCHM/KBPZ OX13 .... 213 K1 🔟
Matlock Rd CAV/SC RG4 .... 332 E3
Mattock Cl HEAD OX3 .... 168 D5
Mattock Wy ABGD OX14 .... 215 F4
Maud Cl BIC OX26 .... 96 D3
Maule Cl RBANSW OX15 .... 37 F5
The Maunds RBANSW OX15 .... 56 B3
Mavor Cl WDSTK OX20 .... 109 H8
Mawles La CHNTN OX7 .... 102 E7
Maxwell Av DID OX11 .... 285 K4
Maxwell Cl WODY RG5 .... 335 G7
Maycroft BIC OX26 .... 97 G3 🔟
Mayfair TLHT RG30 .... 331 H8
Mayfair Rd COW/LTMR OX4 .... 192 B3
Mayfield Av WANT OX12 .... 258 F7
Mayfield Cl BUR/CRTN OX18 .... 157 J6
 STAD OX44 .... 244 B1 🔟
Mayfield Dr CAV/SC RG4 .... 333 J4
Mayfield Rd BAN OX16 .... 29 F5
 OXN/BOT/CM OX2 .... 149 F8
 OXN/BOT/CM OX2 .... 164 D5
Mayott's Rd ABGD OX14 .... 214 C8 🔟
May's Cl RBICN OX27 .... 58 E8
Mckee Sq WTLGN OX49 .... 268 A5
Mckeevor Pl BAN OX16 .... 3 E5 🔟
Mcmullan Cl WGFD OX10 .... 266 E7 🔟
Meaden Hl HEAD OX3 .... 168 B2
Mead La FGDN SN7 .... 253 K5
Meadow Bank FGDN SN7 .... 230 B4
Meadowbank Cl CHNTN OX7 .... 103 J5
 RAYLW HP18 .... 174 C1
Meadow Cl CHNTN OX7 .... 102 E6
 GOR/PANG RG8 .... 322 E1 🔟
 WANT OX12 .... 258 E6
 WIT/EY OX8 .... 164 D4
Meadow La BUR/CRTN OX18 .... 139 F1
 CHNTN OX7 .... 102 E6
 COW/LTMR OX4 .... 5 E6
 WGFD OX10 .... 291 J1
Meadow Prospect
 OXN/BOT/CM OX2 .... 148 B7
Meadow Rd CHNR OX39 .... 225 F1
 HEN RG9 .... 319 G6
 HGHW SN6 .... 252 E5
 READ RG1 .... 333 F6
Meadowside ABGD OX14 .... 238 C1
 CALC RG31 .... 331 F6 🔟
Meadowside Rd GOR/PANG RG8 .... 330 B2
The Meadows WTLGN OX49 .... 246 B5 🔟
Meadow Vw BAN OX16 .... 3 E6
 KID OX5 .... 129 H5
 RBANNS OX17 .... 58 D5
 RBICS/W OX25 .... 114 A4
 WIT/EY OX8 .... 143 J7
Meadow View Rd OX/KTN OX1 .... 191 J7
Meadow Wk WDSTK OX20 .... 127 K1 🔟
Meadow Wy CHNTN OX7 .... 84 A3
 DID OX11 .... 263 G8
 FGDN SN7 .... 230 B5 🔟
 KID OX5 .... 147 K2
 THAME OX9 .... 175 F6 🔟
Mead Platt SKCH HP14 .... 249 F2
Mead Rd RBANSW OX15 .... 37 G8
Meads Cl ABGD OX14 .... 4 A5
The Meads WANT OX12 .... 258 E1
The Mead RBANNS OX17 .... 12 B4
Mead Wy KID OX5 .... 129 H5
The Meadway TLHT RG30 .... 331 J8
Meashill Wy DID OX11 .... 285 H7
Medcroft Rd KID OX5 .... 110 E1
Medill Cl GOR/PANG RG8 .... 314 C7 🔟
Medina Cl DID OX11 .... 264 B6 🔟

Medina Gdns BIC OX26 .... 96 C5
Medlar Rd HGHW SN6 .... 252 C8
Medlicott Dr ABGD OX14 .... 238 A1
Mediock Gv DID OX11 .... 263 K4
Medway Cl MCHM/KBPZ OX13 .... 214 A4
Medway Rd MCHM/KBPZ OX13 .... 214 A4
Melbourne Cl BAN OX16 .... 3 F6
Melford Gn CAV/SC RG4 .... 334 A1 🔟
Mellebourne Cl
 COW/LTMR OX4 .... 193 F6 🔟🔟
Melton Dr DID OX11 .... 263 J6
Melville Cl BIC OX26 .... 96 C5
Membury Wy WANT OX12 .... 258 D7
Memorial Av HEN RG9 .... 329 C5
Mendip Cl WAR/TWY RG10 .... 335 K3
Mendip Hts DID OX11 .... 263 G5
Menmarsh Rd RAYLW HP18 .... 172 B1
Menpes Rd CALC RG31 .... 331 C3
Merchants Pl READ RG1 .... 333 G7 🔟
Mercury Cl BUR/CRTN OX18 .... 183 H4
Mercury Rd COW/LTMR OX4 .... 193 C5
Meredith Cl BIC OX26 .... 96 D4
Mere Dyke Rd MCHM/KBPZ OX13 .... 261 H3
Mereland Rd DID OX11 .... 263 K8
Mere La BUCK/WIN MK18 .... 63 H1
Mere Rd BUCK/WIN MK18 .... 63 G1
 OXN/BOT/CM OX2 .... 148 D7
Merewood Av HEAD OX3 .... 169 G3
Merganser Dr BIC OX26 .... 97 J7
Meriden Ct WGFD OX10 .... 266 E8 🔟
Merlin Cl BUR/CRTN OX18 .... 157 K4
Merlin Rd COW/LTMR OX4 .... 192 E5
 MCHM/KBPZ OX13 .... 213 K5
Merlin Wy BIC OX26 .... 97 H7
 SWDNE SN3 .... 274 B6
Merritt Rd DID OX11 .... 263 G6
Merrivale's La RBANSW OX15 .... 37 F3 🔟
Merrivale Sq OXN/BOT/CM OX2 .... 4 A1 🔟
Merrymouth Rd CHNTN OX7 .... 101 F5
Mersey Wy DID OX11 .... 264 A5
Merthyr V CAV/SC RG4 .... 333 C1
Merton Cl DID OX11 .... 264 B7 🔟
 WIT/EY OX8 .... 145 K8
Merton Rd RBICS/W OX25 .... 115 K4
Merton St BAN OX16 .... 3 E3
 OX/KTN OX1 .... 5 D4
Merton Wy KID OX5 .... 147 K2
Metcalf Cl ABGD OX14 .... 238 C3
Metcalfe Cl RBANSW OX15 .... 19 K7 🔟
Meteor Cl BIC OX26 .... 97 H4 🔟
 WODY RG5 .... 335 J8
Mewburn Rd BAN OX16 .... 2 B4
Mews Cl WTLGN OX49 .... 246 B5 🔟
The Mews HGHW SN6 .... 250 E1 🔟
 HGHW SN6 .... 252 D6 🔟
Meyseys Cl HEAD OX3 .... 169 F8 🔟
Micklands Rd CAV/SC RG4 .... 333 K3
Mickle Wy WHLY OX33 .... 170 A3
Middle Aston La RBICS/W OX25 .... 74 C5
Middle Aston Rd RBICS/W OX25 .... 74 D1
Middle Barton Rd RBICS/W OX25 .... 74 A2
Middle Furlong DID OX11 .... 264 B5
Middle Hl RBANSW OX15 .... 34 A8 🔟
Middle La RBANNS OX17 .... 11 K7
 RBANSW OX15 .... 18 C7
Middle Rd BUR/CRTN OX18 .... 137 F1
 WHLY OX33 .... 151 K8
Middle Rw CHNTN OX7 .... 68 B4 🔟
Middle St KID OX5 .... 130 E6
Middleton Cl BAN OX16 .... 21 J8
 RWWCK/WEL CV35 .... 16 B3
Middleton Rd BAN OX16 .... 3 E3
 BAN OX16 .... 21 J8
 RBANNS OX17 .... 22 C5
 RBICN OX27 .... 78 A8
Middleton Stoney Rd BIC OX26 .... 96 B6
Middle Wy CHNR OX39 .... 224 D1
 KID OX5 .... 130 E6
 OXN/BOT/CM OX2 .... 148 E8
Midget Cl ABGD OX14 .... 238 B2
Midshires Wy CHNR OX39 .... 201 J8
Midsummer Meadow
 CAV/SC RG4 .... 333 F1 🔟
Midway RBANNS OX17 .... 22 E6 🔟
Midwinter Av ABGD OX14 .... 262 A4
Midwinter Ct TLHT RG30 .... 331 J7 🔟
Miles Dr WANT OX12 .... 258 E7
Milestone Av WAR/TWY RG10 .... 335 J3
Milestone Crs WAR/TWY RG10 .... 335 J3
Milestone Rd BUR/CRTN OX18 .... 157 K6
Miles Wy WODY RG5 .... 335 J8
Mileway Gdns HEAD OX3 .... 168 C6 🔟
Milford Pl WDSTK OX20 .... 109 H3
Milking La WIT/EY OX8 .... 142 E4
Millaway La FGDN SN7 .... 257 G2
Millbank OXN/BOT/CM OX2 .... 4 A4
Millbrook Cl DID OX11 .... 288 A6
 WGFD OX10 .... 266 E8
Mill Cl CHNTN OX7 .... 86 E6
 HEN RG9 .... 296 B7
 KID OX5 .... 132 B2
 RBANSW OX15 .... 56 B3
Milldown Av GOR/PANG RG8 .... 312 E8
Milldown Rd GOR/PANG RG8 .... 312 E8
Mill End KID OX5 .... 129 K6

Miller Rd BAN OX16 .... 2 A
 WHLY OX33 170
Miller's Acre OXN/BOT/CM OX2 .... 149 F6
Millers Cl GOR/PANG RG8 312
 STAD OX44 220
Millers La RBANSW OX15 10
Millers Ms WIT/EY OX8 143
Millers Turn CHNR OX39 224
Millfield Av RBICN OX27 99
Millfield Cl RBICN OX27 99
Millford Rd READ RG1 333
Mill On CAV/SC RG4 333
The Millham WANT OX12 284
Mill La ABGD OX14 238
 ABGD OX14 262
 BRACKY NN13 41
 BRACKY NN13 43
 BRACKY NN13 44
 BUR/CRTN OX18 181
 BUR/CRTN OX18 181
 CAV/SC RG4 326
 CHNR OX39 224
 CHNTN OX7 72
 CHNTN OX7 73
 CIR CL7 203
 COW/LTMR OX4 191
 DID OX11 289
 HADM HP17 175
 HEAD OX3 149
 HEN RG9 319
 HEN RG9 329
 KID OX5 111
 KID OX5 132
 RBANNS OX17 14
 RBANNS OX17 14
 RBANNS OX17 21
 RBANNS OX17 38
 RBANNS OX17 39
 RBANSW OX15 19
 RBICS/W OX25 75
 RBICS/W OX25 93
 RBICS/W OX25 113
 RBICS/W OX25 116
 READ RG1 333
 SKCH HP14 248
 STAD OX44 196
 STAD OX44 244
 WANT OX12 257
 WANT OX12 258
 WANT OX12 284
 WANT OX12 285
 WDSTK OX20 109
 WGFD OX10 267
 WGFD OX10 267
 WHLY OX33 152
 WIT/EY OX8 146
Millmoor Crs WIT/EY OX8 146
Mill Orch WANT OX12 259
Mill Paddock ABGD OX14 238
 WANT OX12 282
Mill Rd ABGD OX14 238
 CAV/SC RG4 333
 GOR/PANG RG8 312
 HEN RG9 294
 HEN RG9 329
 MCHM/KBPZ OX13 237
 OXN/BOT/CM OX2 148
 RBICN OX27 80
 SKCH HP14 248
Mills La RBANSW OX15 19
Mill St KID OX5 129
 MCHM/KBPZ OX13 261
 OXN/BOT/CM OX2 4
 WANT OX12 282
 WHLY OX33 151
 WIT/EY OX8 142
 WIT/EY OX8 146
Millway Cl OXN/BOT/CM OX2 148
Millway La MCHM/KBPZ OX13 212
Millwood End WIT/EY OX8 126
Millwood V WIT/EY OX8 126
Millwright Cl BAN OX16 .... 2 B3
Milne Pl HEAD OX3 168
 HEN RG9 319
Milton Cl BIC OX26 .... 96 D4
Milton Crs WHLY OX33 170
Milton Hl ABGD OX14 261
Milton La MCHM/KBPZ OX13 261
Milton Pk ABGD OX14 262
Milton Rd ABGD OX14 262
 COW/LTMR OX4 192
 DID OX11 262
 EARL RG6 334
 RBANSW OX15 37
Milton St BAN OX16 .... 2 C4
Minchery Rd COW/LTMR OX4 192
Minchins Cl ABGD OX14 215
Minnow La BUR/CRTN OX18 139
Minns Rd WANT OX12 259
Minster Riding WIT/EY OX8 141
Minster Rd BUR/CRTN OX18 158
 COW/LTMR OX4 168
Minster St READ RG1 333
Minton Cl TLHT RG30 .... 331 K7
Minty Cl BUR/CRTN OX18 157

Airfield Rd *WIT/EY* OX8 .... 142 C7
Mistletoe Gn *COW/LTMR* OX4 .... 192 E6
Mitchell Cl *MCHM/KBPZ* OX13 .... 213 J1
  THAME OX9 .... 174 E7
Mitchell Wy *WODY* RG5 .... 335 J8
Mixbury Rd *BRACKY* NN13 .... 43 G1
Moat Cl *BUR/CRTN* OX18 .... 158 D4
Moat La *RBICN* OX27 .... 99 H5
Moat's Crs *THAME* OX9 .... 175 F7
The Moat *CHNTN* OX7 .... 84 A1
Mobbs La *WIT/EY* OX8 .... 34 A8
Moberly Cl *COW/LTMR* OX4 .... 5 F5
Mohawk Wy *WODY* RG5 .... 335 K8
Moir Ct *WANT* OX12 .... 282 D2
Mold Crs *BAN* OX16 .... 2 A3
Mole Pl *COW/LTMR* OX4 .... 193 F6
Mollington La *RBANNS* OX17 ..... 11 G3
  RBANNS OX17 .... 11 J7
Mollison Cl *WODY* RG5 .... 335 K7
Molyneux Dr *RBANSW* OX15 ...... 29 G7
Monique Cl *BAN* OX16 .... 20 C6
Monks Cl *COW/LTMR* OX4 .... 192 D5
  WANT OX12 .... 258 E1
  WGFD OX10 .... 242 A6
Monks Lode *DID* OX11 .... 263 K4
Monks Md *WGFD* OX10 .... 266 A5
Monmouth Rd *OX/KTN* OX1 .... 191 H2
Mons Wy *ABGD* OX14 .... 214 B6
Montague St *CAV/SC* RG4 .... 333 J5
  READ RG1 .... 333 K8
Montagu Rd *OXN/BOT/CM* OX2 .. 166 A7
Montgomery Rd *RBICN* OX27 ..... 97 H1
Montpelier Dr *CAV/SC* RG4 .... 334 A2
Monument Rd *STAD* OX44 .... 244 C1
Monument St *BAN* OX16 .... 2 C4
Moody Rd *HEAD* OX3 .... 5 F2
Moor Av *WIT/EY* OX8 .... 142 E6
Moorbank *COW/LTMR* OX4 .... 192 E4
Moorend La *THAME* OX9 .... 175 G5
Moorfield Ct *BAN* OX16 .... 3 E3
Moorgate *CIR* GL7 .... 203 F3
Moor Hart Cl *SKCH* HP14 .... 249 G3
Moorland Cl *WIT/EY* OX8 .... 142 D6
Moorland Rd *WIT/EY* OX8 .... 142 E7
The Moorlands *KID* OX5 .... 129 C5
  WGFD OX10 .... 267 H3
Moor La *RBANSW* OX15 .... 36 A8
Moor Pond Cl *BIC* OX26 .... 97 C5
Moors Cl *WIT/EY* OX8 .... 160 E2
Moran Cl *BAN* OX16 .... 20 B7
Moriston Cl *TLHT* RG30 .... 332 B7
Morlais *CAV/SC* RG4 .... 333 J3
Morland Cl *WHLY* OX33 .... 170 D7
Morland Rd *MCHM/KBPZ* OX13 .. 237 F1
Morlands *WANT* OX12 .... 235 H8
Morrell Av *COW/LTMR* OX4 .... 5 F5
Morrell Cl *KID* OX5 .... 129 C7
Morrell Crs *COW/LTMR* OX4 ...... 192 A5
Morrells Cl *DID* OX11 .... 263 H6
Morris Crs *COW/LTMR* OX4 .... 192 B1
Morris Dr *BAN* OX16 .... 20 B7
Morse Rd *DID* OX11 .... 287 H1
Mortimer Dr *HEAD* OX3 .... 5 E1
Mortimer Rd *COW/LTMR* OX4 .... 191 F7
Morton Av *KID* OX5 .... 129 H8
Morton Cl *ABGD* OX14 .... 215 C7
  KID OX5 .... 129 H7
Mosedale *MIM* GL56 .... 46 B2
Mosquito La *WGFD* OX10 .... 268 B4
Moss Cl *CAV/SC* RG4 .... 333 J4
The Motte *ABGD* OX14 .... 214 D7
Mountfield Rd *GOR/PANG* RG8 .. 312 E8
Mountfield Rd *WIT/EY* OX8 .... 142 C8
Mount Owen Rd *BUR/CRTN* OX18 .. 183 J3
Mount Pl *OXN/BOT/CM* OX2 ..... 4 A3
Mount Pleasant *CIR* GL7 .... 203 G3
Mount St *OXN/BOT/CM* OX2 ..... 4 A3
The Mount *CAV/SC* RG4 .... 333 F4
  THAME OX9 .... 198 B7
Mount Vw *HEN* RG9 .... 319 G4
Mowbray Dr *TLHT* RG30 .... 332 A7
Mowbray Rd *DID* OX11 .... 287 J1
Mowforth Cl *GOR/PANG* RG8 ... 314 C6
Muirfield Cl *READ* RG1 .... 333 G6
The Mulberries *WANT* OX12 ...... 259 G1
Mulberry Dr *BIC* OX26 .... 97 C2
  WHLY OX33 .... 170 D7
Mulcaster Av *KID* OX5 .... 129 J7
Mullard Wy *ABGD* OX14 .... 214 C8
Mullein Cl *BIC* OX26 .... 96 E2
Murcott Rd *RBICS/W* OX25 .... 134 A1
Murdock Cl *RBANSW* OX15 .... 56 B5
Murdock Rd *BIC* OX26 .... 97 G5
The Murren *WGFD* OX10 .... 291 F1
Museum Rd *OX/KTN* OX1 .... 4 C3
Musgrave Rd *CHNR* OX39 .... 201 F8

Musgrave Wk *SKCH* HP14 .... 249 H2
Musson Cl *ABGD* OX14 .... 238 C1
Mustard La *CAV/SC* RG4 .... 335 G6
Myers Cl *RBANNS* OX17 .... 40 C1
Myers Wy *RBANNS* OX17 .... 40 E2
Myrtle Cl *CALC* RG31 .... 331 G4
  WIT/EY OX8 .... 126 C6

N

Naldertown *WANT* OX12 .... 282 C2
Napier Rd *COW/LTMR* OX4 .... 192 D3
  READ RG1 .... 333 J7
Nappins Cl *RAYLW* HP18 .... 174 D2
Nash Dr *ABGD* OX14 .... 238 A1
Nash La *WIT/EY* OX8 .... 126 E8
Neals La *CAV/SC* RG4 .... 316 B5
Neath Gdns *TLHT* RG30 .... 331 K8
Neithrop Av *BAN* OX16 .... 2 B2
Neithrop Cl *BAN* OX16 .... 2 B2
Nell Br *RBANNS* OX17 .... 39 J6
Nelson Cl *WGFD* OX10 .... 266 F7
Nelson Rd *CAV/SC* RG4 .... 333 J5
Nelson St *OXN/BOT/CM* OX2 ..... 4 B3
  THAME OX9 .... 175 F7
Nene Cv *DID* OX11 .... 264 B5
Nene Rd *MCHM/KBPZ* OX13 ..... 214 A5
Netheravon Cl *BUR/CRTN* OX18 . 158 A5
Nethercote La *MCHM/KBPZ* OX13 . 211 J4
Nethercote Rd *KID* OX5 .... 111 F1
Netherton La *MCHM/KBPZ* OX13 . 211 J4
Netherton Rd *MCHM/KBPZ* OX13 . 212 B1
Netherwoods Rd *HEAD* OX3 .... 169 F5
Netherworton Rd *RBANSW* OX15 . 55 F3
Netley Cl *CAV/SC* RG4 .... 334 A1
Netting Rd *RBANSW* OX15 .... 33 K8
Nettlebed Md *COW/LTMR* OX4 ... 192 E6
Nettleton Dr *RBICS/W* OX25 ...... 76 B8
Neville Wy *FGDN* SN7 .... 232 C8
Nevis Rd *CALC* RG31 .... 331 H4
New Bath Rd *WAR/TWY* RG10 .... 335 K2
New Cross Rd *HEAD* OX3 .... 168 E4
Newells Cl *STAD* OX44 .... 218 E6
Newell's La *CAV/SC* RG4 .... 326 B8
Newfield Rd *CAV/SC* RG4 .... 327 F1
Newgate Rd *KID* OX5 .... 132 E2
New High St *HEAD* OX3 .... 168 C5
New Hl *GOR/PANG* RG8 .... 331 G2
New Inn Hall St *OX/KTN* OX1 ..... 4 C4
New Inn Rd *HEAD* OX3 .... 151 G5
Newland *WIT/EY* OX8 .... 143 G7
Newland Cl *WIT/EY* OX8 .... 146 A8
Newland Ml *WIT/EY* OX8 .... 143 G7
Newland Pl *BAN* OX16 .... 3 D4
Newland Rd *BAN* OX16 .... 3 D4
Newlands *RBANNS* OX17 .... 39 K1
Newlands Av *CAV/SC* RG4 .... 333 H4
  DID OX11 .... 263 J8
Newlands Dr *WANT* OX12 .... 258 C7
Newlands La *HEN* RG9 .... 316 A2
Newland St *WIT/EY* OX8 .... 146 A7
Newlin Cl *COW/LTMR* OX4 .... 191 K4
Newman La *ABGD* OX14 .... 237 K5
Newman Rd *COW/LTMR* OX4 ..... 192 D4
Newmans Cl *DID* OX11 .... 287 G4
Newmill La *WIT/EY* OX8 .... 142 C5
Newnham Gn *WGFD* OX10 .... 267 H8
Newnhamhill Bottom *HEN* RG9 .. 316 B1
New Pond La *KID* OX5 .... 132 B2
Newport Cl *KID* OX5 .... 129 C8
Newport Rd *READ* RG1 .... 333 G6
New Rd *ABGD* OX14 .... 215 J4
  BAN OX16 .... 2 C4
  BUR/CRTN OX18 .... 183 H5
  CHNTN OX7 .... 53 J8
  CHNTN OX7 .... 83 J5
  CHNTN OX7 .... 84 A4
  DID OX11 .... 288 A1
  HEN RG9 .... 329 A1
  HGHW SN6 .... 277 G4
  KID OX5 .... 112 A7
  MCHM/KBPZ OX13 .... 236 E1
  MIM GL56 .... 46 A1
  OX/KTN OX1 .... 4 B4
  RBANNS OX17 .... 11 J7
  RBANSW OX15 .... 10 A3
  RBANSW OX15 .... 36 B6
  SKCH HP14 .... 249 H3
  WANT OX12 .... 233 K5
  WANT OX12 .... 256 C7
  WANT OX12 .... 257 F6
  WDSTK OX20 .... 90 E7
  WDSTK OX20 .... 127 J1

WGFD OX10 .... 266 D1
WGFD OX10 .... 267 F8
WIT/EY OX8 .... 126 C6
WIT/EY OX8 .... 142 E1
WTLGN OX49 .... 246 B5
New Rw *RBICN* OX27 .... 78 A8
Newscut La *RBANNS* OX17 .... 13 H5
New St *ABGD* OX14 .... 214 D8
  BIC OX26 .... 97 F4
  CHNTN OX7 .... 68 A4
  HEN RG9 .... 19 G5
  RBANSW OX15 .... 56 C4
Newton Av *CAV/SC* RG4 .... 333 K2
Newton Rd *OX/KTN* OX1 .... 4 C6
Newton Wy *WGFD* OX10 .... 267 J2
Newtown Gdns *HEN* RG9 .... 319 G7
New Town La *HGHW* SN6 .... 298 D2
Newtown Rd *HEN* RG9 .... 319 H7
New Yatt La *WIT/EY* OX8 .... 124 C8
New Yatt Rd *WIT/EY* OX8 .... 143 G5
Niagara Rd *HEN* RG9 .... 319 G7
Nicholas Av *HEAD* OX3 .... 5 F1
Nicholas Rd *HEN* RG9 .... 318 D7
Nichol Ct *FGDN* SN7 .... 230 B4
Nicholson Rd *HEAD* OX3 .... 5 F2
Nightingale Av *COW/LTMR* OX4 .. 193 F6
Nightingale La *SWDNE* SN3 .... 274 E2
Nimrod Cl *WODY* RG5 .... 335 J8
Nine Acres Cl *CHNTN* OX7 .... 106 A3
Nine Acres La *CHNTN* OX7 .... 106 A3
Nineteenth St *DID* OX11 .... 285 H5
Ninety Cut Hl *BUR/CRTN* OX18 .. 140 C3
Ninth Av *HEAD* OX3 .... 169 F8
Ninth St *DID* OX11 .... 285 K4
Nire Rd *CAV/SC* RG4 .... 334 A4
Nixon Rd *COW/LTMR* OX4 .... 191 K2
Nizewell Head *RBICS/W* OX25 ... 74 E7
Nobles Cl *OXN/BOT/CM* OX2 ..... 165 J7
  WANT OX12 .... 258 D6
Nobles La *OXN/BOT/CM* OX2 .... 165 J7
Norbrook Cl *ABGD* OX14 .... 215 G5
Norcot Rd *TLHT* RG30 .... 331 J7
Norfolk Cl *ABGD* OX14 .... 215 H5
Norfolk Rd *TLHT* RG30 .... 332 C8
Norfolk St *OX/KTN* OX1 .... 4 C5
Norham Gdns *OXN/BOT/CM* OX2 . 4 C2
Norham Rd *OXN/BOT/CM* OX2 ... 4 C1
Norman Av *ABGD* OX14 .... 214 E6
  HEN RG9 .... 319 G6
Normandy Crs *COW/LTMR* OX4 .. 192 E2
Norman Pl *READ* RG1 .... 333 H6
Norman Rd *CAV/SC* RG4 .... 333 J3
Norman Smith Rd
  COW/LTMR OX4 .... 193 F6
Normanstead Rd *CALC* RG31 ..... 331 G7
Norman Wy *WGFD* OX10 .... 266 G8
Norreys Av *OX/KTN* OX1 .... 191 H1
Norreys Cl *DID* OX11 .... 263 H8
Norreys Rd *DID* OX11 .... 263 H7
  OXN/BOT/CM OX2 .... 189 H2
Norries Dr *WGFD* OX10 .... 267 F9
Norris Acre *BRACKY* NN13 .... 42 A1
Norris Cl *ABGD* OX14 .... 215 F5
  RBANNS OX17 .... 38 B5
Norris Rd *RBICS/W* OX25 .... 116 B8
Northampton Rd *OX/KTN* OX1 ... 191 H2
North Aston Rd *RBICS/W* OX25 .. 74 B1
North Av *ABGD* OX14 .... 214 E5
North Bar Pl *BAN* OX16 .... 2 C3
North Bar St *BAN* OX16 .... 2 C3
Northbrook Rd *CAV/SC* RG4 ...... 333 K2
North Bush Furlong *DID* OX11 ... 264 B6
North Cl *THAME* OX9 .... 172 D8
Northcourt La *ABGD* OX14 .... 214 E6
Northcourt Rd *ABGD* OX14 .... 214 D6
Northcourt Wk *ABGD* OX14 .... 214 E7
North Cft *DID* OX11 .... 287 K2
North Dr *DID* OX11 .... 286 A3
  WANT OX12 .... 258 E5
Northern By-Pass Rd *HEAD* OX3 . 168 B2
  OXN/BOT/CM OX2 .... 148 B5
  OXN/BOT/CM OX2 .... 149 H7
Northfield Av *HEN* RG9 .... 329 J3
Northfield End *HEN* RG9 .... 319 F4
Northfield Rd *ABGD* OX14 .... 214 E4
  HEAD OX3 .... 168 E3
  HEN RG9 .... 329 K3
  READ RG1 .... 333 G6
Northford Cl *HGHW* SN6 .... 252 C7
Northford Hl *HGHW* SN6 .... 252 D7
North Gn *WANT* OX12 .... 259 F1
North Hinksey La
  OXN/BOT/CM OX2 .... 166 C7
North La *RBICS/W* OX25 .... 113 F5
North Leigh La *WIT/EY* OX8 .... 124 C7
Northmead La *WANT* OX12 .... 254 A8
North Mill Rd *PRR7* HP22 .... 201 J2
Northmoor Rd *OXN/BOT/CM* OX2 . 167 G2
Northolt Rd *BUR/CRTN* OX18 ..... 157 K4
North Parade Av *OXN/BOT/CM* OX2 . 4 B1
North Pl *HEAD* OX3 .... 168 D4
North Quay *ABGD* OX14 .... 238 D3
North Rd *DID* OX11 .... 263 G5
  WGFD OX10 .... 312 B3
North Side *RBICS/W* OX25 .... 74 D6

North St BAN OX16 .... 3 E2
BIC OX26 .... 97 F5
BUR/CRTN OX18 .... 184 C4
CAV/SC RG4 .... 333 H5
CHNTN OX7 .... 73 G7
HGHW SN6 .... 252 D6
KID OX5 .... 130 E6
MCHM/KBPZ OX13 .... 212 E8
RBICN OX27 .... 58 D8
READ RG1 .... 333 F7
THAME OX9 .... 175 F6
North Vw HGHW SN6 .... 252 D6
North Wy HEAD OX3 .... 168 E3
MCHM/KBPZ OX13 .... 261 H3
OXN/BOT/CM OX2 .... 148 D6
Northwood Crs BUR/CRTN OX18 .. 158 A3
Northwood Rd WIT/EY OX8 ... 142 A6
Norton Cl HEAD OX3 .... 168 D5
Norton Rd READ RG1 .... 334 A8
Norton Wy BUR/CRTN OX18 .. 158 B4
Norwich Dr WODY RG5 .... 334 E7
Norwood Av MCHM/KBPZ OX13 .. 210 E6
Norwood Rd READ RG1 .... 333 K8
Nottwood La HEN RG9 .... 316 A2
Nowell Rd COW/LTMR OX4 .... 191 K4
Nuffield Cl BIC OX26 .... 97 G4
DID OX11 .... 264 A7
Nuffield Dr BAN OX16 .... 2 A2
Nuffield Hl WGFD OX10 .... 293 G3
Nuffield La WGFD OX10 .... 292 B2
Nuffield Rd HEAD OX3 .... 168 E7
Nuffield Wy ABGD OX14 .... 214 A8
Nuneham Sq ABGD OX14 .... 214 C7
Nunhide La COR/PANG RG8 .... 330 D6
Nun's Acre GOR/PANG RG8 .... 312 D8
Nurseries Rd KID OX5 .... 129 C7
Nursery Cl HEAD OX3 .... 168 C5
HEN RG9 .... 329 J3
Nursery Dr BAN OX16 .... 2 B2
Nursery Gdns GOR/PANG RG8 .. 331 F2
Nursery La BAN OX16 .... 2 C2
Nursery Rd WIT/EY OX8 .... 125 H8
The Nursery ABGD OX14 .... 238 E7 ⊞
Nursery Vw FGDN SN7 .... 230 D4
Nuthatch Cl COW/LTMR OX4 .. 192 E6 ⊞⊞
Nyatt Rd ABGD OX14 .... 215 C7
Nye Bevan Cl COW/LTMR OX4 .. 168 A7
Nyland Rd SWDNE SN3 .... 274 A8

O

Oak Av ABGD OX14 .... 215 J1
Oak Cl BIC OX26 .... 97 G3
Oakdale Cl CALC RG31 .... 331 G2
Oakdene GOR/PANG RG8 .... 314 D8 ⊞
Oakdown Cl GOR/PANG RG8 ... 324 C4
Oak Dr HGHW SN6 .... 250 D2
KID OX5 .... 129 C7
Oak End Wy CHNR OX39 .... 224 E2
Oakes La OXN/BOT/CM OX2 ... 164 E5
Oakesmere MCHM/KBPZ OX13 .. 212 D1
Oak Farm Cl THAME OX9 .... 198 B8 ⊞
Oakfield Rd BUR/CRTN OX18 .. 157 K6
Oakham Cl CALC RG31 .... 331 H5 ⊞
Oakham Rd MIM GL56 .... 48 C6
Oakland Cl WIT/EY OX8 .... 126 A8
Oakland Rd BAN OX16 .... 29 F5
Oak La RBICS/W OX25 .... 116 A3
Oakley La CHNR OX39 .... 224 D1
Oakley Rd CAV/SC RG4 .... 333 F3
CHNR OX39 .... 224 E1
RAYLW HP18 .... 135 K7
WHLY OX33 .... 153 K3
Oak Mill Cl ABGD OX14 .... 238 B1
Oak Rd HGHW SN6 .... 252 C6
Oaks Rd HEN RG9 .... 329 J3
Oak St CIR GL7 .... 203 G3
Oakthorpe Pl OXN/BOT/CM OX2 .. 167 F1 ⊞
Oakthorpe Rd OXN/BOT/CM OX2 .. 167 F1
Oak Tree Copse CALC RG31 .... 331 J4 ⊞
Oak Tree Rd CALC RG31 .... 331 H5
Oak Tree Wk GOR/PANG RG8.. 331 H2
Oak Vw CALC RG31 .... 331 G7
Oatland Cl DID OX11 .... 263 J7
Oatlands Rd OXN/BOT/CM OX2 .. 166 D6
Observatory Cl WGFD OX10 .... 267 J3
Observatory St OXN/BOT/CM OX2 .. 4 B2
Ock Dr WGFD OX10 .... 241 K2
Ock St ABGD OX14 .... 238 C1
O'Connors Rd WIT/EY OX8 ..... 141 G5 ⊞
Octavian Wy BRACKY NN13 ..... 43 H1
Odiham Av CAV/SC RG4 .... 334 A2
Odiham Cl BUR/CRTN OX18 .... 158 B4 ⊞
Offas Cl WGFD OX10 .... 267 J2
Ogbourne Cl WANT OX12 .... 282 B2 ⊞
Ogmore Cl TLHT RG30 .... 331 J8 ⊞
Okeford Cl SWDNE SN3 .... 274 A8
Old Acre La WAR/TWY RG10 ... 335 K2
Old Arncott Rd RBICS/W OX25 .. 115 K4
Old Barn Cl CAV/SC RG4 .... 333 G1
WGFD OX10 .... 267 J3

Old Bath Rd CAV/SC RG4 .... 334 E6
WAR/TWY RG10 .... 335 J5
Old Bourne Rd DID OX11 .... 263 J4
Old Brewery Wk BRACKY NN13 .. 43 G1
Old Bridge Rd RBANSW OX15 ... 37 F3
Old Buildings WGFD OX10 ...... 267 F8 ⊞
Old Burford Rd CHNTN OX7 ..... 83 J5
Old Chapel Cl KID OX5 .... 129 H6
The Old Coachyard WIT/EY OX8 .. 145 F2 ⊞
Old Copse Gdns HEN RG9 ...... 327 F1
Old Croft Cl CHNR OX39 .... 224 B3
Old Elm Dr TLHT RG30 .... 331 H7 ⊞
Old Farm Cl ABGD OX14 .... 215 G7
RAYLW HP18 .... 172 C2 ⊞
Old Farm Crs CALC RG31 .... 331 G5 ⊞
Old Fld WANT OX12 .... 195 J8
Old Forge Cl CHNTN OX7 .... 83 J5
Old Forge Rd CHNTN OX7 .... 50 D4
Old George Yd BUR/CRTN OX18 .. 138 E2 ⊞
Old Glebe RBANSW OX15 .... 26 C7
Old Greyfriars St OX/KTN OX1 .... 4 C5 ⊞
Old Grimsbury Rd BAN OX16 ...... 3 J3
Old High St HEAD OX3 .... 168 D3
The Old Kiln HEN RG9 .... 294 E5 ⊞
Old London Rd THAME OX9 .... 196 D3
WGFD OX10 .... 267 J3
WHLY OX33 .... 170 E7
Old Manor Cl WANT OX12 ...... 281 K5
Old Marston Rd HEAD OX3 .... 5 F1 ⊞
Old Mill Cl HADM HP17 .... 176 C1
WANT OX12 .... 258 E6
Old Moor ABGD OX14 .... 262 B2
Old Moor Cl WGFD OX10 .... 266 E8 ⊞
Old Nursery Vw OX/KTN OX1 .. 191 H4 ⊞
Old Orch CHNR OX39 .... 201 C5
Old Parr Cl BAN OX16 .... 3 D4
Old Parr Rd BAN OX16 .... 2 C5
Old Place Yd BIC OX26 .... 97 F6
The Old Pound MCHM/KBPZ OX13.. 213 K2
Old Reading Rd WGFD OX10 ... 267 H8
Old Rectory Ct RBICS/W OX25 .. 114 B3
Old Rd CHNTN OX7 .... 53 J8
HEAD OX3 .... 168 D6
RBANSW OX15 .... 9 K3
WANT OX12 .... 285 C1
WHLY OX33 .... 169 K7
Old School Cl RBICN OX27 ...... 79 G8
Old School End RBANSW OX15 .. 33 K8
Old School La WANT OX12 ...... 281 K2
Old School Pl BAN OX16 .... 3 E3 ⊞
Old Stables Yd WANT OX12 ..... 282 A6
Old Tree La RWWCK/WEL CV35 .. 16 B3
Old Wharf Rd RDNG SN7 .... 253 J7
Old Witney Rd WIT/EY OX8 .... 145 J7
Oliver Rd COW/LTMR OX4 .... 192 E2
Olney Rd RWWCK/WEL CV35 ..... 8 E1
One End La WGFD OX10 .... 267 H3
Onslow Dr THAME OX9 .... 175 G6
Onslow Gdns CAV/SC RG4 ...... 333 J4
Oracle Pkwy EARL RG6........... 334 B7
Orange Cl HGHW SN6 .... 250 E1
Orchard Av CAV/SC RG4 .... 326 E2
Orchard Cl BAN OX16 .... 2 A3
CALC RG31 .... 331 F3
CHNTN OX7 .... 67 H2
CIR GL7 .... 203 F3 ⊞
DID OX11 .... 263 J6 ⊞
DID OX11 .... 287 G5
FGDN SN7 .... 208 C7
HEN RG9 .... 319 C6
HEN RG9 .... 329 G5
STAD OX44 .... 220 B8 ⊞
THAME OX9 .... 175 G7
WANT OX12 .... 233 K5
WANT OX12 .... 259 H1
WANT OX12 .... 261 F8
WGFD OX10 .... 242 D8
WHLY OX33 .... 170 D8
WIT/EY OX8 .... 126 B3
WIT/EY OX8 .... 146 E5 ⊞
Orchard Coombe GOR/PANG RG8 .. 324 B4
Orchard Fld CAV/SC RG4 .... 326 C2 ⊞
Orchard Field La WDSTK OX20 .. 128 A3
Orchard Gdns WANT OX12 ...... 281 H2
Orchard Gv CAV/SC RG4 .... 334 A3
RBANSW OX15 .... 36 E4 ⊞
Orchard Hvn WGFD OX10 .... 241 K7
Orchard Hl FGDN SN7 .... 230 A5
Orchard La OX/KTN OX1 .... 190 A6
RBICS/W OX25 .... 75 J7
WANT OX12 .... 285 F1
Orchard Piece RBANNS OX17 ... 12 C4
Orchard Pl BRACKY NN13 .... 44 D3
Orchard Ri BIC OX26 .... 96 A7
BUR/CRTN OX18 .... 138 E3
Orchard Rd FGDN SN7 .... 208 C7
OXN/BOT/CM OX2 .... 165 J7
RBANSW OX15 .... 34 A7
RBICN OX27 .... 77 G3
Orchard Rw BUR/CRTN OX18 .. 139 F1
The Orchard CHNTN OX7 .... 103 J6
RBICS/W OX25 .... 114 E7
WANT OX12 .... 282 A2
WIT/EY OX8 .... 146 B8
Orchard Vw RBANNS OX17 ...... 13 H5 ⊞

Orchard Wy BAN OX16 .... 2 ⊞
BIC OX26 .... 96 ⊞
CHNR OX39 .... 224 ⊞
CHNTN OX7 .... 73 ⊞
CHNTN OX7 .... 84 ⊞
COW/LTMR OX4 .... 192 C
DID OX11 .... 262 E
KID OX5 .... 129 ⊞
MCHM/KBPZ OX13 .... 237 ⊞
RBANNS OX17 .... 39 ⊞
WANT OX12 .... 282 ⊞
WIT/EY OX8 .... 142 E
The Orchids DID OX11 .... 286 ⊞
Ordnance Rd DID OX11 .... 63 ⊞
Oregon Av CALC RG31 .... 331 C
Oriel Ct DID OX11 .... 264 E
Oriel Gv MIM GL56 .... 46 A
Oriel St OX/KTN OX1 .... 5 D4
Orkney Pl WIT/EY OX8 .... 142 ⊞
Ormond Rd THAME OX9 .... 175 ⊞
WANT OX12 .... 282 C
Ormsby St READ RG1 .... 332 ⊞
Orpwood Wy ABGD OX14........ 238 A
Orrin Cl TLHT RG30 .... 332 A
Orts Rd READ RG1 .... 333 ⊞
Orville Cl WODY RG5 .... 335 ⊞
Orwell Cl CAV/SC RG4 .... 333 ⊞
Orwell Dr DID OX11 .... 264 A
Osberton Rd OXN/BOT/CM OX2 .. 148 E6
Osborne Av CALC RG31 .... 331 C
KID OX5 .... 129 C
OXN/BOT/CM OX2 .... 148 D7
Osborne Rd TLHT RG30 .... 332 B
The Osiers WGFD OX10 .... 242 C
Osler Rd HEAD OX3 .... 168 C
Osney Cl RBANSW OX15 .... 33 K8
Osney La OX/KTN OX1 .... 4 ⊞
OXN/BOT/CM OX2 .... 4 A
Osney Md OXN/BOT/CM OX2 ..... 4 A
Osprey Cl BIC OX26 .... 97 ⊞
Osterley Dr CAV/SC RG4 .... 334 A
Osterley Gv BAN OX16 .... 2 E
Oswestry Rd OX/KTN OX1 .... 191 H
Otmoor La HEAD OX3 .... 151 H
KID OX5 .... 132 E
Otters Reach OX/KTN OX1 ...... 191 ⊞
Ottery Wy DID OX11 .... 264 A
Otwell Cl ABGD OX14 .... 215 F5
Ouseley Cl HEAD OX3 .... 5 ⊞
Outram Rd COW/LTMR OX4 .... 192 E
The Oval BIC OX26 .... 96 E
COW/LTMR OX4 .... 192 A
DID OX11 .... 263 C
Overbrooke Gdns
COW/LTMR OX4 .... 193 G5
Overdale Cl HEAD OX3 .... 168 E3
Overdown Rd CALC RG31 .... 331 H
Overlanders End CALC RG31 ... 331 J4
Over Norton Rd CHNTN OX7 ..... 68 E
Overstrand Cl READ RG1 .... 332 A
Overthorpe Rd BAN OX16 .... 3 ⊞
RBANNS OX17 .... 29 ⊞
Overton Dr THAME OX9 .... 175 H6
Owlington Cl OXN/BOT/CM OX2 .. 166 A
Oxen Piece STAD OX44 .... 196 A
Oxeye Ct COW/LTMR OX4........ 192 E
Oxford Canal Wk BAN OX16 .... 3 C
KID OX5 .... 93 ⊞
KID OX5 .... 148 E
OXN/BOT/CM OX2 .... 166 E
RBANNS OX17 .... 29 ⊞
Oxford Cl KID OX5 .... 111 C
Oxford Crs DID OX11 .... 263 C
Oxford Hl WIT/EY OX8 .... 145 ⊞
Oxford La WANT OX12 .... 258 ⊞
Oxford Rd ABGD OX14 .... 214 E
ABGD OX14 .... 240 E
BAN OX16 .... 2 C
BRACKY NN13 .... 43 ⊞
BUR/CRTN OX18 .... 138 E
CALC RG31 .... 331 C
CHNTN OX7 .... 88 E
COW/LTMR OX4 .... 192 E
COW/LTMR OX4 .... 192 E
COW/LTMR OX4 .... 192 E
COW/LTMR OX4 .... 193 F
HEAD OX3 .... 167 K
KID OX5 .... 111 ⊞
KID OX5 .... 129 H
KID OX5 .... 148 E
OXN/BOT/CM OX2 .... 189 H
RBANSW OX15 .... 56 C
RBICS/W OX25 .... 74 E
RBICS/W OX25 .... 95 F
READ RG1 .... 333 F
SKCH HP14 .... 248 D
STAD OX44 .... 193 H
THAME OX9 .... 174 C
THAME OX9 .... 196 B
TLHT RG30 .... 332 E
WDSTK OX20 .... 127 K
WGFD OX10 .... 241 ⊞
WGFD OX10 .... 267 C
WIT/EY OX8 .... 146 E

Oxfordshire Circular Wks
WIT/EY OX8 .... 164 B2
Oxfordshire Cycle Wy
RBANSW OX15 .... 27 H8
Oxfordshire Wy CHNTN OX7 .... 102 C3
HEN RG9 .... 271 K8
KID OX5 .... 112 A4
THAME OX9 .... 222 C3
WHLY OX33 .... 170 D1
WIT/EY OX8 .... 107 K8
WTLGN OX49 .... 246 E5
Oxford Sq HGHW SN6 .... 252 C6
Oxford St CAV/SC RG4 .... 333 C5
MIM GL56 .... 46 A2 🔟
WDSTK OX20 .... 127 H1
Oxhey HI RBANNS OX17 .... 13 F4
Oxhey RI RBANSW OX15 .... 35 G8
Oxhill Rd RWWCK/WEL CV35 .... 16 B3
Oxlease WIT/EY OX8 .... 143 H8
Oxon PI HGHW SN6 .... 298 D3
Oxpens Rd OX/KTN OX1 .... 4 B5

P

Pack & Prime La HEN RG9 .... 318 E5
Packhorse La MCHM/KBPZ OX13 .... 237 F1
Pack La RBICS/W OX25 .... 73 J8
Paddick CI CAV/SC RG4 .... 335 C4
Paddock CI STAD OX44 .... 220 B8 🔟
WANT OX12 .... 283 F1
WGFD OX10 .... 267 J3
Paddock Farm La RBANSW OX15 .... 29 F7
Paddock Rd CAV/SC RG4 .... 333 K6
RBICN OX27 .... 77 C5
WGFD OX10 .... 291 F1
The Paddocks HADM HP17 .... 176 D2
KID OX5 .... 147 K2 🔟
RBANNS OX17 .... 12 B4
RBANSW OX15 .... 56 B3
RBICN OX27 .... 58 D4 🔟
The Paddock DID OX11 .... 286 B7
HGHW SN6 .... 250 E2 🔟
MCHM/KBPZ OX13 .... 210 D6
OX/KTN OX1 .... 191 J8
Paddox CI OXN/BOT/CM OX2 .... 148 E7
Page Furlong WGFD OX10 .... 241 K5 🔟
Pages La RBANSW OX15 .... 18 C1
Pages Orch CAV/SC RG4 .... 326 E2
Paget Rd COW/LTMR OX4 .... 192 E1
Pagisters Rd ABGD OX14 .... 215 G5
Paines HI RBICS/W OX25 .... 74 E7
Painswick CI WIT/EY OX8 .... 142 C6
Painters CI RBANSW OX15 .... 36 E3
Pain Wy WGFD OX10 .... 242 C5
Palmer Av RBICS/W OX25 .... 116 B7
Palmer Rd HEAD OX3 .... 168 E6
Palmers WANT OX12 .... 283 F2
Palmerstone Rd EARL RG6 .... 334 C4
Pampas CI BUR/CRTN OX18 .... 158 A6
Pangbourne HI GOR/PANG RG8 .... 330 A2
Pangbourne Rd TLHT RG30 .... 332 B7
Panters Rd WGFD OX10 .... 290 C6
Paper Mill La DID OX11 .... 289 G2
Papist Wy WGFD OX10 .... 290 D7
The Parade RWDY RG5 .... 335 H7
Paradise La RBANSW OX15 .... 36 A5
Paradise Rd HEN RG9 .... 318 E6
Paradise Sq OX/KTN OX1 .... 4 B5
Park Av HGHW SN6 .... 250 B5
HGHW SN6 .... 252 C6
KID OX5 .... 129 C5
Park CI BAN OX16 .... 2 C3
CAV/SC RG4 .... 327 C5
DID OX11 .... 263 H7
KID OX5 .... 111 J2
KID OX5 .... 147 K3
OXN/BOT/CM OX2 .... 149 F5
RBICS/W OX25 .... 95 F3
WDSTK OX20 .... 127 J4
WIT/EY OX8 .... 144 C1
Park Crs ABGD OX14 .... 214 B8
Park End BRACKY NN13 .... 41 J7
RBANSW OX15 .... 29 G6
Park End Ct RBANSW OX15 .... 29 G6 🔟
Park End PI OX/KTN OX1 .... 4 B4 🔟
Park End St OX/KTN OX1 .... 4 B4
Parkers CI FGDN SN7 .... 230 C4
Parker St COW/LTMR OX4 .... 191 K1
Park HI RBANSW OX15 .... 34 A8
WHLY OX33 .... 170 C6
Parkhill Dr CALC RG31 .... 331 H5 🔟
Parklands BAN OX16 .... 2 B2 🔟
WIT/EY OX8 .... 126 A8
Park La CALC RG31 .... 331 C5
FGDN SN7 .... 256 D1
GOR/PANG RG8 .... 325 J1
HEN RG9 .... 296 A1
MCHM/KBPZ OX13 .... 188 C8
RBANSW OX15 .... 25 J8
RBANSW OX15 .... 27 J3
SKCH HP14 .... 249 C1

WANT OX12 .... 283 K4
WAR/TWY RG10 .... 335 K4
WDSTK OX20 .... 127 H1
WDSTK OX20 .... 127 J5
WIT/EY OX8 .... 126 E5
Park RI RBICS/W OX25 .... 115 K4
Park Rd ABGD OX14 .... 214 C8
BAN OX16 .... 2 B3
CHNTN OX7 .... 68 C3
DID OX11 .... 263 H7
DID OX11 .... 287 H1
FGDN SN7 .... 230 B5
HEN RG9 .... 319 G6
RBANSW OX15 .... 34 A8
WIT/EY OX8 .... 126 C2
WIT/EY OX8 .... 142 D6
WIT/EY OX8 .... 144 B1
WIT/EY OX8 .... 160 E5
Parkside HEN RG9 .... 318 E5
WIT/EY OX8 .... 144 C1
Park Side MCHM/KBPZ OX13 .... 236 E1
WDSTK OX20 .... 127 K1
Parks Rd OX/KTN OX1 .... 4 C2
Park St CHNTN OX7 .... 106 A4
SWDNE SN3 .... 274 A5
THAME OX9 .... 175 F7
WDSTK OX20 .... 127 J5
WDSTK OX20 .... 127 J5
Park Ter THAME OX9 .... 175 G8
The Park DID OX11 .... 286 C1
OXN/BOT/CM OX2 .... 189 G2
Park Vw WANT OX12 .... 282 E2
Park View Dr North
WAR/TWY RG10 .... 335 J1
Park View Dr South
WAR/TWY RG10 .... 335 J2
Park Wk GOR/PANG RG8 .... 331 H2 🔟
Park Wall La GOR/PANG RG8 .... 322 D7
Park Wy HEAD OX3 .... 149 K8
Parkway Dr CAV/SC RG4 .... 335 F4
Parliament Rd THAME OX9 .... 175 F6
Parrs Rd SKCH HP14 .... 249 G3
Parry CI HEAD OX3 .... 5 F7
Parsonage CI WANT OX12 .... 283 C1
Parson's La WGFD OX10 .... 268 D4
Parsons Md ABGD OX14 .... 214 C6
Parsons PI COW/LTMR OX4 .... 168 A7
Parson's St BAN OX16 .... 2 C3
RBANSW OX15 .... 38 D3
Partridge Cha BIC OX26 .... 97 H7
Partridge CI WANT OX12 .... 282 E3
Partridge PI KID OX5 .... 129 F6
Partridge Wk COW/LTMR OX4 .... 193 G6 🔟
Pascali PI BAN OX16 .... 20 C6
Passey Crs WGFD OX10 .... 267 J3
Passmore CI SWDNE SN3 .... 274 C8 🔟
Patemore La HEN RG9 .... 270 E5
Paternoster La WGFD OX10 .... 290 B6 🔟
Patrick Haugh Rd RBICS/W OX25 .. 116 B8
Patrick Rd READ RG1 .... 333 H6
Patricks Orch FGDN SN7 .... 255 F8
Pattison PI READ RG1 .... 333 J8
Pattison PI COW/LTMR OX4 .... 192 A4 🔟
Pauling Rd HEAD OX3 .... 168 E6
Pauls Wy WTLGN OX49 .... 246 B5
Paxmans PI BAN OX16 .... 2 C5
Paynes End RBICN OX27 .... 97 G1
Peachcroft Rd ABGD OX14 .... 215 G5
Peacock La RWWCK/WEL CV35 .... 16 C2
Peacock Rd HEAD OX3 .... 5 F2
Peaks La WIT/EY OX8 .... 107 H8
Pearce Dr CHNTN OX7 .... 68 B5
Pearces Meadow HEN RG9 .... 294 D4 🔟
Pearce's Orch HEN RG9 .... 319 F4
Pearce Wy CAV/SC RG4 .... 335 F4
Pearson Rd CAV/SC RG4 .... 335 H4
Pear Tree La CHNTN OX7 .... 102 C6
Peartree CI COW/LTMR OX4 .... 193 F6 🔟
Peascroft RAYLW HP18 .... 174 B1
Peat Moors HEAD OX3 .... 168 D7
Peeble Dr DID OX11 .... 264 A7
Peel CI CAV/SC RG4 .... 333 K5
WIT/EY OX8 .... 161 F3
Peel PI BUR/CRTN OX18 .... 157 K5
OX/KTN OX1 .... 191 H2
Peep-o-day La ABGD OX14 .... 238 C5
Pegasus Ct CALC RG31 .... 331 G8 🔟
Pegasus Rd COW/LTMR OX4 .... 192 E5
Peg's Gn TLHT RG30 .... 332 B8 🔟
Pelham Rd THAME OX9 .... 175 H6
Pelican PI WIT/EY OX8 .... 146 A7
Pembroke La ABGD OX14 .... 262 A2
Pembroke PI BUR/CRTN OX18 .... 183 H3
CAV/SC RG4 .... 333 J4
Pembroke Sq OX/KTN OX1 .... 4 C5 🔟
Pemscott CI BUR/CRTN OX18 .... 181 J2 🔟
Pendennis Av CAV/SC RG4 .... 334 A1
Pen La ABGD OX14 .... 214 D3
MCHM/KBPZ OX13 .... 214 D2
Penley CI CHNR OX39 .... 224 D1
Penn CI ABGD OX14 .... 215 G5 🔟
CAV/SC RG4 .... 333 G1
Pennine Wy WAR/TWY RG10 .... 335 K3
Pennington PI THAME OX9 .... 175 H6 🔟

Pennycress Rd COW/LTMR OX4 .. 193 G5 🔟
Pennygreen La WGFD OX10 .... 266 A5
Pennyhooks La HGHW SN6 .... 252 B7
Pennypiece GOR/PANG RG8 .... 312 E8
Pennywell Dr OXN/BOT/CM OX2 .. 149 F5
Penpont Water DID OX11 .... 264 A5 🔟
Penrhyn CI BAN OX16 .... 20 A8
Penrose Dr BAN OX16 .... 2 A3
Pensclose WIT/EY OX8 .... 143 G6
Pensfield WGFD OX10 .... 267 G3
Penson's Gdns COW/LTMR OX4 .. 5 E4 🔟
Pentridge CI SWDNE SN3 .... 274 A8 🔟
Pentylands CI HGHW SN6 .... 226 D8
Pentylands La HGHW SN6 .... 226 D7
Pen Wy BAN OX16 .... 20 D6
Peppard HI HEN RG9 .... 317 F7
Peppard La HEN RG9 .... 319 F8
Peppard Rd CAV/SC RG4 .... 327 J8
Pepper Aly BAN OX16 .... 3 D3 🔟
RBANSW OX15 .... 57 H3 🔟
Peppercorn Av HEAD OX3 .... 168 E7 🔟
Percy St COW/LTMR OX4 .... 191 K1
Peregrine CI SWDNE SN3 .... 274 B7 🔟
Peregrine Rd COW/LTMR OX4 .. 192 D5
Peregrine Wy BIC OX26 .... 97 H7 🔟
WANT OX12 .... 258 C6
Periam CI HEN RG9 .... 318 E7
Perimeter Rd DID OX11 .... 286 A5
Periwinkle PI COW/LTMR OX4 .. 193 F5
Perkins OX/KTN OX1 .... 191 H5
Perrinsfield CIR GL7 .... 203 H1
Perrin St HEAD OX3 .... 168 C5
Perrott CI WIT/EY OX8 .... 125 F8
Perry La PRRI HP27 .... 201 K5
Perry's Rd FGDN SN7 .... 232 B7
Perseverance HI HEN RG9 .... 328 C2
Perth CI WODY RG5 .... 335 J6
Peterley Rd COW/LTMR OX4 .... 193 F1
Peter's Wy COW/LTMR OX4 .... 192 C5
Pether Rd HEAD OX3 .... 168 E6
Petre PI KID OX5 .... 129 J6
Pettiwell STAD OX44 .... 193 K7
Pevensey Av CAV/SC RG4 .... 334 A2
Pheasant Wk COW/LTMR OX4 .. 192 A6
The Phelps KID OX5 .... 129 G7
Philcote St RBANSW OX15 .... 56 C3
Phillimore Rd CAV/SC RG4 .... 327 J7
Phillips CI WODY RG5 .... 335 K6
Phipps Rd COW/LTMR OX4 .... 192 D3
Phyllis Court Dr HEN RG9 .... 319 G4
Pickett Av HEAD OX3 .... 168 E8
Picklers HI ABGD OX14 .... 214 E5
Picton Wy CAV/SC RG4 .... 333 H3
Piddington Rd RAYLW HP18 .... 117 K7
The Pieces BUR/CRTN OX18 .... 183 H4
Pierce's HI CALC RG31 .... 331 G6
Pigeon Farm Rd SKCH HP14 .... 249 G2
Pigeon House La WIT/EY OX8 .... 145 H1
Piggott's Rd CAV/SC RG4 .... 333 J6
Piggy La BIC OX26 .... 97 F6
Pikeshaw Wy CALC RG31 .... 331 C5 🔟
Pike Ter OX/KTN OX1 .... 4 C5
Pill La MIM GL56 .... 48 A6
Pimpernel CI COW/LTMR OX4 .. 193 G5 🔟
Pinchgate La KID OX5 .... 112 C8
Pine CI BIC OX26 .... 97 G2
COW/LTMR OX4 .... 193 G4 🔟
Pinecroft BUR/CRTN OX18 .... 157 K5
The Pines FGDN SN7 .... 230 A4
Pinetree Ct CAV/SC RG4 .... 333 C2 🔟
Pine Woods Rd
MCHM/KBPZ OX13 .... 210 B6
Pingle Dr BIC OX26 .... 97 F7
Pinhill Rd BAN OX16 .... 2 B2
Pinkhill La WIT/EY OX8 .... 164 A1
Pinnocks Wy OXN/BOT/CM OX2 .. 165 J7
Pinsley Rd WIT/EY OX8 .... 126 C7
Pioneer Rd FGDN SN7 .... 230 B5
RBICS/W OX25 .... 115 H1
Pipers Cft BAN OX16 .... 2 A5
Piper St HEAD OX3 .... 168 D5
Pipit CI COW/LTMR OX4 .... 192 E6 🔟
Pipitdene SWDNE SN3 .... 274 B8
Pipits Cft BIC OX26 .... 97 H7
Pipkin Wy COW/LTMR OX4 .... 192 A1 🔟
Pitford Rd WODY RG5 .... 335 H7
Pitreavie Av BUR/CRTN OX18 .... 158 A3
Pitts La CHNTN OX7 .... 72 C4
EARL RG6 .... 334 D8
Pitts Rd HEAD OX3 .... 168 E4 🔟
Pixey PI OXN/BOT/CM OX2 .... 148 D7 🔟
Pixton CI DID OX11 .... 263 G7
The Plain Rd RBANSW OX15 .... 26 B1
The Plain OX/KTN OX1 .... 5 E4
Plane Tree Wy WDSTK OX20 .... 127 K1
Plantation Rd DID OX11 .... 285 H7
OXN/BOT/CM OX2 .... 4 B2
Plater Dr OXN/BOT/CM OX2 .... 4 A1
Playfield Rd OX/KTN OX1 .... 191 J8
Playhatch Rd CAV/SC RG4 .... 334 C2
Pleck La CHNR OX39 .... 224 C3 🔟
Plot Rd RBANSW OX15 .... 26 B1
Plough CI WGFD OX10 .... 266 D1
Plough Cnr CHNR OX39 .... 200 B6
Plough La HEN RG9 .... 329 G6

Ploughley Cl *KID* OX5 .... 129 G7 🔲
  RBICN OX27 .... 77 H3 🔲
Ploughley Rd *RBICS/W* OX25 .... 115 K3
Plowden Pk *CHNR* OX39 .... 223 K4
Plowden Wy *HEN* RG9 .... 329 G6
Plum La *CHNTN* OX7 .... 102 E8
Pluto Rd *DID* OX11 .... 285 H7
Plym Rd *DID* OX11 .... 264 A5
Pochard Pl *HADM* OX14 .... 193 F6 🔲🔲
Pococks Cl *BUR/CRTN* OX18 .... 183 H4
Poffley End La *WFY* OX8 .... 143 F2
Polecat End La *WHLY* OX33 .... 170 B3
Polstead Rd *OXN/BOT/CM* OX2....... 4 B1
Polsted Rd *CALC* RG31 .... 331 H6
Poltondale *SWDNE* SN3 .... 274 B8
  WANT OX12 .... 169 C4
Pond Cl *HEAD* OX3 .... 306 A6
Pond End Rd *CAV/SC* RG4 .... 327 C1
Pond Hl *WFY* OX8 .... 147 H8
Pond La *CAV/SC* RG4 .... 331 K1
Ponds La *HEAD* OX3 .... 167 K1
Pony Rd *COW/LTMR* OX4 .... 193 F1
Pool Cl *TLHT* RG30 .... 331 K8
Poole Cl *MIM* GL56 .... 48 A6
Pooles La *CHNTN* OX7 .... 106 A3
Poolgate *RWWCK/WEL* CV35 .... 16 B3
Poolside Cl *BAN* OX16 .... 2 B4
Popes Acre *HADM* HP17 .... 176 B2
Pope's Piece *WFY* OX8 .... 142 D6
Poplar Cl *BAN* OX16 .... 29 G5 🔲
  KID OX5 .... 129 J8 🔲
  STAD OX44 .... 195 J5
Poplar Farm Cl *CHNTN* OX7 .... 102 B6
Poplar Farm Rd *STAD* OX44 .... 220 B8 🔲
Poplar Gv *OX/KTN* OX1 .... 191 J7
Poplar Rd *OXN/BOT/CM* OX2 .... 166 A6
Poplars Cl *RBANNS* OX17 .... 22 E7
Poplars Rd *RBANNS* OX17 .... 22 D3
The Poplars *BIC* OX26 .... 98 A5
Popplechurch Dr *SWDNE* SN3 .... 274 C8 🔲
Portal Dr *RBICS/W* OX25 .... 76 E7 🔲
Portal Dr North *RBICS/W* OX25 ... 76 A7
Portal Dr South *RBICS/W* OX25 .... 76 B8
Port Hl *HEN* RG9 .... 294 B5
Port Hill Rd *WGFD* OX10 .... 267 H2
Portland Cl *TLHT* RG30 .... 331 G8
Portland Gdns *TLHT* RG30 .... 331 K6
Portland Pl *CHNTN* OX7 .... 68 B4 🔲
Portland Rd *OXN/BOT/CM* OX2 .... 149 F8
  RBANSW OX15 .... 36 B5
Portman Rd *TLHT* RG30 .... 332 B6
Portmeirion Gdns *TLHT* RG30 .. 331 K6 🔲
Port Wy *KID* OX5 .... 93 K7
  RBICS/W OX25 .... 93 K1
  WANT OX12 .... 283 G1
  WGFD OX10 .... 291 H2
Portway *BAN* OX16 .... 2 A1
  BRACKY NN13 .... 41 K8
  DID OX11 .... 263 G8
  FGDN SN7 .... 230 B4 🔲
  RBANNS OX17 .... 40 C7
Portway Crs *BRACKY* NN13 .... 41 J8
Portway Dr *BRACKY* NN13........... 41 J8
Portway Gdns *RBANNS* OX17 .... 40 C8
Post Office La *WANT* OX12 .... 282 A6
Potenger Wy *ABGD* OX14 .... 238 D1
Potkiln La *GOR/PANG* RG8 .... 324 C1
Pottery Flds *HEN* RG9 .... 294 E5 🔲
Pottery Piece *COW/LTMR* OX4 .... 192 C6
Pottery Rd *TLHT* RG30 .... 331 K6
Pottle Cl *OXN/BOT/CM* OX2 .... 165 K6
Pott's Cl *STAD* OX44 .... 195 K4
Poultney Pl *BUR/CRTN* OX18 .. 157 K4 🔲
Poulton Pl *COW/LTMR* OX4 .... 193 F4
Pound Bank *CHNTN* OX7 .... 72 D4 🔲
Pound Cl *KID* OX5 .... 111 J3
  KID OX5 .... 147 K2
  WFY OX8 .... 161 F3
Pound Cft *WANT* OX12 .... 258 D7 🔲
Pound Field Cl *HEAD* OX3 .... 168 E2
Pound Hl *CHNTN* OX7 .... 105 K3
Pound La *BUR/CRTN* OX18............ 182 A7
  CAV/SC RG4 .... 335 G5
  DID OX11 .... 287 G5
  RBANSW OX15 .... 24 E5
  WGFD OX10 .... 290 B5
  WHLY OX33 .... 151 J8
  WFY OX8 .... 146 E5
Pound Piece *HGHW* SN6 .... 277 C8
The Pound *RBANSW* OX15 .... 27 H3
  RBANSW OX15 .... 36 E2
  WANT OX12 .... 283 G2
Powell Cl *WHLY* OX33 .... 170 B3
Powys Gv *BAN* OX16 .... 2 A2
Preachers La *OX/KTN* OX1 .... 4 C5 🔲
Prescott Av *BAN* OX16 .... 28 B1
Prescott Cl *BAN* OX16 .... 2 A3
Preston Rd *ABGD* OX14 .... 238 B2
Prestwich Pl *OXN/BOT/CM* OX2 .. 166 D6
Prestwick Burn *DID* OX11 .... 263 K5 🔲
Prichard Rd *HEAD* OX3 .... 168 A4
Priest Cl *HEN* RG9 .... 294 B5
Priestend *THAME* OX9 .... 174 E6
Priest Hl *CAV/SC* RG4 .... 333 G4
Priest Hill La *WFY* OX8 .... 142 D2

Primrose Cl *GOR/PANG* RG8 .... 331 G2 🔲
Primrose Ct *MIM* GL56 .... 46 A2
Primrose Dr *BIC* OX26 .... 96 E3
Primrose La *BUR/CRTN* OX18 .... 183 G5
Primrose Pl *COW/LTMR* OX4 ... 193 F6 🔲🔲
Prince Gv *ABGD* OX14 .... 214 E4
Prince of Wales Av *TLHT* RG30 .. 332 D8
Princes Ride *WDSTK* OX20 .... 127 K1
Princess Gdns *WANT* OX12 .... 258 C7
Princes St *COW/LTMR* OX4 .... 5 F5
  READ RG1 .... 333 J8
Princethorpe Dr *BAN* OX16 .... 3 F2
Prince William Dr *CALC* RG31 ..... 331 G6
Prior's Forge *OXN/BOT/CM* OX2 .. 149 F6
Prior's La *FGDN* SN7 .... 209 K4
Priory Av *CAV/SC* RG4 .... 333 G5
Priory Cl *BIC* OX26 .... 97 G6 🔲
Priory Ct *BIC* OX26 .... 97 F6
Priory Gn *HGHW* SN6 .... 250 E1 🔲
Priory La *BIC* OX26 .... 97 F6
  BUR/CRTN OX18 .... 138 E2
  CHNTN OX7 .... 102 E2
  MCHM/KBPZ OX13 .... 237 F1
Priory Md *FGDN* SN7 .... 253 J5
Priory Ms *WGFD* OX10 .... 267 F8 🔲
Priory Orch *WANT* OX12 .... 282 C2
Priory Rd *BIC* OX26 .... 97 G6 🔲
  CHNTN OX7 .... 102 E2
  COW/LTMR OX4 .... 192 C5
  WANT OX12 .... 282 D3
Priory Vale Rd *BAN* OX16 .... 3 F2
Pritchard Cl *WGFD* OX10 .... 241 K1 🔲
Promenade Rd *READ* RG1 .... 333 G5
Prospect Cl *WFY* OX8 .... 107 H8 🔲
Prospect Rd *BAN* OX16 .... 3 D4
  DID OX11 .... 287 G5
Prospect St *CAV/SC* RG4 .... 333 G5
  READ RG1 .... 333 F8
Puck La *WFY* OX8 .... 143 F6
Puddleduck La *FGDN* SN7 .... 229 H7
Puddicote La *CHNTN* OX7 .... 85 K8
Pudsey Cl *ABGD* OX14 .... 238 C3
Pugsden La *MCHM/KBPZ* OX13 .... 261 J5
Pulker Cl *COW/LTMR* OX4 .... 192 C3 🔲
Pullens Fld *HEAD* OX3 .... 168 A5
Pullens La *HEAD* OX3 .... 168 A5
Pulling Cl *FGDN* SN7 .... 230 B4
Pulpit Hl *WANT* OX12 .... 280 E3
Pumbro *WFY* OX8 .... 107 H8
Purbeck Cl *SWDNE* SN3 .... 274 A8 🔲
Purcell Rd *HEAD* OX3 .... 5 F2
Purley La *GOR/PANG* RG8............. 331 G2
Purley Ri *GOR/PANG* RG8 .... 330 D2
Purley Village *GOR/PANG* RG8 .... 331 G2
Purley Wy *GOR/PANG* RG8 .... 330 C2
Purrants La *WFY* OX8 .... 122 B6
Purslane *ABGD* OX14 .... 215 F7
Pusey La *OX/KTN* OX1 .... 4 C3
Pusey Pl *OX/KTN* OX1 .... 4 C3
Pusey St *OX/KTN* OX1 .... 4 C3
Putman Cl *THAME* OX9 .... 175 H7
Pykes Cl *ABGD* OX14 .... 215 G5
Pym Wk *THAME* OX9 .... 175 F6
Pyrton La *WTLGN* OX49 .... 246 B4
Pytenry Cl *ABGD* OX14 .... 215 F4
Pytt's La *BUR/CRTN* OX18 .... 138 E2 🔲

Q

The Quadrant *ABGD* OX14 .... 215 F8
Quaker La *WGFD* OX10 .... 242 D8
Quakers Mede *HADM* HP17 .... 176 C1
Quantock Av *CAV/SC* RG4 .... 333 K2
Quantock Cl *WAR/TWY* RG10 ... 335 K3 🔲
Quantock Vw *DID* OX11 .... 263 G5
Quarhill Cl *CHNTN* OX7 .... 68 B2
Quarrybrook Cl *SWDNE* SN3 .... 274 C2
Quarry Cl *CHNTN* OX7 .... 88 E2
  RBANSW OX15 .... 36 D5
Quarry Crs *HGHW* SN6 .... 250 D1
Quarry End *KID* OX5 .... 128 E7
Quarry High St *HEAD* OX3 .... 168 E4
Quarry Hollow *HEAD* OX3 .... 168 E5
Quarry La *HEN* RG9 .... 329 J3
Quarry Rd *CHNTN* OX7 .... 86 E6
  HEAD OX3 .... 168 E5
  MCHM/KBPZ OX13 .... 190 E8
  WFY OX8 .... 142 E5
Quarry School Pl *HEAD* OX3 ..... 168 E5 🔲
Quarry Vw *CIR* GL7 .... 178 D4
Quartermain Cl *COW/LTMR* OX4 .. 192 A1 🔲
Quartermain Rd *STAD* OX44 .... 220 A8 🔲
Queen Annes Ga *CAV/SC* RG4 .... 333 J4
Queen Cl *HEN* RG9 .... 319 G6
Queen Elizabeth Cl *DID* OX11 .... 264 A7 🔲
Queen Emmas Dyke *WFY* OX8 .... 142 D7
Queens Av *BIC* OX26 .... 97 F5
  HGHW SN6 .... 250 E1
  KID OX5 .... 129 K7
  WGFD OX10 .... 266 D6
Queensborough Dr *CAV/SC* RG4 .. 332 D2
Queens Cl *OXN/BOT/CM* OX2......... 165 K7

  THAME OX9 .... 175 F🔲
  WGFD OX10 .... 241 K🔲
  WFY OX8 .... 146 A🔲
Queen's Crs *BUR/CRTN* OX18....... 182 A🔲
  RBANSW OX15 .... 19 K🔲
Queen's La *OX/KTN* OX1 .... 5 D🔲
  WFY OX8 .... 146 A🔲
Queen's Rd *BAN* OX16........................ 2 B🔲
  BUR/CRTN OX18 .... 158 A🔲
  CAV/SC RG4 .... 333 H🔲
  READ RG1 .... 333 H🔲
  THAME OX9 .... 175 G🔲
  WGFD OX10 .... 290 B🔲
Queens St *RBANSW* OX15 .... 36 E🔲
Queen St *ABGD* OX14 .... 214 D🔲
  BUR/CRTN OX18 .... 183 H🔲
  CAV/SC RG4 .... 333 G🔲
  HEN RG9 .... 319 G🔲
  OX/KTN OX1 .... 4 C🔲
  RBANNS OX17 .... 22 D🔲
  RBANSW OX15 .... 34 A8 🔲
  WGFD OX10 .... 241 K🔲
  WFY OX8 .... 146 A🔲
Queensway *BAN* OX16 .... 2 B🔲
  CAV/SC RG4 .... 333 K🔲
  DID OX11 .... 263 H🔲
Queens Wy *DID* OX11 .... 265 F7 🔲
Queen Victoria St *READ* RG1 .... 333 H🔲
Quickset Cl *CHNTN* OX7 .... 87 J🔲
Quintan Av *RBICS/W* OX25 .... 116 A🔲

THAME OX9 .... 175 F🔲
WGFD OX10 .... 241 K🔲
WFY/EY OX8 .... 146 A🔲

R

Rack End *WFY* OX8........................... 186 E🔲
Radbone Hl *CHNTN* OX7 .... 68 C🔲
Radburn Cl *MIM* GL56 .... 46 B2 🔲
Radcliffe Rd *OXN/BOT/CM* OX4 .... 191 K🔲
Radcliffe Sq *OX/KTN* OX1 .... 5 D4 🔲
Radcot Cl *WODY* RG5 .... 335 G🔲
Radcot Rd *BUR/CRTN* OX18 .... 206 B🔲
  FGDN SN7 .... 230 B🔲
Radford Cl *COW/LTMR* OX4 .... 191 K🔲
Radley Cl *SWDNE* SN3 .... 274 A🔲
Radley Rd *ABGD* OX14 .... 214 E🔲
Radnor Cl *HEN* RG9 .... 319 G🔲
Radnor Rd *WGFD* OX10 .... 266 D🔲
Radstock Rd *READ* RG1 .... 334 B🔲
Raghouse La *RBICN* OX27 .... 76 E🔲
Raglan Gdns *CAV/SC* RG4 .... 333 J🔲
Ragley Ms *CAV/SC* RG4 .... 335 K1 🔲
Ragnall's La *HEAD* OX3 .... 133 G🔲
Rahere Rd *COW/LTMR* OX4 .... 192 C🔲
Railway La *COW/LTMR* OX4 .... 192 A🔲
Rainbow Wy *ABGD* OX14 .... 215 F🔲
Raincliffe Cl *RBANNS* OX17 .... 40 B8 🔲
Raleigh Crs *WFY* OX8 .... 142 B🔲
Raleigh Park Rd
  OXN/BOT/CM OX2 .... 166 C🔲
Rampion Cl *COW/LTMR* OX4 ..... 193 G5 🔲
Ramsey Rd *HEAD* OX3 .... 168 E🔲
Ramsons Wy *ABGD* OX14 .... 215 G🔲
Randall Rd *COTS* GL54..................... 100 A🔲
Randolph Rd *READ* RG1 .... 333 G🔲
Randolph St *COW/LTMR* OX4........... 5 F🔲
Range Rd *WFY* OX8 .... 141 K🔲
Rannal Dr *CHNR* OX39...................... 224 E🔲
Rattlecombe Rd *RBANSW* OX15 ... 17 G🔲
Rau Ct *RBICN* OX27 .... 79 H🔲
Ravencroft *BIC* OX26 .... 97 H🔲
Raven Rd *SKCH* HP14 .... 249 H🔲
Ravensbourne Dr *WODY* RG5 .... 335 G🔲
Ravenscroft *SWDNE* SN3 .... 274 A🔲
Ravenscroft Rd *HEN* RG9............... 319 F🔲
Ravensmead *BAN* OX16 .... 2 A5 🔲
  CHNR OX39 .... 224 E🔲
Rawlings Cl *SWDNE* SN3 .... 274 C🔲
Rawlings Gv *ABGD* OX14 .... 214 B🔲
Rawlingson Cl *CHNTN* OX7 .... 86 E🔲
Rawlins Cl *RBANNS* OX17 .... 58 D🔲
Rawlinson Rd *OXN/BOT/CM* OX2 .. 167 F🔲
Rawson Cl *OXN/BOT/CM* OX2 .... 148 D6 🔲
Rawthey Av *DID* OX11 .... 263 J🔲
Ray Ct *DID* OX11 .... 264 A🔲
Raymond Rd *BIC* OX26 .... 96 D🔲
Raymund Rd *HEAD* OX3 .... 167 K🔲
Raynham Cl *BUR/CRTN* OX18 ... 158 A3 🔲
Ray Rd *BIC* OX26 .... 96 E🔲
Reade Av *ABGD* OX14 .... 215 F🔲
Reade Cl *CHNTN* OX7...................... 102 C🔲
Reade's La *CAV/SC* RG4 .... 326 E🔲
Reading La *HEN* RG9 .... 270 B🔲
Reading Rd *CAV/SC* RG4 .... 325 K🔲
  DID OX11 .... 286 B🔲
  GOR/PANG RG8 .... 314 D🔲
  GOR/PANG RG8 .... 322 C🔲
  GOR/PANG RG8 .... 330 B🔲
  HEN RG9 .... 319 C🔲
  WANT OX12 .... 284 A🔲
  WGFD OX10 .... 290 C🔲
  WODY RG5 .... 335 F🔲
Recreation Rd *TLHT* RG30 .... 331 J🔲
  WDSTK OX20 .... 127 K🔲

Rectory Cl RBANNS OX17 .... 11 G3
RBICN OX27 .... 99 J4
RBICS/W OX25 .... 75 J6
RBICS/W OX25 .... 114 B3
Rectory Crs CHNTN OX7 .... 73 F7
Rectory Farm La WANT OX12 ...... 235 F8
Rectory HI HEN RG9 .... 270 A6
Rectory La DID OX11 .... 210 B4
MCHM/KBPZ OX13 .... 211 F7
RBANNS OX17 .... 22 D6
RBICN OX27 .... 79 K1
THAME OX9 .... 222 E6
WANT OX12 .... 281 J8
WDSTK OX20 .... 127 H1
Rectory Meadow CHNR OX39 ..... 201 F8
Rectory Rd CAV/SC RG4 .... 333 G5
COW/LTMR OX4 .... 311 J8
GOR/PANG RG8 .... 34 A7
RBANSW OX15 .... 196 A6
STAD OX44 .... 44 A3
Redberry Cl CAV/SC RG4 .... 333 K2
Red Bridge Hollow OX/KTN OX1 . 191 G3
Red Copse La OX/KTN OX1 .... 190 E5
Red Cross Rd GOR/PANG RG8 ..... 322 E1
Rede Cl HEAD OX3 .... 168 E7
Redwood La HEN RG9 .... 328 B2
Red HI HEN RG9 .... 328 B2
Red House Dr CAV/SC RG4 .... 327 F2
Red House Rd RBANSW OX15 .... 29 G7
Redland Rd HEAD OX3 .... 168 B2
Redlands Cl HGHW SN6 .... 314 C6
Red La GOR/PANG RG8 .... 314 A3
WGFD OX10 .... 270 D4
WTLGN OX49 .... 270 D4
Red Lion Dr SKCH HP14 .... 249 F2
Red Lion St RBANNS OX17 .... 5 H5
RBANNS OX17 .... 39 J5
Redmoor Cl BAN OX16 .... 20 B7
Redmoor Cl BIC OX26 .... 96 E5
Red Poll Cl BAN OX16 .... 20 B7
Redwing CI BIC OX26 .... 97 H6
Redwood Cl COW/LTMR OX4 ...... 210 E6
MCHM/KBPZ OX13 .... 210 E6
Redwood Wy CALC RG31 .... 331 H4
Reedmace Cl CAV/SC RG4 .... 331 H4
Reedmace BIC OX26 .... 97 F5
Reeds Cl WANT OX12 .... 282 C2
Regal Wy FDGN SN7 .... 230 B3
Regent Cl READ RG1 .... 333 G7
Regent Gdns DID OX11 .... 264 B7
Regent Ms FGDN SN7 .... 230 B3
Regent St COW/LTMR OX4 .... 5 F6
READ RG1 .... 334 A8
Regis Pl WANT OX12 .... 282 A5
Reid Cl BAN OX16 .... 20 B7
Reid Pl RBICS/W OX25 .... 76 A8
Remenham Church La HEN RG9 . 319 J3
Remenham La HEN RG9 .... 319 H5
Remus Cl BRACKY NN13 .... 43 H1
Rest Harrow COW/LTMR OX4 ..... 193 F5
Retford Cl WODY RG5 .... 335 H6
Retreat Gdns WGFD OX10 .... 267 G8
Rewley Rd OXN/BOT/CM OX2 ...... 4 B4
Reynolds Cl CHNTN OX7 .... 102 E6
Reynolds Wy ABGD OX14 .... 238 C2
WANT OX12 .... 281 K2
Rhigos CAV/SC RG4 .... 333 F1
Rhine Cl CAV/SC RG4 .... 333 K5
Richards La OXN/BOT/CM OX2 ... 148 E8
Richards Wy HEAD OX3 .... 169 F5
Richens Dr BUR/CRTN OX18 .... 157 J5
Richfield Av READ RG1 .... 332 E6
Richfield Pl READ RG1 .... 333 F6
Richman Gdns BAN OX16 .... 20 B7
Richmere Rd DID OX11 .... 263 K8
Richmond Rd CAV/SC RG4 .... 332 E3
OXN/BOT/CM OX2 .... 4 B3
TLHT RG30 .... 332 C7
Richmond St RBANNS OX15 .... 39 K2
Rickyard Cl OXN/BOT/CM OX2 .... 4 B3
The Rickyard RBANSW OX15 .... 285 K2
WANT OX12 .... 285 K2
Riddell Pl OXN/BOT/CM OX2 ...... 148 E6
Riders Wy CHNR OX39 .... 224 E1
The Ride MCHM/KBPZ OX13 .... 212 D2
Ridge Cl BAN OX16 .... 3 D5
Ridgefield Cl COW/LTMR OX4 ..... 168 A8
Ridge Hall Cl CAV/SC RG4 .... 332 E4
Ridgemont Cl
OXN/BOT/CM OX2 .... 148 E8
Ridgemount La CALC RG31 .... 331 F5
The Ridge GOR/PANG RG8 .... 323 H7
KID OX5 .... 111 F1
Ridge Wy WANT OX12 .... 225 G1
Ridgeway CHNR OX39 .... 224 E1
DID OX11 .... 308 D4
DID OX11 .... 310 A2
FGDN SN7 .... 278 E6
GOR/PANG RG8 .... 312 C2
HEN RG9 .... 293 H4
HGHW SN6 .... 299 F5
OX/KTN OX1 .... 190 B6
WANT OX12 .... 302 D1
WANT OX12 .... 304 A2
WGFD OX10 .... 291 G4

WOO/WRO SN4 .... 298 B7
WTLGN OX49 .... 270 A2
Ridgeway Cl HEN RG9 .... 293 H4
Ridgeway Meads PRRI HP27 .... 201 K5
Ridgeway Rd DID OX11 .... 169 F4
HEAD OX3 .... 169 F4
The Ridgeway CAV/SC RG4 .... 333 G4
HEN RG9 .... 294 D5
RBANSW OX15 .... 37 F2
WANT OX12 .... 284 E8
WANT OX12 .... 304 E2
Riding La WIT/EY OX8 .... 122 E7
The Ridings CAV/SC RG4 .... 327 J7
HEAD OX3 .... 169 F7
KID OX5 .... 129 G6
The Riding WIT/EY OX8 .... 122 B5
Ridley Rd COW/LTMR OX4 .... 192 E1
Riely Cl WIT/EY OX8 .... 126 D6
Righton Cl WAR/TWY RG10 .... 335 K4
Riley Cl ABGD OX14 .... 238 E1
Riley Dr BAN OX16 .... 20 B7
Riley Rd TLHT RG30 .... 331 K7
Rimes Cl MCHM/KBPZ OX13 ...... 211 F6
Rimmer Cl HEAD OX3 .... 167 K2
The Ring RBANNS OX17 .... 22 C3
Ringwood Rd HEAD OX3 .... 169 G4
TLHT RG30 .... 331 K6
Ripley Av WIT/EY OX8 .... 141 G6
Ripley Rd TLHT RG30 .... 332 A6
Rippington Ct ABGD OX14 .... 237 K5
Rippington Dr HEAD OX3 .... 5 F1
The Rise CAV/SC RG4 .... 333 H3
KID OX5 .... 130 D6
RBANNS OX17 .... 38 D3
Rissington Cl CALC RG31 .... 331 J4
Rissington Dr WIT/EY OX8 .... 142 C7
Rivacres GOR/PANG RG8 .... 324 C4
River Cl ABGD OX14 .... 238 C2
River Gdns GOR/PANG RG8 .... 331 H2
Rivermead Rd COW/LTMR OX4 ... 191 H3
River Rd CAV/SC RG4 .... 332 D4
Riverside Bank OX1 .... 3 E4
Riverside Gdns WIT/EY OX8 .... 143 F6
Riverside Rd OXN/BOT/CM OX2 .. 166 B8
Rivers Wy HGHW SN6 .... 250 D1
River Vw COW/LTMR OX4 .... 192 A8
OX/KTN OX1 .... 191 J6
WGFD OX10 .... 266 D5
Riverview Rd GOR/PANG RG8 ..... 330 A1
Rivy Cl ABGD OX14 .... 215 G7
Road Eight DID OX11 .... 285 J5
Road Five DID OX11 .... 285 J5
Road Four DID OX11 .... 285 J5
Road One DID OX11 .... 285 J5
Road Six DID OX11 .... 285 K6
Robert Robinson Av
COW/LTMR OX4 .... 192 C5
Robert Sparrow Gdns
WGFD OX10 .... 291 J1
Roberts Rd HADM HP17 .... 176 A1
Robin HI WIT/EY OX8 .... 126 B5
Robins Cl CHNTN OX7 .... 50 E4
RBANSW OX15 .... 55 F2
Robinsgreen SWDNE SN3 .... 274 B8
Robinson Cl BUR/CRTN OX18 ..... 157 K4
DID OX11 .... 288 A7
Robins Platt CHNR OX39 .... 224 D5
Robins Wy BIC OX26 .... 97 H8
Robinswood BAN OX16 .... 2 A5
Robsart Pl OXN/BOT/CM OX2 ..... 189 G3
Rochester Av CAV/SC RG4 .... 335 G6
Rochester Pl CHNTN OX7 .... 106 B4
Rochester Wy RBANNS OX17 ...... 38 C2
Rochford Gdns BIC OX26 .... 97 H3
Rochford Farm Ct CHNTN OX7 ... 68 C4
Rock Cl BUR/CRTN OX18 .... 157 K4
Rock Edge HEAD OX3 .... 168 D6
Rocker Bench HGHW SN6 .... 298 D3
Rock Farm La COW/LTMR OX4 ... 192 B7
Rock HI CHNTN OX7 .... 68 C4
Rockhill Farm Ct CHNTN OX7 ..... 68 C4
Rock Rd BUR/CRTN OX18 .... 157 K4
The Rock RBANSW OX15 .... 55 G1
Rocky La HEN RG9 .... 317 F3
Roding Wy DID OX11 .... 264 A5
Rodway Rd TLHT RG30 .... 331 J6
Roebuck Ct DID OX11 .... 264 A6
Roebuck Ri CALC RG31 .... 331 H4
Roentgen Av DID OX11 .... 219 K4
Rofford St OXN/BOT/CM OX2 ..... 149 F8
Rofle Pl HEAD OX3 .... 168 A4
Rolls Ct WANT OX12 .... 282 D2
Roman Pl DID OX11 .... 263 H5
Roman Rd WHLY OX33 .... 170 E8
Roman Rw HGHW SN6 .... 252 E5
Roman Wk HGHW SN6 .... 252 E5
Roman Wy BIC OX26 .... 97 F5
CIR QL7 .... 203 H2
HEAD OX3 .... 151 H4
WANT OX12 .... 282 C1
Romany Cl TLHT RG30 .... 332 A6
Romany La TLHT RG30 .... 332 A6

Romney Rd BAN OX16 .... 20 B6
Romsey Rd TLHT RG30 .... 332 A6
Romulus Wy BRACKY NN13 .... 43 H1
Rona Ct TLHT RG30 .... 332 B7
Rookery Cl MCHM/KBPZ OX13 ... 213 K6
RBANSW OX15 .... 29 G7
The Rookery KID OX5 .... 129 G7
Rooks La THAME OX9 .... 175 F7
Roosevelt Dr HEAD OX3 .... 168 C6
Roosevelt Rd WIT/EY OX8 .... 126 A7
Roper Rd RBICS/W OX25 .... 76 A7
Rope Wy RBANSW OX15 .... 34 A8
Rosamund Dr WDSTK OX20 .... 109 H8
Rosamund Rd OXN/BOT/CM OX2 . 148 B7
Rose Av ABGD OX14 .... 214 D4
Rose Bank RBANSW OX15 .... 37 F3
Rosebay Crs WANT OX12 .... 258 D7
Rosebery Rd CAV/SC RG4 .... 326 D8
Rose Cl BUR/CRTN OX18 .... 157 K5
WODY RG5 .... 335 K8
Rose Cnr SKCH HP14 .... 249 G2
Rosedale Av BAN OX16 .... 20 C6
Rosedale Crs EARL RG6 .... 334 C7
Rose Gdns OXN/BOT/CM OX2 ..... 166 A7
Rose Hall La RBANNS OX17 .... 22 E7
Rose HI COW/LTMR OX4 .... 192 B3
Rosehill Pk CAV/SC RG4 .... 327 J8
Rose La OX/KTN OX1 .... 5 D4
Rosemary La BUR/CRTN OX18 .... 183 G2
Rosemead Av CALC RG31 .... 331 F4
Rosemont Wy THAME OX9 .... 175 G7
Roses La CHNTN OX7 .... 67 G3
Rose Wk READ RG1 .... 333 G8
Rosina Wk BAN OX16 .... 20 C6
Rossendale Rd CAV/SC RG4 .... 333 K4
Ross Rd READ RG1 .... 333 F6
Rotha Field Rd
OXN/BOT/CM OX2 .... 148 E6
Rotherfield Rd HEN RG9 .... 319 F8
Rotherfield Wy CAV/SC RG4 .... 333 G3
Rother Garth DID OX11 .... 264 A4
Rother Rd BAN OX16 .... 20 B6
Rothwell Gdns WODY RG5 .... 335 H6
Rothwells Cl WGFD OX10 .... 290 C5
Rotten Rw WGFD OX10 .... 241 H6
Round Close Rd RBANNS OX17 ... 33 K8
RBANSW OX15 .... 33 K8
Roundham Cl KID OX5 .... 129 G6
Roundhead Dr THAME OX9 .... 175 F5
Roundhill Rd RBANNS OX17 .... 12 C3
Roundhills Md HGHW SN6 .... 251 F1
Roundtown RBANNS OX17 .... 40 B8
The Roundway HEAD OX3 .... 169 F4
Rouses La CIR QL7 .... 180 B2
Rousham Rd KID OX5 .... 92 E8
Routh Rd HEAD OX3 .... 169 F3
Roves La HGHW SN6 .... 333 F1
Rowallan Cl CAV/SC RG4 .... 333 K1
Rowan Cl BUR/CRTN OX18 .... 157 K3
CAV/SC RG4 .... 327 F3
KID OX5 .... 129 H8
Rowan Wy WODY RG5 .... 335 G7
Rowan Gv COW/LTMR OX4 .... 193 G6
Rowan Rd BIC OX26 .... 96 E4
Rowe Ct TLHT RG30 .... 332 B7
Rowel Dr KID OX5 .... 128 E6
Rowell Wy CHNTN OX7 .... 68 C4
Rowland OXN/BOT/CM OX2 .... 148 B7
WGFD OX10 .... 266 F7
Rowland Rd WGFD OX10 .... 290 C6
Row La CAV/SC RG4 .... 328 A7
Row Leigh La MCHM/KBPZ OX13 . 213 F1
Rowles Cl OX/KTN OX1 .... 191 J6
Rowney Pl COW/LTMR OX4 .... 192 A3
Roxburgh Dr DID OX11 .... 263 H4
Royal Oak La RBANNS OX17 .... 22 E7
Royston Cl TLHT RG30 .... 331 K8
Ruck Keene Cl BIC OX26 .... 96 D5
Rudgeway BRACKY NN13 .... 43 G5
Rufus Isaacs Rd CAV/SC RG4 ...... 333 H5
Rugge Furlong DID OX11 .... 264 B6
Rumbolds Cl WGFD OX10 .... 267 H2
Rupert Cl HEN RG9 .... 319 G4
Rupert Rd COW/LTMR OX4 .... 192 E1
STAD OX44 .... 244 B1
Rupert St READ RG1 .... 333 K8
Rupert Wy THAME OX9 .... 175 G6
Ruscote Av BAN OX16 .... 2 B1
Ruscote Sq BAN OX16 .... 2 B2
Rushall Rd THAME OX9 .... 175 G6
Rushbrook WODY RG5 .... 334 E8
Rushbrook Rd WODY RG5 .... 335 F8
Rushmead Copse ABGD OX14 ..... 215 G5
Ruskin Av ABGD OX14 .... 238 C2
Ruskin Cl DID OX11 .... 264 A7
Ruskin Rd BAN OX16 .... 2 B6
Russell Jackson Cl WGFD OX10 ... 241 H1
Russell Rd CAV/SC RG4 .... 326 D8
Russell St OXN/BOT/CM OX2 ...... 4 A4
READ RG1 .... 333 F8
Russet Cl CAV/SC RG4 .... 326 E2
Russet Gld CAV/SC RG4 .... 327 J8
Russet Rd RBICN OX27 .... 77 H3
Rutherford Av DID OX11 .... 285 J5
Rutherford Cl ABGD OX14 .... 214 E6

Rutherway OXN/BOT/CM OX2 ...... **4** A1
Rutland Rd TLHT RG30 .... **332** D8 🄱
Rutten La KID OX5 .... **147** J1
Rutters CI KID OX5 .... **129** C2
Rycote La THAME OX9 .... **197** G3
Rydal Av TLHT RG30 .... **331** K5
The Rydes RBANSW OX15 .... **29** C7
Rye CI BAN OX16 .... **20** B6
Ryecroft CI WODY RG5 .... **335** C6
Rylstone Rd TLHT RG30 .... **332** D7 🄱
Rymans Crs DID OX11 .... **288** A2
Rymers La COW/LTMR OX4 ...... **192** B2

S

Sackville St READ RG1 .... **333** G7
Saddledon St RWWCK/WEL CV35 .... **16** C2
Sadlers Cft STAD OX44 .... **194** A6 🄱
The Sadlers CALC RG31 .... **331** F6
Saffron Cl ABGD OX14 .... **215** F7 🄱
Sage Cl CALC RG31 .... **331** G4 🄱
Sage Wk COW/LTMR OX4 .... **193** F6
St Alban's Ct READ RG1 .... **267** F8 🔟
St Aldate's OX/KTN OX1 .... **4** C5 🄵
St Amand Dr ABGD OX14 .... **238** C1
St Andrews CI ABGD OX14 .... **215** D5
St Andrews Ct THAME OX9 .... **175** F7
St Andrews La CAV/SC RG4 .... **333** F3
St Andrew's La HEAD OX3 .... **168** D3
St Andrew's Rd CAV/SC RG4 ...... **333** F3
  CHNR OX39 .... **224** E2
  DID OX11 .... **265** K7
  HEAD OX3 .... **168** C3
St Annes CI BIC OX26 .... **97** G4 🄲
  HEN RG9 .... **319** F7
St Annes Ct DID OX11 .... **264** B8 🄱
St Anne's Rd BAN OX16 .... **29** F5
  CAV/SC RG4 .... **333** J5
  HEAD OX3 .... **168** C5
St Barnabas Rd CAV/SC RG4 ..... **333** G1
St Barnabas St OXN/BOT/CM OX2 .... **4** B3 🄱
St Bartholomews Rd EARL RG6 ... **334** B8
St Bernard's Rd OXN/BOT/CM OX2 .... **4** B2
St Christopher's PI
  COW/LTMR OX4 .... **192** C1 🄱
St Clement's St COW/LTMR OX4 .... **5** E5
St Cross Rd OX/KTN OX1 .... **5** D3
St David's CI CAV/SC RG4 .... **333** F2
St Denys CI FGDN SN7 .... **232** B2
St Ebbes St OX/KTN OX1 .... **4** C5 🄸
St Edburg's CI BIC OX26 .... **96** D5
St Edmund's La ABGD OX14 .... **238** D1 🄱
St Edward's Av OXN/BOT/CM OX2 .. **148** E8
St George's Cl MIM GL56 .... **46** A2
St George's Crs BAN OX16 .... **2** C5
St George's Gn WGFD OX10 ...... **266** E6
St George's Rd FGDN SN7 .... **208** B7
  TLHT RG30 .... **332** B7
  WGFD OX10 .... **266** E7
St Giles KID OX5 .... **111** K7
  OX/KTN OX1 .... **4** C3
St Giles CI RBICS/W OX25 .... **114** B3
St Helen's Av WGFD OX10 .... **267** F8
St Helen's Ct ABGD OX14 .... **238** D1
St Helen's Crs WGFD OX10 .... **267** F8
St Helen's Whf ABGD OX14 .... **238** D1
St Hilda's CI BIC OX26 .... **97** G3
  DID OX11 .... **264** B8
St Hughs CI BAN OX16 .... **2** B6
  BIC OX26 .... **97** G3
St Hugh's PI SKCH HP14 .... **249** H3 🄲
St Hughs Ri DID OX11 .... **264** B8
St Ives Rd WANT OX12 .... **258** E7
St James WANT OX12 .... **282** D1
St James CI WIT/EY OX8 .... **107** H8 🄷
St James Rd ABGD OX14 .... **215** J4
  BRACKY NN13 .... **43** F2
St John's CI DID OX11 .... **264** A7
  MCHM/KBPZ OX13 .... **211** H6
  WODY RG5 .... **335** H7
St John's Dr BUR/CRTN OX18 .... **157** K4
  KID OX5 .... **129** J6
St John's HI READ RG1 .... **333** J8
St John's La WIT/EY OX8 .... **123** H5
St John's Rd ABGD OX14 .... **214** E7
  BAN OX16 .... **2** C4
  CAV/SC RG4 .... **333** J5
  KID OX5 .... **111** F1
  WANT OX12 .... **258** E6
  WGFD OX10 .... **266** E8
St John's St BIC OX26 .... **97** F5
  CIR GL7 .... **203** H3
  READ RG1 .... **333** J8
St John St OX/KTN OX1 .... **4** C3
St John's Wy RBANSW OX15 ...... **55** J3
St Katherine CI SWDNE SN3 ...... **274** C8 🄷
St Katherine's Rd HEN RG9 .... **319** F8
St Kenelm's CI WIT/EY OX8 .... **141** G5 🄶
St Lawrence CI WGFD OX10 ...... **242** D7 🄱
St Lawrence Rd CIR GL7 .... **203** G3

  OX/KTN OX1 .... **191** F2 🄱
St Leonard's CI BAN OX16 .... **3** E3
  WTLGN OX49 .... **246** B5
St Leonard's La WGFD OX10 ..... **267** F8
St Leonard's Rd HEAD OX3 .... **168** D5
St Leonard's Sq WGFD OX10 ..... **267** F8 🄱🄱
St Lucian's La WGFD OX10 .... **291** F1
St Luke's Rd COW/LTMR OX4 .... **192** C2
St Lukes Wy CAV/SC RG4 .... **333** H5
St Margaret's Rd OXN/BOT/CM OX2 .. **4** B1
St Mark's Rd HEN RG9 .... **319** F7
St Martin's La COW/LTMR OX4 ... **192** A4
St Martin's St WGFD OX10 .... **267** F8
St Mary's Av GOR/PANG RG8 .... **331** G2
St Mary's Butts READ RG1 .... **333** G8
St Mary's CI BIC OX26 .... **96** E6 🄴
  HEN RG9 .... **318** C7
  KID OX5 .... **129** H6
  STAD OX44 .... **244** B1 🄱
  WHLY OX33 .... **170** D7 🄳
St Mary's Gn ABGD OX14 .... **214** C6
St Mary's La CHNTN OX7 .... **52** D4
St Marys Md WIT/EY OX8 .... **143** F8
St Mary's Rd COW/LTMR OX4 .... **5** F6
  RBANNS OX17 .... **38** B4
  WANT OX12 .... **285** G2
St Mary's St WGFD OX10 .... **267** F8
St Michael's Av ABGD OX14 .... **214** C8
  HGHW SN6 .... **250** E1 🄱
St Michaels CI CHNTN OX7 .... **102** D7
  RBICN OX27 .... **80** A1
St Michael's La KID OX5 .... **128** C7
St Michael's Rd TLHT RG30 .... **331** J8 🄱
St Michael's St OX/KTN OX1 ...... **4** C4
St Michael's Wy
  MCHM/KBPZ OX13 .... **261** H3
St Nicholas' Gn ABGD OX14 .... **214** C6
St Nicholas Rd COW/LTMR OX4 .. **192** B5
  KID OX5 .... **111** F1
  WGFD OX10 .... **266** E7
St Omer Rd COW/LTMR OX4 ...... **192** C2
St Patrick's Av WAR/TWY RG10 .. **335** J2
St Paul's Crs OXN/BOT/CM OX2 .. **166** E7 🄱
St Peter's Av CAV/SC RG4 .... **333** H5
St Peter's CI MCHM/KBPZ OX13 .. **213** K1
  WIT/EY OX8 .... **147** F5
St Peter's Crs BIC OX26 .... **97** G3
St Peter's HI CAV/SC RG4 .... **333** F4
St Peter's PI WGFD OX10 .... **267** F8 🄱🄱
St Peter's Rd ABGD OX14 .... **215** G6
  DID OX11 .... **263** J7
  OXN/BOT/CM OX2 .... **148** D7
St Peter's St WGFD OX10 .... **267** F8 🄱🄱
St Ronans Rd TLHT RG30 .... **332** B7
St Ruald's CI WGFD OX10 .... **267** F8 🄱🄱
St Rumbolds Dr RBANNS OX17 .. **39** K2
St Rumbold's Rd WGFD OX10 .... **267** F8 🄱🄵
St Stephens CI READ RG1 .... **333** H5
St Swithun's Rd OX/KTN OX1 ..... **191** J7
St Thomas' St FGDN SN7 .... **209** K5
St Thomas' St OX/KTN OX1 .... **4** B4
  RBANSW OX15 .... **56** C4
Salegate La COW/LTMR OX4 ...... **192** D2
Salesian Gdns COW/LTMR OX4 .. **192** D1 🄱
Salford Rd HEAD OX3 .... **5** E1
Salisbury Crs OXN/BOT/CM OX2 .. **149** D2
Salisbury Rd TLHT RG30 .... **332** E7
Salmon CI RBANSW OX15 .... **37** G1
Salmons La RBANNS OX17 .... **23** F7 🄱
Salop CI HGHW SN6 .... **276** B3 🄱
Salter CI OX/KTN OX1 .... **4** C6
Salt La THAME OX9 .... **222** E5
Salt Wy RBANSW OX15 .... **29** F6
Salvia CI BAN OX16 .... **20** C6
Samian Wy WGFD OX10 .... **241** K7 🄱
Samor Wy DID OX11 .... **263** H7
Samphire Rd COW/LTMR OX4 .... **193** F6
Sanctuary CI TLHT RG30 .... **331** J7
Sandcroft Rd CAV/SC RG4 .... **332** E1
Sandell CI BAN OX16 .... **2** B4
Sanderling Wk BAN OX16 .... **3** E6
Sandfield Rd HEAD OX3 .... **168** B4
Sandfine Rd RBANSW OX15 .... **27** G5
Sandleigh Rd MCHM/KBPZ OX13 .. **213** J1
Sandpiper Br SWDNE SN3 .... **274** C8
Sandpiper CI BIC OX26 .... **97** H7
Sandpit HI BUCK/WIN MK18 .... **63** J1
Sandpit La CAV/SC RG4 .... **328** A6
  PRRI HP27 .... **201** K3
Sandpits CI RWWCK/WEL CV35 .. **16** A3
Sandpits Rd RWWCK/WEL CV35 .. **16** B3

Sandringham Rd DID OX11 .... **264** A
  RBANNS OX17 .... **39** J
Sands La RBANSW OX15 .... **36** A
Sands Rd DID OX11 .... **289** F
The Sands CHNTN OX7 .... **102** B
  WGFD OX10 .... **268** A
Sands Wy WGFD OX10 .... **267** H
Sand Vw FGDN SN7 .... **230** B5
Sandy La COW/LTMR OX4 .... **192** E
  FGDN SN7 .... **231** K
  HGHW SN6 .... **276** B
  KID OX5 .... **129** F
  MCHM/KBPZ OX13 .... **210** E
  OX/KTN OX1 .... **190** A
  RAYLW HP18 .... **174** B
  THAME OX9 .... **196** D
  WGFD OX10 .... **290** A
Sandy La West COW/LTMR OX4 .. **192** C
Sankey Gv MIM GL56 .... **46** A
Sarajac Av WANT OX12 .... **281** K
Sarsden CI CHNTN OX7 .... **86** E
Sarum CI BUR/CRTN OX18 .... **158** B
Satwell CI HEN RG9 .... **317** G
Saunders CI WTLGN OX49 .... **246** B5
Saunders Rd COW/LTMR OX4 .... **192** B
Saunders Wood Copse
  SKCH HP14 .... **249** H3
Savernake CI TLHT RG30 .... **331** K8
Savile Wy WANT OX12 .... **258** C
Saw CI STAD OX44 .... **220** A8
Sawpit Rd COW/LTMR OX4 .... **192** E
Sawpits La MIM GL56 .... **65** F
Saxel CI BUR/CRTN OX18 .... **184** C
Saxifrage Sq COW/LTMR OX4 .... **192** E6 🄱
Saxon Orch HGHW SN6 .... **266** E8
Saxon PI WANT OX12 .... **282** B
Saxons Wy DID OX11 .... **264** A8
Saxon Wy HEAD OX3 .... **168** B
  WIT/EY OX8 .... **142** E6
Saxton Rd ABGD OX14 .... **238** B
Sayers Orch DID OX11 .... **263** H6
Scafell CI CALC RG31 .... **331** F
Scampton CI BIC OX26 .... **97** J4
Schofield Av WIT/EY OX8 .... **142** E
Schofield Gdns WIT/EY OX8 ...... **142** E4
Schofields Wy RBANSW OX15 .... **37** F
Scholar PI OXN/BOT/CM OX2 .... **166** A8
Scholars Acre BUR/CRTN OX18 .. **157** K
Scholars CI CAV/SC RG4 .... **333** F4
Schongau CI ABGD OX14 .... **238** B
School La MCHM/KBPZ OX13 ..... **210** C
  MCHM/KBPZ OX13 .... **261** H
  RAYLW HP18 .... **172** E
  SHPSTR CV36 .... **49** C
School Ct OXN/BOT/CM OX2 ..... **4** B3
School End RBANNS OX17 .... **40** B8
Schooler's La MIM GL56 .... **65** H
School HI RBANNS OX17 .... **12** B
  WIT/EY OX8 .... **141** H
School La ABGD OX14 .... **239** K
  ABGD OX14 .... **262** A
  ABGD OX14 .... **262** B
  BAN OX16 .... **2** C
  BRACKY NN13 .... **43** C
  BUR/CRTN OX18 .... **182** B
  CAV/SC RG4 .... **333** H
  CHNR OX39 .... **224** A
  CHNTN OX7 .... **104** C
  DID OX11 .... **262** C
  GOR/PANG RG8 .... **315** K
  HEN RG9 .... **273** H
  HGHW SN6 .... **228** B
  MCHM/KBPZ OX13 .... **210** E
  RAYLW HP18 .... **173** H
  RBANNS OX17 .... **11** C
  RBANNS OX17 .... **13** F
  RBANSW OX15 .... **27** H
  RBICN OX27 .... **78** C
  RBICS/W OX25 .... **75** J7 🄱
  RBICS/W OX25 .... **95** F
  READ RG1 .... **333** C
  STAD OX44 .... **218** E
  WIT/EY OX8 .... **141** G
School Paddock RBICN OX27 ..... **78** A7
School PI OX/KTN OX1 .... **191** H1 🄱
School Rd CALC RG31 .... **331** H7
  CHNTN OX7 .... **124** B1
  KID OX5 .... **129** H6
  WANT OX12 .... **259** F1
  WANT OX12 .... **283** K2
School Ter READ RG1 .... **333** K7
School Vw BAN OX16 .... **3** E3
Scotland End RBANSW OX15 ...... **33** K8
Scotsgrove HI HADM HP17 .... **175** G4
Scott CI BIC OX26 .... **96** D4
  CAV/SC RG4 .... **333** C2
  KID OX5 .... **129** C7 🄱
  WODY RG5 .... **335** J8
Scott Rd OXN/BOT/CM OX2 ...... **149** F7
Scotts CI RBICN OX27 .... **99** K4
Scotts La RBICN OX27 .... **99** H5
Scours La TLHT RG30 .... **332** B6
Seacourt Rd OXN/BOT/CM OX2 .. **166** A6
Sealham Rd WIT/EY OX8 .... **160** E3

Second Av DID OX11 .... 263 H6
Second St BRACKY NN13 .... 59 K1
  DID OX11 .... 286 A4
Sedgefield Cl CAV/SC RG4 .... 327 F1
Sedgemoor Dr THAME OX9 .... 175 G6
Sedgewell Rd CAV/SC RG4 .... 327 F2
Sefton Pl RBANSW OX15 .... 29 G8
Sefton Rd HEAD OX3 .... 168 E4
Segsbury Rd WANT OX12 .... 188 D7
Selborne Gdns TLHT RG30 .... 332 A6
Selcourt Cl WODY RG5 .... 335 F7
Sellwood Dr BUR/CRTN OX18 .... 158 A4
Sellwood Rd ABGD OX14 .... 214 E5
Selsdon Av WODY RG5 .... 335 H7
Selwyn Crs ABGD OX14 .... 215 J5
Send Rd CAV/SC RG4 .... 333 J6
Sermon Cl HEAD OX3 .... 169 G5
Seven Acres THAME OX9 .... 175 G7
Sevenfields HGHW SN6 .... 226 E7
Seventeenth St DID OX11 .... 285 J5
Seventh Av HEAD OX3 .... 169 F7
Severalls Cl WGFD OX10 .... 267 F6 ▣
Severn Cl BIC OX26 .... 96 C4
Severn Rd DID OX11 .... 285 K6
  MCHM/KBPZ OX13 .... 214 B5
Sewell Cl ABGD OX14 .... 215 G5
Sewell's La CHNR OX39 .... 200 A7
Shackleton Cl BIC OX26 .... 97 H3 ▣
Shackleton Wy WODY RG5 .... 335 J8
Shadwell Rd WGFD OX10 .... 241 H2
Shaftesbury Rd TLHT RG30 .... 332 B7
Shaftsbury Rd HEAD OX3 .... 168 E2
Shakespeare Cl CAV/SC RG4 ..... 333 K2 ▣
Shakespeare Dr BIC OX26 .... 96 C5
Shakespeare Rd WIT/EY OX8 .... 145 K7
Shanes Castle Rd
  RWWCK/WEL CV35 .... 8 E1
Shannon Cl WANT OX12 .... 259 F6
Shannon Rd BIC OX26 .... 96 C5
Shapwick Cl SWDNE SN3 .... 274 A8 ▣
Sharland Cl WANT OX12 .... 258 E7
Sharman Beer Ct THAME OX9 ..... 174 E7 ▣
Shaw Cl DID OX11 .... 96 D5
Shaw's Copse ABGD OX14 .... 215 K5
Sheards La FGDN SN7 .... 232 C8
The Shearings RBANSW OX15 ...... 33 K8 ▣
Shearwater Dr BIC OX26 .... 97 J7
Sheen Cl RBICN OX27 .... 97 G1
Sheepstead Rd MCHM/KBPZ OX13.. 212 E7
Sheep St BIC OX26 .... 97 F5 ▣
  BUR/CRTN OX18 .... 138 D2
  CHNTN OX7 .... 106 A4
  HGHW SN6 .... 250 E1
Sheep Wk CAV/SC RG4 .... 333 H3
Sheepwash La MCHM/KBPZ OX13 ... 261 J3
Sheepway Ct COW/LTMR OX4 ...... 192 A3 ▣
Sheepways La CAV/SC RG4 .... 326 D7
Sheerstock HADM HP17 .... 176 A1
Shefford Rd RWWCK/WEL CV35 .... 8 E1
Sheldon Rd RAYLW HP18 .... 172 D4
Sheldons Piece WTLGN OX49 .... 246 A5
Sheldon Wy COW/LTMR OX4 .... 192 C4
Shelford Pl HEAD OX3 .... 168 D6 ▣
Shelley Cl ABGD OX14 .... 214 B6
  BAN OX16 .... 2 A6 ▣
  BIC OX26 .... 96 D4
  HEAD OX3 .... 169 F5
Shelley Rd COW/LTMR OX4 .... 192 B1
Shepard Wy CHNTN OX7 .... 68 C4 ▣
Shepherds Av EARL RG6 .... 334 D7
Shepherds Cl WANT OX12 .... 238 A1
Shepherds Ct EARL RG6 .... 334 D7
Shepherds Hl COW/LTMR OX4 .... 193 F6
  EARL RG6 .... 334 E7 ▣
Shepherd's House La EARL RG6 .. 334 C7 ▣
Shepherds La CAV/SC RG4 .... 332 D1
Sheraton Dr CALC RG31 .... 331 F6
Sherborne Cl CIR GL7 .... 203 G3
Sherbourne Cl DID OX11 .... 263 K5 ▣
Sherbourne Dr WODY RG5 .... 335 H7
Sherbourne Rd WIT/EY OX8 .... 142 B7
Sheridan Av CAV/SC RG4 .... 333 F7
Sheriff's Dr OXN/BOT/CM OX2 .... 148 D7 ▣
Sherwood Av ABGD OX14 .... 214 E8
Sherwood Cl BIC OX26 .... 98 A5
Sherwood Gdns HEAD RG9 .... 318 E7
Sherwood Rd GOR/PANG RG8 .... 331 F3
Sherwood Rd DID OX11 .... 263 H7
Sherwood St TLHT RG30 .... 332 C7
Shifford La WIT/EY OX8 .... 186 B6
Shillbrook Av BUR/CRTN OX18 ...... 157 J2
Shilldeane Dr BUR/CRTN OX18 ... 157 K3 ▣
Shilton Rd BUR/CRTN OX18 .... 138 E4
  BUR/CRTN OX18 .... 157 J2
Shiplake Bottom HEN RG9 .... 316 E8
Shipley Cl WODY RG5 .... 335 J6
Shipston Rd RWWCK/WEL CV35 ...... 16 B3
Ship St OX/KTN OX1 .... 4 C4 ▣
Shipton Cl CALC RG31 .... 331 C5
Shipton Rd CHNTN OX7 .... 102 C6
  WDSTK OX20 .... 128 A1
Shirburn Rd WTLGN OX49 .... 246 C5
Shire Lake Cl OX/KTN OX1 .... 4 C5 ▣1
Shirvell's Hl GOR/PANG RG8 .... 314 B8
Shogmoor La HEN RG9 .... 273 K7

Shooter's Hl GOR/PANG RG8 .... 323 H7
Short Furlong DID OX11 .... 264 B5 ▣
Shortlands Hl WGFD OX10 .... 311 J3
Short St CAV/SC RG4 .... 333 H5
  GOR/PANG RG8 .... 330 B2 ▣
  HGHW SN6 .... 252 D6
The Short CAV/SC RG8 .... 331 H2
Shotover FGDN SN7 .... 278 E1
Shotover Kilns HEAD OX3 .... 169 F6
Shrieves Cl ABGD OX14 .... 215 F4 ▣
Shrivenham Rd FGDN SN7 .... 253 J6
  HGHW SN6 .... 250 E3
Shute Av HGHW SN6 .... 252 D7
Shutford Rd RBANSW OX15 .... 26 E8
Sibford Rd RBANSW OX15 .... 25 J4
  RBANSW OX15 .... 34 A8 ▣
Sideleigh Rd RBANSW OX15 .... 29 G7
Sidings Rd CHNTN OX7 .... 84 E2
Sidmouth Grange Rd EARL RG6 ..... 334 D8
Sidmouth Grange Rd EARL 334 D8
Sidmouth St READ RG1 .... 333 J8
Sidney St COW/LTMR OX4 .... 5 F6
Signet End BUR/CRTN OX18 ...... 138 E3
Silkdale Cl COW/LTMR OX4 ...... 192 D2 ▣
Silver La WANT OX12 .... 281 H2
Silvermead RAYLW HP18 .... 172 B3
Silver Rd COW/LTMR OX4 .... 168 A8
Silver St FGDN SN7 .... 254 C5
  HGHW SN6 .... 276 A5
  RBANSW OX17 .... 19 H7
  RBANSW OX15 .... 198 B7
  THAME OX9 .... 198 B7
Silver St North RBANNS OX17 .... 22 C3
Silverthorne Dr CAV/SC RG4 .... 332 D1
Simmonds Flds WAR/TWY RG10 ..... 335 K4
Simmons Hl HEN RG9 .... 319 F4
Simmons Wy THAME OX9 .... 175 F6 ▣
Simons Cl CALC RG31 .... 331 C5 ▣
  WHLY OX33 .... 170 C7 ▣
Simons La CHNTN OX7 .... 102 E8
Simpsons Wy OX/KTN OX1 .... 191 J7
Sinclair Av BAN OX16 .... 2 A2
Sinclair Rd BAN OX16 .... 2 A2
Singers Cl HEN RG9 .... 319 G7
Sinnels Fld CHNTN OX7 .... 103 F7
Sinodun Rd DID OX11 .... 263 K8
  WGFD OX10 .... 266 E6
Sinodun Vw WGFD OX10 .... 242 D7
Sint Niklaas Cl ABGD OX14 .... 238 B3 ▣
Sires Hl ABGD OX14 .... 264 C2
Sir Georges La RBANNS OX17 .... 38 D4
Siskin Rd BIC OX26 .... 97 H6
Sixpenny La STAD OX44 .... 244 C1
Sixteenth St DID OX11 .... 285 K8
Sixth St BRACKY NN13 .... 41 K8
  DID OX11 .... 285 K4
Skarries Vw CAV/SC RG4 .... 326 D7
Skerritt Wy GOR/PANG RG8 .... 331 H3
Skilton Rd CALC RG31 .... 331 G4
Skimmingdish La RBICN OX27 .... 97 G1
Skinner Rd BIC OX26 .... 98 A5
Skippett La CHNTN OX7 .... 123 K3
Skippon Wy THAME OX9 .... 175 F5
Skittle Aly RBANNS OX17 .... 40 D8 ▣
Skittle Gn PRRI HP27 .... 201 J5
Skye Cl HGHW SN6 .... 226 D8
Slade Cl HEAD OX3 .... 168 D6
Slade Rd DID OX11 .... 265 G7
  SKCH HP14 .... 249 G3
  WGFD OX10 .... 290 C5
The Slade CHNTN OX7 .... 106 B3
  HEAD OX3 .... 168 D6
  RBANNS OX17 .... 6 B6
Slave Hl HADM HP17 .... 176 B2
Slaymaker Cl HEAD OX3 .... 169 F5 ▣
The Slopes CAV/SC RG4 .... 333 K5
Small House RBANSW OX15 .... 25 F8
Smarts La RWWCK/WEL CV35 .... 16 E3
Smith Barry Crs COTS GL54 .... 100 A3
Smith Barry Rd COTS GL54 .... 100 A3
Smith Cl CAV/SC RG4 .... 327 F2
Smith's Cl BUR/CRTN OX18 .... 184 C5 ▣
Smith's Hl WANT OX12 .... 303 J2
Smiths Rickyard WANT OX12 .... 261 F8
Snakehill La RBANSW OX15 .... 55 J2
Snowdon Mede HEAD OX3 .... 168 A3 ▣
Snowshill Dr WIT/EY OX8 .... 142 B7
Snowswick La FGDN SN7 .... 203 J8
Snuff La RBANNS OX17 .... 11 J7
Snuggs La WANT OX12 .... 235 H8
Soane End CAV/SC RG4 .... 333 G1
Soden Rd RBICS/W OX25 .... 76 C7
Somerstown Ct READ RG1 .... 333 F8 ▣
Somerton Rd RBICN OX27 .... 77 F3
  RBICS/W OX25 .... 56 E8
Somerville DID OX11 .... 264 B7
Somerville Cl RBANNS OX17 .... 39 G4
Somerville Dr BIC OX26 .... 97 G3
Songers Cl OXN/BOT/CM OX2 .... 165 K8
Sonning La CAV/SC RG4 .... 335 F5
Sonning Mdw CAV/SC RG4 .... 334 E6
Soot La RBANNS OX17 .... 11 G3
Sopwith Cl WODY RG5 .... 335 J8 ▣
Sorrel Rd COW/LTMR OX4 .... 193 F4

Sotwell St WGFD OX10 .... 266 B5
Southampton St FGDN SN7 .... 230 B3 ▣
Southam Rd BAN OX16 .... 2 C2
  RBANSW OX17 .... 6 B8
South Av ABGD OX14 .... 214 D5
  HEN RG9 .... 319 G7
  KID OX5 .... 148 C1
South Bar St BAN OX16 .... 2 C4
Southby BUR/CRTN OX18 .... 183 H3
Southby Cl MCHM/KBPZ OX13 ...... 188 C7
South Cl KID OX5 .... 148 D2
Southcroft HEAD OX3 .... 167 K1
Southdale Rd OXN/BOT/CM OX2 ... 149 F7
Southdown Ct FGDN SN7 .... 332 C8
Southdown Rd CAV/SC RG4 .... 334 E6
South Dr CAV/SC RG4 .... 286 A3
  DID OX11 .... 50 D4
South End CHNTN OX7 .... 50 D4
  HADM HP17 .... 176 B2 ▣
Southend STAD OX44 .... 194 A6
Southern By-Pass Rd OX/KTN OX1.. 190 E1
  OXN/BOT/CM OX2 .... 166 B7
Southerndene Cl CALC RG31 ...... 331 H5 ▣
Southern Rd THAME OX9 .... 174 E7
Southfield La RBICN OX27 .... 58 E8 ▣
Southfield Rd COW/LTMR OX4 .... 168 A7
Southlands BUR/CRTN OX18 .... 184 C5
Southlawn WIT/EY OX8 .... 142 D8
South Leigh Rd WIT/EY OX8 .... 143 K8
South Meadow RBICS/W OX25 ... 115 K4 ▣
South Mere BUR/CRTN OX18 .... 158 E4
Southmoor Pl OXN/BOT/CM OX2 .. 4 B1 ▣
Southmoor Rd OXN/BOT/CM OX2 .. 4 A2
Southmoor Wy ABGD OX14 .... 214 C7
South Newington Rd
  RBANSW OX15 .... 36 C6
South Pde OXN/BOT/CM OX2 .... 166 E1
South Park Av DID OX11 .... 263 H8
South Parks Rd OX/KTN OX1 .... 5 D3
South Rd HEN RG9 .... 316 B6
Southrop Rd RBANSW OX15 .... 52 A1
South Rw DID OX11 .... 286 B7
South Side RBICS/W OX25 .... 74 D7
South Stoke Rd WGFD OX10 .... 313 J4
South St BAN OX16 .... 3 E2
  CHNTN OX7 .... 73 G7
  DID OX11 .... 288 A7
  HGHW SN6 .... 252 D6
  OXN/BOT/CM OX2 .... 4 A5
  OXW/SC OX25 .... 94 A2
  READ RG1 .... 333 H5
  WANT OX12 .... 282 A6
South Vw RBANNS OX17 .... 13 F8
South View Av CAV/SC RG4 .... 333 H5
South View Pk CAV/SC RG4 .... 333 J5
Southwold BIC OX26 .... 97 G3 ▣
Southwood Rd WIT/EY OX8 .... 142 A6
Sovereign Cl DID OX11 .... 264 A7
Spa Cl HGHW SN6 .... 227 F8
Span Hl HEN RG9 .... 328 D8
Spareacre La WIT/EY OX8 .... 145 K7
Sparsey Pl OXN/BOT/CM OX2 .... 149 F6
Sparsholt St WANT OX12 .... 280 D5
The Spears KID OX5 .... 147 K1
  KID OX5 .... 147 K2
Spencer Av KID OX5 .... 147 K2
Spencer Crs COW/LTMR OX4 .... 192 A3
Spencer Gdns BRACKY NN13 .... 43 F1
Spencers St FGDN SN7 .... 232 C8
Spenlove Cl ABGD OX14 .... 214 D5
Spenser Cl BIC OX26 .... 96 D4
Spey Rd MCHM/KBPZ OX13 .... 214 A4
  TLHT RG30 .... 332 A7
Speyside Cl BUR/CRTN OX18 .... 157 K2
Spier's La RBICN OX27 .... 99 J5
Spindleberry Cl COW/LTMR OX4 .. 192 E5 ▣
Spindlers KID OX5 .... 129 J3
Spindleside BIC OX26 .... 97 G3 ▣
Spinney Cl CAV/SC RG4 .... 327 H8 ▣
Spinney Dr BAN OX16 .... 3 E6
Spinney Fld COW/LTMR OX4 ..... 192 E6 ▣3
Spinneys Cl ABGD OX14 .... 215 K4
The Spinneys CHNTN OX7 .... 88 E2 ▣
The Spinney ABGD OX14 .... 214 B6
  BIC OX26 .... 97 K5
  CIR GL7 .... 203 G3
  WANT OX12 .... 285 F1
Spitfire Cl BIC OX26 .... 97 H4 ▣
Spitfire Sq WGFD OX10 .... 335 J8
Spitfire Wy WODY RG5 .... 335 J8
Spode Cl TLHT RG30 .... 331 J7
Spooner Cl HEAD OX3 .... 168 E4
Spriggs Molly La SKCH HP14 .... 225 J6
Spring Copse OX/KTN OX1 .... 191 G4
Springdale WGFD OX10 .... 266 E8
Springfield RBANNS OX17 .... 20 B3
Springfield Av BAN OX16 .... 2 C6
Springfield Cl HGHW SN6 .... 276 B1 ▣
  WTLGN OX49 .... 246 C6
Springfield Dr ABGD OX14 .... 214 C7
Springfield End GOR/PANG RG8 ... 312 E7 ▣
Springfield Gdns CHNR OX39 .... 200 E8
Springfield Ov WIT/EY OX8 .... 142 D5
Springfield Pk WIT/EY OX8 .... 142 D6
Springfield Rd KID OX5 .... 129 J7
  OXN/BOT/CM OX2 .... 166 A7 ▣

RBICN OX27 .... 79 C8
SKCH HP14 .... 249 H3
WANT OX12 .... 282 E3
Spring Gdns ABCD OX14 .... 214 B8
CIR GL7 .... 203 C3
Spring Hi MCHM/KBPZ OX13 .... 210 B7
Springhill Rd GOR/PANG RG8 .... 312 E7
Spring Hill Rd KID OX5 .... 128 C7
Spring La CAV/SC RG4 .... 334 D1
CHNTN OX7 .... 101 C3
COW/LTMR OX4 .... 192 D5
DID OX11 .... 288 E7
HEAD OX3 .... 169 F4
RBANNS OX17 .... 21 F2
WHLY OX33 .... 169 J8
WTLGN OX49 .... 246 C6
Spring Pth THAME OX9 .... 174 E2
Spring Rd ABGD OX14 .... 214 B8
The Springs WIT/EY OX8 .... 142 E8
Spring St CHNTN OX7 .... 68 B4
Springwell Hi KID OX5 .... 111 K5
Springwood La HEN RG9 .... 317 F7
Spruce Dr BIC OX26 .... 97 G2
Spruce Gdns COW/LTMR OX4 .... 192 E7
Spruce Rd KID OX5 .... 129 H8
Square Firs WIT/EY OX8 .... 126 B2
The Square RAYLW HP18 .... 174 C1
RBANNS OX17 .... 39 J2
RBANNS OX17 .... 40 B8
RBANSW OX15 .... 25 K7
RWWCK/WEL CV35 .... 16 B2
WIT/EY OX8 .... 161 F3
Squires La BUR/CRTN OX18 .... 158 E4
Squires Rd HGHW SN6 .... 252 D6
Squire's Wk WGFD OX10 .... 291 F1
Squitchey La OXN/BOT/CM OX2 .... 148 E7
Stable CI BUCK/WIN MK18 .... 63 F1
OXN/BOT/CM OX2 .... 4 B3
Stable Rd BIC OX26 .... 97 F4
Staddlestone CI CALC RG31 .... 331 C5
Stadhampton Rd WGFD OX10 .... 242 D2
Stadium Wy TLHT RG30 .... 332 B6
Stafford Cl WODY RG5 .... 335 H8
Staffordshire Cl TLHT RG30 .... 331 K6
Stainer PI HEAD OX3 .... 5 F1
Stainfield Cl HEAD OX3 .... 168 B2
Stainswick La HGHW SN6 .... 276 C1
Stallpits Rd HGHW SN6 .... 252 A8
Stanbridge Cl BAN OX16 .... 2 A4
Standlake Rd WIT/EY OX8 .... 161 F4
WIT/EY OX8 .... 187 G5
Stanford Dr ABGD OX14 .... 214 D8
Stanford Rd FGDN SN7 .... 230 D4
Stanham Rd TLHT RG30 .... 331 K7
Stanier PI BAN OX16 .... 3 E2
Stanley Cl OXN/BOT/CM OX2 .... 166 B7
Stanley Gv READ RG1 .... 332 E7
Stanley Rd COW/LTMR OX4 .... 5 F6
Stanley St READ RG1 .... 333 F7
Stanmore Crs BUR/CRTN OX18 .... 158 A4
Stanmore Rd KSCL RG20 .... 308 C8
Stansfeld PI HEAD OX3 .... 168 E6
Stansfield Cl HEAD OX3 .... 169 F6
Stanshawe Rd READ RG1 .... 333 C7
Stanton Cl WIT/EY OX8 .... 142 C7
Stanton Harcourt Rd
WIT/EY OX8 .... 143 H7
WIT/EY OX8 .... 162 D2
Stanton Rd OXN/BOT/CM OX2 .... 190 C1
WHLY OX33 .... 170 A2
Stanville Rd OXN/BOT/CM OX2 .... 165 K8
Stanway Cl WIT/EY OX8 .... 142 B6
Stanway Rd HEAD OX3 .... 169 F4
Stanwell Cl RBANNS OX17 .... 22 E6
Stanwell Dr RBANNS OX17 .... 22 B6
Stanwell La RBANNS OX17 .... 13 F7
Stanwell Lea RBANNS OX17 .... 22 E5
Stapleton Cl HGHW SN6 .... 250 D2
Stapleton Rd HEAD OX3 .... 168 C5
Starina Cft RBANNS OX17 .... 20 C6
Star La HGHW SN6 .... 252 C6
Starnham Rd WIT/EY OX8 .... 160 E3
Star Rd CAV/SC RG4 .... 333 J5
Station Ap BIC OX26 .... 97 G7
KID OX5 .... 129 F5
Station Hi READ RG1 .... 333 G7
Station La WIT/EY OX8 .... 160 E1
Station Rd ABGD OX14 .... 239 K4
BIC OX26 .... 98 C4
BUR/CRTN OX18 .... 159 F7
BUR/CRTN OX18 .... 182 A3
BUR/CRTN OX18 .... 183 G1
CHNR OX39 .... 200 E8
CHNTN OX7 .... 68 A5
CHNTN OX7 .... 83 K6
CHNTN OX7 .... 103 F6
CIR GL7 .... 203 H2
DID OX11 .... 263 J5
DID OX11 .... 287 G5
FGDN SN7 .... 230 B4
FGDN SN7 .... 255 G8
GOR/PANG RG8 .... 322 E1
HADM HP17 .... 176 A2
HEN RG9 .... 319 G6
HEN RG9 .... 329 J3

HGHW SN6 .... 250 E1
HGHW SN6 .... 276 B2
KID OX5 .... 111 K7
MIM GL56 .... 46 A1
RBANNS OX17 .... 13 H6
RBANSW OX15 .... 34 B7
RBANSW OX15 .... 57 K1
RBICN OX27 .... 77 H4
RBICN OX27 .... 99 J4
RBICS/W OX25 .... 93 F7
RBICS/W OX25 .... 116 D4
READ RG1 .... 333 G7
WANT OX12 .... 259 F6
WGFD OX10 .... 266 E7
WGFD OX10 .... 290 B6
WHLY OX33 .... 170 C7
WIT/EY OX8 .... 146 A8
WIT/EY OX8 .... 162 C2
Station Yd MCHM/KBPZ OX13 .... 261 J3
Staunton Rd HEAD OX3 .... 175 G8
Staverton Rd OXN/BOT/CM OX2 .... 167 F2
Steady's La WIT/EY OX8 .... 163 H8
Steeple Cl RBANSW OX15 .... 37 F3
Steepness Hi RBANSW OX15 .... 55 G3
Steep Ri HEAD OX3 .... 168 C3
Steggles CI WODY RG5 .... 335 F7
Stenton Cl ABGD OX14 .... 238 C2
Stephen Rd HEAD OX3 .... 168 C4
Stephenson Rd WANT OX12 .... 258 A7
Steptoe Cl WANT OX12 .... 258 D5
Sterling Cl BIC OX26 .... 97 H4
Sterling Rd KID OX5 .... 129 H7
Sterling Road Ap KID OX5 .... 129 H6
Sterling Wy TLHT RG30 .... 332 A6
Stert Rd CHNR OX39 .... 224 B3
Stert St ABGD OX14 .... 214 D8
Stevens La HEN RG9 .... 316 D7
Stevenson Cl BIC OX26 .... 96 D4
Stevenson Dr ABGD OX14 .... 214 B6
Steventon Rd ABGD OX14 .... 237 J7
WANT OX12 .... 235 J8
Stewart St OX/KTN OX1 .... 191 C1
Stile Rd HEAD OX3 .... 168 D4
Stileway Rd WANT OX12 .... 285 H5
Stimpsons Cl OXN/BOT/CM OX2 .... 165 J6
Stirling Cl BUR/CRTN OX18 .... 157 J5
CAV/SC RG4 .... 333 K1
WANT OX12 .... 282 E2
Stirling Ct BAN OX16 .... 28 B1
Stirling Rd SWDNE SN3 .... 274 A1
Stirlings Rd WANT OX12 .... 282 D2
Stockey End ABGD OX14 .... 215 G5
Stockham Pk WANT OX12 .... 282 C2
Stocking La RBANSW OX15 .... 117 H5
Stockleys Rd HEAD OX3 .... 168 A2
Stockmore St COW/LTMR OX4 .... 5 F5
Stocks La MCHM/KBPZ OX13 .... 261 H3
Stocks Tree Cl KID OX5 .... 147 K2
Stockwell Furlong HADM HP17 .... 176 C1
Stockwells MIM GL56 .... 46 A2
Stonebridge Rd
MCHM/KBPZ OX13 .... 261 H2
Stoneburge Crs BIC OX26 .... 97 F4
Stone Cl OXN/BOT/CM OX2 .... 165 K6
Stone Ct CHNTN OX7 .... 50 D4
Stonefield Cl HGHW SN6 .... 276 C1
Stonefield Dr HGHW SN6 .... 250 E2
Stone Hi RBANSW OX15 .... 36 E3
Stonehill La ABGD OX14 .... 238 A3
MCHM/KBPZ OX13 .... 210 D7
Stone House Cl
MCHM/KBPZ OX13 .... 210 E6
Stoneleigh Cl CHNTN OX7 .... 86 E6
Stoneleigh Dr BUR/CRTN OX18 .... 157 F2
Stone Quarry La
COW/LTMR OX4 .... 192 A3
Stonesfield Cl DID OX11 .... 264 A8
Stonesfield La CHNTN OX7 .... 106 B5
Stonesfield Riding WIT/EY OX8 .... 107 J6
Stonesfield Rd WIT/EY OX8 .... 126 A2
Stone St COW/LTMR OX4 .... 168 A7
TLHT RG30 .... 332 B6
Stoney La STAD OX44 .... 221 H6
Stonhouse Crs ABGD OX14 .... 215 J5
Stonor Cl DID OX11 .... 263 J6
Stonor Gn WTLGN OX49 .... 246 B6
Stonor PI HEAD OX3 .... 168 B5
Stort Cl DID OX11 .... 263 K4
Stour Cl DID OX11 .... 264 A6
TLHT RG30 .... 332 A7
Stoutsfield Cl KID OX5 .... 147 J2
Stow Av WIT/EY OX8 .... 142 B7
Stowford Rd HEAD OX3 .... 169 F3
Stowood Cl HEAD OX3 .... 168 E3
Stow Rd CHNTN OX7 .... 83 H5
HEN RG9 .... 319 H7
St Patrick's Br WAR/TWY RG10 .... 335 H1

Strachey Cl GOR/PANG RG8 .... 330 A
Strafford Wy THAME OX9 .... 175 G7
Strainges Cl WIT/EY OX8 .... 161 F3
Strangers La BUCK/WIN MK18 .... 63 K
Stratfield Rd KID OX5 .... 148 C
OXN/BOT/CM OX2 .... 149 F
Stratford Br WDSTK OX20 .... 109 H
Stratford Dr WIT/EY OX8 .... 145 K
Stratford La WDSTK OX20 .... 109 J
Stratford Rd RBANSW OX15 .... 18 A
Stratford St COW/LTMR OX4 .... 5 E
Stratfords Wy HADM HP17 .... 176 B
Stratheden PI READ RG1 .... 333 F7
Strathmore Cl BUR/CRTN OX18 .... 158 A
Strathmore Dr WAR/TWY RG10 .... 335 J
Strathy Cl TLHT RG30 .... 332 B
Stratton Audley Rd RBICN OX27 .... 78 C
Stratton Wy ABGD OX14 .... 214 D8
Strawberry Hi RBANSW OX15 .... 37 F
Strawberry Ter RBANSW OX15 .... 37 F
Stream Rd DID OX11 .... 287 G
Streatley Hi GOR/PANG RG8 .... 322 A
The Street GOR/PANG RG8 .... 312 D3
RBICN OX27 .... 78 C
WGFD OX10 .... 267 G8
WGFD OX10 .... 291 G6
WGFD OX10 .... 292 A8
WGFD OX10 .... 312 C
Stroma Wy HGHW SN6 .... 226 C8
Stuart Cl CAV/SC RG4 .... 333 H
Stuart Wy THAME OX9 .... 175 G7
Stubble Cl OXN/BOT/CM OX2 .... 165 J7
Stubbs Av HEAD OX3 .... 168 E8
Studdridge Ct SKCH HP14 .... 248 E3
Stud Farm Cl RBANNS OX17 .... 14 C6
Sturges Cl HEAD OX3 .... 168 E3
Sturt Cl CHNTN OX7 .... 106 B5
Sturt Rd CHNTN OX7 .... 106 B5
Styles Cl RBICN OX27 .... 99 H5
The Styles DID OX11 .... 262 B8
Sudbury La MCHM/KBPZ OX13 .... 210 C4
Suffolk Ct RBICN OX27 .... 99 J5
Suffolk Rd TLHT RG30 .... 332 C8
Suffolk Wy ABGD OX14 .... 238 B
Sugarswell La RBANSW OX15 .... 16 E4
Sugworth Crs ABGD OX14 .... 215 J1
Sugworth La MCHM/KBPZ OX13 .... 215 F
Sulham La GOR/PANG RG8 .... 330 C2
Summerfield OX/KTN OX1 .... 191 H1
Summerfield Ri GOR/PANG RG8 .... 313 F8
Summerhill Rd OXN/BOT/CM OX2 .... 149 F6
Summers Cl RBANNS OX17 .... 38 D2
Summerside Rd FGDN SN7 .... 208 C2
Summerton PI CHNTN OX7 .... 68 C4
Summertown WANT OX12 .... 259 G1
Summertown Ct
OXN/BOT/CM OX2 .... 148 E8
Sunderland Av OXN/BOT/CM OX2 .... 148 D6
Sunderland Cl WODY RG5 .... 335 K7
Sunderland Dr BIC OX26 .... 97 H5
Sundew Cl COW/LTMR OX4 .... 193 G5
Sunningwell Rd
MCHM/KBPZ OX13 .... 214 D1
OX/KTN OX1 .... 191 H2
Sunny Ri WHLY OX33 .... 193 K1
Sunnyside COW/LTMR OX4 .... 192 D1
WGFD OX10 .... 267 H2
WHLY OX33 .... 170 E7
Sun Rising Hi RBANSW OX15 .... 8 E6
Sun St READ RG1 .... 333 K8
Surley Rw CAV/SC RG4 .... 333 G2
Sussex Dr BAN OX16 .... 20 B7
Sussex Gdns WODY RG5 .... 335 G8
Sutherland Beck DID OX11 .... 263 J4
Sutton Cl ABGD OX14 .... 214 D8
Sutton Courtenay La ABGD OX14 .... 262 D2
Sutton La WIT/EY OX8 .... 163 H5
Sutton Rd ABGD OX14 .... 262 B1
HEAD OX3 .... 168 B2
Suttons Park Av EARL RG6 .... 334 B7
READ RG1 .... 334 A7
Sutton Wick La ABGD OX14 .... 237 K5
Suzan Crs WANT OX12 .... 282 E2
Swalcliffe Lea RBANSW OX15 .... 26 B5
Swalcliffe Rd RBANSW OX15 .... 26 B7
Swale Dr DID OX11 .... 264 A5
Swallow Cl BIC OX26 .... 97 H7
COW/LTMR OX4 .... 193 F6
Swallowdale SWDNE SN3 .... 274 B8
Swanbrook SWDNE SN3 .... 274 B7
Swan Cl CIR GL7 .... 203 C3
RBANNS OX17 .... 22 D7
WANT OX12 .... 258 C6
Swan Close Rd BAN OX16 .... 3 D4
Swan Gdns THAME OX9 .... 198 B7
Swanhall La WIT/EY OX8 .... 143 F1
Swan La BUR/CRTN OX18 .... 138 E2
FGDN SN7 .... 230 D3
RBANNS OX17 .... 13 F7
RBICN OX27 .... 99 K4
WIT/EY OX8 .... 126 C6
Swan Lane Cl BUR/CRTN OX18 .... 138 E2
Swan PI READ RG1 .... 333 C8
Swansea Rd READ RG1 .... 333 G6
Swansea Ter CALC RG31 .... 331 H6

Swansfield *CIR* GL7 .... 203 H1 🖫
Swanston Fld *GOR/PANG* RG8 .... 324 B8
Swan St *OXN/BOT/CM* OX2 .... 4 A4
 WIT/EY OX8 .... 146 A8
Swan's Wy *CHNR* OX39 .... 225 F2
 WGFD OX10 .... 313 J1
 WTLGN OX49 .... 246 E6
Sweeps La *BUR/CRTN* OX18 .... 138 E2
Sweet Briar *MCHM/KBPZ* OX13 ...... 256 E1
Sweetmans Rd *OXN/BOT/CM* OX2 .. 166 B8
Swerford Rd *RBANSW* OX15 .... 52 A2
Swift *CI BIC* OX26 .... 96 D3
 COW/LTMR OX4 .... 193 F6
Swift *CI WGFD* OX10 .... 268 B4
Swinbourne Rd *COW/LTMR* OX4 ..... 192 B5
Swinbrook *CI CALC* RG31 .... 331 H4
Swinbrook Rd *BUR/CRTN* OX18 ...... 157 K2
 CHNTN OX7 .... 103 F8
Swinburne Rd *ABGD* OX14 .... 214 E7
 COW/LTMR OX4 .... 191 K1
Swindon Rd *HGHW* SN6 .... 250 C5
Swindon St *HGHW* SN6 .... 250 E2
Swinford Bridge (Toll)
 WIT/EY OX8 .... 164 C1
Swingburn Pl *WIT/EY* OX8 .... 142 E7 🖫
Swin La *BUR/CRTN* OX18 .... 140 A2
Swiss Cottage La *CALC* RG31 .... 331 C7 🖫
Sworford La *WHLY* OX33 .... 195 H1
Sycamore *CI MCHM/KBPZ* OX13 ..... 213 K6
 RAYLW HP18 .... 174 C1
 RBANSW OX15 .... 24 E7
 WIT/EY OX8 .... 143 G5
 WTLGN OX49 .... 246 A5 🖫
Sycamore Crs *OX/KTN* OX1 .... 191 J8
Sycamore Dr *BAN* OX16 .... 29 F5
 BUR/CRTN OX18 .... 157 K4
 THAME OX9 .... 174 D7
Sycamore Gdns *BIC* OX26 .... 97 G3 🖫
Sycamore Rd *BIC* OX26 .... 98 A5
 OXN/BOT/CM OX2 .... 166 B8
 RBICS/W OX25 .... 115 K3
Sydenham Gv *CHNR* OX39 .... 200 A7
Sylvester *CI BUR/CRTN* OX18 .... 138 E2
Sympson *CI ABGD* OX14 .... 238 C1
Synderford *CI DID* OX11 .... 264 A5
Sywell Rd *SWDNE* SN3 .... 274 A7

T

Tackley Pl *OXN/BOT/CM* OX2 .... 4 B1
Tacks La *HADM* HP17 .... 176 B1
Tadmarton Rd *RBANSW* OX15 .... 36 B2
Tadpole Br *BUR/CRTN* OX18 .... 208 A2
Taff Wy *TLHT* RG30 .... 332 A8
Taggs Ga *HEAD* OX3 .... 169 F3
Tait Dr *RBICS/W* OX25 .... 76 A8
Talbot *CI BAN* OX16 .... 20 B7
 CAV/SC RG4 .... 333 K5
Talbot *CI READ* RG1 .... 333 G8 🖫
Talbot Rd *OXN/BOT/CM* OX2 .... 148 E5
Talbot Wy *CALC* RG31 .... 331 G4 🖫
Talisman Rd *BIC* OX26 .... 97 C7
Tamar Crs *BIC* OX26 .... 96 C4
Tamarisk Gdns *BIC* OX26 .... 97 F2 🖫
Tamar Wy *DID* OX11 .... 264 A5
Tangmere Av *BUR/CRTN* OX18 .. 158 A3 🖫
Tangmere *CI BIC* OX26 .... 97 J3
Tanners Ct *CHNTN* OX7 .... 106 A4
Tanner's La *BUR/CRTN* OX18 .... 138 D3
 CAV/SC RG4 .... 327 F7
 RBANSW OX17 .... 38 C4
 WIT/EY OX8 .... 146 B8
Tannery *CI BUR/CRTN* OX18............. 138 E2
Taphouse Av *WIT/EY* OX8 .... 143 F5
Tarragon Dr *COW/LTMR* OX4 .... 193 H6
Tarrant Av *WIT/EY* OX8 .... 143 G4
Taston Rd *CHNTN* OX7 .... 87 K7
Tatham Rd *ABGD* OX14 .... 214 D6
Tatlings Rd *MCHM/KBPZ* OX13 .... 261 H2
Taverner Pl *HEAD* OX3 .... 5 F1
Tavistock Av *DID* OX11 .... 263 H8
Tavy *CI DID* OX11 .... 263 K4
Tawney St *COW/LTMR* OX4 .... 168 A7
Tawny Owl *CI SWDNE* SN3 .... 274 A7 🖫
Tay Gdns *BIC* OX26 .... 96 D4 🖫
Taylor *CI BIC* OX26 .... 97 F5
Tay Rd *TLHT* RG30 .... 332 A8
Tays Gtwy *RBANSW* OX15 .... 56 C5 🖫
Teal *CI BAN* OX16 .... 3 E6
 COW/LTMR OX4 .... 195 F6 🖫
 WANT OX12 .... 258 D6
Teale *CI RBICS/W* OX25 .... 116 B8
Tealsbrook *SWDNE* SN3 .... 274 C8 🖫
Teescroft *DID* OX11 .... 264 A4
Telford Crs *WODY* RG5 .... 335 H6
Telford Rd *BIC* OX26 .... 97 J4
Templar Rd *OXN/BOT/CM* OX2 ...... 149 F6 🖫
Templars *CI WHLY* OX33 .... 170 C7 🖫
Temple Ms *WODY* RG5 .... 335 H8
Temple Rd *COW/LTMR* OX4 .... 192 C1
Temple St *COW/LTMR* OX4 .... 5 E5
 RAYLW HP18 .... 135 K7

Tenby Av *CAV/SC* RG4 .... 333 K2
Tenlands *RBANNS* OX17 .... 22 D7
The Tennis *WIT/EY* OX8 .... 146 E5
Tennyson *CI BAN* OX16 .... 2 A6 🖫
Tennyson Dr *ABGD* OX14 .... 238 A2
Tenpenny *WGFD* OX10 .... 241 K7 🖫
Tenth St *DID* OX11 .... 285 K4
Tern *CI TLHT* RG30 .... 332 A8
Tern Wk *COW/LTMR* OX4 .... 192 E6
Terrington La *ABGD* OX14 .... 214 D5
Tessa Rd *READ* RG1 .... 333 F6
Test *CI TLHT* RG30 .... 332 A7 🖫
Tetbury Dr *WIT/EY* OX8 .... 142 B6
Teviot Rd *TLHT* RG30 .... 331 J8
The Tewer *WIT/EY* OX8 .... 107 H8
Tew La *WDSTK* OX20 .... 109 G1
Thackley End *OXN/BOT/CM* OX2 ..... 167 F2 🖫
Thame Br *THAME* OX9 .... 174 E5
Thame La *ABGD* OX14 .... 239 G3
Thame Park Rd *THAME* OX9 .... 175 G8
Thame Rd *CHNR* OX39 .... 200 C7
 HADM HP17 .... 175 H3
 RAYLW HP18 .... 174 C1 🖫
 RBICS/W OX25 .... 116 C4
 STAD OX44 .... 195 H8
 STAD OX44 .... 196 A5
 STAD OX44 .... 196 C7
 THAME OX9 .... 175 K8
 WGFD OX10 .... 242 D8
Thames Av *BIC* OX26 .... 96 D4
 GOR/PANG RG8 .... 330 B1
 READ RG1 .... 333 G6
Thames Ct *READ* RG1 .... 332 E6
 BUR/CRTN OX18 .... 206 C2
 CIR GL7 .... 203 F4
 FGDN SN7 .... 208 E4
 GOR/PANG RG8 .... 312 E7
 HEN RG9 .... 329 K1
 OXN/BOT/CM OX2 .... 4 A3
 READ RG1 .... 332 E5
 WGFD OX10 .... 267 F8 🖫
 WGFD OX10 .... 267 G5
 WIT/EY OX8 .... 147 H6
 WIT/EY OX8 .... 186 E8
Thames Reach *GOR/PANG* RG8 ...... 331 H3
Thames Rd *DID* OX11 .... 285 J4
 GOR/PANG RG8 .... 322 D1
Thames Side *HEN* RG9 .... 319 C5
Thames Side Prom *READ* RG1 .... 333 G5 🖫
Thames St *ABGD* OX14 .... 335 F3
 CAV/SC RG4 .... 203 G4
 CIR GL7 .... 4 C5
 OX/KTN OX1 .... 4 C5
 WGFD OX10 .... 267 F8
 WIT/EY OX8 .... 146 A8 🖫
Thames Vw *ABGD* OX14 .... 214 E8
Thames View Rd *COW/LTMR* OX4 .. 191 K5
Thame Valley Wk *RAYLW* HP18 ...... 174 E1
 THAME OX9 .... 197 G1
Thatchers *CI RBANSW* OX15 .... 24 E2
Thenford Rd *RBANNS* OX17 .... 23 H7
Theobald *CI CALC* RG31 .... 331 H5
Thesiger Rd *ABGD* OX14 .... 214 D7
Thetford Ms *CAV/SC* RG4 .... 333 K1 🖫
Thicket Rd *TLHT* RG30 .... 331 J7
Third Acre Ri *OXN/BOT/CM* OX2 ... 165 K7
Third St *BRACKY* NN13 .... 59 K1
 DID OX11 .... 285 K5
Thirlmere Av *TLHT* RG30 .... 331 K6
Thirteenth St *DID* OX11 .... 285 J5
Thistlecroft *CI ABGD* OX14 .... 215 F5 🖫
Thistledown *CALC* RG31 .... 331 C6 🖫
Thistle Dr *COW/LTMR* OX4 .... 193 G5
Thompson Dr *RBICN* OX27 .... 79 G8
Thomson Av *ABGD* OX11 .... 285 J4
Thomson Ter *COW/LTMR* OX4 .... 192 A5
Thorn Av *WAR/TWY* RG10 .... 335 K2
Thornbury Ri *BAN* OX16 .... 28 B2
Thornbury Rd *WIT/EY* OX8 .... 145 K8
Thorncliffe Rd *OXN/BOT/CM* OX2 . 167 F1
Thorne *CI KID* OX5 .... 129 F6
Thorne La *WGFD* OX10 .... 265 K5
Thorney Leys *WIT/EY* OX8 .... 160 C1
Thornhill *RBANNS* OX17 .... 22 C3
Thornhill *CI WANT* OX12 .... 282 D2
Thornhill Wk *ABGD* OX14 .... 214 C6
Thorningdown *DID* OX11 .... 286 B7 🖫
Thorn La *READ* RG1 .... 333 H8 🖫
Thorn St *READ* RG1 .... 333 G8
Thornton Ms *TLHT* RG30 .... 332 C7 🖫
Thorpe *CI BAN* OX16 .... 3 F3
Thorpe Dr *BAN* OX16 .... 3 F3
Thorpe La *BAN* OX16 .... 3 F3
Thorpe Md *BAN* OX16 .... 3 F4
Thorpe Rd *RBANNS* OX15 .... 22 C5
Thorpes Fld *BUR/CRTN* OX18 .... 181 J2
Thorpe St *DID* OX11 .... 288 E6
Thorpe Wy *BAN* OX16 .... 3 F3
Thrale Ms *TLHT* RG30 .... 332 B7
Three Corners Rd *COW/LTMR* OX4 .. 193 G5

Three Fields Rd *HEAD* OX3 .... 168 E7 🖫
Three Gables La *GOR/PANG* RG8 ..... 312 C8
Three Pigeons *CI WANT* OX12 .... 282 E3
Thrift Pl *COW/LTMR* OX4 .... 193 F5 🖫
Thrupp La *ABGD* OX14 .... 215 H7
Thrupp Rd *ABGD* OX14 .... 215 J6
Thrupp Turn *FGDN* SN7 .... 206 C6
Thurne Vw *DID* OX11 .... 264 A6 🖫
Thurso *CI TLHT* RG30 .... 332 A7
Thurston *CI ABGD* OX14 .... 238 C1
Tichborne *CI THAME* OX9 .... 175 C7 🖫
Ticknell Piece Rd *CHNTN* OX7 .... 106 B3
Tidmarsh La *OX/KTN* OX1 .... 4 B4 🖫
Tidmarsh Rd *GOR/PANG* RG8 .... 330 A3
Tidmarsh St *TLHT* RG30 .... 332 D7
Tidmore La *GOR/PANG* RG8 .... 314 D6
Tiger *CI WODY* RG5 .... 335 K8
Tilbury *CI CAV/SC* RG4 .... 333 J4
Tilbury La *OXN/BOT/CM* OX2 .... 166 A5
Tilebarn *CI HEN* RG9 .... 318 E6
Tilehouse *CI HEAD* OX3 .... 168 E4 🖫
Tilehurst Rd *READ* RG1 .... 332 E8
 TLHT RG30 .... 332 D8
Tilgarsley Rd *WIT/EY* OX8 .... 145 K7
Tilling *CI CALC* RG31 .... 331 F5
Tilsley Rd *CHNTN* OX7 .... 68 A6
Timbers La *HEN* RG9 .... 295 H5
Timber Wy *CHNR* OX39 .... 224 E1
Timms Rd *BAN* OX16 .... 29 F5
Timothy Wy *COW/LTMR* OX4 ..... 193 F5 🖫
Tinkerbush La *WANT* OX12 .... 282 D1
Tinker's *CI MIM* GL56 .... 46 A2
Tippings *SKCH* OX44 .... 249 G2
Tippings La *WODY* RG5 .... 335 J6
Tirrold Wy *WANT* OX12 .... 283 F2
Titchener *CI BIC* OX26 .... 96 E4
Tite La *RBANSW* OX15 .... 34 A8
Tithe Ct *BAN* OX16 .... 2 A4
Tithe La *RBANSW* OX15 .... 57 F1
Titup Hall Dr *HEAD* OX3 .... 168 E6
Tiverton *CI WODY* RG5 .... 335 G6
Tofrek Ter *TLHT* RG30 .... 332 C8
Tokers Green La *CAV/SC* RG4 .... 326 D6
Tollbrook Cnr *KID* OX5 .... 112 B7
Tollgate Rd *ABGD* OX14 .... 239 F5
Tollington Ct *FGDN* SN7 .... 230 A6
Tompkins La *RBICN* OX27 .... 99 H5
Toot Hill Butts *HEAD* OX3 .... 169 F4
Torridge Dr *DID* OX11 .... 264 A5
Tothill *CHNTN* OX7 .... 102 E6 🖫
Totterdown *CI SWDNE* SN3 .... 274 C8
Towcester Rd *SWDNE* SN3 .... 274 A7
Tower *CI ABGD* OX14 .... 238 B1
 CAV/SC RG4 .... 327 J8
 MCHM/KBPZ OX13 .... 237 F1
Tower Gdns *DID* OX11 .... 263 G5
Tower Hl *WIT/EY* OX8 .... 142 D7
Tower Rd *WGFD* OX10 .... 241 K1
Towersey Dr *THAME* OX9 .... 175 H8
Towersey Rd *THAME* OX9 .... 175 H7
Tower Vw *FGDN* SN7 .... 230 B5 🖫
Town *CI ABGD* OX14 .... 238 E8
Town End Rd *FGDN* SN7 .... 230 B5
Town Furlong *MCHM/KBPZ* OX13 .. 188 C7
 RBANSW OX15 .... 29 F7
Town Furze *HEAD* OX3 .... 168 D8
The Town On *KID* OX5 .... 129 J6
Townhill *RBANSW* OX15 .... 10 A4
Town Pond La *MCHM/KBPZ* OX13 .. 210 D7
Townsend *ABGD* OX14 .... 238 D2
 BAN OX16 .... 2 B3
 DID OX11 .... 262 C8
 DID OX11 .... 286 B6
 RBANSW OX15 .... 55 F2
 RBICN OX27 .... 99 H5
Townsend La *RBANNS* OX17 .... 23 K1
 RBICN OX27 .... 99 G5
Townsend Rd *GOR/PANG* RG8 .... 312 C8
 HGHW SN6 .... 276 B1
Townsend Sq *COW/LTMR* OX4 .. 191 K1 🖫
Townside *HADM* HP17 .... 176 B2
Town Well End *RBICN* OX27 .... 58 D7
Toy La *CHNTN* OX7 .... 67 K5
Toynbee *CI OXN/BOT/CM* OX2 .... 166 B8
Trafford Br *RBANNS* OX17 .... 15 H3
Trafford Rd *HEAD* OX3 .... 168 E4
 READ RG1 .... 333 F6
Traitor's Ford La *RBANSW* OX15 ...... 33 F4
Trajan Rd *SWDNE* SN3 .... 274 A6
Tramway Rd *BAN* OX16 .... 3 E4
Treadwells *FGDN* SN7 .... 232 C8 🖫
Tredegar Rd *CAV/SC* RG12 .... 333 F2
Tree *CI TLHT* RG30 .... 331 H7 🖫
Tree Close Bay *COW/LTMR* OX4 .... 192 A3 🖫
Treeground Pl *KID* OX5 .... 129 H7
Tree La *COW/LTMR* OX4 .... 192 A3
Trefoil Pl *COW/LTMR* OX4 .... 195 G5 🖫
Treforgan *CAV/SC* RG4 .... 333 F2 🖫
Trelawney Dr *CALC* RG31 .... 331 F6
Trenchard Av *ABGD* OX14 .... 262 A4
Trenchard Cir *RBICS/W* OX25 .... 76 C7
Trenchard Rd *WGFD* OX10 .... 290 C1 🖫
Trent Crs *BIC* OX26 .... 96 C4
Trent *CI DID* OX11 .... 264 A5
Trevor Pl *COW/LTMR* OX4 .... 192 B2

Trinder Rd WANT OX12 ... 282 E3
Tring Rd CALC RG31 ... 331 G4
Trinity Cl ABGD OX14 ... 215 F5
  BAN OX16 ... 20 B7
Trinity Pl READ RG1 ... 333 F8
Trinity Rd HEAD OX3 ... 168 E5
Trinity St OX/KTN OX1 ... 4 B5
Trinity Wy RBANNS OX17 ... 39 G4
Tristram Rd WIT/EY OX8 ... 161 F3
Troika Cl BAN OX16 ... 20 C6
Trout Cl EARL RG6 ... 334 C7
Troy Cl HEAD OX3 ... 168 E8
Troy La KID OX5 ... 111 J4
Truelocks Wy WANT OX12 ... 283 F1
Truemper Gv RBICN OX27 ... 79 G8
Trust Cnr HEN RG9 ... 319 G7
Tubb Cl BIC OX26 ... 96 D5
Tubbs Cl WANT OX12 ... 258 D7
Tucker Rd COW/LTMR OX4 ... 192 E6
Tuckers La WOO/WRO SN4 ... 298 A4
Tuckers Rd FGDN SN7 ... 230 C4
Tuck's La MCHM/KBPZ OX13 ... 210 B4
Tudor Cl BAN OX16 ... 29 F5
Tudor Ct OXN/BOT/CM OX2 ... 165 J7
Tudor Rd READ RG1 ... 333 G6
The Tuer WIT/EY OX8 ... 146 A8 🖾
Tulbrook Stones RBANNS OX17 ... 23 F8 🖾
Tullis Cl ABGD OX14 ... 238 D8
Tulwick La WANT OX12 ... 259 F5
Tumbledown Hl
  OXN/BOT/CM OX2 ... 189 F1
Tuns La HEN RG9 ... 319 G5
Turberville Cl ABGD OX14 ... 238 C1
Turley La WIT/EY OX8 ... 123 K7
Turnagain La ABGD OX14 ... 238 D1
Turnberry Cl BIC OX26 ... 97 H4
Turner Cl COW/LTMR OX4 ... 192 D1
Turner Rd ABGD OX14 ... 238 B2
Turners Cl ABGD OX14 ... 215 G5
Turnfields RAYLW HP18 ... 172 E4
Turnpike Rd HGHW SN6 ... 250 E1
  OXN/BOT/CM OX2 ... 189 K1
  RBICN OX27 ... 97 H1
Turnstone Gn BIC OX26 ... 97 H7
Tuscan Cl TLHT RG30 ... 331 J7
Tuxford Ms TLHT RG30 ... 332 B8 🖾
Tweed Cl BIC OX26 ... 96 C4
Tweed Dr DID OX11 ... 263 K3
Twelfth St DID OX11 ... 285 K4
Twelve Acre Dr ABGD OX14 ... 215 F4
Twentieth St DID OX11 ... 285 H5
Twin Oaks CAV/SC RG4 ... 333 H1
Two Tree Hl HEN RG9 ... 318 D7
Twyford Av RBANNS OX17 ... 38 D1
Twyford Cl RBANNS OX17 ... 38 D1
Twyford Rd RBANNS OX17 ... 38 D1
Twynhams Rd KID OX5 ... 111 F1 🖾
Tyburn Gln DID OX11 ... 263 K5
Tyler Cl CAV/SC RG4 ... 332 E2
Tyle Rd TLHT RG30 ... 331 H7 🖬
Tylers Pl TLHT RG30 ... 331 K7 🖾
Tylorstown CAV/SC RG4 ... 333 F1
Tyndale Cl WHLY OX33 ... 170 E7 🖾
Tyndale Rd COW/LTMR OX4 ... 5 E5
Tyne Av DID OX11 ... 263 K5
Tyne Rd MCHM/KBPZ OX13 ... 214 A4
Tyrell Cl FGDN SN7 ... 232 B8
Tyrrells Cl DID OX11 ... 286 C1
Tyrrell's Wy ABGD OX14 ... 262 C1
Tyte End CHNTN OX7 ... 50 E4

U

Uffington Cl CALC RG31 ... 331 G7
Ulfgar Rd OXN/BOT/CM OX2 ... 148 D7
Ullswater Dr CALC RG31 ... 331 H4
Ulster Cl CAV/SC RG4 ... 333 K2
Underhill WGFD OX10 ... 312 B3
Underhill Circ HEAD OX3 ... 169 F3 🖾
Unicorn St RBANSW OX15 ... 36 E5 🖾
Union St BAN OX16 ... 2 B3
  COW/LTMR OX4 ... 5 F5
  WDSTK OX20 ... 127 J1
Union Wy WIT/EY OX8 ... 142 D7
Unity Cl CAV/SC RG4 ... 333 H1
Untons Pl FGDN SN7 ... 230 B4
Upavon Wy BUR/CRTN OX18 ... 157 J4
Upland Park Rd
  OXN/BOT/CM OX2 ... 148 E7
Upland Ri RBANNS OX17 ... 21 F2
Uplands Rd CAV/SC RG4 ... 332 E2
Upper Astrop Rd RBANNS OX17 ... 39 K2
Upper Brook Hl WDSTK OX20 ... 127 J1 🖾
Upper Campsfield Rd KID OX5 ... 128 B2
Upper Common La FGDN SN7 ... 255 F8
Upper Craie FGDN SN7 ... 232 B7
Upper Crs WIT/EY OX8 ... 141 G5
Upper Cross La DID OX11 ... 287 K2 🖾
Upper End BUR/CRTN OX18 ... 120 A8
  CHNTN OX7 ... 120 E1
Upper Fisher Rw OX/KTN OX1 ... 4 B4
Upper Gn FGDN SN7 ... 232 C7 🖾

Upper High St THAME OX9 ... 175 F7
Upper Red Cross Rd
  GOR/PANG RG8 ... 312 E8
Upper Rd OX/KTN OX1 ... 191 H5
Upper St BUCK/WIN MK18 ... 63 K1
Upper Warren Av CAV/SC RG4 ... 332 C6
Upperway Furlong DID OX11 ... 264 B5 🖾
Upper Windsor St BAN OX16 ... 2 C5
Upper Woodcote Rd CAV/SC RG4 ... 332 D2
Uppingham Dr WODY RG5 ... 335 H6
Uppingham Gdns CAV/SC RG4 ... 333 K1 🖾
Upthorpe Dr WANT OX12 ... 282 E1
Upton Cl ABGD OX14 ... 214 E6
  COW/LTMR OX4 ... 192 C5
  HEN RG9 ... 319 G6
Upton Rd TLHT RG30 ... 332 A8
Upway Rd HEAD OX3 ... 168 B2
Upwood Dr BUR/CRTN OX18 ... 158 A3
Urquhart La WGFD OX10 ... 292 E8
Usk Wy DID OX11 ... 264 A4
Uxmore Rd GOR/PANG RG8 ... 315 J3

V

Vachel Rd READ RG1 ... 333 G7
Vale Av WANT OX12 ... 258 G7
Vale Crs TLHT RG30 ... 331 J6
Valence Crs WIT/EY OX8 ... 142 B7
Valentia Cl KID OX5 ... 111 J7
Valentia Rd HEAD OX3 ... 168 B5
  TLHT RG30 ... 332 D7
Valentine Crs CAV/SC RG4 ... 333 J3
Vale Rd DID OX11 ... 285 K4
  WIT/EY OX8 ... 142 C7
Valetta Wy WGFD OX10 ... 268 B4
Vale Vw WAR/TWY RG10 ... 335 K3
Valley Cl CAV/SC RG4 ... 333 G5
  GOR/PANG RG8 ... 322 E1 🖾
Valley Rd BAN OX16 ... 3 D5
  BUCK/WIN MK18 ... 63 G1
  HEN RG9 ... 318 D7
  WHLY OX33 ... 193 K1
Valley Vw RBANNS OX17 ... 13 F7
  RBICS/W OX25 ... 93 H1
Valpy St READ RG1 ... 333 H7
Vanbrugh Cl WDSTK OX20 ... 109 H8
Van Dieman's Cl FGDN SN7 ... 232 B7
Van-Dieman's La
  COW/LTMR OX4 ... 192 C4 🖾
Van Dieman's Rd THAME OX9 ... 175 F8
Van Diemens Cl CHNR OX39 ... 200 E8
Vane Rd THAME OX9 ... 175 H7
Vanner Rd WIT/EY OX8 ... 143 G4
Vastern Rd READ RG1 ... 333 G6
Vauxhall Wy DID OX11 ... 263 H5
Venables Cl OXN/BOT/CM OX2 ... 4 B2 🖾
Venetia Cl CAV/SC RG4 ... 327 J8
Venners Water DID OX11 ... 264 A5
Ventnor Rd CALC RG31 ... 331 H6 🖾
Venvell Cl CHNTN OX7 ... 88 E2 🖾
Verbena Wy COW/LTMR OX4 ... 192 E6 🖾
Verlam Cu DID OX11 ... 264 B5
Vermont Dr WDSTK OX20 ... 109 H8 🖾
Verney Ms TLHT RG30 ... 332 C8
Vernon Av OXN/BOT/CM OX2 ... 190 C1
Verulam Cl SWDNE SN3 ... 274 B7
Vespasian Cl SWDNE SN3 ... 274 A7
Vestry Cl WANT OX12 ... 258 D5 🖾
Vetch Pl COW/LTMR OX4 ... 193 G5
Vicarage Cl COW/LTMR OX4 ... 192 B5
  STAD OX44 ... 220 B8
  WANT OX12 ... 258 E6
Vicarage Gdns RBANNS OX17 ... 13 H5 🖾
Vicarage Hl WANT OX12 ... 282 A3
Vicarage La HGHW SN6 ... 250 E1
  HGHW SN6 ... 276 C1
  OX/KTN OX1 ... 191 G1 🖾
  RBICS/W OX25 ... 135 H1
  SHPSTR CV36 ... 49 C1
Vicarage Rd DID OX11 ... 263 K7
  HEN RG9 ... 319 G7
  KID OX5 ... 129 J6
  MCHM/KBPZ OX13 ... 261 G3
  OX/KTN OX1 ... 191 G1
Vicarage Wood Wy CALC RG31 ... 331 F6 🖾
Vickers Rd COTS GL54 ... 100 A2
Victoria Cl BIC OX26 ... 97 G6
Victoria Md THAME OX9 ... 175 G8
Victoria Pl BAN OX16 ... 3 E5 🖾
Victoria Rd ABGD OX14 ... 214 B8
  BIC OX26 ... 97 G5
  CALC RG31 ... 331 H7
  CAV/SC RG4 ... 333 G4
  OXN/BOT/CM OX2 ... 149 F7
Victoria St READ RG1 ... 333 K8
Victoria Ter RBANSW OX15 ... 56 C3
Victor St OXN/BOT/CM OX2 ... 4 B3
Victor Wy WODY RG5 ... 335 J8
Viking Dr DID OX11 ... 264 A8
Viking Ter WGFD OX10 ... 268 B4
Village Farm Ct RBICS/W OX25 ... 113 F5
Village Rd RBANNS OX17 ... 11 G3

Villeboys Cl ABGD OX14 ... 215 G
Villiers La COW/LTMR OX4 ... 192 A
Villiers Rd BIC OX26 ... 96 E
Viner Cl WIT/EY OX8 ... 143 G
The Vine RAYLW HP18 ... 173 H
Vineyard ABGD OX14 ... 214 D
Vineyard Cl BAN OX16 ... 2 C
Violet Wy COW/LTMR OX4 ... 192 E
Virginia Wy ABGD OX14 ... 238 B
Viscount Wy SWDNE SN3 ... 274 A
  WODY RG5 ... 335 H
Vorda Rd HGHW SN6 ... 226 E
Vulcan Cl WODY RG5 ... 335 K

W

Wadard's Meadow WIT/EY OX8 ... 143 G
Wadham Cl BIC OX26 ... 97 G
  CIR GL7 ... 178 D
Wagtail Cl SWDNE SN3 ... 274 A
Waingels Rd WODY RG5 ... 335 J
Wainwrights RAYLW HP18 ... 174 D
Waites Cl BUR/CRTN OX18 ... 184 C
Wales St COR/PANG RG8 ... 314 C6
Walker Dr THAME OX9 ... 199 H
Walkers Cl WIT/EY OX8 ... 145 G
Walker's Height CHNTN OX7 ... 124 B
Walkers Pl TLHT RG30 ... 332 C
The Walk KID OX5 ... 130 E6
Wallace Cl ABGD OX14 ... 238 C
Waller Ct CAV/SC RG4 ... 333 H
Waller Dr BAN OX16 ... 2 A
Wallingford Rd GOR/PANG RG8 ... 312 C
  WGFD OX10 ... 266 D
  WGFD OX10 ... 290 C
Walmer Rd WODY RG5 ... 335 H
Walnut Cl BIC OX26 ... 97 G
  CAV/SC RG4 ... 326 E
  RBANSW OX15 ... 57 H
  WDSTK OX20 ... 109 G
Walnut Ct FGDN SN7 ... 230 B
Walnut Paddocks
  RWWCK/WEL CV35 ... 16 B
Walnut Ri RBICS/W OX25 ... 75 J1
Walnut Tree Ct GOR/PANG RG8 ... 322 E1
Walnut Trees Hl HGHW SN6 ... 277 H
Walnut Wy TLHT RG30 ... 331 H
Walpole Cl BIC OX26 ... 96 D
Walronds Ct MARL SN8 ... 321 F
Walrus Cl WODY RG5 ... 335 K
Walterbush Rd CHNTN OX7 ... 68 A
Waltham Gdns BAN OX16 ... 29 J1
Walton Av HEN RG9 ... 319 G
  RBANNS OX17 ... 38 E
Walton Cl RBANSW OX15 ... 29 G
  WODY RG5 ... 334 E
Walton Crs OXN/BOT/CM OX2 ... 4 B
Walton La OX/KTN OX1 ... 4 B
Walton St OXN/BOT/CM OX2 ... 4 B
Walton Well Rd OXN/BOT/CM OX2 ... 4 A
Wanborough Rd SWDNE SN3 ... 274 A
  WOO/WRO SN4 ... 274 C
Wanbourne La HEN RG9 ... 294 D
Wandhope Wy CALC RG31 ... 331 G
Wansbeck Dr BIC OX26 ... 96 C
Wansbeck Wd DID OX11 ... 264 A
Wantage Rd DID OX11 ... 263 G
  DID OX11 ... 286 B
  GOR/PANG RG8 ... 312 B
  TLHT RG30 ... 332 C
  WGFD OX10 ... 266 D
Wapping RAYLW HP18 ... 174 D
Warborough Av CALC RG31 ... 331 F
Warborough Rd WANT OX12 ... 282 A
  WGFD OX10 ... 266 D
Warbreck Dr CALC RG31 ... 331 F
Warburg Crs COW/LTMR OX4 ... 193 F
Wardington Rd RBANNS OX17 ... 22 B
Wardle Av CALC RG31 ... 331 H
Wards Crs RBANSW OX15 ... 29 G
Ward's La CHNTN OX7 ... 124 B
Wards Rd CHNTN OX7 ... 68 C
Ware Leys Cl RBICN OX27 ... 99 H
Ware Rd FGDN SN7 ... 232 A
Wargrave Rd HEN RG9 ... 319 J
Warkworth Cl BAN OX16 ... 20 B
Warkworth Rd RBANNS OX17 ... 22 B
Warley Ri CALC RG31 ... 331 F
Warmans Cl WANT OX12 ... 282 B
Warnborough Rd OXN/BOT/CM OX2 ... 4 B
Warneford La HEAD OX3 ... 168 B
Warneford Pl MIM GL56 ... 46 A
Warneford Rd COW/LTMR OX4 ... 168 A
Warner Crs DID OX11 ... 263 H
Warnford Rd TLHT RG30 ... 331 K
Warren Crs HEAD OX3 ... 168 D
Warren Hl STAD OX44 ... 218 E
Warren Rd WODY RG5 ... 335 F
The Warren ABGD OX14 ... 215 F
  CAV/SC RG4 ... 332 C
  READ RG1 ... 333 F

Warren Vw *STAD* OX44 .... 195 H8 🔲
Warwick Cl *ABGD* OX14 .... 214 E7
  BUR/CRTN OX18 .... 157 J5
  FGDN SN7 .... 232 C8 🔲
Warwick Ct *BIC* OX26 .... 97 H3 🔲
Warwick Rd *BAN* OX16 .... 2 C3
  RBANNS OX17 .... 20 A3
Wasbrough Av *WANT* OX12 .... 282 C1 🔲
Washford Gln *DID* OX11 .... 264 A5
Washington Rd *CAV/SC* RG4 .... 333 H5
Wastie Dr *RBANNS* OX17 .... 23 F7
Wastie's Orch *WIT/EY* OX8 .... 126 C5
Watcombe Rd *WTLGN* OX49 .... 246 B6
Water Eaton Rd
  OXN/BOT/CM OX2 .... 149 G7
Water La *CHNTN* OX7 .... 71 F1
  RBANNS OX17 .... 38 C4
  RBANSW OX17 .... 37 F2
  RBICN OX27 .... 77 G5
  RBICS/W OX25 .... 74 D7
  WGFD OX10 .... 242 D2
Waterloo Cl *WGFD* OX10 .... 290 C8
Waterloo Dr *BAN* OX16 .... 3 E3
Waterman Pl *READ* RG1 .... 333 G6
Waterman's Rd *HEN* RG9 .... 319 G7
Watermead *KID* OX5 .... 129 K7
  SWDNE SN3 .... 274 A5 🔲
Watermill Wy *HEAD* OX3 .... 169 G3
Waterperry Rd *RAYLW* HP18 .... 172 B2
Water Rd *TLHT* RG30 .... 332 B8
Waterside Dr *CAV/PANG* RG8 .... 331 H2
Waterside Gdns *READ* RG1 .... 333 C8 🔲
Waterside Pens *HADM* HP17 .... 176 A1
Waters La *RBANNS* OX17 .... 23 F5
Water Stratford Rd
  BUCK/WIN MK18 .... 45 K8
Water St *RBICS/W* OX25 .... 75 J1
Watery La *ABGD* OX14 .... 240 D3
  HEN RG9 .... 273 J5
  RBANSW OX15 .... 33 K8
  WANT OX12 .... 280 D3
Wates Wy *BAN* OX16 .... 3 E1
Watling La *WGFD* OX10 .... 241 K6
Watlington Rd *COW/LTMR* OX4 .... 193 F4
  STAD OX44 .... 193 H6
  WGFD OX10 .... 267 H3
  WTLGN OX49 .... 246 D4
Watlington St *READ* RG1 .... 333 J8
Watson Crs *MCHM/KBPZ* OX13 .... 189 J8
Watsons Cl *BUR/CRTN* OX18 .... 158 A6 🔲
Watt's La *DID* OX11 .... 288 A7
Waveney Cl *BIC* OX26 .... 96 C5
  DID OX11 .... 264 A6 🔲
Waverley Av *KID* OX5 .... 129 K7
Waverley Rd *SWDNE* SN3 .... 274 A6
  TLHT RG30 .... 332 B8
Wavers Gnd *BUR/CRTN* OX18 .... 158 B4 🔲
Waxes Cl *ABGD* OX14 .... 215 G5
Wayfaring Cl *COW/LTMR* OX4 .... 192 E7 🔲
Wayfarings *BIC* OX26 .... 97 F2 🔲
Wayland Av *WANT* OX12 .... 258 A7
Wayland Crs *DID* OX11 .... 286 A6
Wayland Rd *WANT* OX12 .... 258 D6
Waylen St *READ* RG1 .... 333 F8
Waynflete Rd *HEAD* OX3 .... 169 F3
Wayside Gn *GOR/PANG* RG8 .... 314 C7 🔲
Wealden Wy *TLHT* RG30 .... 331 J7
Weald Ri *TLHT* RG30 .... 331 K5
Weald St *BUR/CRTN* OX18 .... 183 F6
Wear Rd *BIC* OX26 .... 96 C5
Weaver Cft *DID* OX11 .... 264 A4
Weavers Cl *WIT/EY* OX8 .... 142 E8
Webb Cl *BAN* OX16 .... 3 E2
Webb Crs *CHNTN* OX7 .... 68 A5
Webbs Cl *CHNTN* OX7 .... 86 E6
  OXN/BOT/CM OX2 .... 148 B7
Webb's Wy *KID* OX5 .... 129 J6
Webster Cl *THAME* OX9 .... 175 F6
Websters *WIT/EY* OX8 .... 145 G1
Wedgewood Wy *TLHT* RG30 .... 331 K6 🔲
Wedgwood Rd *BIC* OX26 .... 97 H4
Weedon Cl *WGFD* OX10 .... 290 C7
Weedon Ct *WGFD* OX10 .... 266 E8 🔲
Weeping Cross *RBANSW* OX15 .... 29 C7
Weighbridge Rw *READ* RG1 .... 333 F6
Weir La *RBICS/W* OX25 .... 116 D2
Weirs La *OX/KTN* OX1 .... 191 H2
Welchman Rd *RWWCK/WEL* CV35 .... 16 C3
Welch Wy *WIT/EY* OX8 .... 142 E7
Weldale St *READ* RG1 .... 333 F7
Weldon Rd *HEAD* OX3 .... 5 F1
Weldon Wy *THAME* OX9 .... 175 G7
Welford Dr *SWDNE* SN3 .... 274 A7
Welford Gdns *ABGD* OX14 .... 214 E5
Welford Rd *WODY* RG5 .... 335 J7
Welland Av *DID* OX11 .... 264 B5
Welland Cl *CALC* RG31 .... 351 C6
  MCHM/KBPZ OX13 .... 214 A5
Welland Cft *BIC* OX26 .... 96 C4
Well Bank *RBANSW* OX15 .... 34 A8
Wellesbourne Cl *ABGD* OX14 .... 215 F7
Wellesley Cl *BAN* OX16 .... 3 E3 🔲
Wellfield Cl *CALC* RG31 .... 331 C8 🔲

Well HI *CHNTN* OX7 .... 124 B2
Wellington Av *BAN* OX16 .... 3 E2
Wellington Cl *BIC* OX26 .... 97 H3
Wellington Rd *MIM* GL56 .... 46 B2
Wellington Sq *HGHW* SN6 .... 252 D6
Wellington St *OXN/BOT/CM* OX2 .... 4 B3 🔲
  THAME OX9 .... 175 F7
Well La *RBANSW* OX15 .... 17 K5
  WIT/EY OX8 .... 107 H8
  WIT/EY OX8 .... 160 A2
Wellshead La *DID* OX11 .... 286 C1
Wellsprings *WGFD* OX10 .... 266 A5
Well Vw *HEN* RG9 .... 315 K3 🔲
Welsh Rd *RBANNS* OX17 .... 15 G1
Wendover Wy *TLHT* RG30 .... 331 H8
Wenlock Cl *DID* OX11 .... 263 G5
Wenlock Edge *WAR/TWY* RG10 .... 335 K3
Wenman Rd *THAME* OX9 .... 199 G1
  WIT/EY OX8 .... 142 C7
Wenrisc Dr *WIT/EY* OX8 .... 141 G5
Wensum Crs *BIC* OX26 .... 96 C4
Wensum Dr *DID* OX11 .... 264 A5
Wentworth Rd *OXN/BOT/CM* OX2 .... 149 F7
  THAME OX9 .... 175 G7
Wesley Cl *BIC* OX26 .... 96 D3 🔲
  COW/LTMR OX4 .... 192 E5
Wesley Dr *BAN* OX16 .... 2 B5
Wesley Pl *RBANNS* OX17 .... 22 C3
Wessex Cl *FGDN* SN7 .... 230 C4
Wessex Rd *DID* OX11 .... 263 K7
Wessex Wy *HGHW* SN6 .... 227 F8
Westacott Rd *RBICS/W* OX25 .... 115 H1
West Av *ABGD* OX14 .... 214 E5
West Bar St *BAN* OX16 .... 2 C4
Westbeech Ct *BAN* OX16 .... 2 C4
Westbourne Ct *RBANSW* OX15 .... 37 F4
Westbourne Ter *TLHT* RG30 .... 332 C8
Westbrook *FGDN* SN7 .... 230 B4
  WANT OX12 .... 258 E5
Westbrook Gn *DID* OX11 .... 287 K7
Westbrook Rd *TLHT* RG30 .... 332 C6 🔲
Westbrook St *DID* OX11 .... 287 K7
Westbury Crs *COW/LTMR* OX4 .... 192 B5
Westbury La *GOR/PANG* RG8 .... 330 E1
West Chiltern *GOR/PANG* RG8 .... 314 C7 🔲
Westcote Cl *WIT/EY* OX8 .... 142 B8
Westcot La *WANT* OX12 .... 280 C3
Westcott *BAN* OX16 .... 2 C4
West Cft *CAV/SC* RG4 .... 335 G5
West Cft *WGFD* OX10 .... 241 H2
Westdene Crs *CAV/SC* RG4 .... 332 E5
West Dr *CAV/SC* RG4 .... 335 F6
  DID OX11 .... 285 J4
West Edge *RBICN* OX27 .... 99 H5
West End *BIC* OX26 .... 98 A6
  CHNTN OX7 .... 68 B6
  CHNTN OX7 .... 84 A2
  RBANSW OX15 .... 18 C1
  WDSTK OX20 .... 109 G4
  WGFD OX10 .... 265 K5
  WGFD OX10 .... 290 A6
  WIT/EY OX8 .... 126 B3
  WIT/EY OX8 .... 143 F5
West End Cl *BIC* OX26 .... 98 A6
West End La *HGHW* SN6 .... 298 C3
  RBICS/W OX25 .... 114 E7
Western Av *HEN* RG9 .... 319 G7
  WODY RG5 .... 335 F7
Western By-Pass Rd
  OXN/BOT/CM OX2 .... 148 A8
Western Crs *BAN* OX16 .... 3 E5
Western Elms Av *TLHT* RG30 .... 332 E8
Western Oaks *CALC* RG31 .... 331 J5
Western Rd *HEN* RG9 .... 319 G7
  OX/KTN OX1 .... 4 C6
Westfield *DID* OX11 .... 262 B8
Westfield Cl *COW/LTMR* OX4 .... 192 B1
  WANT OX12 .... 258 D7
  WGFD OX10 .... 267 J3
Westfield Crs *HEN* RG9 .... 329 K4
Westfield Rd *ABGD* OX14 .... 240 C8
  READ RG1 .... 333 H5
  WGFD OX10 .... 267 H2
  WHLY OX33 .... 311 K1
  WHLY OX33 .... 170 C6
  WIT/EY OX8 .... 142 E5
Westfields *ABGD* OX14 .... 214 B7
Westfield Wy *WANT* OX12 .... 283 F1
West Hawthorne Rd
  RBICS/W OX25 .... 116 A3
West HI *WANT* OX12 .... 282 C3
Westhill Cl *HGHW* SN6 .... 250 D2
Westholme Ct *BIC* OX26 .... 97 G6
Westland Rd *FGDN* SN7 .... 230 B4
Westlands Av *RBICS/W* OX25 .... 113 F5
Westlands Dr *HEAD* OX3 .... 168 B2
Westland Wy *WDSTK* OX20 .... 109 H8
West La *HEN* RG9 .... 319 F5 🔲
  PRRI HP27 .... 201 J6
Westleigh Dr *CAV/SC* RG4 .... 327 G3
Westminster Ct *BRACKY* NN13 .... 43 G1
Westminster Wy *BAN* OX16 .... 3 F2
  OXN/BOT/CM OX2 .... 166 D3 🔲
Westonbirt Dr *CAV/SC* RG4 .... 332 E4 🔲
Weston Ct *SHPSTR* CV36 .... 49 H1
Weston La *THAME* OX9 .... 173 K7

Weston Rd *THAME* OX9 .... 222 E6
  WTLGN OX49 .... 223 G7
Westridge Av *GOR/PANG* RG8 .... 331 G2 🔲
West Rd *HEN* RG9 .... 316 B5 🔲
Westrop *HGHW* SN6 .... 250 E1
Westrup Cl *HEAD* OX3 .... 5 F2 🔲
West Saint Helen St *ABGD* OX14 .... 238 D1
West St *BAN* OX16 .... 3 E2
  BIC OX26 .... 96 E4
  CHNTN OX7 .... 68 B5
  CHNTN OX7 .... 84 A2
  HEN RG9 .... 319 F5
  OXN/BOT/CM OX2 .... 4 A4
  RBANSW OX15 .... 26 A2
  READ RG1 .... 333 G7
  WANT OX12 .... 280 D3
Westwater Wy *DID* OX11 .... 264 B5
West Wy *CIR* GL7 .... 205 G2
  OXN/BOT/CM OX2 .... 166 A6
Westway *GOR/PANG* RG8 .... 312 E7 🔲
West Well La *BUCK/WIN* MK18 .... 63 K1
Westwood Cl *CALC* RG31 .... 331 G7
Westwood Rd *CALC* RG31 .... 331 H6
  WIT/EY OX8 .... 142 A6
Westwood Rw *CALC* RG31 .... 331 G5
Wesy Quay *ABGD* OX14 .... 238 D3
Wetherby Cl *CAV/SC* RG4 .... 333 J1
Weycroft *DID* OX11 .... 264 A4 🔲
Weyland Rd *HEAD* OX3 .... 168 E5
Wey Rd *WGFD* OX10 .... 241 J2
Whales La *RBICN* OX27 .... 99 H5
Wharf Cl *ABGD* OX14 .... 238 C1
Wharfe La *HEN* RG9 .... 319 G5
Wharf La *CIR* GL7 .... 203 H3
  RBICN OX27 .... 57 K4
  RBICS/W OX25 .... 75 J1 🔲
Wharf Rd *WGFD* OX10 .... 266 C1
The Wharf *WANT* OX12 .... 282 D2
Wharton Rd *HEAD* OX3 .... 168 D4
Whatleys Orch *HGHW* SN6 .... 298 C3
Wheatcroft *ABGD* OX14 .... 214 E5 🔲
Wheatfields *DID* OX11 .... 263 G8
Wheatley Br *WHLY* OX33 .... 171 G8
Wheatley Cl *BAN* OX16 .... 29 G5
Wheatley Rd *KID* OX5 .... 130 E7
  STAD OX44 .... 194 A5
  WHLY OX33 .... 170 B3
Wheatley Rd *KID* OX5 .... 335 F7
Wheeler Ct *CALC* RG31 .... 331 J6
Wheelers End *CHNR* OX39 .... 224 E1 🔲
Wheeler's Ri *BRACKY* NN13 .... 41 H7
Whilestone Wy *SWDNE* SN3 .... 274 A6
Whimbrel Cl *BIC* OX26 .... 97 H6
Whimbrel Wy *BAN* OX16 .... 3 F6
Whirlpool Arch *RAYLW* HP18 .... 172 B4
Whirlwind Wy *WGFD* OX10 .... 268 B4
Whitby Gn *CAV/SC* RG4 .... 333 H1
Whitchurch Rd *GOR/PANG* RG8 .... 330 B1
Whitecross *MCHM/KBPZ* OX13 .... 214 A2
Whitecross Rd *HADM* HP17 .... 176 B2
Whitegates La *EARL* RG6 .... 334 C8
Whitehall Cl *WIT/EY* OX8 .... 141 F5
Whitehall La *GOR/PANG* RG8 .... 315 H4
White Hart Cl *WGFD* OX10 .... 267 H3 🔲
White Hart La *HADM* HP17 .... 176 B2
White Hart Wk *FGDN* SN7 .... 230 B4 🔲
White HI *BUR/CRTN* OX18 .... 139 H4
  HEN RG9 .... 319 J5
  HEN RG9 .... 328 C2
  WODY/WRO SN4 .... 298 A5
White HiI La *OX/KTN* OX1 .... 189 J6
Whitehills Gn *GOR/PANG* RG8 .... 322 E1
Whitehorns Farm Rd *WANT* OX12 .... 283 G2
Whitehorns Wy *ABGD* OX14 .... 237 J6
White Horse *FGDN* SN7 .... 255 F8
White Horse Crs *WANT* OX12 .... 258 C7
White Horse Ms *BUR/CRTN* OX18 .... 138 E3
Whitehouse Cl *MCHM/KBPZ* OX13 .... 214 A6
Whitehouse Rd *GOR/PANG* RG8 .... 314 C7
  OX/KTN OX1 .... 4 C6
White House Rd *WGFD* OX10 .... 291 G6
White La *HEN* RG9 .... 296 A8
White Leys Cl *DID* OX11 .... 263 K6
Whitelock Rd *ABGD* OX14 .... 214 D6
White Lodge Cl *CALC* RG31 .... 331 F4
White Post Rd *RBANSW* OX15 .... 29 G6
White Rd *COW/LTMR* OX4 .... 192 E2
  WANT OX12 .... 261 G8
Whites Forge *MCHM/KBPZ* OX13 .... 188 C7
White Shoot *DID* OX11 .... 310 A1
White's La *ABGD* OX14 .... 215 H4
White Wy *KID* OX5 .... 129 H7
Whiteway *RBANNS* OX17 .... 12 B3
Whitings La *WIT/EY* OX8 .... 124 D7
Whitley Crs *BIC* OX26 .... 97 H4
Whitley Dr *RBICS/W* OX25 .... 76 B7 🔲
Whitley Rd *WGFD* OX10 .... 266 D8
Whitson Pl *COW/LTMR* OX4 .... 168 A8 🔲
Whittall St *RBANNS* OX17 .... 39 J2
Whittington Pl *BUR/CRTN* OX18 .... 157 K6 🔲
Whittle Rd *THAME* OX9 .... 175 H7
Whittons Cl *RBANSW* OX15 .... 34 A2
Wick Cl *ABGD* OX14 .... 215 G5
  HEAD OX3 .... 168 E3
Wick Gn *WANT* OX12 .... 258 D5

Wicks Cl BUR/CRTN OX18 .... 182 A7
Widmore La CAV/SC RG4 .... 327 G1
Widnell La RBICS/W OX25 .... 116 E8
Wigginton Rd RBANSW OX15 .... 35 K8
Wigmore La TLHT RG30 .... 332 B6
Wigod Wy WGFD OX10 .... 266 E6
Wilberforce St HEAD OX3 .... 168 D5
Wilcher Cl DID OX11 .... 287 K1
Wilcote Riding CHNTN OX7 .... 124 B2
Wilcote Rd HEAD OX3 .... 169 F3
Wilcote Vw WIT/EY OX8 .... 125 H8
Wilcox Rd CHNTN OX7 .... 85 F5
Wilder Av GOR/PANG RG8 .... 330 C2
Wilding Rd WGFD OX10 .... 266 E6
Wildmere Cl BAN OX16 .... 3 E1
Wildmoor Ga ABGD OX14 .... 214 B6
Wilkins Rd COW/LTMR OX4 .... 192 D2
Willes Cl FGDN SN7 .... 230 D4
William Bliss Av CHNTN OX7 .... 68 B5
William Cl BAN OX16 .... 20 B8
William Kimber Crs HEAD OX3 .... 168 E4
William Orchard Cl HEAD OX3 ..... 168 C3
Williamscot Hl RBANNS OX17 ...... 21 K1
William Smith Cl CHNTN OX7 ...... 85 F3
William Wy COW/LTMR OX4 .... 192 A5
William St HEAD OX3 .... 5 F2
........................READ OX1 .... 333 F7
Willis Ct CHNTN OX7 .... 102 E6
Willis Rd HADM HP17 .... 176 C2
Willoughby Rd BAN OX16 .... 29 F5
Willow Brook ABGD OX14 .... 214 B8
Willowbrook WIT/EY OX8 .... 163 F7
Willow Cl KID OX5 .... 147 J1
........................STAD OX44 .... 193 J5
........................WTLGN OX9 .... 246 A5
Willow Court La MCHM/KBPZ OX13 . 214 A6
Willow Dr BIC OX26 .... 97 F3
Willow End MIM CL56 .... 48 B6
Willow Gdns CALC RG31 .... 331 F5
Willow La ABGD OX14 .... 262 B2
........................WANT OX12 .... 282 D4
Willow Md STAD OX44 .... 244 B1
Willow Rd BAN OX16 .... 29 F6
........................CHNR OX39 .... 224 E1
........................RBICS/W OX25 .... 115 K3
........................THAME OX9 .... 175 F6
Willows Edge WIT/EY OX8 .... 145 K8
Willowside WODY RG5 .... 335 G6
The Willows HGHW SN6 .... 250 E6
........................RBANNS OX17 .... 39 K1
........................READ RG1 .... 333 G5
........................WIT/EY OX8 .... 145 G6
Willow Tree Cl MCHM/KBPZ OX13 . 214 A6
Willow Wk WANT OX12 .... 282 D1
Willow Wy ABGD OX14 .... 191 J8
........................KID OX5 .... 128 D7
Wills Rd DID OX11 .... 263 G6
Wilmington Cl WODY RG5 .... 335 G7
Wilmot Cl WIT/EY OX8 .... 160 D1
Wilmots STAD OX44 .... 217 G1
Wilmot Wy WANT OX12 .... 283 F1
Wilsdon Wy KID OX5 .... 129 G6
Wilsham Rd ABGD OX14 .... 238 D1
Wilson Av HEN RG9 .... 319 G7
Wilson Rd TLHT RG30 .... 332 C8
Wilson Wy RBICN OX27 .... 79 G8
Wilton Rd TLHT RG30 .... 332 C7
Wilwyne Cl CAV/SC RG4 .... 333 J4
Wimblestraw Rd WGFD OX10 .... 241 J2
Wimborne Av BAN OX16 .... 2 B3
Wimborne Gdns TLHT RG30 .... 332 A6
Winaway DID OX11 .... 286 B1
Winchelsea Cl BAN OX16 .... 20 B6
Winchester Cl BAN OX16 .... 3 F2
Winchester Rd OXN/BOT/CM OX2 . 4 B1
Winchester Wy WANT OX12 .... 282 C2
Wincroft Rd CAV/SC RG4 .... 332 E2
Windale Av COW/LTMR OX4 .... 192 E5
Windle Gdns BIC OX26 .... 96 D5
Windmill Cl BAN OX16 .... 3 D5
........................RBANSW OX15 .... 56 B3
........................THAME OX9 .... 176 A8
........................WIT/EY OX8 .... 144 B2
Windmill Hts WIT/EY OX8 .... 144 B1
Windmill La WHLY OX33 .... 170 B8
Windmill PI WANT OX12 .... 281 K3
Windmill Rd HADM HP17 .... 176 B1
........................HEAD OX3 .... 168 D5
........................THAME OX9 .... 175 F8
........................THAME OX9 .... 176 A7
........................WIT/EY OX8 .... 144 B1
Windmill St RAYLW HP18 .... 135 K6
........................RBANSW OX15 .... 56 B3
Windmill Wy RWWCK/WEL CV35 .. 16 B3
Windrush HGHW SN6 .... 250 D1
Windrush Cl BIC OX26 .... 96 E6
........................BUR/CRTN OX18 .... 138 C2
........................WANT OX12 .... 258 D6
........................WIT/EY OX8 .... 142 C6
Windrush Ms DID OX11 .... 264 A4
Windrush Park Rd WIT/EY OX8 .... 142 A6
Windrush Rd WGFD OX10 .... 241 J3
Windrush Valley Rd WIT/EY OX8 . 142 C6

Windrush Wy ABGD OX14 .... 215 F6
........................TLHT RG30 .... 332 B8
........................WIT/EY OX8 .... 186 C2
Windsor Cl BUR/CRTN OX18 .... 157 J5
........................RBANNS OX17 .... 39 J1
Windsor Crs DID OX11 .... 287 K1
........................HEAD OX3 .... 167 J2
Windsor St BAN OX16 .... 3 D4
........................HEAD OX3 .... 168 D5
Windsor Ter BAN OX16 .... 3 D4
Windy Rdg FGDN SN7 .... 230 C4
Wingate Cl COW/LTMR OX4 .... 192 E4
Wingfield Cl WGFD OX10 .... 268 D3
The Winnyards OXN/BOT/CM OX2 . 189 G3
Winsmore La ABGD OX14 .... 214 D8
Winston Cl KID OX5 .... 129 H8
Winston Crs BRACKY NN13 .... 43 G1
Winterberry Wy CAV/SC RG4 ...... 332 E1
Winterborne Rd ABGD OX14 .... 214 B8
Winterbrook WGFD OX10 .... 291 F2
Winterbrook La WGFD OX10 .... 290 E2
Wintergreen La WGFD OX10 .... 290 E2
Winter La WANT OX12 .... 235 F8
Winter's Fld WGFD OX10 .... 267 H8
Winters Wy RBANSW OX15 .... 36 E3
Wintringham Wy GOR/PANG RG8 . 331 H2
Wise Av KID OX5 .... 129 G6
Wise Cl RBANSW OX15 .... 29 H7
Wise Crs RBICN OX27 .... 79 K1
Wiston Ter READ RG1 .... 333 H7
Witan Wy WANT OX12 .... 282 D1
........................WIT/EY OX8 .... 143 F8
Withers Cl CHNTN OX7 .... 68 B5
Withington Ct ABGD OX14 .... 214 D8
Withington Rd BIC OX26 .... 97 G5
Withycombe Dr BAN OX16 .... 20 B8
Witney Hl WIT/EY OX8 .... 142 C5
Witney La WIT/EY OX8 .... 122 C4
Witney Rd BUR/CRTN OX18 .... 158 E2
........................CHNTN OX7 .... 123 K2
........................WIT/EY OX8 .... 122 E6
........................WIT/EY OX8 .... 126 B6
........................WIT/EY OX8 .... 142 D4
........................WIT/EY OX8 .... 145 K7
........................WIT/EY OX8 .... 160 E2
........................WIT/EY OX8 .... 186 A3
Witney St BUR/CRTN OX18 .... 138 E2
Wittenham Av CALC RG31 .... 331 F7
Wittenham Cl GOR/PANG RG8 ..... 314 D7
........................WGFD OX10 .... 267 H5
Wittenham La WGFD OX10 .... 241 K7
Woburn Cl BAN OX16 .... 3 F1
........................CAV/SC RG4 .... 332 E3
Wokingham Rd EARL RG6 .... 334 A8
Wolseley Cl BAN OX16 .... 2 A1
Wolsey Ct KID OX5 .... 128 B4
Wolsey Rd OXN/BOT/CM OX2 ..... 149 H1
........................READ RG1 .... 333 G6
Wolvercote Gn OXN/BOT/CM OX2 . 148 C7
Woodbine PI OX/KTN OX1 .... 4 B4
Woodbridge Cl BUR/CRTN OX18 . 184 E5
Woodcote La CHNTN OX7 .... 124 A4
Woodcote Rd CAV/SC RG4 .... 332 E3
........................GOR/PANG RG8 .... 313 F3
........................RBICN OX27 .... 79 H8
Woodcote Wy CAV/SC RG4 .... 332 D2
Woodcroft OX/KTN OX1 .... 191 J6
Wood End BAN OX16 .... 3 E6
Wood Farm Rd HEAD OX3 .... 168 E7
Woodfield BAN OX16 .... 2 B1
Woodfield Dr CHNTN OX7 .... 106 A4
Woodfield Rd BIC OX26 .... 97 F4
Woodford Cl CAV/SC RG4 .... 332 E3
Woodgate St WANT OX12 .... 258 D6
Wood Gn GOR/PANG RG8 .... 314 C7
Woodgreen Av BAN OX16 .... 2 A4
Wood Green Cl TLHT RG30 .... 332 E8
Woodgreen Hl WIT/EY OX8 .... 143 F6
Woodhall Dr BAN OX16 .... 29 G5
Woodhill Dr WANT OX12 .... 258 D7
Woodhill La WANT OX12 .... 258 A8
Woodhouse Wy COW/LTMR OX4 .. 192 A2
Woodland Dr TLHT RG30 .... 331 H8
Woodland Ri WIT/EY OX8 .... 125 H1
Woodlands WIT/EY OX8 .... 126 B8
........................WIT/EY OX8 .... 186 D4
Woodlands Av WODY RG5 .... 335 F8
Woodlands Cl CHNTN OX7 .... 102 C6
........................HEAD OX3 .... 168 B4
Woodlands Dr RBANSW OX15 ...... 52 A1
Woodlands Gv CAV/SC RG4 .... 333 K3
Woodlands Rd CAV/SC RG4 .... 326 E1
........................HEAD OX3 .... 168 B4
........................HEN RG9 .... 529 G3
........................WIT/EY OX8 .... 143 G5
The Woodlands BIC OX26 .... 96 A8
Wood La CAV/SC RG4 .... 326 B3
........................GOR/PANG RG8 .... 314 B7
........................WIT/EY OX8 .... 123 H6
Wood Lane Cl CAV/SC RG4 .... 327 F2
Woodley Cl ABGD OX14 .... 214 D4
Woodley Gn WODY RG5 .... 335 H7
Woodpecker Gn
........................COW/LTMR OX4 .... 193 F6
Woodperry Rd HEAD OX3 .... 151 H3

Woodpiece Rd RBICS/W OX25 ..... 134 B
Woodruff Cl COW/LTMR OX4 ...... 193 F5
Wood's Farm Rd WANT OX12 .... 261 F
Woodside WIT/EY OX8 .... 144 C1
Woodside Dr BUR/CRTN OX18 .... 138 C8
Woodside La CAV/SC RG4 .... 326 C2
Woodside Rd SWDNE SN3 .... 250 A
Woods Rd CAV/SC RG4 .... 333 K
Woodstock Cl OXN/BOT/CM OX2 . 148 E
Woodstock Rd CHNTN OX7 .... 106 B8
........................KID OX5 .... 128 D
........................OXN/BOT/CM OX2 ..... 148 C5
........................SWDNE SN3 .... 274 A6
........................WDSTK OX20 .... 128 B
........................WIT/EY OX8 .... 107 J8
........................WIT/EY OX8 .... 143 C5
Woodstock Rd West KID OX5 ...... 128 C6
Woodstock St READ RG1 .... 333 K8
Wood St WGFD OX10 .... 267 F8
Woodview FGDN SN7 .... 230 A3
Woodview Rd GOR/PANG RG8 ..... 330 B2
Woodville CHNR OX39 .... 224 E4
Woodwaye WODY RG5 .... 335 F8
Woodway Rd CHNTN OX7 .... 73 F7
........................DID OX11 .... 310 A1
........................RBANSW OX15 .... 24 E8
Woodways HADM HP17 .... 176 C9
Woolstone Rd FGDN SN7 .... 254 E8
Wootton Cl CALC RG31 .... 331 C7
Wootton End WIT/EY OX8 .... 107 H7
Wootton Rd HEN RG9 .... 318 E7
........................MCHM/KBPZ OX13 ... 214 B3
Worcester Dr DID OX11 .... 264 B7
Worcester Pl
........................MCHM/KBPZ OX13 ... 210 D6
........................OX/KTN OX1 .... 4 B3
Worcester Rd CHNTN OX7 .... 67 J5
Worcester St OX/KTN OX1 .... 4 B4
Wordsworth Dr BIC OX26 .... 96 D3
........................FGDN SN7 .... 232 B7
Wordsworth Rd ABGD OX14 .... 238 B2
Workhouse La RBANSW OX15 ...... 36 E2
Wormald Rd WGFD OX10 .... 290 E1
Worminghall Rd RAYLW HP18 ..... 172 D4
Wormsley Crs SKCH HP14 .... 248 E8
Wortham Rd DID OX11 .... 263 H5
Worthington Wy WANT OX12 .... 282 D1
Worton Rd CHNTN OX7 .... 73 F6
Wrde Hl HGHW SN6 .... 250 D2
Wren Cl WHLY OX33 .... 170 D7
Wrenfield Dr CAV/SC RG4 .... 333 F2
Wren Rd OXN/BOT/CM OX2 .... 149 G7
Wrenswood SWDNE SN3 .... 274 B7
Wretchwick Wy BIC OX26 .... 97 J8
Wrightson Cl WHLY OX33 .... 193 J1
Wroslyn Rd WIT/EY OX8 .... 126 A7
Wroxham Rd WODY RG5 .... 335 F7
Wyatt Rd OXN/BOT/CM OX2 .... 149 F6
Wychcotes READ RG1 .... 333 F5
Wychwood Cl BUR/CRTN OX18 ... 157 K2
........................CHNTN OX7 .... 102 B7
........................CHNTN OX7 .... 106 B3
........................WGFD OX10 .... 267 J3
........................WIT/EY OX8 .... 142 C7
Wychwood Dr CHNTN OX7 .... 102 B7
Wychwood Gdns BAN OX16 .... 2 A5
Wychwood La HEAD OX3 .... 169 G5
Wychwood Paddocks
........................CHNTN OX7 .... 106 A3
Wychwood Vw WIT/EY OX8 .... 141 G5
Wycombe Rd SKCH HP14 .... 249 J3
Wycombe Wy BUR/CRTN OX18 ... 158 A5
Wye Cl BIC OX26 .... 96 C4
Wyfold La CAV/SC RG4 .... 316 A8
........................HEN RG9 .... 316 E7
Wykeham Crs COW/LTMR OX4 .... 192 B3
Wykeham Ga HADM HP17 .... 176 B2
Wykeham Pk THAME OX9 .... 175 G7
Wykeham Ri CHNR OX39 .... 225 F1
Wykeham Wy HADM HP17 .... 176 B1
Wykham Gdns BAN OX16 .... 2 B5
Wykham La BAN OX16 .... 28 D6
Wykham PI BAN OX16 .... 2 B6
Wylie Cl HEAD OX3 .... 168 D7
Wynbush Rd COW/LTMR OX4 ...... 192 A4
The Wyncies HGHW SN6 .... 298 D3
Wyndale Cl HEN RG9 .... 319 G6
Wyndham Crs WODY RG5 .... 335 F6
Wyndham Gdns WGFD OX10 .... 291 F1
Wyndham Wy OXN/BOT/CM OX2 . 148 E7
Wyndyke Furlong ABGD OX14 ..... 214 A7
Wyre Cl HADM HP17 .... 176 C2
Wyre St CALC RG31 .... 331 G4
Wysdom Wy BUR/CRTN OX18 ..... 138 E5
Wytham Cl WIT/EY OX8 .... 146 A7
Wytham St OX/KTN OX1 .... 191 H2
Wytham Vw WIT/EY OX8 .... 146 A7

Y

Yare Cl DID OX11 .... 264 B6
Yarnell's Hl OXN/BOT/CM OX2 .... 166 B8

Yarnell's Rd *OXN/BOT/CM* OX2 .... 166 C7
Yarnton Cl *CAV/SC* RG4 .... 333 J1
Yarnton Ct *KID* OX5 .... 129 H7
Yarnton La *KID* OX5 .... 148 B1
Yarnton Rd *WIT/EY* OX8 .... 147 F4
Yealm Cl *DID* OX11 .... 263 K3
Yeates Cl *THAME* OX9 .... 175 F6
Yeats Cl *COW/LTMR* OX4 .... 192 E1 ▣
Yeftly Dr *COW/LTMR* OX4 .... 192 A6
Yeld Hall Rd *ABGD* OX14 .... 215 F5 ▣
Yew Cl *BIC* OX26 .... 97 F2
Yew Tree Cl *RBANNS* OX17 .... 22 E7

THAME OX9 .... 198 B7 ▣
Yew Tree Ct *GOR/PANG* RG8 ...... 322 E1 ▣
Yew Tree Gdns *SWDNE* SN3 ...... 274 C3 ▣
Yewtree Ms *ABGD* OX14 .... 214 D8 ▣
Yew Tree Ri *BRACKY* NN13............ 41 J7
Yield Hall La *READ* RG1 .... 333 H8 ▣
Yield Hall Pl *READ* RG1 .... 333 H8 ▣
Yolsum Cl *HADM* HP17 .... 176 A1
York Av *HEAD* OX3 .... 168 E6
York Cl *BIC* OX26 .... 97 H4
York Pl *HEAD* OX3 .... 5 E4
York Rd *BUR/CRTN* OX18 .... 158 A3
DID OX11 .... 287 G3

HEAD OX3 .... 168 E5
HEN RG9 .... 319 F5
READ RG1 .... 333 G6
Youghal Cl *HGHW* SN6 .... 276 B1 ▣
Ypres Wy *ABGD* OX14 .... 214 B6

Z

Zinzan St *READ* RG1 .... 333 F8

Index - featured places

Abacus College
  OX/KTN OX1 .... 4 C4
Abbey Chiropody Clinic
  ABGD OX14 .... 214 C8
Abbey Sports Centre
  WGFD OX10 .... 241 J2
Abingdon College
  ABGD OX14 .... 214 C6
Abingdon Museum
  ABGD OX14 .... 214 D8
Abingdon Rugby Football Club
  ABGD OX14 .... 238 C3
Abingdon School
  ABGD OX14 .... 214 C8
The Abingdon Surgery
  ABGD OX14 .... 214 D8
The Acland Hospital
  OXN/BOT/CM OX2 .... 4 C2
All Saints C of E Primary School
  DID OX11 .... 264 A5
All Saints Infants School
  READ RG1 .... 332 E8
Alvescot Health Centre
  BUR/CRTN OX18 .... 157 K5
Apollo Theatre
  OX/KTN OX1 .... 4 C4
Aquinas Tutorial College
  COW/LTMR OX4 .... 5 E5
Arcade Gallery
  GOR/PANG RG8 .... 322 D1
Ardington Gallery
  WANT OX12 .... 283 K2
The Argyle Clinic
  TLHT RG30 .... 332 E8
Army Medical Centre
  RBICS/W OX25 .... 115 K3
Art Gallery
  HEN RG9 .... 319 G5
The Art Gallery
  READ RG1 .... 333 H8
Arthur Hill Memorial
  Swimming Baths
  READ RG1 .... 333 K8
Artworks School of Art & Design
  COW/LTMR OX4 .... 5 F6
Asbury Medical Centre
  DID OX11 .... 264 A5
Ashmolean Museum
  OX/KTN OX1 .... 4 C3
Aston Rowant C of E
  Primary School
  WTLGN OX49 .... 224 A4
Aston Rowant Cricket Club
  CHNR OX39 .... 224 A4
Auction Market
  READ RG1 .... 333 F7
Avenue Three
  WIT/EY OX8 .... 161 F1
Avenue Two
  WIT/EY OX8 .... 161 F1
Aynhoe Park House
  RBANNS OX17 .... 40 B8
Badgemore CP School
  HEN RG9 .... 318 E5
Balliol College
  OX/KTN OX1 .... 4 C3
The Bampton Clinic
  BUR/CRTN OX18 .... 183 H4
Bampton C of E Primary School
  BUR/CRTN OX18 .... 183 G3
Bampton Surgery
  BUR/CRTN OX18 .... 183 G3
Banbury County Court
  BAN OX16 .... 2 C3
Banbury Golf Club
  RBANNS OX17 .... 39 G6

Banbury Museum
  Heritage Centre
  BAN OX16 .... 3 F3
Banbury Road Medical Centre
  OXN/BOT/CM OX2 .... 167 F1
Banbury Road North
  Sports Ground
  OXN/BOT/CM OX2 .... 148 E5
Banbury Rugby Union
  Football Club
  RBANNS OX17 .... 29 H7
Banbury School
  BAN OX16 .... 2 C6
Banbury Town Hall
  BAN OX16 .... 3 D3
Banbury Twenty Cricket Club
  BAN OX16 .... 21 J7
Banbury West End Lawn
  Tennis Club
  RBANNS OX17 .... 38 C3
Bardwell School
  BIC OX26 .... 97 G3
Barley Hill County
  Primary School
  THAME OX9 .... 175 F6
The Barn Gallery
  THAME OX9 .... 175 F7
Barn Surgery
  WTLGN OX49 .... 246 D6
Bartholomew School
  WIT/EY OX8 .... 145 K7
Barton Village First School
  HEAD OX3 .... 168 E2
Basildon House
  GOR/PANG RG8 .... 323 G6
Battle Farm Trading Estate
  TLHT RG30 .... 332 D6
Battle Primary School
  TLHT RG30 .... 332 D8
Batt School
  WIT/EY OX8 .... 142 E7
Bayswater Middle School
  HEAD OX3 .... 169 F4
Beachborough School
  BRACKY NN13 .... 44 D3
Beadle Trading Estate
  WGFD OX10 .... 266 D8
Beaumont Business Centre
  BAN OX16 .... 20 E6
Beechwood County Junior
  & Infant School
  WODY RG5 .... 335 G8
The Bell Surgery
  HEN RG9 .... 319 F5
Benson C of E Junior School
  WGFD OX10 .... 267 H3
Benson County Primary School
  WGFD OX10 .... 268 B5
Berinsfield Health Centre
  WGFD OX10 .... 241 H2
Berinsfield Primary School
  WGFD OX10 .... 241 J2
Bernwood First School
  HEAD OX3 .... 168 E3
Bessels Leigh School
  MCHM/KBPZ OX13 .... 188 E8
Bicester Community College
  BIC OX26 .... 96 E5
Bicester Community Hospital
  BIC OX26 .... 97 F6
Bicester Health Centre
  BIC OX26 .... 97 F6
Bicester & Ploughley
  Sports Centre
  BIC OX26 .... 96 E5

Bicester Sports Club
  BIC OX26 .... 96 E6
Bicester Town Council
  BIC OX26 .... 97 G6
Birch Copse Primary School
  CALC RG31 .... 331 G7
Bishop Carpenter C of E
  Primary School
  RBANSW OX15 .... 27 H3
Bishop Loveday C of E
  Primary School
  BAN OX16 .... 29 G6
Bishopstone C of E School
  HCHW SN6 .... 298 D3
Blackbird Leys Health Centre
  COW/LTMR OX4 .... 192 E5
Blackbird Leys Leisure Centre
  COW/LTMR OX4 .... 192 E5
The Blake C of E Primary School
  WIT/EY OX8 .... 143 G7
Bledington County
  Primary School
  CHNTN OX7 .... 83 J5
Bledlow Cricket Club
  PRRI HP27 .... 201 J6
Blenheim Palace
  WDSTK OX20 .... 127 H2
Blessed George Napier
  RC School
  BAN OX16 .... 2 C6
Bletchingdon Parochial
  Controlled Primary School
  KID OX5 .... 112 A7
Blewbury C of E Primary School
  DID OX11 .... 287 K6
Bloxham C of E School
  RBANSW OX15 .... 36 D3
Bloxham Museum
  RBANSW OX15 .... 37 F3
Bloxham School
  RBANSW OX15 .... 37 F2
Boathouse Surgery
  GOR/PANG RG8 .... 322 D1
Bohun Gallery
  HEN RG9 .... 319 G6
Borocourt Hospital
  CAV/SC RG4 .... 316 A6
Botley County Primary School
  OXN/BOT/CM OX2 .... 166 B6
Botley Medical Centre
  OXN/BOT/CM OX2 .... 166 A6
Boundary Business Park
  STAD OX44 .... 194 B4
Brackley Town Football Club
  BRACKY NN13 .... 43 G1
Bradstocks Way Surgery
  ABGD OX14 .... 262 D1
Brasenose College
  Sports Ground
  OX/KTN OX1 .... 5 D6
Breakspear Clinic
  CHNTN OX7 .... 102 C6
The Brian Sinfield Gallery
  BUR/CRTN OX18 .... 138 E2
Bridge House Gallery
  CIR GL7 .... 203 F3
Brightwell C of E
  Primary School
  WGFD OX10 .... 266 A5
Britannia County Infants School
  BAN OX16 .... 3 D4
Brize Norton County
  Primary School
  BUR/CRTN OX18 .... 158 E3
Bromag Industrial Estate
  WIT/EY OX8 .... 141 K5

Brookfields School
CALC RG31 .... **331** G4
Brookside Primary School
BIC OX26 .... **97** F5
Broughton Castle
RBANSW OX15 .... **27** H6
Broughton & North
Newington Sports Club
RBANSW OX15 .... **27** K4
Buckland School
FGDN SN7 .... **208** D7
Buckland University College
HEAD OX3 .... **168** A4
The Bulmershe School
EARL RG6 .... **334** E8
Burford Cottage Hospital
BUR/CRTN OX18 .... **138** D2
The Burford Gallery
BUR/CRTN OX18 .... **138** E2
Burford Golf Club
BUR/CRTN OX18 .... **138** D4
Burford Primary School
BUR/CRTN OX18 .... **138** E2
Burford School
BUR/CRTN OX18 .... **138** E2
Burford Surgery
BUR/CRTN OX18 .... **138** D2
Bury Knowle Health Centre
HEAD OX3 .... **168** D4
Bushell Business Park
WCFD OX10 .... **290** D1
Business School
OX/KTN OX1 .... **4** B4
Bygones Museum
RBANNS OX17 .... **7** F6
Caldecott Primary School
ABGD OX14 .... **238** B2
Camp Industrial Estate
THAME OX9 .... **197** F3
Cardinal Newman Middle School
COW/LTMR OX4 .... **192** A1
Carswell CP School
ABGD OX14 .... **214** C8
Carswell Golf Club
FGDN SN7 .... **207** K8
Carterton Community College
BUR/CRTN OX18 .... **157** K3
Carterton County
Primary School
BUR/CRTN OX18 .... **158** A4
Carterton Industrial Estate
BUR/CRTN OX18 .... **158** A6
Carterton Surgery
BUR/CRTN OX18 .... **157** K5
Carterton Town Football Club
BUR/CRTN OX18 .... **157** K1
Castle Hill Clinic
READ RG1 .... **333** F8
Caversham Park Primary School
CAV/SC RG4 .... **334** A1
Caversham Primary School
CAV/SC RG4 .... **333** G4
Centenary Business Park
HEN RG9 .... **319** H6
Central Swimming Pool
READ RG1 .... **333** F8
Century Galleries
HEN RG9 .... **319** G5
Chacombe C of E Aided School
RBANNS OX17 .... **22** D3
Chadlington C of E School
CHNTN OX7 .... **87** F6
Chalgrove County
Primary School
STAD OX44 .... **244** B1
Chandlings Manor School
MCHM/KBPZ OX13 .... **191** F8
Chapel
THAME OX9 .... **197** H1
Chapel Hill Surgery
CALC RG31 .... **331** G7
Charlbury Museum
CHNTN OX7 .... **106** A3
Charlbury Primary School
CHNTN OX7 .... **106** B3
The Charlbury Surgery
CHNTN OX7 .... **106** A3
Charlton County Primary School
WANT OX12 .... **283** F2
Charlton on Otmoor
Parochial School
KID OX5 .... **132** B2
Chatham Street Surgery
READ RG1 .... **333** F8

Checkendon C of E Aided
Primary School
GOR/PANG RG8 .... **315** G4
Chenderit School
RBANNS OX17 .... **22** E6
Cheney School
HEAD OX3 .... **168** B6
Cherwell District Council
BAN OX16 .... **2** A3
Cherwell District Council
BAN OX16 .... **3** D3
Cherwell District Council
BIC OX26 .... **97** G6
Cherwell District Council
RBANSW OX15 .... **29** G6
The Cherwell School
OXN/BOT/CM OX2 .... **167** G1
Chesterton C of E
Primary School
BIC OX26 .... **96** B7
Chesterton Country Golf Club
BIC OX26 .... **95** K7
Chiltern Business Centre
COW/LTMR OX4 .... **192** E3
Chiltern Edge Secondary School
CAV/SC RG4 .... **326** E3
Chilterns Fine Art Gallery
WGFD OX10 .... **267** F8
Chilton County Primary School
DID OX11 .... **286** A7
Chinnor Rugby Football Club
THAME OX9 .... **175** J6
Chipping Norton Football Club
CHNTN OX7 .... **68** B6
Chipping Norton Golf Club
CHNTN OX7 .... **69** G5
Chipping Norton Rugby Club
CHNTN OX7 .... **68** C7
Chipping Norton School
CHNTN OX7 .... **68** C5
Chipping Norton War
Memorial Hospital
CHNTN OX7 .... **68** B4
Cholsey County Primary School
WGFD OX10 .... **290** A5
Christ Church College
OX/KTN OX1 .... **5** D5
Christchurch Sports Ground
OX/KTN OX1 .... **5** E5
Christopher Rawlins C of E School
RBANNS OX17 .... **38** D3
Christs Hospital
ABGD OX14 .... **214** D8
Church Cowley St James School
COW/LTMR OX4 .... **192** C3
Churchill Hospital
HEAD OX3 .... **168** C6
Church of England
Primary School
WIT/EY OX8 .... **126** B8
Clanfield Parish School
BUR/CRTN OX18 .... **182** B7
Clarendon Centre
OX/KTN OX1 .... **4** C4
Clearway House Industrial Estate
BAN OX16 .... **21** J8
Clifton Hampden C of E
Primary School
ABGD OX14 .... **240** C3
Cogges Hill Surgery
WIT/EY OX8 .... **143** G8
Cogges Manor Farm Museum
WIT/EY OX8 .... **143** G7
Cokethorpe School
WIT/EY OX8 .... **161** J6
College Oak
ABGD OX14 .... **215** F5
College of Further Education
COW/LTMR OX4 .... **192** E5
Colston House Tennis Club
CIR GL7 .... **180** D4
Combe C of E Primary School
WIT/EY OX8 .... **126** B3
Convent Senior School
ABGD OX14 .... **214** E7
Cooper School
BIC OX26 .... **97** G3
Corn Exchange Theatre
WGFD OX10 .... **267** C4
Corpus Christi College
OX/KTN OX1 .... **5** D5
Cothill Old School
MCHM/KBPZ OX13 .... **213** H3
Cotswold Business Park
WIT/EY OX8 .... **142** A6
Council Offices
MIM GL56 .... **46** A1

The County Gallery
WIT/EY OX8 .... **145** K
County Hall
OX/KTN OX1 .... **4** C
County Trading Estate
COW/LTMR OX4 .... **193** F
Covingham Park County
Junior & Infant School
SWDNE SN3 .... **274** A
Cranford House School
WGFD OX10 .... **312** B
Crescent School
OXN/BOT/CM OX2 .... **148** E
Cropredy C of E School
RBANNS OX17 .... **13** H
Croughton C of E School
BRACKY NN13 .... **41** J
Crowmarsh Gifford
C of E School
WGFD OX10 .... **291** H
Crown Trading Estate
SWDNE SN3 .... **274** B
Culham College Institute
ABGD OX14 .... **238** D
Culham Parochial
Primary School
ABGD OX14 .... **239** F
Cumnor C of E Primary School
OXN/BOT/CM OX2 .... **189** G
Cutteslowe Primary School
OXN/BOT/CM OX2 .... **149** G
Dashwood County
Primary School
BAN OX16 .... **2** C
David Lloyd Sports Centre
EARL RG6 .... **334** C
Deddington Health Centre
RBANSW OX15 .... **56** C
Deddington Primary School
RBANSW OX15 .... **56** B
Deer Park Medical Centre
WIT/EY OX8 .... **142** B
Denman College
MCHM/KBPZ OX13 .... **236** E
Didcot Girls School
DID OX11 .... **263** G
Didcot Health Centre
DID OX11 .... **263** J
Didcot Hospital
DID OX11 .... **263** G
Didcot Leisure Centre
DID OX11 .... **263** K
Didcot Power Station
DID OX11 .... **263** C
Didcot Railway Centre
DID OX11 .... **263** J
Didcot Town Football Club
DID OX11 .... **263** K
Donnington Middle School
COW/LTMR OX4 .... **192** A
Dorchester Sailing Club
WGFD OX10 .... **241** J
Dorchester St Birinus
C of E School
WGFD OX10 .... **241** K
Dormer House PNEU School
MIM GL56 .... **46** A
D'overbroecks College
OXN/BOT/CM OX2 .... **4** C
Downs Way School
CALC RG31 .... **331** G
Dragon School
OXN/BOT/CM OX2 .... **4** C
Drayton County Primary School
ABGD OX14 .... **237** K
Drayton Golf Club
ABGD OX14 .... **237** G
Drayton School
RBANSW OX15 .... **20** A
Dr Radcliffes C of E
Primary School
RBICS/W OX25 .... **74** E
Dr Souths C of E Primary School
KID OX5 .... **130** E
Dryleas Sports Ground
HEN RG9 .... **319** F
Dry Sandford County
Primary School
MCHM/KBPZ OX13 .... **213** H
Ducklington C of E New
Primary School
WIT/EY OX8 .... **161** F
Duffield Road CP School
WODY RG5 .... **335** H
Dunmore County Infant School
ABGD OX14 .... **214** D

Easington Sports Club
BAN OX16 .... 2 C6

East Challow C of E School
WANT OX12 .... 281 K3

East Hanney C of E
Primary School
WANT OX12 .... 235 G8

East Oxford First School
COW/LTMR OX4 .... 5 F5

Eastrop County Infant School
HGHW SN6 .... 250 E2

Eaton Practice
MCHM/KBPZ OX13 .... 188 D4

Edith Moorhouse
Primary School
BUR/CRTN OX18 .... 157 K5

Edward Field Primary School
KID OX5 .... 129 J8

Edward Street Business Centre
BAN OX16 .... 3 F4

Elm Tree Surgery
HGHW SN6 .... 252 C8

Emmanuel Christian School
COW/LTMR OX4 .... 192 B5

Emmer Green Clinic
CAV/SC RG4 .... 333 H2

Emmer Green CP School
CAV/SC RG4 .... 333 H1

Emmer Green Surgery
CAV/SC RG4 .... 333 G1

English Martyrs RC
Primary School
TLHT RG30 .... 332 A8

Enstone Primary School
CHNTN OX7 .... 88 E2

E P Collier School
READ RG1 .... 333 G6

Exeter College
OX/KTN OX1 .... 4 C4

Exeter College Sports Ground
HEAD OX3 .... 5 E1

Eye Hospital Radcliffe Infirmary
OXN/BOT/CM OX2 .... 4 B3

Eynsham County Primary School
WIT/EY OX8 .... 146 B7

Eynsham Medical Centre
WIT/EY OX8 .... 146 A8

Fairleigh Dickinson University
RBANSW OX15 .... 19 H7

Fair Mile Hospital
WGFD OX10 .... 290 D7

Fairview Trading Estate
HEN RG9 .... 319 H7

Faringdon Health Centre
FGDN SN7 .... 230 A4

Faringdon Infant School
FGDN SN7 .... 230 A3

Faringdon Junior School
FGDN SN7 .... 230 A3

Faringdon Leisure Centre
FGDN SN7 .... 230 B6

Faringdon School
FGDN SN7 .... 230 B5

Ferndale Preparatory School
FGDN SN7 .... 230 B4

Ferry Sports Centre
OXN/BOT/CM OX2 .... 167 F1

Finmere C of E School
BUCK/WIN MK18 .... 63 G1

Finstock C of E Primary School
CHNTN OX7 .... 124 A2

Fire Service Technical College
MIM GL56 .... 46 D1

Fire Station
OXN/BOT/CM OX2 .... 4 B4

Fir Tree County Junior School
WGFD OX10 .... 266 D7

Fitzharrys County
Secondary School
ABGD OX14 .... 214 D6

Fitzwaryn School
WANT OX12 .... 282 C1

Five Acres School
RBICS/W OX25 .... 116 A3

Food Gallery
READ RG1 .... 334 A8

Football Club
HEN RG9 .... 319 H7

Foscote Private Hospital
BAN OX16 .... 3 D5

Fosse Way Business Centre
MIM GL56 .... 46 A1

Frank Wise School
BAN OX16 .... 2 A4

Frideswide Middle School
OXN/BOT/CM OX2 .... 167 G1

Frilford Heath Golf Club
MCHM/KBPZ OX13 .... 212 C6

Fringford C of E School
RBICN OX27 .... 79 K1

Fritwell C of E School
RBICN OX27 .... 58 E8

The Gallery
CAV/SC RG4 .... 334 D2

Garsington C of E
Primary School
STAD OX44 .... 193 K5

Garsington Sports Club
STAD OX44 .... 194 B5

Gateway School
BUR/CRTN OX18 .... 158 A5

Geoffrey Walton Practice
CHNTN OX7 .... 106 A3

Gillotts School
HEN RG9 .... 318 D8

Glory Farm County
Primary School
BIC OX26 .... 97 H3

Goring C of E Primary School
GOR/PANG RG8 .... 312 E8

Goring & Streatley Golf Club
GOR/PANG RG8 .... 312 A8

Gosford All Blacks Rugby
Football Club
KID OX5 .... 128 E5

Gosford Hill Medical Centre
KID OX5 .... 129 J8

Gosford Hill School
KID OX5 .... 129 J8

Grange County Primary School
BAN OX16 .... 3 D6

Great Milton C of E School
STAD OX44 .... 196 A4

Great Rollright C of E
Primary School
CHNTN OX7 .... 50 E4

Great Tew School
CHNTN OX7 .... 53 H8

Green College
OXN/BOT/CM OX2 .... 4 B2

Greenmere County
Primary School
DID OX11 .... 263 J7

Gresham Way Industrial Estate
TLHT RG30 .... 332 A5

Greys Gallery
HEN RG9 .... 319 G6

Greystones Gallery
CIR GL7 .... 203 G3

Grimsbury St Leonards
C of E Primary School
BAN OX16 .... 3 F3

Grove Further
Education College
WANT OX12 .... 258 D5

Grovelands Surgery
TLHT RG30 .... 332 B7

Grove Primary School
WANT OX12 .... 258 E5

Groves Industrial Estate
CHNTN OX7 .... 102 C6

Gun Street Gallery
READ RG1 .... 333 H8

Haddenham County
First School
HADM HP17 .... 176 C1

Haddenham First School
HADM HP17 .... 176 C3

Haddenham Health Centre
HADM HP17 .... 176 C1

Haddenham Middle School
HADM HP17 .... 176 C1

Hadden Hill Golf Club
DID OX11 .... 264 C6

Hagbourne C of E
Primary School
DID OX11 .... 287 J2

Hailey C of E Primary School
WIT/EY OX8 .... 142 E1

Hailey Road County
Primary School
WIT/EY OX8 .... 142 E4

Hanborough Business Park
WIT/EY OX8 .... 127 F6

Hardwick County
Primary School
BAN OX16 .... 2 A1

Harriers Ground County School
BAN OX16 .... 2 C5

Harris Manchester College
OX/KTN OX1 .... 5 D3

The Hart Surgery
HEN RG9 .... 319 F5

Harwell County Primary School
DID OX11 .... 262 B8

Haseley Trading Estate
STAD OX44 .... 196 A6

Headington County
Secondary Modern School
HEAD OX3 .... 168 D5

Headington Quarry School
HEAD OX3 .... 168 E5

Headington School
HEAD OX3 .... 168 B5

Hemdean House School
CAV/SC RG4 .... 333 G4

The Hendreds Primary School
WANT OX12 .... 284 E1

The Henley College
HEN RG9 .... 318 E6

The Henley College
HEN RG9 .... 319 F6

Henley District Indoor
Sports Centre
HEN RG9 .... 318 D8

Henley Golf Club
HEN RG9 .... 329 F1

Henley Town Football Club
HEN RG9 .... 319 H7

Henry Box School
WIT/EY OX8 .... 142 E8

Hernes Estate
HEN RG9 .... 318 B7

Hertford College
OX/KTN OX1 .... 5 D4

Hertford College Sports Ground
HEAD OX3 .... 5 E1

Highdown School
CAV/SC RG4 .... 333 G2

Hightown Surgery
BAN OX16 .... 2 C6

Highworth Golf Club
HGHW SN6 .... 250 D3

Highworth Recreation Centre
HGHW SN6 .... 250 D2

The Hill Primary School
CAV/SC RG4 .... 333 J2

Hillview County Primary School
BAN OX16 .... 2 A2

Hinksey Business Centre
OXN/BOT/CM OX2 .... 166 B6

Hinksey Pools Swimming
OX/KTN OX1 .... 191 G1

HM Prison
READ RG1 .... 333 J7

Hollow Way Medical Centre
COW/LTMR OX4 .... 192 D2

Holy Trinity RC School
CHNTN OX7 .... 68 C4

Holywell Business Centre
OXN/BOT/CM OX2 .... 4 A5

Hook Norton C of E
Primary School
RBANSW OX15 .... 34 A7

Hook Norton Surgery
RBANSW OX15 .... 34 A8

Horse Fair Surgery
BAN OX16 .... 2 C4

Horspath C of E Primary School
WHLY OX33 .... 169 J8

Horton General Hospital
NHS Trust
BAN OX16 .... 3 D5

Huntercombe Golf Club
HEN RG9 .... 293 J4

Ibis Sports Club
CAV/SC RG4 .... 332 B5

Ibstone C of E First School
SKCH HP14 .... 273 F1

Ickford CP School
RAYLW HP18 .... 172 D4

Icknield Community School
WTLGN OX49 .... 246 B5

Iffley Mead School
COW/LTMR OX4 .... 191 K2

Independent Business Park
SKCH HP14 .... 248 E2

The Infirmary
ABGD OX14 .... 215 H3

Institute of Virology
& Environmental Microbiology
OX/KTN OX1 .... 5 D3

Isis Business Centre
COW/LTMR OX4 .... 193 F1

Isis Clinic
COW/LTMR OX4 .... 191 K3

Isis Middle School
COW/LTMR OX4 .... 191 J1

Jericho Health Centre
OXN/BOT/CM OX2 .... 4 B2

Jesus College
OX/KTN OX1 .... **4** C4
Jesus College Sports Ground
COW/LTMR OX4 .... **168** B8
John Blandy Primary School
MCHM/KBPZ OX13 .... **210** E6
John Hampden County
Primary School
THAME OX9 .... **175** F8
John Mason School
ABGD OX14 .... **214** C7
John Radcliffe Hospital
HEAD OX3 .... **168** B3
John Watson School
WHLY OX33 .... **170** C7
Jordan Hill Business Park
OXN/BOT/CM OX2 .... **148** E5
Joscas Preparatory School
MCHM/KBPZ OX13 .... **212** C8
Keble College
OX/KTN OX1 .... **4** C3
Kennet Surgery
READ RG1 .... **334** A8
Kennington Health Centre
OX/KTN OX1 .... **191** J6
Kenton Theatre
HEN RG9 .... **319** G5
Kidlington & Gosford
Sports Centre
KID OX5 .... **129** J8
Kidlington Health Centre
KID OX5 .... **129** H7
Kidlington Parish Council
KID OX5 .... **129** H7
Kidmore End Primary School
CAV/SC RG4 .... **326** D4
King Alfred School East
WANT OX12 .... **283** F3
King Alfreds Grammar School
WANT OX12 .... **282** D3
King Alfreds School West
WANT OX12 .... **282** B3
Kingfisher School
ABGD OX14 .... **238** C1
Kingfisher Special School
ABGD OX14 .... **215** F7
Kingham County Primary School
CHNTN OX7 .... **84** B2
Kingham Hill School
CHNTN OX7 .... **66** C6
Kings Meadow County
Primary School
BIC OX26 .... **96** D4
Kings School
WIT/EY OX8 .... **143** G4
Kings School Oxford
COW/LTMR OX4 .... **192** D1
Kings School Seniors
WIT/EY OX8 .... **143** F7
Kings Sutton County
Primary School
RBANNS OX17 .... **39** K2
Kirtlington C of E Primary School
KID OX5 .... **111** K3
Ladygrove Park Primary School
DID OX11 .... **263** K4
Langford Medical Practice
BIC OX26 .... **97** H7
Langford Village County
Primary School
BIC OX26 .... **97** H7
Langtree Secondary School
GOR/PANG RG8 .... **314** D7
Larkmead School
ABGD OX14 .... **214** A7
Larkrise First School
COW/LTMR OX4 .... **192** A1
Launton Business Centre
BIC OX26 .... **97** H4
Leafield C of E School
WIT/EY OX8 .... **122** C4
Lewknor C of E School
WTLGN OX49 .... **223** G7
Linacre College
OX/KTN OX1 .... **5** D2
Lincoln College
OX/KTN OX1 .... **4** C4
Lincoln College Sports Ground
COW/LTMR OX4 .... **168** B8
Little Milton School
STAD OX44 .... **219** H1
The Loddon Vale Practice
WODY RG5 .... **335** J8
Long Compton Junior
& Infant School
SHPSTR CV36 .... **49** G1

Longfields Primary School
BIC OX26 .... **97** G5
Long Furlong Medical Centre
ABGD OX14 .... **214** E4
Long Furlong Primary School
ABGD OX14 .... **214** E4
Long Hanborough Surgery
WIT/EY OX8 .... **126** C6
Long Lane Primary School
GOR/PANG RG8 .... **331** F3
Long Wittenham C of E
Primary School
ABGD OX14 .... **240** D6
Longworth Undenominational
Primary School
MCHM/KBPZ OX13 .... **210** C3
Lord Williams Lower School
THAME OX9 .... **175** H7
Lord Williams Upper School
THAME OX9 .... **174** D7
Lyneham Golf Club
CHNTN OX7 .... **102** D1
Mabel Prichard School
COW/LTMR OX4 .... **192** B5
Magdalen College
OX/KTN OX1 .... **5** E4
Magdalen College School
COW/LTMR OX4 .... **5** E5
Magdalen College Sports Ground
HEAD OX3 .... **5** F3
Magna Gallery
OX/KTN OX1 .... **5** D4
The Malthouse Surgery
ABGD OX14 .... **214** D8
Manor County Infants School
DID OX11 .... **263** J6
Manor County Junior School
DID OX11 .... **263** H6
The Manor County
Primary School
WIT/EY OX8 .... **126** C6
The Manor Preparatory School
MCHM/KBPZ OX13 .... **214** A6
Manor Surgery
HEAD OX3 .... **168** C4
Mansfield College
OX/KTN OX1 .... **5** D3
Mapledurhamhouse
CAV/SC RG4 .... **331** J1
Marantha Christian School
WHLY SN6 .... **250** C6
Marcham C of E School
MCHM/KBPZ OX13 .... **237** F1
Marcham Health Centre
ABGD OX14 .... **238** A1
Marlborough College
OX/KTN OX1 .... **4** C4
Marlborough School
WDSTK OX20 .... **127** K1
Marsh Baldon C of E
Primary School
STAD OX44 .... **217** G3
Marsh Gibbon C of E
First School
RBICN OX27 .... **99** J4
Marston Health Centre
HEAD OX3 .... **168** A2
Marston Middle School
HEAD OX3 .... **167** J2
Matthew Arnold County
Secondary School
OXN/BOT/CM OX2 .... **166** A8
Mckay Trading Estate
BIC OX26 .... **97** G6
Meadway Comprehensive
School
TLHT RG30 .... **331** K8
Melrose Surgery
READ RG1 .... **333** J8
Mereland County Infants School
DID OX11 .... **263** J7
Mereland Road Surgery
DID OX11 .... **263** K7
Merriscourt Gallery
CHNTN OX7 .... **85** G7
Merton College
OX/KTN OX1 .... **5** D4
Micklands CP School
CAV/SC RG4 .... **333** K3
Middle Barton Primary School
CHNTN OX7 .... **73** H7
Middleton Cheney County
Primary School
RBANNS OX17 .... **22** D7
Milham Ford School for Girls
HEAD OX3 .... **168** A4

The Mill at Sonning (Theatre)
CAV/SC RG4 .... **334** E
Millbrook County Junior School
WANT OX12 .... **258** D
Millbrook House School
ABGD OX14 .... **262** B
Mill Lane County Primary School
CHNR OX39 .... **200** D
Mill Stream Surgery
WGFD OX10 .... **267** H
Milton C of E Primary School
ABGD OX14 .... **262** A
Milton Manor
ABGD OX14 .... **262** A
Minster Industrial Estate
WIT/EY OX8 .... **141** K
Montgomery House Surg
BIC OX26 .... **97** G
Monument Business Park
STAD OX44 .... **220** D
Moorlands Primary School
TLHT RG30 .... **331** J
Moreton Wanderers
Football Club
MIM GL56 .... **46** B
Morland House Surgery
WHLY OX33 .... **170** D
The Motorsports Centre
BRACKY NN13 .... **44** E
Moulsford Preparatory School
GOR/PANG RG8 .... **312** C
Museum of Modern Art
OX/KTN OX1 .... **4** C
Museum of Oxford
OX/KTN OX1 .... **4** C
Neithrop County Junior
& Infant School
BAN OX16 .... **28** B
Nettlebed CP School
HEN RG9 .... **294** D
Newbottle & Charlton
Primary School
RBANNS OX17 .... **40** E
New College
OX/KTN OX1 .... **5** D
New College School
OX/KTN OX1 .... **5** D
New Hinksey School
OX/KTN OX1 .... **191** G
New Marston School
HEAD OX3 .... **168** A
Newtown Junior
& Infant School
READ RG1 .... **333** K
New Yatt Business Centre
WIT/EY OX8 .... **124** E
North Bicester Surgery
BIC OX26 .... **97** F
Northbourne C of E
Primary School
DID OX11 .... **263** J
Northern House School
OXN/BOT/CM OX2 .... **148** E
Northfield School
COW/LTMR OX4 .... **192** D
North Hinksey C of E School
OXN/BOT/CM OX2 .... **166** C
North Kidlington School
KID OX5 .... **129** H
North Leigh C of E School
WIT/EY OX8 .... **144** B
North Leigh Football Club
WIT/EY OX8 .... **144** D
North Oxford Medical Centre
OXN/BOT/CM OX2 .... **167** F
North Oxfordshire
Agricultural College
BAN OX16 .... **2** B
North Oxfordshire College
BIC OX26 .... **97** F
Northview Primary School
HGHW SN6 .... **227** F
Northway Health Centre
HEAD OX3 .... **168** B
Northway Sports Centre
HEAD OX3 .... **168** A
The Norton Practice
READ RG1 .... **333** J
Nuffield College
HEN RG9 .... **293** K
Nuffield College
OX/KTN OX1 .... **4** C
Nuffield Health Centre
WIT/EY OX8 .... **142** E
Nuffield Hospital Management
Committee
HEAD OX3 .... **168** C

uffield Industrial Estate
COW/LTMR OX4 .... 192 C5
ythe Primary School
SWDNE SN3 .... 274 A8
akfield Industrial Estate
WIT/EY OX8 .... 163 K2
ak Tree Health Centre
DID OX11 .... 263 K5
deon Theatre
READ RG1 .... 333 G8
ld Fire Station Theatre
OX/KTN OX1 .... 4 B4
he Old Gaol Leisure Centre
ABGD OX14 .... 238 D1
ld Rectory Surgery
HEAD OX3 .... 62 E5
he Open University
OX/KTN OX1 .... 190 B6
ne Oratory Preparatory School
GOR/PANG RG8 .... 324 B3
ne Oratory School
GOR/PANG RG8 .... 314 E7
he Orchard Health Centre
BAN OX16 .... 2 C3
he Orchard Surgery
BAN OX16 .... 2 C3
riel College
OX/KTN OX1 .... 5 D4
riel College Sports Ground
COW/LTMR OX4 .... 168 B7
rmerod School
HEAD OX3 .... 169 G4
sney Mead Industrial Estate
OXN/BOT/CM OX2 .... 4 A5
ur Lady of Lourdes RC School
WIT/EY OX8 .... 142 C8
ur Ladys RC School
COW/LTMR OX4 .... 192 C2
verthorpe Hall (School)
RBANNS OX17 .... 22 A7
xford Brookes University
HEAD OX3 .... 168 A5
xford Brookes University
WHLY OX33 .... 171 F6
xford Business Centre
OX/KTN OX1 .... 4 B5
xford Bus Museum Trust
WIT/EY OX8 .... 127 F6
xford City Council
COW/LTMR OX4 .... 192 C1
xford City Council
OX/KTN OX1 .... 4 C5
xford City Council
OX/KTN OX1 .... 191 H1
xford City Council
OXN/BOT/CM OX2 .... 149 G5
xford City Football Club
HEAD OX3 .... 168 A2
xford College
of Further Education
OX/KTN OX1 .... 4 B5
xford Community
Health NHS Trust
COW/LTMR OX4 .... 192 A2
xford Crown & County Court
OX/KTN OX1 .... 4 C5
xford Gallery
OX/KTN OX1 .... 4 C4
xford High School for Girls
OXN/BOT/CM OX2 .... 167 G1
xford Ice Rink
OX/KTN OX1 .... 4 B5
xford Marathon Rugby Club
COW/LTMR OX4 .... 193 G1
xford Old Boys Rugby
Football Club
OXN/BOT/CM OX2 .... 167 G1
xford Radcliffe Hospital
HEAD OX3 .... 168 C4
xford Rd Surgery
READ RG1 .... 333 F8
xford Regional
Health Authority
COW/LTMR OX4 .... 192 E4
xford Retail Park
COW/LTMR OX4 .... 192 E4
xford Road Primary School
READ RG1 .... 332 E8
xford Rugby Football Club
OXN/BOT/CM OX2 .... 166 D8
xford School
COW/LTMR OX4 .... 168 B8
xfordshire Community
Health NHS Trust
ABGD OX14 .... 214 A8

Oxfordshire Community
Health NHS Trust
COW/LTMR OX4 .... 168 A7
Oxfordshire County Council
ABGD OX14 .... 238 C1
Oxfordshire County Council
COW/LTMR OX4 .... 5 F5
Oxfordshire County Council
HEAD OX3 .... 168 D6
Oxfordshire County Council
KID OX5 .... 129 F5
Oxfordshire County Council
KID OX5 .... 147 J2
Oxfordshire County Council
OX/KTN OX1 .... 4 B4
Oxfordshire County Council
THAME OX9 .... 196 E4
Oxfordshire County Council
WIT/EY OX8 .... 142 E6
The Oxfordshire County Museum
WDSTK OX20 .... 127 H1
The Oxfordshire Golf Club
THAME OX9 .... 197 G1
Oxfordshire Health Authority
ABGD OX14 .... 214 C8
Oxfordshire Health Authority
HEAD OX3 .... 168 C6
Oxfordshire Mental
Healthcare NHS Trust
COW/LTMR OX4 .... 168 C7
Oxfordshire Mental
Healthcare NHS Trust
COW/LTMR OX4 .... 192 B6
Oxford Spires Business Park
KID OX5 .... 128 E4
Oxford United Football Club
HEAD OX3 .... 168 C4
Oxford University
OXN/BOT/CM OX2 .... 4 B2
Oxford University Press
OXN/BOT/CM OX2 .... 4 B3
Oxford University
Rugby Football Club
OX/KTN OX1 .... 5 E6
Paddock Road Industrial Estate
CAV/SC RG4 .... 333 K5
Pangbourne Infants School
GOR/PANG RG8 .... 330 C2
Pangbourne Medical Centre
GOR/PANG RG8 .... 330 A1
Paradise Street Business Centre
OX/KTN OX1 .... 4 B4
Paramins Business Centre
MCHM/KBPZ OX13 .... 261 J6
Park Hospital for Children
HEAD OX3 .... 168 C6
Park Lane Primary School
CALC RG31 .... 331 G7
Park Road Industrial Estate
FGDN SN7 .... 230 B4
Parkside Business Park
WODY RG5 .... 335 G7
Parkside Gallery
BRACKY NN13 .... 43 F1
The Park Sports Centre
WHLY OX33 .... 170 D6
Peachcroft Shopping Centre
ABGD OX14 .... 215 F5
Pegasus First School
COW/LTMR OX4 .... 193 F5
Pembroke College
OX/KTN OX1 .... 4 C5
Pendon Museum
ABGD OX14 .... 240 C8
Penhill Industrial Park
BAN OX16 .... 20 D6
Peppard C of E School
HEN RG9 .... 317 G7
Physiotherapy Surgery
GOR/PANG RG8 .... 330 B1
Pinewood School
HCHW SN6 .... 275 K5
Plater College
HEAD OX3 .... 168 B5
The Players Theatre
THAME OX9 .... 175 F7
Primsdown Industrial Estate
CHNTN OX7 .... 67 K4
Prospect Foot Clinic
CAV/SC RG4 .... 333 G4
Purley C of E School
GOR/PANG RG8 .... 331 G2
Quarry Surgery
HEAD OX3 .... 168 D4
Queen Annes School
CAV/SC RG4 .... 333 H4

Queens College
OX/KTN OX1 .... 5 D4
Queens College
STAD OX44 .... 217 G4
Queens College Sports Ground
OX/KTN OX1 .... 5 D6
Queens Dyke County
Primary School
WIT/EY OX8 .... 142 D8
Queensway County
Primary School
BAN OX16 .... 2 A5
Radcliffe Camera
OX/KTN OX1 .... 5 D4
Radcliffe Infirmary NHS Trust
OXN/BOT/CM OX2 .... 4 B2
Radley C of E Primary School
ABGD OX14 .... 215 J4
Radley College
ABGD OX14 .... 215 H3
R A F & Wallingford Rowing Club
WGFD OX10 .... 267 F8
Ranikhet Primary School
TLHT RG30 .... 332 A7
Reading Adult College
TLHT RG30 .... 332 C7
Reading Adult
& Community College
READ RG1 .... 333 G5
Reading Blue Coat School
CAV/SC RG4 .... 334 E4
Reading Business Centre
READ RG1 .... 333 H8
Reading Clinic
READ RG1 .... 333 J8
Reading County Court
READ RG1 .... 333 H7
Reading Retail Park
TLHT RG30 .... 332 B6
Reading School
READ RG1 .... 333 K8
Regents Park College
OX/KTN OX1 .... 4 C3
Rhodes House
OX/KTN OX1 .... 4 C3
The Ridgeway C E
Primary School
WANT OX12 .... 281 F4
Ridgeway Day Hospital
DID OX11 .... 263 G7
Rivermead Leisure Centre
READ RG1 .... 333 F5
The River & Rowing Museum
at Henley
HEN RG9 .... 319 H6
Rockfort Industrial Estate
WGFD OX10 .... 266 D8
Rose Hill Primary School
COW/LTMR OX4 .... 192 A4
Rousham House
RBICS/W OX25 .... 92 E2
Royal Berkshire
& Battle Hospital
TLHT RG30 .... 332 D7
Royal Military College
of Science
HGHW SN6 .... 252 E8
Rupert House School
HEN RG9 .... 319 G4
Rush Common County
Primary School
ABGD OX14 .... 215 F6
Ruskin College
OXN/BOT/CM OX2 .... 4 B3
Russell Street Surgery
READ RG1 .... 333 F8
Rycotewood College
THAME OX9 .... 174 E6
Rye St Antony School
HEAD OX3 .... 168 B4
Sacred Heart RC School
HEN RG9 .... 319 F6
St Aldates College
OX/KTN OX1 .... 4 C5
St Aloysius First School
OXN/BOT/CM OX2 .... 4 B1
St Andrews C of E School
CHNR OX39 .... 200 E8
St Andrews C of E School
HEAD OX3 .... 168 D4
St Andrews School
WANT OX12 .... 282 E3
St Annes College
OXN/BOT/CM OX2 .... 4 C2
St Annes RC Primary School
CAV/SC RG4 .... 333 H5

Tom Browns School Museum
   FGDN SN7 .... 254 E8
Tower Hill County
   Primary School
   WIT/EY OX8 .... 142 D6
Town Hall & Museum
   READ RG1 .... 333 H7
Townlands Hospital
   HEN RG9 .... 318 E5
Training Standards Council
   COW/LTMR OX4 .... 192 D3
Trinity College
   OX/KTN OX1 .... 4 C3
Trinity College Sports Ground
   HEAD OX3 .... 5 F3
Trinity Primary School
   HEN RG9 .... 319 G6
Tudor Hall School
   BAN OX16 .... 28 C7
Two Rivers Industrial Estate
   WIT/EY OX8 .... 161 F1
Tysoe C of E Primary School
   RWWCK/WEL CV35 .... 16 B2
Uffington Castle
   FGDN SN7 .... 278 D6
Uffington C of E (Controlled)
   Primary School
   FGDN SN7 .... 254 E8
Uffington Trading Estate
   FGDN SN7 .... 255 G6
University College
   OX/KTN OX1 .... 5 D4
University College Sports Ground
   OX/KTN OX1 .... 191 H1
University of Oxford
   COW/LTMR OX4 .... 5 F5
University of Oxford
   KID OX5 .... 128 E8
University of Oxford
   OX/KTN OX1 .... 4 C2
University of Oxford
   OX/KTN OX1 .... 191 H2
University of Oxford
   OXN/BOT/CM OX2 .... 4 A4
The University
   & Pitt Rivers Museum
   OX/KTN OX1 .... 4 C2
University Science Area
   OX/KTN OX1 .... 5 D2
Upcroft Primary School
   TLHT RG30 .... 331 K7
Vale & Downland Museum
   & Visitor Centre
   WANT OX12 .... 282 C3
Vale of White Horse
   District Council
   ABGD OX14 .... 214 D8
Vale of White Horse
   District Council
   FGDN SN7 .... 255 F8
Valley Road Primary School
   HEN RG9 .... 318 E7
Van Alloys Industrial Estate
   HEN RG9 .... 315 K3
Vets Surgery
   COW/LTMR OX4 .... 168 A8
Victoria House Surgery
   BIC OX26 .... 97 G5
Viscount Industrial Estate
   BUR/CRTN OX18 .... 159 F7
Wadham College
   OX/KTN OX1 .... 4 C3
Waingels Copse School
   WODY RG5 .... 335 J5
Wallingford
   Community Hospital
   WGFD OX10 .... 290 E1
Wallingford Infant School
   WGFD OX10 .... 266 E7
Wallingford Lower School
   WGFD OX10 .... 267 F7
Wallingford Medical Practice
   WGFD OX10 .... 290 E1
Wallingford Museum
   WGFD OX10 .... 267 F7
Wallingford School
   WGFD OX10 .... 266 E7
Wantage C of E Infant School
   WANT OX12 .... 282 C3
Wantage C of E School
   WANT OX12 .... 282 D4

Wantage Health Centre
   WANT OX12 .... 282 E2
Wantage Hospital
   WANT OX12 .... 282 E2
Wantage Leisure Centre
   WANT OX12 .... 282 D3
Wantage Town Football
   & Social Club
   WANT OX12 .... 282 D4
The Warriner School
   RBANSW OX15 .... 37 C1
Waterstock Golf Club
   WHLY OX33 .... 196 A1
Watlington County
   Primary School
   WTLGN OX49 .... 246 B6
Watlington & District Hospital
   WTLGN OX49 .... 246 C7
Watlington Industrial Estate
   WTLGN OX49 .... 246 A6
Welfare Clinic
   TLHT RG30 .... 331 H7
Wellbeing Clinic
   OXN/BOT/CM OX2 .... 4 A2
Wellington House Practice
   CHNR OX39 .... 200 E8
Well Place Zoo
   WGFD OX10 .... 292 D8
Wesley Green School
   COW/LTMR OX4 .... 192 E5
Wesley Lane Clinic
   BIC OX26 .... 97 F5
West Bar Surgery
   BAN OX16 .... 2 C4
Westbury Court Business Centre
   RBICN OX27 .... 99 F3
West End Industrial Estate
   WIT/EY OX8 .... 143 F6
Western Elms Surgery
   TLHT RG30 .... 332 E8
Westgate Shopping Centre
   OX/KTN OX1 .... 4 C4
West Kidlington Primary School
   KID OX5 .... 129 H8
West Oxford Health Centre
   OXN/BOT/CM OX2 .... 166 D6
West Oxford Primary School
   OXN/BOT/CM OX2 .... 166 D6
West Oxfordshire
   District Council
   WIT/EY OX8 .... 142 E8
West Oxfordshire
   District Council
   WIT/EY OX8 .... 143 F5
West Oxfordshire
   Industrial Park
   BUR/CRTN OX18 .... 158 B4
West Oxfordshire
   Technical College
   WIT/EY OX8 .... 142 E7
Westrop School
   HGHW SN6 .... 250 D1
Westrop Surgery
   HGHW SN6 .... 250 D1
The West Street Practice
   HEN RG9 .... 319 F5
West Street Surgery
   CHNR OX7 .... 68 B5
West Way Health Centre
   OXN/BOT/CM OX2 .... 166 A7
West Witney County
   Primary School
   WIT/EY OX8 .... 142 C7
Westwood Farm County
   Junior School
   CALC RG31 .... 331 G4
Westwood Road Health Centre
   CALC RG31 .... 331 H6
W & G Industrial Estate
   WANT OX12 .... 281 J1
Wheatley Business Centre
   WHLY OX33 .... 170 E7
Wheatley Parish Council
   WHLY OX33 .... 170 D7
Wheatley Park School
   WHLY OX33 .... 170 D5
Wheatley Rugby Club
   WHLY OX33 .... 170 D5
Whitchurch Primary School
   GOR/PANG RG8 .... 324 C8

White Horse Business Park
   FGDN SN7 .... 231 K8
White House Surgery
   CHNTN OX7 .... 68 B4
Wildmere Road Industrial Estate
   BAN OX16 .... 21 G6
William Fletcher School
   KID OX5 .... 147 J2
William Morris County
   Primary School
   BAN OX16 .... 20 B8
Wilson Junior & Infant School
   TLHT RG30 .... 332 C8
Windale First School
   COW/LTMR OX4 .... 192 E6
Windmill First School
   HEAD OX3 .... 168 D5
Windrush Health Centre
   WIT/EY OX8 .... 142 E7
Windrush Surgery
   BAN OX16 .... 2 C4
Windrush Valley School
   CHNTN OX7 .... 103 K5
Winterbourne House Clinic
   TLHT RG30 .... 332 E6
The Wiseman Gallery
   OXN/BOT/CM OX2 .... 149 F8
The Witney Clinic
   WIT/EY OX8 .... 142 E6
Witney Community Hospital
   WIT/EY OX8 .... 142 E6
Witney Leisure Centre
   WIT/EY OX8 .... 143 F7
Witney Museum
   WIT/EY OX8 .... 143 F6
Witney Rugby Football Club
   WIT/EY OX8 .... 142 E3
Witney Town Football Club
   WIT/EY OX8 .... 141 K7
Wolfson College
   OXN/BOT/CM OX2 .... 167 G2
Wolvercote First School
   OXN/BOT/CM OX2 .... 148 D7
Wolvercote Surgery
   OXN/BOT/CM OX2 .... 148 C7
Woodcote CP School
   GOR/PANG RG8 .... 314 C6
Woodfarm Council Offices
   HEAD OX3 .... 168 E6
Woodfarm First School
   HEAD OX3 .... 168 E6
Woodfarm Health Centre
   HEAD OX3 .... 168 E7
Woodgreen
   Comprehensive School
   WIT/EY OX8 .... 143 H6
Woodlands Surgery
   BAN OX16 .... 3 E2
Woodley Centre Surgery
   WODY RG5 .... 335 C8
Woodley C of E Primary School
   WODY RG5 .... 335 K7
Woodley Park Estate
   WODY RG5 .... 335 F7
Woodley Town Council
   WODY RG5 .... 335 G7
Woodstock C of E
   Primary School
   WDSTK OX20 .... 127 K1
Woodstock Swimming Pool
   WDSTK OX20 .... 128 A1
Woolgate Shopping Centre
   WIT/EY OX8 .... 143 F7
Wootton C of E Primary School
   OX/KTN OX1 .... 189 K7
Wootton C of E Primary School
   WDSTK OX20 .... 109 G3
Worcester College
   OX/KTN OX1 .... 4 B3
Wrag Barn Golf & Country Club
   HGHW SN6 .... 251 F4
Wroxton C of E Primary School
   RBANSW OX15 .... 19 G7
Wychwood County
   Primary School
   CHNTN OX7 .... 102 D7
Wychwood School
   OXN/BOT/CM OX2 .... 4 C1
Wykeham Park Day Hospital
   THAME OX9 .... 175 G7

Page 3

E3
1 Junction Rd
2 Mckeevor Pl
3 Moorfield Ct
4 Old School Pl
5 Victoria Pl
6 Wellesley Cl

Page 4

C5
1 Albion Pl
2 Baltic Whf
3 Blackfriars Rd
4 Brewer St
5 Butterwyke Pl
6 Cobden Crs
7 Faulkner St
8 Luther Ct
9 Old Greyfriars St
10 Pembroke Sq
11 Preachers La
12 St Aldate's
13 St Ebbes St
14 Shire Lake Cl

Page 96

D3
1 Coleridge Cl
2 Cowper Cl
3 Fleming Cl
4 Goldsmith Cl
5 Keats Cl
6 Kingsley Rd
7 Walpole Cl
8 Wesley Cl
9 Wordsworth Cl

D4
1 Huxley Cl
2 Longfellow Cl
3 Macaulay Cl
4 Mackenzie Cl
5 Masefield Cl
6 Milton Cl
7 Stevenson Cl
8 Tay Gdns

E6
1 Bourne Cl
2 Chalvey Cl
3 Cherwell Cl
4 Evenlode Cl
5 Finchley La
6 Kennet Cl
7 St Mary's Cl
8 Windrush Cl

Page 97

F5
1 Chichester Cl
2 Crockwell Cl
3 Crumps Butts
4 Draymans' Cft
5 Sheep St

F6
1 Church La

H4
1 Beaufort Cl
2 Bisley Cl
3 Defiant Cl
4 Lysander Cl
5 Meteor Cl
6 Spitfire Cl
7 Sterling Cl

Page 129

G7
1 Belgrove Cl
2 Bellenger Wy
3 Bowerman Cl
4 Fernhill Cl
5 Grovelands
6 The Hornestead
7 Morrell Cl
8 Ploughley Cl
9 The Rookery
10 Scott Cl

Page 167

F4
1 Arthur Garrard Cl
2 Blomfield Pl
3 Cardigan St
4 Cranham Ter
5 Leckford Pl
6 Venables Cl

F7
1 Abbey Pl

G6
1 Blue Boar St
2 Brasenose La
3 Broad St
4 Castle St
5 Cornmarket St
6 George St
7 Gloucester St
8 Magdalen St
9 Ship St

G7
1 Albion Pl
2 Baltic Whf
3 Blackfriars Rd
4 Brewer St
5 Butterwyke Pl
6 Cobden Crs
7 Faulkner St
8 Luther Ct
9 Old Greyfriars St
10 Pembroke Sq
11 Preachers La
12 St Aldate's
13 St Ebbes St
14 Shire Lake Cl

G8
1 Hodges Ct

K8
1 Eyot Pl
2 Hawkins St

Page 168

A7
1 Ablett Cl
2 Cosin Cl
3 East Av
4 Manzil Wy

C8
1 Acland Cl
2 Desmesne Furze
3 Mileway Gdns

E3
1 The Beeches
2 Gurden Pl
3 Gurl Cl
4 Overdale Cl
5 Sturges Cl

E4
1 Bankside
2 Chequers Pl
3 Colemans Hl
4 Tilehouse Cl

E5
1 Coppock Cl
2 Quarry School Pl

E7
1 Abbots Wood (East)
2 Abbots Wood (West)
3 Cinnaminta Rd
4 Holland Pl
5 Peppercorn Av
6 Three Fields Rd

Page 192

B4
1 Elm Tree Cl
2 Hardings Cl

C3
1 Compass Cl
2 Lewin Cl
3 Pulker Cl

D3
1 Burgan Cl

E5
1 Spindleberry Cl

E6
1 Aspen Sq
2 Bergamont Pl
3 Brooklime Wk
4 Choswell Spring
5 Cleavers Sq
6 Cotton Grass Cl
7 Forget-me-not Wy
8 Foxglove Cl
9 Nettlebed Mead
10 Nuthatch Cl
11 Pipit Cl
12 Saxifrage Sq
13 Spinney Fld
14 Verbena Wy

E7
1 Anemone Cl
2 Hyacinth Wk
3 Spruce Gdns
4 Wayfaring Cl

Page 193

F6
1 Andromeda Cl
2 Blacksmiths Meadow
3 Bluebell Ct
4 Buttercup Sq
5 Celandine Pl
6 Chaffinch Wk
7 Hobby Ct
8 Jack Argent Cl
9 Marigold Cl
10 Mellebourne Cl
11 Norman Smith Rd
12 Peartree Cl
13 Pochard Pl
14 Primrose Pl
15 Swallow Cl
16 Teal Cl
17 Woodpecker Gn

G5
1 Honeysuckle Gv
2 Hornbeam Dr
3 Marjoram Cl
4 Overbrooke Gdns
5 Pennycress Rd
6 Pimpernel Cl
7 Rampion Cl
8 Reedmace Cl
9 Trefoil Pl

Page 230

B4
1 Bennett Rd
2 Bromsgrove
3 Coxwell Gdns
4 Hart Av
5 The Lees
6 Nichol Ct
7 Portway
8 Station Rd
9 White Hart Wk
10 Willes Cl

Page 267

F8
1 Bosley Crs
2 Cherwell Cl
3 Crispin Pl
4 Hart St
5 Kinecroft
6 Market Pl
7 New Rd
8 Old Buildings
9 Priory Ms
10 St Alban's Ct
11 St Leonard's Sq
12 St Peter's Pl
13 St Peter's St
14 St Ruald's Cl
15 St Rumbold's Rd
16 Thames Pth

Page 274

C8
1 Blackmore Cl
2 Eagle Cl
3 Forsey Cl
4 Passmore Cl
5 Popplechurch Dr
6 St Andrews Gn
7 St Katherine Gn
8 Tealsbrook
9 Totterdown Cl

Page 314

D7
1 Abbots Cl
2 Baldons Cl
3 Beckley Cl
4 Beeson Cl
5 Bensgrove Cl
6 Birchen Cl
7 The Close
8 Cuddesdon Cl
9 Hagbourne Cl
10 Sandford Cl
11 Wittenham Cl

Page 331

F3
1 Carew Cl

F5
1 Hawthornes
2 Kernham Dr
3 The Knoll
4 Ridgemount Cl
5 Willow Gdns

F6
1 Meadowside
2 Vicarage Wood Wy

F8
1 Chaffinch Cl

G3
1 Brierley Pl
2 Duncan Gdns
3 Goodliffe Gdns
4 Huckleberry Cl
5 Huscarle Wy
6 The Hydes
7 Simons Cl

G5
1 Bowfell Cl
2 Marling Cl
3 Old Farm Crs
4 Pikeshaw Wy
5 Staddlestone Cl

G7
1 Enborne Cl
2 Heathway
3 Holford Cl
4 Little Oak Dr
5 Swiss Cottage Cl
6 Wootton Cl

H2
1 Church Ms
2 Lilac Cl
3 Park Wk

H5
1 Mapledurham Vw
2 Oakham Cl
3 Parkhill Dr
4 Southerndene Cl

H7
1 Alford Cl
2 Dunstall Cl
3 Green Acre Mt
4 Lambourne Cl
5 Old Elm Dr
6 Tree Cl
7 Tyle Rd

J4
1 Ferndale Cl
2 Oak Tree Copse
3 Overlanders End

J8
1 Cadogan Cl
2 Hollicombe Cl
3 Hursley Cl
4 Ogmore Cl
5 St Michael's Rd

K6
1 Dresden Wy
2 Holkam Cl
3 Portmeirion Gdns
4 Staffordshire Cl
5 Wedgewood Wy

K7
1 Atherton Cl
2 Delft Cl
3 Minton Cl
4 Stanham Rd
5 Tylers Pl

K8
1 Lambeth Ct
2 Logan Cl
3 Neath Gdns
4 Savernake Cl

Page 333

F6
1 Denbeigh Pl
2 Richfield Pl

J1
1 Birchwood Cl
2 Burleigh Ms
3 Carlsbrooke Cl

J8
1 Bembridge Pl
2 Blakes Cottages

K2
1 Shakespeare Cl

Notes